Microsoft Project 2013

Step by Step

Carl Chatfield
Timothy Johnson

PUBLISHED BY
Microsoft Press
A Division of Microsoft Corporation
One Microsoft Way
Redmond, Washington 98052-6399

Library of Congress Control Number: 2013933461
ISBN: 978-0-7356-6911-6

Printed and bound in the United States of America.

Seventh Printing: September 2015

Microsoft Press books are available through booksellers and distributors worldwide. If you need support related to this book, email Microsoft Press Book Support at mspinput@microsoft.com. Please tell us what you think of this book at http://www.microsoft.com/learning/booksurvey.

Acquisitions Editor: Rosemary Caperton
Developmental Editor: Valerie Woolley
Project Editor: Valerie Woolley
Editorial Production: Waypoint Press
Technical Reviewer: Shawn Kim; Technical Review services provided by Content Master, a member of CM Group, Ltd.
Indexer: Christina Yeager
Cover: Microsoft Press Brand Team

Contents

Introduction xi

    Who this book is for. xi

    How this book is organized xi

    Download the practice files xii

    Your settings in Project xiii

    Your companion ebook. xiv

    Get support and give feedback xiv

        Errata xv

        We want to hear from you xv

        Stay in touch xv

PART 1

Introduction to Microsoft Project

1   Microsoft Project, project management and you   2

Meet the Project application 3

Meet the Project family. 4

New features in Project 2013 5

        What was new in Project 2010. 6

        What was new in Project 2007. 8

You as a project manager. 9

        Let's get started!. 10

2   A guided tour of Project   12

The Project interface: Finding your way around 14
The Backstage view: Managing files and setting options 17
The ribbon and tabs: Finding the features you want 21
Views: Working with schedule details the way you want 27
Reports: Seeing project status in new ways 33
Key points 37

PART 2

Simple Scheduling Basics

3   Starting a new plan   40

Starting a new plan, and setting its start date 42
Setting nonworking days in the project calendar 45
Entering the plan's title and other properties 48
Key points 50

4   Building a task list   52

Entering task names 54
Entering task durations 57
Entering a milestone task 62
Creating summary tasks to outline the plan 63
Creating task dependencies with links 66
Switching task scheduling from manual to automatic 72
Checking the plan's duration and finish date 76
Documenting tasks with notes and hyperlinks 78
Key points 81

5   Setting up resources   82

Entering work resource names. 84

Entering resources' maximum capacity 87

Entering resource pay rates 89

Adjusting working time in a resource calendar. 92

Setting up cost resources 97

Documenting resources with notes. 98

Key points 101

6   Assigning resources to tasks   102

Assigning work resources to tasks. 104

Controlling work when adding or removing resource assignments 112

Assigning cost resources to tasks 116

Checking the plan's duration, cost, and work 118

Key points 122

7   Formatting and sharing your plan   124

Customizing a Gantt Chart view 126

Customizing a Timeline view 133

Customizing reports 136

Copying views and reports. 139

Printing views and reports 144

Key points 149

8   Tracking progress   150

Saving a baseline of your plan. 153

Tracking a plan as scheduled through a specific date 156

Entering a task's completion percentage. 157

Entering actual values for tasks 160

Key points 165

PART 3

Advanced Scheduling Techniques

9   Advanced task scheduling   170

See task relationships with Task Path 170
Adjusting task link relationships 173
Setting task constraints 179
Interrupting work on a task 185
Adjusting working time for individual tasks 187
Control task scheduling with task types 191
Key points 197

10   Fine-tuning task details   198

Entering deadline dates 200
Entering fixed costs 202
Setting up a recurring task 204
Viewing the project's critical path 208
Scheduling summary tasks manually 211
Key points 215

11   Fine-tuning resource and assignment details   216

Setting up resource availability to apply at different times 218
Entering multiple pay rates for a resource 221
Setting up resource pay rates to apply at different times 223
Setting up material resources 225
Delaying the start of assignments 226
Applying contours to assignments 229
Applying different pay rates to assignments 234
Assigning material resources to tasks 236
Viewing resource capacity 238

Adjusting assignments in the Team Planner view. 241
Key points 247

12   Fine-tuning the Project plan   248

Examining resource allocations over time 250
Resolving resource overallocations manually 255
Leveling overallocated resources. 259
Checking the plan's cost and finish date 267
Inactivating tasks 271
Key points 273

13   Organizing project details   274

Sorting Project details. 276
Grouping Project details. 280
Filtering Project details 285
Creating new tables. 290
Creating new views 294
Key points 297

14   Tracking progress on tasks and assignments   298

Updating a baseline. 300
Tracking actual and remaining values for tasks and assignments 305
Tracking timephased actual work for tasks and assignments. 312
Rescheduling incomplete work 317
Key points 320

15   Viewing and reporting project status   322

Identifying tasks that have slipped 324
Examining task costs 330
Examining resource costs 333
Reporting project cost variance with a stoplight view. 336
Key points 341

16 Getting your project back on track   342

Troubleshooting time and schedule problems 345
Troubleshooting cost and resource problems. 353
Troubleshooting scope-of-work problems 357
Key points 360

PART 4

In-Depth and Special Subjects

17 Applying advanced formatting and printing   362

Formatting a Gantt chart view. 364
Formatting a Timeline view 371
Formatting a Network Diagram view. 373
Formatting a Calendar view 378
Printing and exporting views 381
Key points 387

18 Advanced report formatting   388

Formatting tables in a report. 390
Formatting charts in a report. 399
Creating a custom report 406
Key points 415

19 Customizing Project   416

Sharing custom elements between plans 418
Recording macros 423
Editing macros 429
Customizing the ribbon and Quick Access Toolbar 434
Key points 440

20 Sharing information with other programs   442

Copying Project data to other programs 444
Opening other file formats in Project 449
Saving to other file formats from Project 454
Generating visual reports with Excel and Visio 460
Key points 465

21 Consolidating projects and resources   466

Creating a resource pool 468
Viewing assignment details in a resource pool 474
Updating assignments in a sharer plan 476
Updating a resource's information in a resource pool 478
Updating all plans' working times in a resource pool 482
Linking new plans to a resource pool 485
Changing sharer plan assignments and updating a resource pool 489
Consolidating plans 493
Creating dependencies between plans 494
Key points 502

Appendices

A A short course in project management   505

Understanding what defines a project 505
The project triangle: Viewing projects in terms of time, cost, and scope 506
    Time 507
    Cost 508
    Scope 508
Time, cost, and scope: Managing project constraints 509
Managing your projects with Project 512

B   Developing your project-management skills   513

Joining a Project learning community 514
Joining a project-management learning community. 515
Final words 516

C   Collaborating: Project, SharePoint, and PWA   517

Introduction to sharing your plan with SharePoint 517
Introduction to team collaboration with Project Web App 521
Introduction to Enterprise Project Management 526

D   Using this book in a classroom   529

Matching content to instructional needs. 529
Teaching project management with Project 531

Glossary. 533

Index 543

About the authors 558

Introduction

Microsoft Project 2013 is a powerful tool for creating and managing projects. *Microsoft Project 2013 Step by Step* offers a comprehensive look at the features of Project that most people will use most frequently.

Who this book is for

Microsoft Project 2013 Step by Step and other books in the Step by Step series are designed for beginning to intermediate-level computer users. Examples shown in the book generally pertain to small and medium organizations but teach skills that can be used in organizations of any size. Whether you are already comfortable working in Project and want to learn about new features in Project 2013 or are new to Project, this book provides invaluable hands-oYon experience so that you can plan, track, and manage projects.

How this book is organized

This book is divided into four parts:

- Part 1 introduces you to the rich field of project management and shows you the major parts of the Project 2013 interface.

- Part 2 takes you through a complete project life cycle (planning, tracking, and managing) with a streamlined use of Project features and capabilities.

- In Part 3, you complete another project life cycle, this time with more in-depth use of the powerful capabilities of Project.

- Part 4 wraps up your training with Project with activities that can be applied at any point in a project life cycle.

In addition, this book includes several appendices. The appendices give you broader exposure to the field of project management, collaboration features in Project that are enhanced with SharePoint and Project Web App, and some suggestions for using this book in a classroom setting.

This book's iterative focus on completing a full project life cycle takes you through planning and then into the areas of tracking progress and responding to variance, where Project's feature set really shines.

This book has been designed to lead you step by step through all the tasks you're most likely to want to perform with Project 2013. If you start at the beginning and work your way through all the exercises, you will gain enough proficiency to manage complex projects. However, each topic is self-contained, so you can jump in anywhere to acquire exactly the skills you need.

Download the practice files

Before you can complete the exercises in this book, you need to download the book's practice files to your computer. These practice files can be downloaded from the following page:

http://aka.ms/Project2013sbs/files

The same set of practice files works with both Microsoft Project Professional 2013 and Microsoft Project Standard 2013. Differences between the two editions of Project are explained where needed throughout the book.

> **IMPORTANT** The Project 2013 program is not available from this website. You should purchase and install that program before using this book.

The following table lists the practice files for this book.

Chapter	File
Chapter 1: Microsoft Project, project management and you	No practice file
Chapter 2: A guided tour of Project	Guided Tour_Start.mpp
Chapter 3: Starting a new plan	No practice file
Chapter 4: Building a task list	Simple Tasks_Start.mpp
Chapter 5: Setting up resources	Simple Resources_Start.mpp
Chapter 6: Assigning resources to tasks	Simple Assignments_Start.mpp
Chapter 7: Formatting and sharing your plan	Simple Formatting_Start.mpp
Chapter 8: Tracking progress	Simple Tracking_Start.mpp
Chapter 9: Advanced task scheduling	Advanced Tasks_Start.mpp
Chapter 10: Fine-tuning task details	Fine Tuning Tasks_Start.mpp

Chapter	File
Chapter 11: Fine-tuning resource and assignment details	Advanced Resources_Start.mpp
	Advanced Assignments_Start.mpp
Chapter 12: Fine-tuning the Project plan	Advanced Plan_Start.mpp
Chapter 13: Organizing project details	Advanced Organizing_Start.mpp
Chapter 14: Tracking progress on tasks and assignments	Advanced Tracking A_Start.mpp
	Advanced Tracking B_Start.mpp
	Advanced Tracking C_Start.mpp
	Advanced Tracking D_Start.mpp
Chapter 15: Viewing and reporting project status	Reporting Status_Start.mpp
Chapter 16: Getting your project back on track	Back on Track_Start.mpp
Chapter 17: Applying advanced formatting and printing	Advanced Formatting_Start.mpp
Chapter 18: Advanced report formatting	Advanced Reporting_Start.mpp
Chapter 19: Customizing Project	Customizing A_Start.mpp
	Customizing B_Start.mpp
Chapter 20: Sharing information with other programs	Sharing_Start.mpp
	Sample Task List.xlsx
Chapter 21: Consolidating projects and resources	Consolidating A_Start.mpp
	Consolidating B_Start.mpp

Your settings in Project

There are many settings that can affect the results you see as you complete the exercises in this book—especially settings relating to how Project calculates schedules. When working with Project, there are two levels of detail at which such settings apply:

- Settings unique to the Project file
- Settings that apply to all Project files you work with in Project

We've already made all the necessary settings possible in the practice files you'll use with this book. However, your installation of Project might have settings that differ from the "factory default" settings, and it could produce results that differ from what's shown in this book. If you don't get the results you expect, check these settings.

This setting	Should be
File > Options >General tab >Default View	Gantt with Timeline
File > Options >Display tab >Show Indicators and Options Buttons For	All options here should be selected
File > Options > Schedule tab > Show Assignment Units As A	Percentage
File > Options > Schedule tab >Calculation > Calculate Project After Each Edit	On
File > Options > Save tab > Save Files In This Format	Project (*.mpp)
File > Options > Advanced tab > Edit	All options here should be selected
File > Options > Advanced tab > Display > Show Status Bar	Selected
File > Options > Advanced tab > Display > Show Scroll Bars	Selected
Resources > Level > Leveling Options > Leveling Calculations	Manual
Resources > Level > Leveling Options > Look for Overallocations On A	Day By Day

Your companion ebook

With the ebook edition of this book, you can do the following:

- Search the full text
- Print
- Copy and paste

To download your ebook, see the instruction page at the back of the book.

Get support and give feedback

The following sections provide information about getting help with this book and contacting us to provide feedback or report errors.

Errata

We've made every effort to ensure the accuracy of this book and its companion content. Any errors that have been reported since this book was published are listed on our Microsoft Press site, which you can find at:

http://aka.ms/Project2013sbs/errata

If you find an error that is not already listed, you can report it to us through the same page.

If you need additional support, email Microsoft Press Book Support at *mspinput@microsoft.com*.

Please note that product support for Microsoft software is not offered through the addresses above.

We want to hear from you

At Microsoft Press, your satisfaction is our top priority, and your feedback our most valuable asset. Please tell us what you think of this book at:

http://www.microsoft.com/learning/booksurvey

The survey is short, and we read every one of your comments and ideas. Thanks in advance for your input!

Stay in touch

Let's keep the conversation going! We're on Twitter at: *http://twitter.com/MicrosoftPress*.

Introduction to Microsoft Project

1 Microsoft Project, project
management, and you   3

2 A guided tour of Project   12

Microsoft Project, project management and you

1

IN THIS CHAPTER, YOU WILL LEARN HOW TO

- Describe the high-level benefits of a dedicated project planning and management tool like Project.

- Distinguish between Project Standard and Project Professional.

- Identify the major new features introduced in the 2013 edition, as well as in the several prior releases of Project, and where in this book you'll find hands-on activities with those features.

- Begin to develop your own skills development strategy for mastering Project in the context of good project-management practice.

Thank you for adding this book to your Microsoft Project 2013 skills development plan. This book is designed as a self-paced tutorial, and you can also use it as a reference. Most of the chapters that follow include hands-on activities in Project.

This chapter does not involve hands-on work in Project. Instead, read it to better understand how Project and project management fit with your personal skills development goals. This chapter introduces you to Microsoft Project 2013 and the field of project management.

Meet the Project application

Microsoft Project 2013 can be the go-to tool in your project-management toolbox. This book explains how to use Project to build schedules (which we'll generally call *plans*) complete with *tasks* and *resources*, use the extensive formatting features in Project to organize and format the plan's details, track actual work against the plan, share status, and take corrective action when things get off track.

TIP Terms formatted *like this* are defined in the Glossary at the end of this book.

Project is a powerful application that helps you plan and manage a wide range of projects. From meeting crucial deadlines and budgets to selecting the right resources, you can be more productive and realize better results using the set of features Project offers. You can use Project to do the following:

- Create plans at the level of detail that's right for your project. Work with summary data initially, or shift to a more detailed approach when it's convenient.

- Control what tasks Project can schedule automatically or that you'll schedule manually.

- Manage tasks, costs, work, and resources at whatever level of detail is appropriate for your project's needs.

- Work with your plan's data in a variety of views and reports.

- Track and manage your plan throughout the life of the project.

- Collaborate and share data with others in your organization using rich view and report formatting options.

- Use resource pools, consolidated projects, and cross-project links to extend your project-management focus across multiple projects.

Project 2013 builds on previous versions to provide powerful project-management tools. The section "New features in Project 2013" later in the chapter catalogs the major new features from the last several releases of Project and includes cross-references to relevant, hands-on exercises in this book.

Meet the Project family

Project 2013 for your computer is available in two different editions:

- Project Standard is the entry-level desktop application with which you can create and modify plans.

- Project Professional includes all the functionality of Project Standard plus a few additional features you can use to create and modify plans. In addition, Project Professional can connect to Project Web App (PWA), the browser-based interface of Microsoft Project Server.

In addition to installing Project on your computer, you have other options for accessing Project and related services:

- Project Pro for Office 365 is an online subscription.

- Project Online is the online subscription to Microsoft's Project and Portfolio Management (PPM) solution built on Project Web App and Project Server.

- Project Online with Project Pro for Office 365.

TIP For more information about using Project with the SharePoint and PWA services, see Appendix C, "Collaborating: Project, SharePoint and PWA." To learn more about Project Online and Office 365 offerings, visit *office.microsoft.com/*.

This book focuses on the features in the Project Standard and Project Professional applications. When a feature that is unique to Project Professional appears, you'll see special instructions for users of both Project Standard and Project Professional.

New features in Project 2013

The 2013 version includes several new features as well as some improved ones, including the following:

- **Reports**   Project 2013 replaces the old tabular reports feature with an entirely new way of visualizing your Project data. The new reports feature includes a dynamic mix of tables, charts, and textual content, and it's highly customizable. For more information, see, "Customizing reports" in Chapter 7, "Formatting and sharing your plan," and Chapter 18, "Advanced report formatting." The Microsoft Excel–supported and Microsoft Visio–supported visual reports feature remains in Project 2013, and it's described in "Generating visual reports with Excel and Visio" in Chapter 20, "Sharing Project information with other programs."

- **Task Path**   Use this feature to quickly identify the Gantt bars of the selected task's predecessors and successors. For more information, see "See task relationships with Task Path" in Chapter 9, "Advanced task scheduling."

- **Redesigned Backstage and SkyDrive integration**   Like other Microsoft Office 2013 applications, quick access to SkyDrive storage is now integrated into the Project 2013 Backstage view. For more information, see "The Backstage: Managing files and setting options" in Chapter 2, "A guided tour of Project."

- **A much later project finish date**   The latest possible date Project can work with has been moved from December 31, 2049 to December 31, 2149.

- **Support for touch input**   Like other Office 2013 applications, you can optimize the Project interface (primarily the commands on the ribbon) for either touch or mouse input.

- **New cleaner look**   As you use Project 2013, you will notice a flatter, cleaner interface. This new look is shared with other Office 2013 applications. Other new visual elements, such as the handy horizontal guidelines extending from the selected task across the chart portion of a Gantt Chart view, are unique to Project.

- **Lync integration (Project Professional only)**   In Project Professional, you can import resource details from Active Directory. (To do this, on the Resource tab, in the Insert group, click Add Resources and then click Active Directory.) In Project, you can then view resource presence information (including availability and whatever other details are supported by your organization's implementation of Active Directory). You can also start a Lync chat or create an email message to the resource directly from Project.

- **Support for apps for Office**   Project 2013 supports third-party add-ins and apps available from the Office Store, located at *office.microsoft.com/store*.

If you're upgrading to Project 2013 from a previous version, you're probably most interested in the differences between the old and new versions and how they will affect you. The following sections list new features introduced in Project 2010 and Project 2007. These features are also present in Project 2013 and, depending on the version of Project from which you are upgrading, might be new to you.

What was new in Project 2010

The 2010 version included several new features and some improved ones, including the following:

- **The Microsoft Office Fluent interface (the "ribbon")**   No more hunting through menus, submenus, and dialog boxes. This new interface organizes all the commands that most people use in a new way, making them quickly accessible from tabs at the top of the application window. For more information, see "The ribbon and tabs: Finding the features you want" in Chapter 2.

- **The Backstage view**   All the tools you need to work with your files are accessible from one location. For more information, see "The Backstage: Managing files and setting options" in Chapter 2.

- **Manually scheduled tasks**   Begin creating tasks with whatever information (numeric or text data) you might have, and don't worry about automatic scheduling of tasks until you're ready. Manually scheduled tasks are not affected by changes in duration, start or finish dates, dependencies, or other issues that otherwise would cause Project to reschedule a task. You can then switch individual tasks or an entire plan from manual to automatic scheduling. For more information, see "Entering task names" and "Switching task scheduling from manual to automatic" in Chapter 4, "Building a task list."

- **Timeline view**   Create a "project at a glance" view that includes just the summary tasks, tasks, and milestones that you choose. Easily copy the Timeline view as a graphic image to paste into other applications. For more information, see "Customizing a Timeline view" in Chapter 7.

- **Better pasting to Excel and Word**   Paste Project data into Excel or Word and preserve the column headings and outline structure of your Project data. For more information, see "Copying Project data to other programs" in Chapter 20.

- **Customizable ribbon**   Create your own tabs and groups to suit the way you work. For more information, see Chapter 19, "Customizing Project."

- **Custom fields**   Just start typing a numeric value, date value, or text string into the rightmost column in a table, and Project will identify the right data type. For more information, see "Create custom fields" in Chapter 13, "Organizing project details."

- **AutoFilter improvements**   Use Excel-like filtering, as well as sorting and grouping, right from AutoFilter arrows on column headings. For more information, see "Filtering Project details" in Chapter 13, "Organizing Project details."

- **Save as PDF or XPS**   Create PDF or XPS format documents directly from Project. For more information, see "Printing and exporting views" in Chapter 17, "Applying advanced formatting and printing."

- **Team Planner view (Project Professional only)**   Perform actions like reassigning a task from one resource to another with simple drag and drop actions in the Team Planner view. For more information, see "Adjusting assignments in the Team Planner view" in Chapter 11, "Fine-tuning resource and assignment details."

- **Inactivate tasks (Project Professional only)**   Disable (but don't delete) selected tasks from a plan so that they have no effect on the overall schedule but can be reactivated later if you need them. For more information, see "Inactivating tasks" in Chapter 12, "Fine-tuning the project plan."

- **SharePoint Task List integration (Project Professional only)**   Publish and synchronize tasks between Project and a Microsoft SharePoint list. For more information, see Appendix C.

What was new in Project 2007

The 2007 version included several new features and some improved ones, including the following:

- **Visual reports**   Export Project task, resource, or assignment details to Excel or Visio in a highly structured graphical format. For more information, see "Generating visual reports with Excel and Visio" in Chapter 20.

- **Change highlighting**   See what values changed throughout a plan immediately after you make a change to a calculated task, resource, or assignment value. ·

- **Cost resources**   Assign this special type of resource to tasks to accrue categories of costs you want to track, like travel or entertainment. For more information, see "Assigning cost resources to tasks" in Chapter 6, "Assigning resources to tasks."

- **Task Inspector pane**   Called the Task Driver pane in Project 2007, the Task Inspector pane shows you details that affect the scheduling of a selected task. For more information, see "Adjusting task link relationships" in Chapter 9.

- **Multi-Level Undo**   Back out of a series of actions when you need to.

- **Calendar working-time exceptions**   Record not just the date, but also an explanation of a resource or project calendar working-time exception. For more information, see "Setting nonworking days in the project calendar" in Chapter 3, "Starting a new plan."

You as a project manager

Project management is a broadly practiced art and science. If you're reading this book, chances are that you're either seriously involved in project management or you want to be.

Project is unique among the Microsoft Office applications in that Project is a specialized tool designed for the specific domain of project management. You might be invested in your professional identity as a project manager, or you might not identify yourself with project management at all. Either way, your success as a user of Project, to a large degree, will be related to your success as a project manager. Let's take a moment to explore this subject.

At its heart, project management is a combination of skills and tools that help you predict and control the outcomes of endeavors undertaken by your organization. Your organization might be involved in other work apart from projects. *Projects* (such as publishing a new children's book) are distinct from *ongoing operations* (such as running payroll services). Projects are defined as *temporary endeavors undertaken to create some unique deliverable or result*. With a good project-management system in place, you should be able to answer such questions as the following:

- What tasks must be performed, and in what order, to produce the deliverable of the project?
- When should each task be performed, and what is the final *deadline*?
- Who will complete these tasks?
- How much will it cost?
- What if some tasks are not completed as scheduled?
- What's the best way to communicate project details to those who have an interest or stake in the project?

Good project management does not guarantee the success of every project, but poor project management often leads to failure.

A core principle of this book's instructional strategy is that success with Project is built on success with basic project-management practice. Although Project is a feature-rich application, mastery of its features alone is no guarantee of success in project management.

For this reason, you will find material about project-management practice throughout this book. See, for example, the following:

- The many "Project management focus" sidebars throughout the chapters
- Appendix A, "A short course in project management"
- Appendix B, "Developing your project-management skills"

Let's get started!

Throughout this book, you will play the role of a project manager at a fictitious children's book publishing company, Lucerne Publishing. Each new book (even this one) constitutes its own project; in fact, some are complex projects involving costly resources and aggressive deadlines. We think you'll be able to recognize many of the scheduling problems that the project managers at Lucerne Publishing encounter and transfer their strategies and solutions to your own scheduling needs.

We've been working with Project since it debuted for Microsoft Windows, and each version has offered something that made project planning and management a little easier. Project 2013 continues that tradition for desktop project management, and we look forward to showing you around.

Chapter at a glance

Manage

Explore the Backstage view, the interface for file management and other features, page 17.

Navigate

Walk through the tabs and ribbon of the Project interface, page 21.

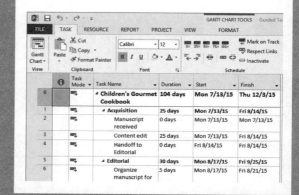

View

Use different views to see Project data the way you want it, page 27.

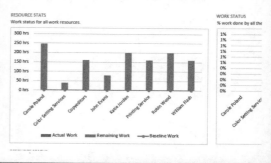

Report

Convey your plan's data in compelling new formats, page 33.

A guided tour of Project 2

IN THIS CHAPTER, YOU WILL LEARN HOW TO

- Use the Backstage view to share and manage Project files.

- Work with commands on different tabs of the ribbon interface.

- Apply different views to see information presented in different ways.

- Use reports to quickly communicate the status of your plan.

This chapter leads you on a fast-paced tour of Microsoft Project 2013. If you are new to Project, you'll see the essential features and activities that make it such a powerful application. In this chapter, you'll be introduced to many of the Project features and conventions that you'll work with throughout this book.

PRACTICE FILES Before you can complete the exercises in this chapter, you need to copy the book's practice files to your computer. A complete list of practice files is provided in "Download the practice files" at the beginning of this book. For each exercise that has a practice file, simply browse to where you saved the book's practice file folder.

IMPORTANT If you are running Project Professional with Project Web App/Project Server, take care not to save any of the practice files you work with in this book to Project Web App (PWA). For more information, see Appendix C, "Collaborating: Project, SharePoint, and PWA."

The Project interface: Finding your way around

You can start Project from the Start menu (in Windows 7) or Start screen (in Windows 8), or by opening a Microsoft Project file. In this exercise, you'll start Project without opening a file and then examine the major parts of the interface.

1   Do one of the following:

- If you are running Windows 7: On the **Start** menu, point to **All Programs**, click **Microsoft Office**, and then click **Project 2013**.

- If you are running Windows 8: On the Start screen, tap or click **Project 2013**.

Project's start screen appears. Here you can quickly open a plan that was recently opened, open some other plan, or create a new plan based on a template.

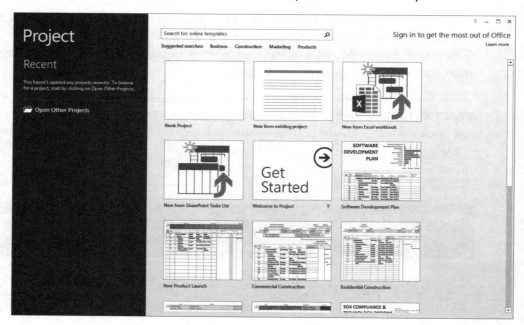

TIP If the start screen did not appear when you started Project, do the following. On the File tab, click Options. In the Project Options dialog box, click General, and under Start Up Options, click Show The Start Screen When This Application Starts.

2   Click **Blank Project.**

Your screen should look similar to the following illustration:

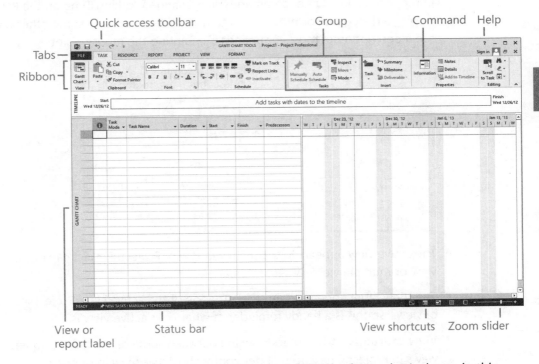

The Project window you see on your screen might differ from what's shown in this book. This might depend on your screen resolution and any previous customizations made to Project on your computer.

Let's walk through the major parts of the Project interface:

- The **Quick Access Toolbar** is a customizable area of the interface where you can add your favorite or frequently used commands. For more information, see Chapter 19, "Customizing Project."

- **Tabs** on the **ribbon** replace the pull-down menus and toolbars that you might be familiar with. Tabs group high-level focus areas of Project together. The *ribbon* contains the commands you use to perform actions in Project.

- **Groups** are collections of related commands. Each tab is divided into multiple groups.

- **Commands** are the specific features you use to perform actions in Project. Each tab contains several commands. Some commands, like Cut on the Task tab, perform an immediate action. Other commands, like Change Working Time on the Project tab, display a dialog box or prompt you to take further action in some other way. You can see a description of most commands by pointing the mouse pointer at the command.

Point at a command to see
a description in a tooltip.

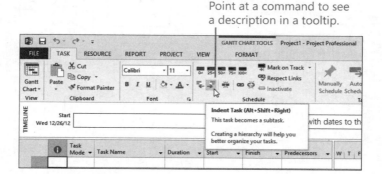

- The active view appears in the main window of Project. Project can display a single view or multiple views in separate panes.

- The **View label** appears along the left edge of the active view. Project includes dozens of views, so this is a handy reminder of what your active view is.

- **View shortcuts** let you quickly switch between some of the more frequently used views in Project. The **Zoom Slider** zooms the active view in or out.

- The **Status bar** displays some important details like the scheduling mode of new tasks (manual or automatic) and whether a filter has been applied to the active view.

- *Shortcut menus* and **Mini Toolbars** are accessible via right-clicking most items you see in a view.

  TIP Here's a good general practice. When you're not sure what actions you can perform with something you see in Project, right-click on the item and see what commands are available for that item.

Shortcut menu   Mini toolbar

Next, you'll use the Backstage view to open a sample plan.

The Backstage view: Managing files and setting options

The *Backstage view* is a part of the Project interface, and you will see a similar Backstage view in most other Office 2013 applications. The Backstage view contains customization and sharing options, as well as the essential commands for file management like Open, New, and Save.

In this exercise, you navigate to the Backstage view and see its major parts.

1   Click the **File** tab.

Project displays the Backstage view.

2   If the Open screen is not already visible, on the left side of the Backstage view click the **Open** tab.

Project displays options for opening files, as well as a list of recently opened files.

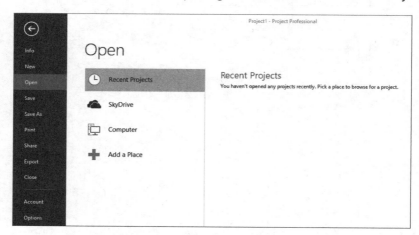

Here is a brief list of the tabs in the Backstage view. In most cases, you can click the tab name to see more options:

- **Info** gives you access to the Organizer, a feature used to share customized elements like views between plans; the Organizer is described in Chapter 19. Info also shows you information about the active plan like its start and finish date, statistics, and advanced properties. You work with advanced properties in Chapter 3, "Starting a new plan." If you're using Project Professional with the Project Web App, you also have access to your account details.

- **New** displays options for creating a new plan, either from scratch or based on a template. You'll use the New command in the next section.

- **Open, Save, Save As**, and **Close** are standard file-management commands.

- **Print** includes options for printing a plan, as well as the print preview. You'll work with printing options in Chapter 7, "Formatting and sharing your plan" and in Chapter 17, "Applying advanced formatting and printing."

- **Share** includes options for SharePoint synchronization and attaching a plan to an e-mail message.

- **Export** includes options for generating a Portable Document Format (PDF) or XML Paper Specification (XPS) format file of the plan, and other options for exporting content. You'll work with these features in Chapter 20, "Sharing Project information with other programs."

- **Account** displays connected services as well as information about Project such as version information. With a Microsoft account, you can use services such as streaming Office applications, SkyDrive file storage, and roaming personal settings. When you are signed in, your user information appears in the upper-right corner of the Project window.

- **Options** displays the Project Options dialog box. This dialog box itself contains several tabs through which you can adjust a wide range of behaviors in Project, such as whether you want to see the start screen when Project starts.

TIP To exit the Backstage view, click the Back button in the upper-left corner of the Backstage screen. You can also press the Escape key.

Next, you'll open the practice file that you'll work with through the rest of this chapter. Recall from earlier that you need to copy the book's practice files to your computer. A complete list of practice files is provided in "Download the practice files" at the beginning of this book.

3 If the Open screen is not already visible in the Backstage, click **Open**.

4 Click **Computer**, click **Browse**, and then navigate to the Chapter02 practice file folder.

5 Open **Guided Tour_Start** from the Chapter02 practice file folder.

The practice file opens.

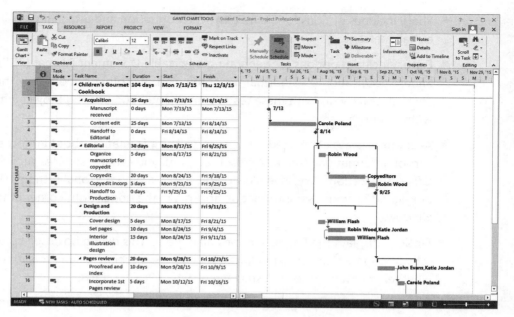

To conclude this exercise, you'll save the practice file with a different name.

6   On the **File** tab, click **Save As**.

7   Click **Computer**, click **Browse**, and then navigate to the Chapter02 practice file folder.

8   In the **File name** box, type **Guided Tour**, and then click **Save**.

Templates: Avoid reinventing the wheel

Instead of creating a plan from scratch, you might be able to use a *template* that includes much of the initial information you need, like task names and relationships. Sources of templates include:

- Templates installed with Project. These can vary depending on the installation options that were selected when Project was installed on your computer.

- Templates from the Office Online website, *www.office.com*. Microsoft makes a large number of Project templates available for free download via the web.

- Templates within your organization. You might be in an organization that has a central library of templates. Often, such templates contain detailed task definitions, resource assignments, and other details that are unique to the organization.

To see available templates, click the File tab and then click New. Templates also appear on Project's start screen.

In addition, Project can generate a new file based on existing files from Project or other applications. (On the File tab, click New, and then click New From Existing Project, New From Excel Workbook, or New From SharePoint Tasks List.)

You can also create templates from your plans for later use or to share. One common concern with sharing plans is they might contain sensitive information like resource pay rates. You can save a plan as a template and clear such information, as well as schedule progress.

1   On the **File** tab, click **Save As.**
2   Navigate to the folder where you want to create the new template based on your plan.
3   In the **Save as type** box, click **Project Template**.
4   In the **File Name** box, enter the template file name that you want, and then click **Save**.
5   When the **Save As Template** dialog box appears, select the types of information, such as resource pay rates, that you want removed from the template.

The original plan is not affected.

The ribbon and tabs: Finding the features you want

Similar to other Office 2013 applications, Project 2013 uses the Fluent interface, commonly called the *ribbon*. The most prominent parts of this interface are the tabs and ribbon that span the top of the Project window. In this section, you'll work with the tabs to see how they are organized.

These tabs logically group the commands that apply to major parts of Project together:

▪ The **Task** and **Resource** tabs relate to the data you frequently work with in Project.

▪ The **Report** tab contains commands you can use to view reports and compare two plans.

- The **Project** tab contains commands that usually apply to the entire plan, such as setting the plan's working time.

- The **View** tab helps you control what you see in the Project window and how that information appears.

- Contextual tabs, such as the **Format** tab (other contextual tabs you might see include **Design** and **Layout**) will vary, depending on what kind of information is displayed in the active view, or what kind of item is selected at the time. For example, when a task view like the *Gantt Chart view* is displayed, the commands on the Format contextual tab apply to tasks and Gantt Chart items like Gantt bars. The current context of the Format tab appears above the tab label—Gantt Chart Tools, for example.

TIP You can double-click a tab label to collapse or expand the ribbon. You can also view a collapsed tab by single-clicking the tab label, and then selecting the command you want.

Let's look more closely at the tabs.

Like all tabs, the Task tab contains a large number of commands, and these commands are organized into groups. The Task tab includes the View, Clipboard, Font, and other groups.

If you enabled touch input (on the Quick Access Toolbar in the upper-left corner of the Project window, click the Touch/Mouse Mode button), the commands on the ribbon appear larger and some lack text labels.

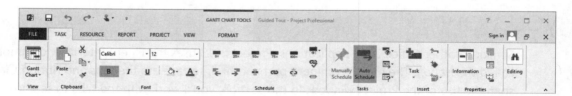

Some commands perform an immediate action, while other commands lead you to more options. Next, you'll look at different tabs and types of command buttons.

1 Click the **Resource** tab label.

   The Resource tab replaces the Task tab.

2   In the **Assignments** group, click **Assign Resources**.

This command has an immediate effect; it displays the Assign Resources dialog box.

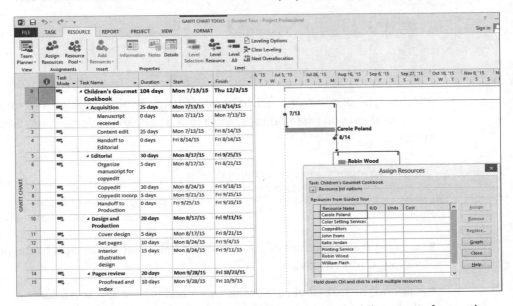

You can leave the Assign Resources dialog box displayed while you perform other actions in Project. For now, though, you'll close it.

3   In the **Assign Resources** dialog box, click **Close**.

4   Click the **View** tab label.

This tab contains a mixture of command types. As you can see, some commands, like New Window, just have a command label and icon.

 Clicking this type of command performs an immediate action.

In most cases, such commands perform an immediate action.

Other commands, like Sort, include a label and an arrow.

Clicking this type of command displays more options.

5   On the **View** tab, in the **Data** group, click **Sort**.

This command displays a list of sorting options.

Another type of command, called a *split button*, can either perform an immediate action or show you more options. You'll look at one example now: the Gantt Chart button.

Clicking the image part of this command performs the command's current setting.

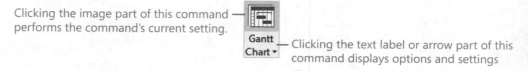

Clicking the text label or arrow part of this command displays options and settings

- Clicking the image part of this command immediately switches to the previously viewed Gantt chart view.

- Clicking the text label part of this command (or just the arrow for commands that have an arrow but no text label) shows you the available settings for that command.

6   On the **Task** tab, in the **View** group, click the **Gantt Chart** text label below the button image.

7   In the list of views that appears, click **Calendar**.

Project switches to the Calendar view.

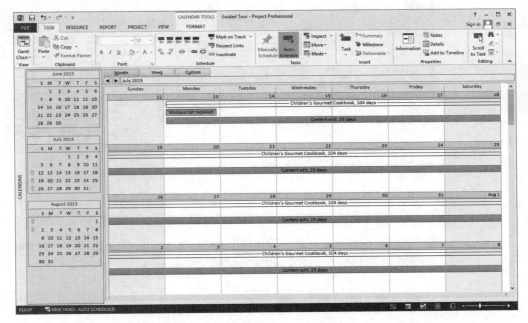

The Calendar view resembles a traditional "month-at-a-glance" calendar and displays tasks as bars spanning the days on which they are scheduled to occur.

Next, you'll switch back to the Gantt Chart view.

8   On the **Task** tab, in the **View** group, click the image part of the **Gantt Chart** button.

TIP Throughout this book, when you see an instruction to click a command that has a graphic image as well as an arrow that displays more options, we mean to click the graphic image (unless otherwise noted).

Next, you will examine other button types.

9   On the **Format** tab, in the **Gantt Chart Style** group, click the **More** button to display the predefined color styles.

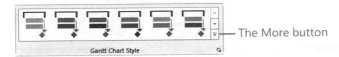
The More button

A gallery of preformatted Gantt bar options appears.

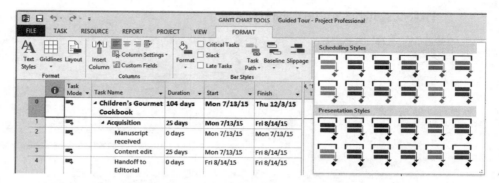

You'll work with these options in Chapter 7.

10 Press the Esc key or click the **Format** tab to close the gallery.

To see more Gantt bar formatting options, you'll next use a different type of button.

11 On the **Format** tab, in the **Gantt Chart Style** group, click the **Format Bar Styles** button in the lower-right corner of the group.

The Bar Styles dialog box appears.

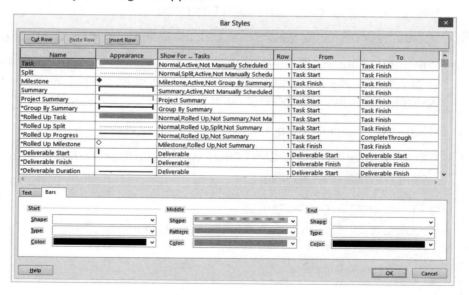

The Format Bar Styles button is an example of a *dialog box launcher*. Unlike the Assign Resources dialog box you saw earlier, you must close the Bar Styles dialog box before you can perform other actions outside of this dialog box.

12   Click **Cancel** to close the **Bar Styles** dialog box.

There are other ways of accessing commands in Project, but what you've seen in this exercise covers most command interfaces in Project.

> **TIP** Keyboard shortcuts are supported throughout Project. To see the keyboard shortcuts for the available commands, press the Alt key. Other keyboard shortcuts, such as Project's multilevel undo (Ctrl+Z) are generally available at all times.

Next, you'll change the active view and other details you work with in Project.

Views: Working with schedule details the way you want

The working space in Project is called a *view*. Project includes many types of views. Some examples of views include tables with graphics, tables with timescales, just tables, charts and diagrams, and forms. With some views, you can filter, sort, or group data, as well as customize what types of data is displayed. You can use and customize the views that come with Project as well as create your own.

Project contains dozens of views, but you normally work with just one view (or sometimes two) at a time. You use views to enter, edit, analyze, and display your project information. The default view—the one you see when you create a new plan—is the Gantt with Timeline view.

In general, views focus on task, resource, or *assignment* details. The Gantt Chart view, for example, lists task details in a table on the left side of the view and graphically represents each task as a bar in the chart on the right side of the view. The Gantt Chart view is a common way to represent a schedule. This type of view is also useful for entering and fine-tuning task details and for analyzing your project.

In this exercise, you'll start at the Gantt Chart view and then switch to other views that focus on different aspects of a plan.

1   On the **View** tab, in the **Zoom** group, click the down arrow next to the **Timescale** box and click **Days**.

Project adjusts the timescale to show individual days. Nonworking days, such as weekends, are formatted in light gray.

You can adjust the timescale to change how much of your plan is visible in the chart portion.

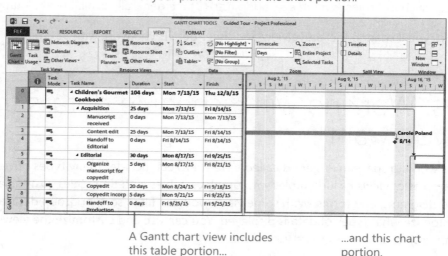

A Gantt chart view includes this table portion...

...and this chart portion.

You can adjust the timescale in the Gantt Chart view in several ways. Here, you used the Timescale box on the View tab. You can also use the Zoom Slider in the lower-right corner of the status bar.

Next, you'll display a view that is a handy way of seeing the "big picture" of the plan.

2   On the **View** tab, in the **Split View** group, select the **Timeline** check box.

Project displays the Timeline view in the pane above the Gantt Chart view.

This Timeline view has been populated for you with some details from the plan. You'll create a custom Timeline view in Chapter 7.

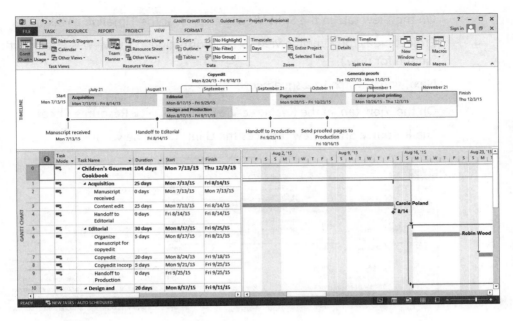

3   Click anywhere in the **Timeline** view.

Note that the label above the Format tab changed to Timeline Tools. The commands displayed on the Format tab now are specific to the Timeline view. Throughout this exercise, as you see different views, note when the label above the Format tab changes accordingly.

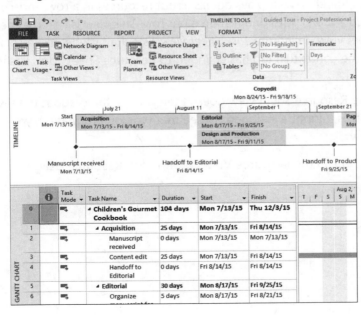

4   On the **View** tab, in the **Split View** group, clear the **Timeline** check box.

Project hides the Timeline view. (The information in the view is not lost; it's just hidden for now.)

Next, you'll switch to a sheet view.

5   On the **View** tab, in the **Resource Views** group, click **Resource Sheet**.

The Resource Sheet view replaces the Gantt Chart view.

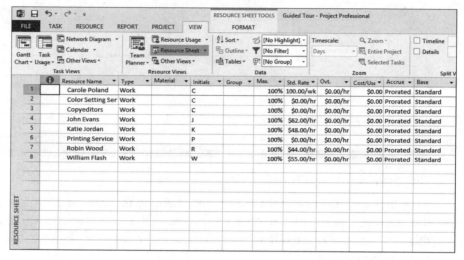

The Resource Sheet view displays details about resources in a row-and-column format (called a *table*), with one resource per row. This view is called a *sheet view*. Another sheet view, called the *Task Sheet view*, lists the task details. Also, notice that the label of the contextual tab has changed to Resource Sheet Tools based on the active view.

Note that the Resource Sheet view doesn't tell you anything about the tasks to which resources might be assigned. To see that type of information, you'll switch to a different view.

6   On the **View** tab, in the **Resource Views** group, click **Resource Usage**.

The Resource Usage view replaces the Resource Sheet view. This usage view groups the tasks to which each resource is assigned and shows you the work assignments per resource on a timescale, such as daily or weekly.

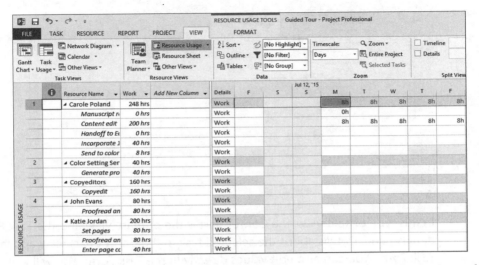

In the timescaled grid on the right side of the usage table, you can see some of Carole Poland's work assignments in the plan. Currently, this usage view's timeline shows assigned work per day. As with the Gantt Chart timescale, you can adjust this timescale using the Timescale command on the View tab or the Zoom Slider controls on the status bar in the lower-right corner of the Project window.

Another usage view, the Task Usage view, flips the data around to display all the resources assigned to each task. You'll work more with usage views in Chapter 9, "Advanced task scheduling."

7   On the **View** tab, in the **Task Views** group, click **Gantt Chart**.

The Gantt Chart view appears.

To conclude this exercise, you'll display a different split view.

8   If necessary, vertically scroll the Gantt Chart view so that task 12 is near the top of the view.

9   In the **Task name** column, click the name of task 12, *Set pages*.

10   On the **View** tab, in the **Split View** group, click **Details**.

The Task Form appears below the Gantt Chart view.

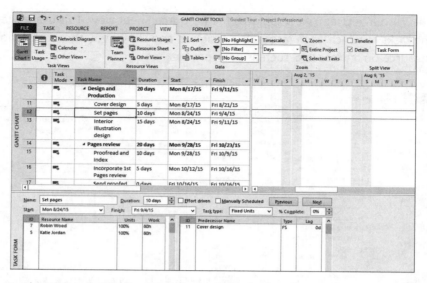

In this type of split view, the Gantt Chart is the primary view and the Task Form is the details pane. Details about the selected task in the Gantt Chart view appear in the Task Form. You can also edit values directly in the Task Form. You will work with the Task Form in Chapter 6, "Assigning resources to tasks," and with the similar Resource Form in Chapter 5, "Setting up resources."

11 On the **View** tab, in the **Split View** group, clear the **Details** check box.

The Task Form is hidden.

There are many other views in Project. You can see them by clicking the Other Views command and then clicking More Views in the Task Views or Resource Views group on the View tab. Keep in mind that, in all these views as well as all the other views in Project, you are looking at different aspects of the same set of details about a plan. Even a simple plan can contain too much data to display at one time. Use views to help you focus on the specific details you want.

Reports: Seeing project status in new ways

Previous editions of Project supported tabular reports that were primarily designed for printing. In Project 2013, *reports* have been greatly enhanced, enabling you to convey your plan's data in compelling new formats. Reports now include elements such as charts, tables, and images to communicate the status of your plan, and they are highly customizable. You can print or view reports directly in the Project window just like any view. You can also copy reports and paste them into other applications such as Microsoft PowerPoint.

In this exercise, you will explore a report.

1   On the **Report** tab, in the **View Reports** group, click **Resources** and then click **Resource Overview**.

The Resource Overview report appears.

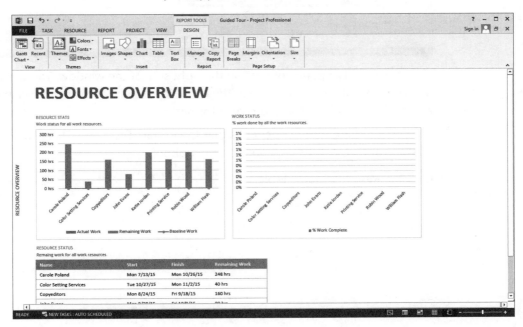

2   Vertically scroll to see all of the report's content.

As you can see, this report includes two charts and a table.

3   Click the *Resource Stats* chart.

You see a couple of things happen when you do this.

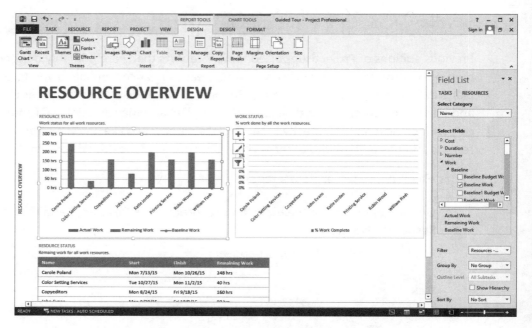

First, the Field List pane appears on the right side of the window. You use this pane to determine what data to include in the chart. You will customize reports in Chapter 7 and in Chapter 18, "Advanced report formatting."

The second thing that happened is that the Report Tools and Chart Tools and their related contextual tabs appeared on the ribbon.

4   Click the *Resource Status* table.

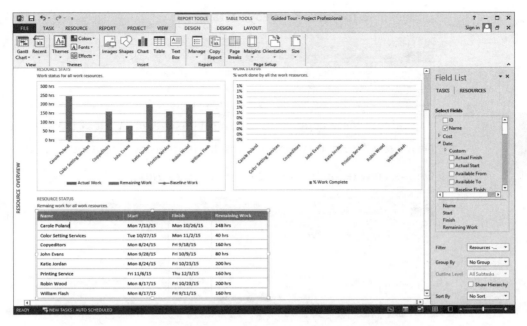

Again, you see the Field List pane and the contextual tabs update to reflect that you now have a table selected in the report rather than a chart.

Next, you will explore the contextual tabs.

5 Under **Report Tools**, click the **Design** tab.

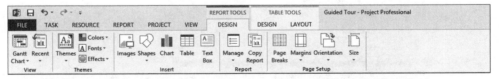

Here you can see commands that relate to the overall design of the report.

6 Under **Table Tools**, click the **Design** tab.

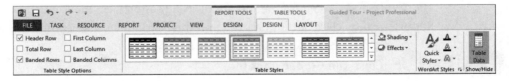

Now you see commands that apply to the selected table in this report.

7   Under **Table Tools**, click the **Layout** tab.

You can use these commands to control the overall layout of the selected table.

Next, we will split the window to display both a view and a report at the same time.

8   On the **View** tab in the **Split V**iew group, click **Timeline**.

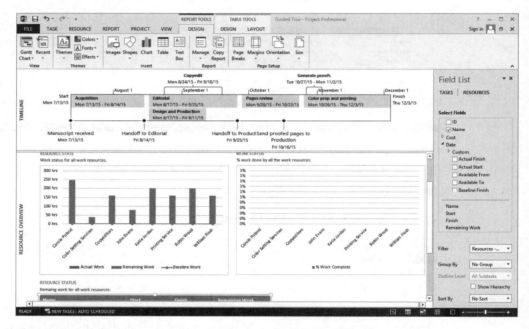

This split view includes a top-level summary in the Timeline view and an overview of your resources in the Resource Overview report.

TIP To see additional information about using reports, on the Report tab, in the View Reports Group, click Getting Started and then click any of the commands listed.

❌ CLEAN UP Close the Guided Tour file.

Key points

- The Backstage view is the central location for managing files and customizing Project.

- The ribbon includes several tabs. On each tab, commands are grouped for quick access.

- The main working space in Project is a view. One view (or sometimes two views) is typically displayed at a time. The Gantt with Timeline view is the default; the Gantt Chart is probably the best-known view in Project, and the Gantt chart is a well-known visual representation in project management as a whole.

- Reports include a variety of elements, such as charts and tables to help convey schedule details in compelling formats.

2

Simple Scheduling Basics

3 Starting a new plan   40

4 Building a task list   52

5 Setting up resources   82

6 Assigning resources to tasks   102

7 Formatting and sharing your plan   124

8 Tracking progress   150

Chapter at a glance

Create

Create a new plan, page 42.

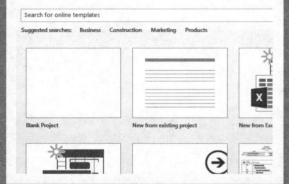

Start

Set the new plan's start date, page 43.

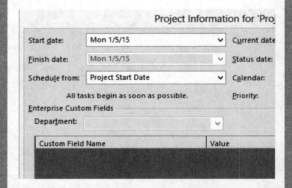

Holiday

Set working-time exceptions in the project calendar, page 45.

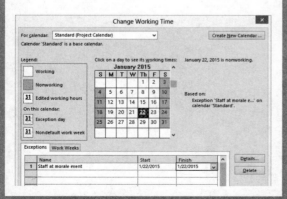

Detail

Enter properties like the plan's title, page 48.

Starting a new plan

3

IN THIS CHAPTER, YOU WILL LEARN HOW TO

- Start a new plan, set its start date, and save it.

- Review the available base calendars, and then create a working-time exception in the project calendar.

- Enter some properties about the plan.

A project's schedule or plan is essentially a model that you construct of some aspects of a project you are anticipating—what you think will happen, or what you want to happen. This model focuses on some, but not all, aspects of a project—tasks, resources, time frames, and possibly their associated costs. Note that throughout this book, we'll refer to the types of documents that Microsoft Project 2013 works with as *plans*, not documents or schedules.

PRACTICE FILES Before you can complete the exercises in this chapter, you need to copy the book's practice files to your computer. A complete list of practice files is provided in "Download the practice files" at the beginning of this book. For each exercise that has a practice file, simply browse to where you saved the book's practice file folder.

IMPORTANT If you are running Project Professional with Project Web App/Project Server, take care not to save any of the practice files you work with in this book to Project Web App (PWA). For more information, see Appendix C, "Collaborating: Project, SharePoint, and PWA."

Starting a new plan, and setting its start date

As you might expect, Project focuses primarily on time. Sometimes you might know the planned start date of a project, the planned finish date, or both. However, when working with Project, you specify only one date, not both: the project start date or the project finish date. Why? Because after you enter the project start or finish date and other project details, Project calculates the other date for you. Remember that Project is not just merely a static repository of your schedule information or a Gantt chart drawing tool—it is an active scheduling engine.

Most plans should be scheduled from a start date, even if you know that the project should finish by a certain deadline date. Scheduling from a start date causes all tasks to start as soon as possible, and it gives you the greatest scheduling flexibility. In this and later chapters, you will see this flexibility in action as you work with a project that is scheduled from a start date.

Now that you've had a brief look at the major parts of the Project interface in Part 1, "Introduction to Microsoft Project," you are ready to create the plan you will use throughout Part 2 of this book, "Simple scheduling basics."

The scenario: Throughout this book, you'll play the role of a project manager at Lucerne Publishing, a book publisher that specializes in children's books. Lucerne is about to publish a major new book, and you've been asked to develop a plan for the book launch.

In this exercise, you create a new plan, set its start date, and save it.

 SET UP **You don't need practice files to complete this exercise; just follow the steps.**

1   Do one of the following:

- In Project, if you see the **File** tab, click it, and then click **New**.

- If you already see a list of available templates in the Start screen, continue to the next step.

Project displays your options for creating a new plan. These options include using templates installed with Project or that are available on the web. You see this same list of templates in the Start screen when you start Project, and in the New screen on the File tab.

For this exercise, you will create a new blank plan.

To create a new plan, click here.

2   In the list of available templates, click **Blank Project**.

Project creates a new plan. You might see a status bar message at the bottom of the window reminding you that new tasks are created in the *manually scheduled* mode. This information remains visible on the status bar.

Notice the thin green vertical line in the chart portion of the Gantt Chart view. This indicates the current date. When you create a new plan, Project sets the plan's start date to the current date. Next you'll change the plan's start date.

3   On the **Project** tab, in the **Properties** group, click **Project Information**.

The Project Information dialog box appears.

> **IMPORTANT** If you are using Project Professional rather than Project Standard, the Project Information dialog box and some other dialog boxes contain additional options relating to Project Server. Throughout this book, we won't use Project Server, so you can ignore these options. For more information about Project Server, see Appendix C, "Collaborating: Project, SharePoint, and PWA."

4   In the **Start Date** box, type **1/5/15**, or click the down arrow to display the calendar and select January 5, 2015.

TIP In the calendar, you can use the left and right arrows to navigate to any month and then click the date you want, or click Today to quickly choose the current date.

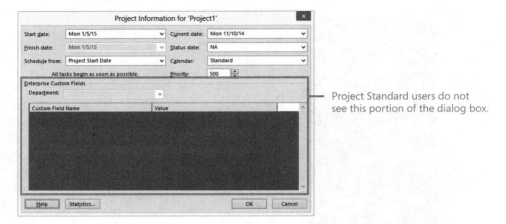

Project Standard users do not see this portion of the dialog box.

Note in the Schedule From drop-down list the *Project Start Date* value. As noted previously, because this plan is scheduled from the start date, you enter the start date and Project calculates the finish date based on the schedule details contained in the plan.

5   Click **OK** to accept this start date and close the Project Information dialog box.

Project scrolls the chart portion of the Gantt Chart view to show the project start date. The start date is shown as a thin dashed vertical line.

TIP You can set Project to automatically display the Project Information dialog box each time you create a new plan. To make this change, on the File tab click Options. In the Project Options dialog box, click the Advanced tab, and then under General, select Prompt For Project Info For New Projects.

6   On the **File** tab, click **Save**.

Because this plan has not been previously saved, the Save As screen appears.

7   Under **Save and Sync**, click **Computer**, and then click **Browse**.

8   Locate the Chapter03 folder in the Project 2013 Step by Step folder on your hard disk.

9   In the **File name** box, type Simple Plan.

10   Click **Save** to save the plan and close the Save As dialog box.

TIP You can instruct Project to automatically save the active plan at predefined intervals, such as every 10 minutes. On the File tab, click Options. In the Project Options dialog box, click Save, select the Auto Save Every check box, and then specify the time interval you want.

Setting nonworking days in the project calendar

Calendars are the primary means by which you control when each task and resource can be scheduled for work in Project. In later chapters, you will work with other types of calendars; in this chapter, you work only with the project calendar.

The *project calendar* defines the general working and nonworking days and time for tasks. Project includes multiple calendars, called *base calendars*, any one of which can serve as the project calendar for a plan. You select the base calendar that will be used as the project calendar in the Project Information dialog box. Think of the project calendar as your organization's normal working hours. For example, this might be Monday through Fridays, 8 A.M. through 5 P.M., with a one-hour lunch break each day. Your organization or specific resources might have exceptions to this normal working time, such as holidays or vacation days. You'll address resource vacations in Chapter 5, "Setting up resources."

You manage calendars through the Change Working Time dialog box (accessed on the Project tab). Use this dialog box to set normal working schedules and working-time exceptions for individual resources or, as you'll do here, the entire plan.

The scenario: At Lucerne Publishing, you need to account for an upcoming date on which the entire Lucerne staff will be unavailable to work on the book launch project.

In this exercise, you'll review the available base calendars and then create a working-time exception in the project calendar:

1   On the **Project** tab, in the **Properties** group, click **Project Information**.

    The Project Information dialog box appears.

2   In the **Calendar** box, click the down arrow.

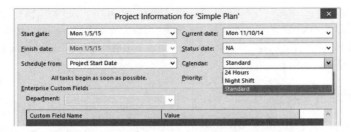

The list that appears contains the three base calendars included with Project:

- **24 Hours**   Has no nonworking time

- **Night Shift**   Covers a "graveyard" shift schedule of Monday night through Saturday morning, 11 P.M. to 8 A.M., with a one-hour break each day

- **Standard**   The traditional working day and week, Monday through Friday from 8 A.M. to 5 P.M., with a one-hour break each day

Only one of the base calendars serves as the project calendar. For this project, you'll use the Standard base calendar as the project calendar, so leave it selected.

3   Click **Cancel** to close the Project Information dialog box without making any changes.

You know the entire Lucerne staff will be at a morale event on January 22; therefore, no work should be scheduled that day. You will record this as a calendar exception.

4   On the **Project** tab, in the **Properties** group, click **Change Working Time**.

The Change Working Time dialog box appears.

5   In the **Name** field on the **Exceptions** tab in the lower portion of the dialog box, type **Staff at morale event**, and then click in the **Start** field.

TIP You don't need to name calendar exceptions, but it's a good practice for you or others to identify the reason for the exception.

6   In the **Start** field, type **1/22/15**, and then click the **Finish** field or press the Right Arrow key.

TIP You can also select the date you want in the calendar above the Exceptions tab or from the drop-down calendar in the Start field.

Here you can see that the Standard base calendar is designated as the Project Calendar.

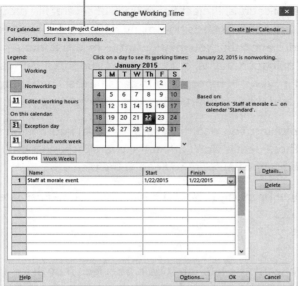

The date is now scheduled as nonworking time for the project. In the dialog box, the date appears underlined and color formatting is applied to indicate an exception day.

7   Click **OK** to close the Change Working Time dialog box.

To verify the change to the project calendar, note in the chart portion of the Gantt Chart view that Thursday, January 22, is now formatted as gray to indicate nonworking time (just like the weekends).

In this section, you made just one specific day a nonworking day for the entire plan. Other common examples of working time adjustments include:

- Recurring holidays or other times off that follow a known pattern, such as weekly, monthly, or annually. To set up recurring nonworking times, click the Details button on the Exceptions tab in the Change Working Time dialog box.

- Vary working times per week, for example, to address seasonal changes in working times. To set up custom work weeks, on the Work Weeks tab of the Change Working Time dialog box, enter the date range you want, click the Details button, and then set the working time adjustments you want.

- Unique working hours for a resource. You'll make such settings in Chapter 5.

Entering the plan's title and other properties

Like other Microsoft Office applications, Project keeps track of several file properties. Some of these properties are statistics, such as how many times the file has been revised. Other properties include information that you might want to record about a plan, such as the project title, the project manager's name, or keywords to support a file search. Some of these properties are used in views, in reports and in page headers and footers when printing. You can see and record these properties in the Advanced Properties dialog box.

The scenario: At Lucerne Publishing, you want to record top-level information about the new book launch plan. These details won't affect the overall schedule but relate to important supplemental information you want to keep in the plan.

In this exercise, you enter some properties about the plan that you will use later when printing and for other purposes:

1 Click the **File** tab.

   The Backstage view appears. The Info tab should be selected by default. On the right side of the screen, under Project Information, note the key statistics, such as the start date on the right side of the Backstage view. Notice that many of the fields you see here are the same fields you see in the Project Information dialog box. You can edit these fields in either place.

2 Click **Project Information**. In the menu that appears, click **Advanced Properties**.

   The Properties dialog box appears with the Summary tab visible.

3 In the **Subject** box, type New book launch schedule.

4 In the **Manager** box, type Carole Poland.

5 In the **Company** box, type Lucerne Publishing.

6 In the **Comments** box, type New children's book for spring release.

7   Click **OK** to close the dialog box.

To conclude this exercise, you will save the Simple Plan file, and then close it.

8   On the **File** tab click **Save**.

Project management focus: Project is part of a larger picture

Depending on your needs and the information to which you have access, the plans that you develop might not deal with other important aspects of your projects. For example, many large projects are undertaken in organizations that have a formal change-management process. Before a major change to the scope of a project is allowed, it must be evaluated and approved by the people managing and implementing the project. Even though this is an important project-management activity, it is not something done directly within Project.

CLEAN UP Close the Simple Plan file.

Key points

- Scheduling a plan from a start date (as opposed to a finish date) gives you the most flexibility.

- You use calendars in Project to control when work can be scheduled to occur.

- You should record file properties in a plan for later use when printing views and reports.

Chapter at a glance

Define

Create a task list, page 54.

	ⓘ	Task Mode ▾	Task Name ▾	Duration ▾	Start ▾
1		✗?	Assign launch team members		
2		✗?	Design and order marketing material		
3		✗?	Distribute advance copies		
4		✗?	Coordinate magazine feature articles		
5		✗?	Launch public web portal for book		

Outline

Create summary tasks to give your plan an outline structure, page 63.

	ⓘ	Task Mode ▾	Task Name	Duration ▾
1		⬛▸	◢ **Planning Phase**	**1 day?**
2		✗?	Assign launch team members	1 day
3		✗?	Design and order marketing	*Check with Marketing*
4		✗?	Planning complete	0 days
5		⬛▸	◢ **Public Launch Phase**	**6 days?**
6		✗?	Distribute advance copies	2 days
7		✗	Coordinate	6 days

Link

Link tasks and create dependencies, page 66.

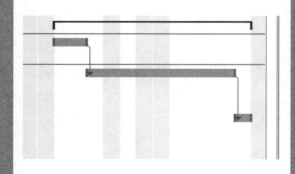

Schedule

Control if tasks are manually or automatically rescheduled, page 72.

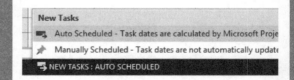

New Tasks
⬛▸ Auto Scheduled - Task dates are calculated by Microsoft Proje
✗ Manually Scheduled - Task dates are not automatically updatε
⬛▸ NEW TASKS : AUTO SCHEDULED

Building a task list

IN THIS CHAPTER, YOU WILL LEARN HOW TO

- Enter task names, durations, and start and finish values.

- Create milestone tasks.

- Create summary tasks to outline a task list.

- Link tasks to create task dependencies between them.

- Convert individual tasks to automatic scheduling, and then change the default to have new tasks automatically scheduled.

- Check a plan's overall duration and scheduled finish date.

- Enter task notes and hyperlinks.

Tasks are the most basic building blocks of any project's plan. Tasks represent the *work* to be done to accomplish the goals of the plan. Tasks describe work in terms of *dependencies*, *duration*, and resource requirements. In Microsoft Project 2013, there are several kinds of tasks. These include summary tasks, subtasks, and milestones (all discussed in this chapter). More broadly, what are called *tasks* in Project are sometimes more generally called *activities* or *work packages*.

PRACTICE FILES Before you can complete the exercises in this chapter, you need to copy the book's practice files to your computer. A complete list of practice files is provided in "Download the practice files" at the beginning of this book. For each exercise that has a practice file, simply browse to where you saved the book's practice file folder.

IMPORTANT If you are running Project Professional with Project Web App/Project Server, take care not to save any of the practice files you work with in this book to Project Web App (PWA). For more information, see Appendix C, "Collaborating: Project, SharePoint, and PWA."

Entering task names

As mentioned previously, tasks represent the work to be done to accomplish the goals of the project. For this reason, it's worth developing good practices about how you name tasks in your plans.

Task names should be recognizable and make sense to the people who will perform the tasks and to other stakeholders who will see the task names. Here are some guidelines for creating good task names:

- Use short verb phrases that describe the work to be done, such as "Edit manuscript."
- If tasks will be organized into an outline structure, don't repeat details from the summary task name in the subtask name unless it adds clarity.
- If tasks will have resources assigned to them, don't include resource names in the task names.

Keep in mind that you can always edit task names later, so don't worry about getting exactly the right task names when you're initially entering them into a plan. Do aim to use concise, descriptive phrases that communicate the required work and make sense to you and others who will perform the work or review the plan. When necessary, you can also add more details in task notes, described later in this chapter.

TIP As you enter a task name, you are creating a new task. Every task in Project has one of two scheduling modes that controls how the task is scheduled: manual (the default) or automatically scheduled. You'll work with automatic scheduling in "Switching task scheduling from manual to automatic" later in this chapter.

The scenario: At Lucerne Publishing, you have collected the initial task names for the new book launch. You know you don't have all the details you'll eventually need, but you have enough detail now to start with.

In this exercise, you enter the names of tasks.

 SET UP You need the Simple Tasks_Start file in your Chapter04 practice file folder to complete this exercise. Open the Simple Tasks_Start file, and save it as Simple Tasks.

1 Click the cell directly below the **Task Name** column heading.

2 Type **Assign launch team members**, and then press the Enter key.

The task you entered is given an ID number. Each task has a unique ID number, but it does not necessarily represent the order in which tasks occur. Your screen should look similar to the following illustration.

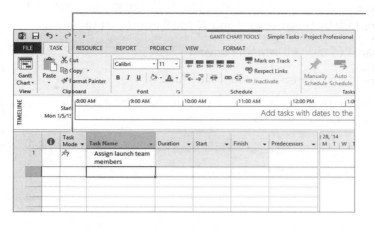

The indicators in this column tell you whether a task is manually or automatically scheduled.

Because this is a manually scheduled task (as indicated in the Task Mode column), no duration or date values appear, and the task does not yet have a Gantt bar in the chart portion of the Gantt Chart view. Later you will work with automatically scheduled tasks that always have duration, start, and finish dates.

Think of a manually scheduled task as an initial placeholder you can create at any time without affecting the rest of the schedule. You might not know more than a task name at this time, and that's OK. As you discover or decide more details about the task, such as when it should occur, you can add those details to the plan.

3   Enter the following task names, pressing Enter after each task name:

> Design and order marketing material
>
> Distribute advance copies
>
> Coordinate magazine feature articles
>
> Launch public web portal for book

Your screen should look similar to the following illustration:

While reviewing the tasks you entered, you realize that you missed a task. You want to enter this task between tasks 2 and 3. You'll insert that task next.

4   Click the name of task 3, *Distribute advance copies*.

5   On the **Task** tab, in the **Insert** group, click **Task**.

Project inserts a row for a new task and renumbers the subsequent tasks. Project names the new task *<New Task>*.

6   With *<New Task>* selected type **Public Launch Phase**, and then press Enter.

The new task is added to your plan.

TIP To delete a task, right-click the task name and in the shortcut menu that appears, click Delete Task.

Project management focus: Defining the right tasks for the deliverable

Every project has an ultimate goal or intent: the reason that the project was started. This is called the project's *deliverable*. This deliverable might be a tangible product, such as a new book, or a service or event, such as a product launch party. Defining the right tasks to create the deliverable is an essential skill for a project manager. The task lists you create in Project should describe all the work required, and only the work required, to complete the project successfully.

When developing your task lists, you might find it helpful to distinguish product scope from project scope. *Product scope* describes the quality, features, and functions of the deliverable of the project. In the scenario used in Part 2, "Simple scheduling basics," for example, the deliverable is a new children's book, and the product scope might include its number of pages and illustrations. *Project scope*, on the other hand, describes the work required to deliver such a product or service. In the scenario in this chapter, the project scope includes detailed tasks relating to generating publicity and advance reviews for the book.

Scope as a component (along with time and cost) of the project manager's focus is described more in Appendix A, "A short course in project management."

Entering task durations

A task's *duration* represents the amount of time you expect it will take to complete the task. Project can work with task durations that range from minutes to months. Depending on the scope of your plan, you'll probably want to work with task durations on the scale of hours, days, and weeks. Giving your tasks duration values is one of the benefits of using a scheduling tool like Project over a simple checklist or to-do approach to organizing work.

Let's explore task durations with an example. Let's say a plan has a project calendar with working time defined as 8 A.M. through 5 P.M. with one hour off for lunch breaks Monday through Friday, leaving nonworking time defined as evenings (after 5 P.M.) and weekends. (If you need a refresher on the *project calendar*, see "Setting nonworking days in the project calendar" in Chapter 3, "Starting a new plan.") If you estimate that a task will take 16 hours of working time, you could enter its duration as "2d" to schedule work over two eight-hour workdays. You should then expect that starting the task at 8 A.M. on a Friday means that it will not be completed until 5 P.M. on the following Monday. No work would be scheduled over the weekend because Saturday and Sunday have been defined as nonworking time.

You can use abbreviations when entering durations.

If you enter this abbreviation	It appears like this	And it means
30m	30 mins	30 minutes
6h	6 hrs	6 hours
4d	4 days	4 days
3w	3 wks	3 weeks
2mo	2 mons	2 months

As noted earlier, Project handles task scheduling in two ways. Automatically scheduled tasks always have a duration (one day by default). Manually Scheduled tasks, however, do not initially have any duration. A task's duration is essential for Project to schedule a task, so it makes sense that a manually scheduled task, which is not scheduled by Project, does not require a duration. You can, however, enter duration values for manually scheduled tasks—you'll do so in this section.

With manually scheduled tasks, you can enter regular duration values using the abbreviations shown in the preceeding table—for example, "3d" for three days. You can also enter text values, such as "Check with Bob." Such text values are replaced with the default 1-day duration value when you convert a task from manual to automatic scheduling.

TIP Project will not allow you to enter a text value for an automatically scheduled task's duration, start, or finish value.

Project uses standard values for minutes and hours for durations: 1 minute equals 60 seconds, and 1 hour equals 60 minutes. For the durations of days, weeks, and months, you can use Project's defaults (for example, 20 days per month) or set your own values. To do this, on the File tab, click Options, and in the Project Options dialog box, click Schedule, as illustrated here:

With a setting of 8 hours per day, entering a two-day task duration (2d) is the same as entering 16 hours (16h).

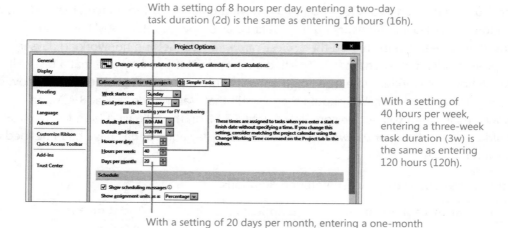

With a setting of 40 hours per week, entering a three-week task duration (3w) is the same as entering 120 hours (120h).

With a setting of 20 days per month, entering a one-month task duration (1mo) is the same as entering 160 hours (8 hours per day × 20 days per month).

The exercises in this chapter use Project's default values: 8 hours per day, 40 hours per week, and 20 days per month.

TIP If needed, you can schedule tasks to occur during nonworking as well as working time. To do this, enter an elapsed duration to a task. You enter elapsed duration by preceding the duration abbreviation with an "e". For example, type "1ed" to indicate one full 24-hour day, or "1ew" to equal seven 24-hour days, or "1emo" to equal thirty 24-hour days.

You might use an elapsed duration for a task that goes on around the clock rather than just during normal working hours. For instance, a construction project might have the tasks "Pour foundation concrete" and "Remove foundation forms." If so, you might also want a task called "Wait for concrete to cure" because you don't want to remove the forms until the concrete has cured. The task "Wait for concrete to cure" should have an elapsed duration because the concrete will cure over a contiguous range of days, whether they are working or nonworking days. If the concrete takes 48 hours to cure, you can enter the duration for that task as "2ed," schedule the task to start on Friday at 9 A.M., and expect it to be complete by Sunday at 9 A.M. In most cases, however, you'll work with nonelapsed durations in Project.

The scenario: At Lucerne Publishing, you showed your initial task list to the resources who will perform the work and to other project stakeholders. They gave you their preliminary (although incomplete) feedback on some task durations and dates that you'd like to record in the new book launch plan.

In this exercise, you enter various task duration, start, and finish values for the manually scheduled tasks you created.

1   Click the cell below the **Duration** column heading for task 1, *Assign launch team members*.

The Duration field for task 1 is selected.

2   Type **1d**, and then press Enter.

TIP You can also click the up and down arrows to enter or change the value in the Duration field.

The value *1 day* appears in the Duration field. Project draws a Gantt bar for the task, starting at the project start date you previously set in Chapter 3.

Until the tasks are linked or a specific start or finish date is set, Project will set all new tasks that have a duration value to start at the project start date. This is true whether the tasks are manually or automatically scheduled.

3   Enter the following durations or text phrases for the following tasks:

Task ID	Task name	Duration
2	Design and order marketing material	Check with Marketing team
3	Public Launch Phase	(press Enter to skip this task for now)
4	Distribute advance copies	2d

For task 5, *Coordinate magazine feature articles*, you'll enter start and finish dates, and Project will calculate the duration.

4   In the **Start** field (not the **Duration** field) for task 5, type 1/19/15, and then press the Tab key.

TIP You can also select the date you want in the Start field. Click the down arrow button, and in the calendar that appears navigate to the month you want. Then click the date you want.

5   In the **Finish** field for the same task, type or select 1/27/15, and then press Enter.

Project calculates the duration as six days. Note that this is six working days: Monday through Wednesday, and Friday of the first week, and then Monday and Tuesday of the following week. Project also draws the Gantt bar for the task to span these working days plus the nonworking days (the Thursday, January 22 morale event you set up in Chapter 3, plus the weekend) between them, as shown here:

The project calendar's nonworking days—in this case, this Thursday as well as Saturdays and Sundays—are formatted in gray.

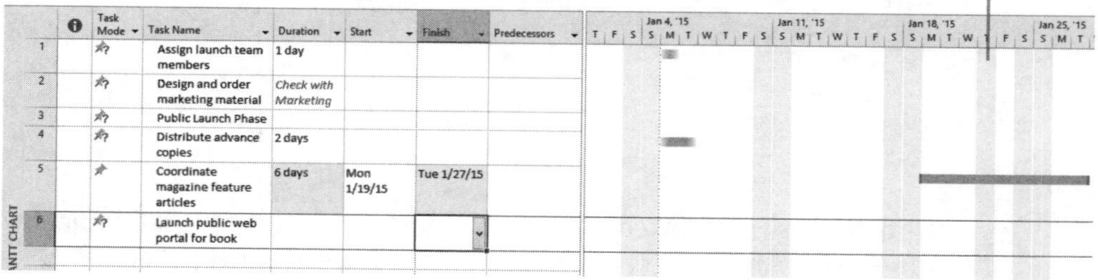

6   For task 6, *Launch public web portal for the book*, you don't know a duration or start or finish date yet, but you can still capture what you do know.

7   In the **Start** field for task 6, type About two weeks before launch complete, and then press Enter.

As with the duration value of a manually scheduled task, you can also enter a text string for a start or finish date, or both. When the task is switched to be automatically scheduled, the text strings will be replaced with specific dates.

Project management focus: How do you come up with accurate task durations?

You should consider two general rules when estimating task durations:

- Overall project duration often correlates to task duration; long projects tend to have tasks with longer durations than do tasks in short projects.

- If you track progress against your plan (described in Chapter 8, "Tracking progress," and in Part 3, "Advanced scheduling techniques"), you need to consider the level of detail you want to apply to your plan's tasks. If you have a multiyear project, for example, it might not be practical or even possible to track tasks that are measured in minutes or hours. In general, you should measure task durations at the lowest level of detail or control that is important to you, but no lower.

For the projects you work on in this book, the durations are supplied for you. For your projects, you will often have to estimate task durations. Good sources of task duration estimates include

- Historical information from previous, similar projects

- Estimates from the people who will complete the tasks

- The expert judgment of people who have managed similar projects

- The standards of professional or industrial organizations that carry out projects similar to yours

One rule of thumb to consider is called the *8/80 rule*. This rule suggests that task durations between 8 hours (or one day) and 80 hours (10 working days, or two weeks) are generally sized about right. Tasks shorter than one day might be too granular, and tasks longer than two weeks might be too long to manage properly. There are many legitimate reasons to break this rule, but for most tasks in your projects, it's worth considering.

For complex, long-duration projects or projects involving a large number of unknowns, you might be able to make detailed duration estimates only of tasks to be started and completed soon (for example, within two to four weeks). You then might have only very general duration estimates for tasks that will start later (for example, after two to four weeks). You could hold a recurring task-duration estimating session with the team in a regular cadence as time progresses.

For complex projects, you probably would combine these and other strategies to estimate task durations. Because inaccurate task duration estimates are a major source of *risk* in any project, making good estimates is well worth the effort expended.

Entering a milestone task

In addition to entering tasks to be completed, you might want to account for an important event for your project's plan, such as the end of a major phase of the project. To do this, you will create a milestone task.

Milestones are significant events that are either reached within the plan (such as the completion of a phase of work) or imposed upon the plan (such as a deadline by which to apply for funding). Because the milestone itself doesn't normally include any work, milestones are represented as tasks with zero duration.

The scenario: At Lucerne Publishing, you just learned the date by which the new book launch's planning activities needs to be completed for the book launch to occur on time. You want this date to have visibility in the plan.

In this exercise, you create a milestone task.

1   Click the name of task 3, *Public Launch Phase*.

2   On the **Task** tab, in the **Insert** group, click **Milestone**.

    Project inserts a row for a new task and renumbers the subsequent tasks. Project names the new task *<New Milestone>* and gives it a zero-day duration. As with the other new tasks, the milestone is initially scheduled at the project start date of January 5.

3   With <New Milestone> selected, type Planning complete! and then press Enter.
The milestone task is added to your plan.

On the Gantt chart, the milestone appears as a diamond.

	ⓘ	Task Mode ▾	Task Name ▾	Duration ▾	Start ▾	Finish ▾	Predecessors ▾	T	F	S	S	M	T	W
1		🗓?	Assign launch team members	1 day							▪			
2		🗓?	Design and order marketing material	Check with Marketing										
3		🗓?	Planning complete!	0 days						◆ 1/5				
4		🗓?	Public Launch Phase											
5		🗓?	Distribute advance copies	2 days							▪			

TIP You can mark a task of any duration as a milestone. Double-click the task name to display the Task Information dialog box, and then click Advanced and select the Mark Task As Milestone option.

4

Creating summary tasks to outline the plan

You'll find it helpful to organize groups of closely related tasks into an outline using summary tasks. When the summary tasks are sequenced over time, the highest level summary tasks are called *phases*.

When reviewing a project's plan, seeing tasks organized in an outline structure helps you and your *stakeholders* think in terms of major work items. For example, it is common to divide book publishing projects into Editorial, Design, and Production phases. With an outline structure applied, you can then expand or collapse the outline to show just the level of detail you want. You create an outline structure by indenting and outdenting tasks. In Project, the tasks indented below a summary task are called *subtasks*.

Summary tasks are automatically scheduled and not manually scheduled by default. The duration of an automatically scheduled summary task is calculated by Project as the span of time from the earliest start date to the latest finish date of its subtasks. If you directly edit the duration of an automatically scheduled summary task, or its start or finish date, it will be switched to a manually scheduled task.

When a summary task is manually scheduled, its duration will be calculated based on its subtasks, just like the duration of an automatically scheduled summary task. However, you can edit the duration of a manually scheduled summary task and Project will keep track of both the manual duration that you entered and the calculated duration.

TIP You will work with summary tasks with both manual and automatically calculated durations in Chapter 10, "Fine-tuning task details."

The highest level of a plan's outline structure is called the *project summary task*. Project automatically generates the project summary task but does not display it by default. Because the project summary task is at the highest level of the plan's outline structure, it includes rolled-up details from all subtasks. It also represents the full duration of the plan so it's a handy way of seeing some essential details, such as the plan's overall duration.

Project management focus: Top-down and bottom-up planning

Two common approaches to developing tasks and phases are top-down and bottom-up planning:

- *Top-down planning* identifies major phases or components of the project's plan before filling in all the details required to complete those phases, represented as summary tasks. Complex plans can have several layers of nested summary tasks. This approach works from general to specific.

- *Bottom-up planning* identifies as many of the bottom-level detailed tasks as possible before outlining them into logical groups called *phases* or *summary tasks*. This approach works from specific to general.

Creating accurate tasks and phases for most complex plans requires a combination of top-down and bottom-up planning. Typically, a project manager begins with established, broad phases for a plan (top-down planning), and the resources who will execute the plan provide the detailed tasks that fill out each phase (bottom-up planning).

The scenario: At Lucerne Publishing, the new book launch plan is put together enough to now organize the plan into two sequential phases.

In this exercise, you outline your task list by creating summary tasks:

1   Select the names of tasks 5 through 7.

     These are the tasks you want to make subtasks of the public launch phase.

2   On the **Task** tab, in the **Schedule** group, click **Indent Task**.

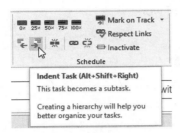

Indent Task (Alt+Shift+Right)
This task becomes a subtask.

Creating a hierarchy will help you
better organize your tasks.

Project promotes task 4 to a summary task and switches it to automatic scheduling.
Or you can think of it as Project demoting tasks 5 through 7 to subtasks; either way,
the plan now includes a summary task and subtasks.

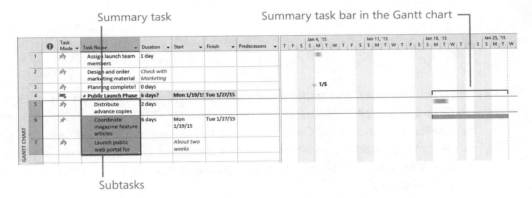

Summary task

Summary task bar in the Gantt chart

Subtasks

TIP If you want to demote a summary task back to a subtask, you must change the
outline structure of the subtasks below the summary task. Select all subtasks, and
then click the Outdent command.

Notice the scheduling effect of creating the summary task. Because task 6 had
specific start and finish dates already, Project set the start date of the summary task
(and its other subtask with a duration) to the same date, January 19.

Next you'll create another summary task in a different way.

3   Select the names of tasks 1 through 3.

4   On the **Task** tab, in the **Insert** group, click **Summary**.

Project inserts a row for a new task, indents the task directly below it, and renumbers
the subsequent tasks. Project names the new task *<New Summary Task>*.

5   With *<New Summary Task>* selected, type Planning Phase and press Enter. Now the plan is organized into two phases of work.

	ⓘ	Task Mode ▾	Task Name ▾	Duration ▾	Start ▾	Finish ▾	Predecessors ▾		T	F	S	S	M	T	W
1		⭑	◢ **Planning Phase**	**1 day?**	**Mon 1/5/15**	**Mon 1/5/15**						□		
2		⭑?	Assign launch team members	1 day								▪		
3		⭑?	Design and order marketing	*Check with Marketing*										
4		⭑?	Planning complete	0 days								◆ 1/5		
5		⭑	◢ **Public Launch Phase**	**6 days?**	**Mon 1/19/15**	**Tue 1/27/15**								
6		⭑?	Distribute advance copies	2 days										
7		⭑	Coordinate magazine feature articles	6 days	Mon 1/19/15	Tue 1/27/15								
8		⭑?	Launch public web portal for	*About two weeks*										

(GANTT CHART — Jan 4, '15)

Creating task dependencies with links

When you link tasks, you create scheduling relationships between the tasks. These task relationships are called *dependencies*, as in "the start of this task is dependent upon the completion of a prior task." Once you create task dependencies (also called *links*), Project can automatically adjust the scheduling of linked tasks as changes occur in your plan. Creating dependencies by linking tasks is crucial to getting the full benefit of Project's scheduling engine.

Let's look at one type of dependency relationship you can create between two tasks. Most plans require tasks to be performed in a specific order. For example, the task of writing a chapter of a book must be completed before the task of editing the chapter can occur. These two tasks have a finish-to-start relationship, which has two aspects:

- The second task must occur after the first task; this is a sequence.
- The second task can occur only if the first task is completed; this is a dependency.

In Project, the first task ("Write the chapter") is called the *predecessor* because it precedes tasks that depend on it. The second task ("Edit the chapter") is called the *successor* because it succeeds, or follows, tasks on which it is dependent. Any task can be a predecessor for one or more successor tasks. Likewise, any task can be a successor to one or more predecessor tasks.

Although this might sound complicated, two tasks can have one of only four types of task relationships.

This task relationship	Means	Looks like this in the Gantt chart	Example
Finish-to-start (FS)	The finish date of the predecessor task determines the start date of the successor task. This is the default task relationship.		A book chapter must be written before it can be edited.
Start-to-start (SS)	The start date of the predecessor task determines the start date of the successor task.		Ordering prepress and ordering paper are closely related, and they should start simultaneously.
Finish-to-finish (FF)	The finish date of the predecessor task determines the finish date of the successor task.		Tasks that require specific equipment must end when the equipment rental period ends.
Start-to-finish (SF)	The start date of the predecessor task determines the finish date of the successor task.		The time when the print run is scheduled to start determines when a binder selection task must end.

TIP You can adjust the schedule relationship between predecessor and successor tasks with lead and lag times. For example, you can set a two-day lag between the end of a predecessor task and the start of its successor task. For more information, see Chapter 9, "Advanced task scheduling."

Representing task relationships and handling changes to scheduled start and finish dates are two areas where the use of a scheduling engine such as Project really pays off. For example, you can change task durations or add or remove tasks from a chain of linked tasks, and Project will reschedule tasks accordingly.

Task relationships appear in several ways in Project, including the following:

- In Gantt chart and *Network Diagram* views, task relationships appear as the lines connecting tasks.

- In tables, such as the *Entry table*, task ID numbers of predecessor tasks appear in the Predecessor fields of successor tasks. (You might need to drag the vertical divider bar to the right to see the Predecessor column.)

The scenario: At Lucerne Publishing, the new book launch plan is coming together nicely. Tasks have been outlined under summary tasks, and you're now ready to create task relationships.

In this exercise, you link tasks to create task dependencies between them:

1   Select the names of tasks 2 and 3.

2   On the **Task** tab, in the **Schedule** group, click **Link the Selected Tasks**.

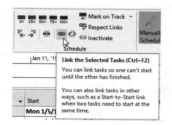

Tasks 2 and 3 are linked with a finish-to-start relationship.

The change highlighting indicates values that are affected after you make a change to a project.

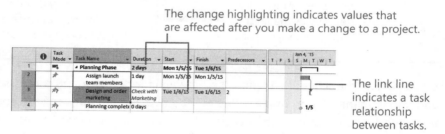

The link line indicates a task relationship between tasks.

Note that task 3 previously had no start or finish date, but by making it a successor of task 2, you gave Project enough information to give task 3 a start date: January 6, the next working day following the end of task 2.

Have you noticed the light blue highlighting of some of the Duration, Start, and Finish fields as you linked tasks? Project highlights the values that are affected after each scheduling change you make in a plan.

TIP To unlink tasks, select the tasks you want to unlink and then click Unlink Tasks in the Schedule group on the Task tab.

Next, you'll link tasks 3 and 4 using a different technique.

3   Select the name of task 4, *Planning complete!*

4   On the **Task** tab, in the **Properties** group, click **Information**.

The Task Information dialog box appears.

5   Click the **Predecessors** tab.

6   Click the empty cell below the **Task Name** column heading, and then click the down arrow that appears.

7   In the **Task Name** list, click *Design and order marketing material.*

8   Click **OK** to close the Task Information dialog box.

	❶	Task Mode	Task Name	Duration	Start	Finish	Predecessors	T	F	S	Jan 4, '15 S	M	T	W	T
1		🔲	⊿ Planning Phase	2 days	Mon 1/5/15	Wed 1/7/15									
2		⚲	Assign launch team members	1 day	Mon 1/5/15	Mon 1/5/15									
3		⚲?	Design and order marketing	*Check with Marketing*	Tue 1/6/15	Tue 1/6/15	2								
4		⚲	Planning complete	0 days	Wed 1/7/15	Wed 1/7/15	3				◆ 1/7				

Tasks 3 and 4 are linked with a finish-to-start relationship.

TIP Recall that any task can have multiple predecessor tasks. One way you can specify additional predecessor tasks is to add them on the Predecessors tab of the Task Information dialog box. For finish-to-start relationships (the default link type), the predecessor with the later finish date determines the start date of the successor task. This predecessor task is sometimes called the "driving predecessor" because it determines or drives the start date of its successor task. Project includes a feature that helps you see driving predecessor and successor relationships more easily. The feature is called Task Path and is described in Chapter 9.

Next you'll link all the subtasks under Public Launch Phase in one action.

9   Select the names of tasks 6 through 8.

10   On the **Task** tab, in the **Schedule** group, click **Link the Selected Tasks**.

Tasks 6 through 8 are linked.

TIP Tasks 6 through 8 are adjacent to each other. To select tasks that are not adjacent, select the first task, hold down the Ctrl key, and then select additional tasks.

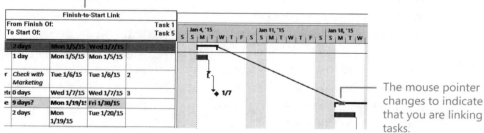

There are several ways of linking tasks, and you'll use one more to link the two phases of the new book launch plan. Notice that Project replaced the text value in the start date field of task 8 with a scheduled date, and supplied a one-day duration. Project did so because it requires a date value for the task once it was linked to another task. The question mark following the duration value indicates that this is an estimated duration; it has no effect on the scheduling of the task.

11   In the chart portion of the Gantt Chart view, point the mouse pointer at the summary task bar for task 1, *Planning Phase*, and then click and drag down and to the right to the Gantt bar for task 5, *Public Launch Phase*.

Note that as you drag the mouse pointer, it changes to a link icon and pop-up window that updates with information as you hover over other task bars.

This tooltip can help you link tasks using the mouse.

The mouse pointer changes to indicate that you are linking tasks.

12   When the mouse pointer is over the summary task bar for task 5, release the mouse pointer.

The summary tasks 1 and 5 are linked with a finish-to-start relationship.

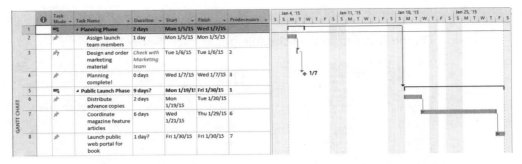

So far, you've used three different techniques to link tasks. Another simple way to create a task relationship is to enter the predecessor's task ID in the Predecessors field of the successor task. As you use Project more, you'll probably find you prefer one of these or another way of linking tasks.

TIP When working with summary tasks, you can either link summary tasks directly (as you did previously) or link the latest task in the first phase with the earliest task in the second phase. The scheduling result is the same in either situation. Under no circumstances, however, can you link a summary task to one of its own subtasks. Doing so creates a circular scheduling problem, so Project doesn't allow it.

To conclude this exercise, you'll enter a specific duration value for task 3. The Lucerne marketing team has reported that its estimate is that task 3 should have a two-week duration.

13   In the duration field for task 3, type **2w**, and then press Enter.

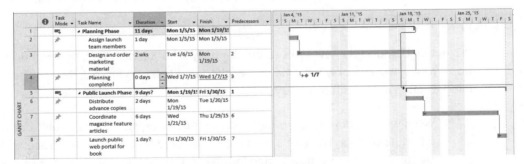

Notice that the new duration for task 3 caused the Planning Phase summary task's duration to increase, but it did not affect the scheduling of the task 4 milestone. Why not? Remember that this task is still manually scheduled. You can force Project to adjust the start and finish dates of this task while leaving it as manually scheduled.

14   Select the name of task 4.

15   On the **Task** tab, in the **Schedule** group, click **Respect Links**.

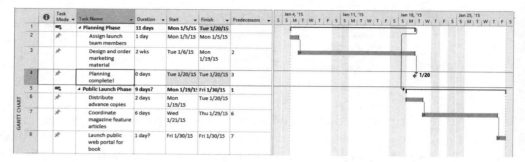

Project reschedules task 4 to start following the completion of its predecessor, task 3.

You might have noticed that the start of the Public Launch Phase summary task does not respect its link to its predecessor, the Planning Phase summary task. Clicking the Respect Link button with the Public Launch Phase summary task selected will not cause it to be rescheduled, as it did for task 4. That's because the start and finish dates of the summary task are driven by the earliest start and latest finish dates of its subtasks, which in this case are still manually scheduled. You'll address this issue next by switching to automatic scheduling.

Switching task scheduling from manual to automatic

Project by default sets new tasks to be manually scheduled. In fact, so far in Part 2 of this book you've worked only with manually scheduled tasks. In Project, you control the scheduling of tasks in two different ways:

- Work with *manually scheduled* tasks to quickly capture some details but without scheduling tasks. Think of a manually scheduled task as an initial placeholder you can create at any time without affecting the rest of the plan. You might not initially know more than a task's name, and that's OK. As you discover or decide more details about the task, such as when it should occur, you can add those details to the plan.

- Work with *automatically scheduled* tasks to take full advantage of the powerful scheduling engine in Project.

With automatic scheduling, Project updates calculated schedule values such as task durations, start dates, and finish dates automatically in response to changes in a plan. Changes to factors such as constraints, task relationships, and calendars can also cause Project to recalculate affected tasks.

The scenario: At Lucerne Publishing, the new book launch plan has been reviewed by the resources who will carry out the work and by other project stakeholders. Although you expect the plan to change somewhat as you learn more about the book launch, you now have enough confidence in the plan overall to switch from manual to automatic task scheduling.

In this exercise, you convert tasks to automatic scheduling and then change the default scheduling mode to have new tasks automatically scheduled:

1   Select the names of tasks 2 through 4.

These tasks are currently set to be manually scheduled, as indicated by the push-pin indicator in the Task Mode column.

2   On the **Task** tab, in the **Tasks** group, click **Auto Schedule**.

Project switches these tasks to be automatically scheduled.

Project changes the Task Mode icons and formatting of the tasks' Gantt bars to indicate that they are now automatically scheduled. Next you'll use a different method to change the scheduling mode for a task.

3   Click the **Task Mode** field of task 6, and then click the arrow that appears.

4   In the list that appears, click **Auto Scheduled**.

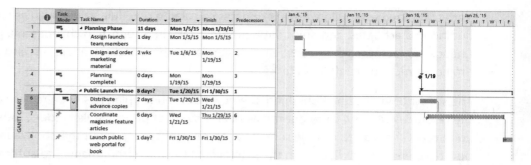

This time, task 6 was rescheduled to start later. Why did this happen? Recall the dependency between the two summary tasks. The dependency said, in effect, that the Public Launch Phase should start once the Planning Phase was finished. However, because task 6 and the other subtasks of the Public Launch Phase were manually scheduled, Project did not reschedule the subtasks to account for this dependency. As soon as you set task 6 to automatic scheduling, however, Project did just that and adjusted the start date of its summary task as well.

The remaining subtasks 7 and 8 are still manually scheduled, so Project did not reschedule them. You'll switch these tasks next.

5   Select the names of tasks 7 and 8.

6   On the **Task** tab, in the **Tasks** group, click **Auto Schedule**.

Project reschedules the remaining tasks. This extends the duration of the Public Launch Phase and of the overall project.

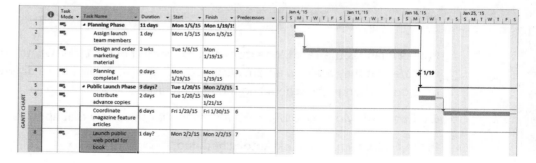

Right now, this plan is set to treat any new tasks you might enter as manually scheduled. You could leave this setting as is and then switch specific tasks to be automatically scheduled. However, this plan is developed enough now to switch to automatic scheduling and later set some specific tasks to manually scheduled as needed.

7   On the **Task** tab, in the **Tasks** group, click **Mode** and then click **Auto Schedule**.

TIP You can toggle the scheduling mode of the plan currently open in Project by clicking the New Tasks status bar text and then picking the other scheduling mode.

You can also change the default scheduling mode Project applies to all new plans. To do this, on the File tab click Options and then click the Schedule tab. In the Scheduling Options For This Project box, click All New Projects, and then in the New Tasks Created box, click Auto Scheduled.

Next you'll see automatic scheduling in action when you add a new task to the plan.

8   In the **Task Name** field, below task 8, type Launch social media programs for book and then press Enter.

Project adds the new task to the plan. By default, it is not linked to any other task, is given a one-day duration, and is scheduled to start at its summary task's start date. Unlike manually scheduled tasks, automatically scheduled tasks get a duration and start and finish dates when added to the plan.

To end this exercise, you'll link two tasks.

9   Select the names of tasks 8 and 9.

10   On the **Task** tab, in the **Schedule** group, click **Link the Selected Tasks**.

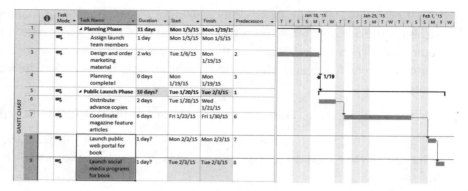

Project links the two tasks. Notice that the duration of the Public Launch Phase summary task was updated automatically from 9 to 10 days.

Checking the plan's duration and finish date

At any time in the planning or execution of a project, you and other project stakeholders very likely will want to know how long the project is expected to take. You don't directly enter a total project *duration* or finish date in a plan, and you don't need to. Project calculates these values based on the task durations, dependencies, project calendar adjustments, and many other factors you have recorded in a plan.

An easy way to view the plan's duration and scheduled start and finish dates is via the Timeline view, the project summary task, and the Project Information dialog box.

The scenario: At Lucerne Publishing, your plan for the new book launch is helping the team to get organized for the upcoming work. You are frequently asked to provide the currently scheduled duration and finish date for the book launch.

In this exercise, you check the plan's overall duration and scheduled finish date based on the task durations and relationships you entered.

1   In the Timeline view above the Gantt Chart view, note the plan's current start and finish dates.

The Timeline view is a handy way of seeing the big picture of the plan. Here you're looking just at start and finish dates, but in later chapters, you'll work with the Timeline view in different ways.

Next you'll get a closer look at the plan's duration.

2   On the **Project** tab, in the **Properties** group, click **Project Information**.

The Project Information dialog box appears.

Here again you see the finish date: 2/3/15. You can't edit the finish date directly because this plan is set to be scheduled from the start date. Project calculates the plan's finish date based on the span of working days required to complete the tasks, starting at the plan's start date. Any change to the start date causes Project to recalculate the finish date.

Next, let's look at the duration information in more detail.

3   Click **Statistics**.

Project Statistics for 'Simple Tasks'				
	Start		Finish	
Current	Mon 1/5/15		Tue 2/3/15	
Baseline	NA		NA	
Actual	NA		NA	
Variance	0d		0d	
	Duration	Work	Cost	
Current	21d?	0h	$0.00	
Baseline	0d	0h	$0.00	
Actual	0d	0h	$0.00	
Remaining	21d?	0h	$0.00	

Percent complete:
Duration: 0%   Work: 0%   [Close]

You don't need to understand all of these numbers yet, but the current duration is worth noting. The duration is the number of working days (not elapsed days) between the plan's start date and finish date.

4   Click **Close** to close the Project Statistics dialog box.

Next you will display the project summary task in the Gantt Chart view.

5   Click anywhere in the Gantt Chart view.

With the focus now on the Gantt Chart view, the contextual label of the Format tab changes to Gantt Chart Tools.

6   On **Format** tab, in the **Show/Hide** group, select the **Project Summary Task** check box.

Project displays the project summary task at the top of the Gantt Chart view with an ID of 0. Here you'll see the same duration and start and finish values displayed in Project Statistics as well as a Gantt bar that's drawn from the start and finish dates of the overall plan.

Documenting tasks with notes and hyperlinks

You can record additional information about a task in a *note*. For example, you might have detailed descriptions of a task but want to keep the task's name succinct. You can add such details to a task note rather than to the task's name. That way, the information resides in the plan and can be easily viewed or printed.

There are three types of notes: task notes, resource notes, and assignment notes. You can enter and review task notes on the Notes tab in the Task Information dialog box. Notes in Project support a wide range of text formatting options; you can even link to or store graphic images and other types of files in notes.

TIP You will work with resource notes in Chapter 5, "Setting up resources."

Sometimes you might want to associate a task in a plan with information stored in a different document or on a webpage. *Hyperlinks* allow you to connect a specific task to additional information that resides outside of the plan.

The scenario: At Lucerne Publishing, you have some details about a few tasks in the new book launch plan that you'd like to record in the plan. This will help you later by keeping such details right in the plan, and it will also be valuable for any other project stakeholders who might work with the plan in the future.

In this exercise, you enter task notes and hyperlinks to document important information about some tasks:

1   Select the name of task 6, *Distribute advance copies*.

2   On the **Task** tab, in the **Properties** group, click **Notes**.

> **TIP** You can also right-click the task name and click Notes in the shortcut menu that appears.

Project displays the Task Information dialog box with the Notes tab visible.

3   In the **Notes** box, type Get recipient list from publicist.

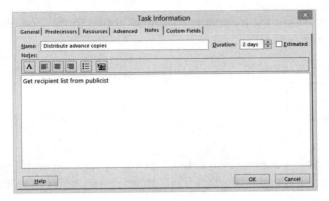

4   Click **OK**.

A note icon appears in the Indicators column.

5   Point to the note icon for task 6.

The note appears in a ScreenTip. For notes that are too long to appear in a ScreenTip, you can double-click the note icon to display the full text of the note.

You might notice a note icon for task 0, the project summary task. We'll look at that next.

6   Point to the note icon on task 0.

You might recognize this note that appears in the ScreenTip from "Entering the plan's title and other properties" in Chapter 3. This text was entered in the Comments field of the Properties dialog box. As you can see, text entered in Comments appears as a note on the project summary task. If you add or change a note on the project summary task as you did earlier, your change will appear in the Comments field in the Properties dialog box.

To conclude this exercise, you will create a hyperlink.

7   Right-click the name of task 8, *Launch public Web portal for book*, and then click **Hyperlink** on the shortcut menu.

The Insert Hyperlink dialog box appears.

8   In the **Text to display** box, type Add to spring catalog here.

9   In the **Address** box, type http://www.lucernepublishing.com/

10   Click **OK**.

A hyperlink icon appears in the Indicators column. Pointing to the icon displays the descriptive text you typed earlier.

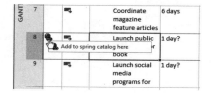

To open the webpage in your browser, either click the hyperlink icon or right-click on the hyperlink icon and in the shortcut menu that appears point to Hyperlink, and then click Open Hyperlink.

TIP You can quickly remove notes, hyperlinks or formatting from selected tasks. On the Task tab, in the Editing group, click Clear (looks like an eraser), and then select the command you want.

✖ CLEAN UP Close the Simple Tasks file.

Key points

- Good task names should be short verb phrases that will make sense to those who will review the plan or perform the work.

- Essential aspects of tasks in a plan include their duration and order of occurrence.

- In Project, phases of a schedule are represented as summary tasks.

- Task links, or relationships, cause the start or end of one task to affect the start or end of another task. A common task relationship is a finish-to-start relationship, in which the completion of one task controls the start of another task.

- Tasks can be manually or automatically scheduled. For manually scheduled tasks, you can record whatever information you might have about a task's duration, start, and finish values without affecting the overall plan.

- You can document additional details using task notes and create hyperlinks to the web.

4

Chapter at a glance

List

Create a list of resources, page 84.

	ⓘ	Resource Name ▾	Type ▾	Mate
1		Jun Cao	Work	
2		Sharon Salavaria	Work	
3		Toby Nixon	Work	
4		Toni Poe	Work	
5		Zac Woodall	Work	

Capacity

Change a resource's capacity to perform work, page 87.

ls ▾	Group ▾	Max. ▾	Std. Rate ▾
		100%	$0.00/hr
		50%	$0.00/hr
		100%	$0.00/hr
		100%	$0.00/hr
		100%	$0.00/hr
		400%	$0.00/hr

Rates

Enter resource pay rates, page 89.

) ▾	Max. ▾	Std. Rate ▾	Ovt. ▾
	100%	$42.00/hr	$0.00/hr
	50%	$1,100.00/wk	$0.00/hr
	100%	$2,700.00/wk	$0.00/hr
	100%	$0.00/hr	$0.00/hr
	100%	$55.00/hr	$0.00/hr
	400%	$45.00/hr	$0.00/hr

Exceptions

Change a resource's working time, page 92.

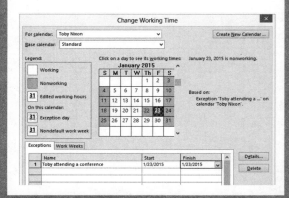

Setting up resources

IN THIS CHAPTER, YOU WILL LEARN HOW TO

- Set up basic resource information for the people who work on projects.

- Adjust the maximum capacity of a resource to do work.

- Enter standard and overtime pay rates for work resources.

- Change a resource's working and nonworking time.

- Create cost resources for financial tracking.

- Record additional information about a resource in a note.

Microsoft Project 2013 supports three types of *resources*. These are work resources, as well as two special-purpose resources: cost and material. Briefly, here is how to think about the three resource types:

- *Work resources* include the people and equipment needed to complete the tasks in a project's plan.

- *Cost resources* represent a financial cost associated with a task you need to account for in the plan. Examples include categories of expenses like travel, entertainment, and so on.

- *Material resources* are consumables you use up as the project proceeds. For example, a construction project might need to track steel or concrete as it is used throughout the project.

In this chapter, you will set up work and cost resources. You will work with material resources in Chapter 11, "Fine-tuning resource and assignment details."

Effective resource management is one of the most significant advantages of using Project rather than task-focused planning tools, such as paper-based organizers. You do not need to set up resources and assign them to tasks in Project; however, without making this information available in Project, you might be less effective in managing your project. Setting up resource information in Project takes a little effort, but the time is well spent if your project is primarily driven by time or cost constraints (and nearly all projects are driven by one, if not both, of these factors).

PRACTICE FILES Before you can complete the exercises in this chapter, you need to copy the book's practice files to your computer. A complete list of practice files is provided in "Download the practice files" at the beginning of this book. For each exercise that has a practice file, simply browse to where you saved the book's practice file folder.

IMPORTANT If you are running Project Professional with Project Web App/Project Server, take care not to save any of the practice files you work with in this book to Project Web App (PWA). For more information, see Appendix C, "Collaborating: Project, SharePoint, and PWA."

Entering work resource names

Work resources are the people and equipment doing the work of the project. Project focuses on two aspects of work resources: their availability and their costs. Availability determines when specific resources can work on tasks and how much work those resources can perform. Costs refer to the financial cost incurred by resources performing work on the project.

Some examples of how you can enter work resource names are listed in this table:

Work Resource	Example
Individual people identified by name.	Jun Cao; Zac Woodall
Individual people identified by job title or function.	Publisher; Contract specialist
Groups of people who have common skills. (When assigning such interchangeable resources to a task, you might not be concerned about who the individual resource is as long as they have the right skills.)	Copyeditors; Typesetters
Equipment.	Offset lithography press

Equipment resource considerations

In Project, you set up people and equipment resources in exactly the same way; they are both examples of work resources. However, you should be aware of important differences in how you can schedule these two work resources. Most people resources have a typical working day of 8 hours and usually no more than 12 hours, but equipment resources might have much more varied capacities for work, ranging from short durations (followed by maintenance) to around-the-clock sessions without interruption. Moreover, people resources might be flexible in the tasks they can perform, but equipment resources tend to be more specialized. For example, a content editor for a book project might also act as a copyeditor in a pinch, but a desktop copy machine cannot replace a printing press.

You do not need to track every piece of equipment that will be used in your plan, but you might want to set up equipment resources when

- Multiple teams or people might need a piece of equipment to accomplish different tasks simultaneously, and the equipment might be overbooked.

- You want to plan and track costs associated with the equipment.

Consider these issues if your plans involve equipment resources.

Project can help you make smarter decisions about managing work resources and monitoring financial costs.

TIP If you and your team members have Lync 2010 or later installed, you can start instant messaging, voice calls, or video calls directly from resource lists in Project. Point to the presence indicator next to resource names.

The scenario: At Lucerne Publishing, you have a good start on the new book launch's task list. You are now ready to set up the work resources needed to complete the new book launch at Lucerne Publishing. As with the task list, you expect some future changes to the resource details as you learn more about the project, but you have enough information to get started now.

In this exercise, you enter the names of several work resources.

SET UP You need the Simple Resources_Start file located in your Chapter05 practice file folder to complete this exercise. Open the Simple Resources_Start file, and save it as Simple Resources.

1   On the **View** tab, in the **Resource Views** group, click **Resource Sheet**.

     You will use the Resource Sheet view to enter the initial list of resources for the new book launch project.

2   Click the cell directly below the **Resource Name** column heading.

3   Type **Jun Cao**, and press the Enter key.

     Project creates a new resource.

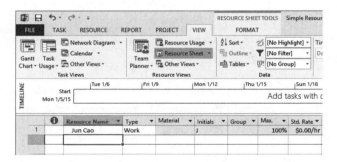

4   In the next empty rows in the **Resource Name** column, enter the following names:

     Sharon Salavaria

     Toby Nixon

     Toni Poe

     Zac Woodall

When you create a new work resource, Project assigns it 100% Max. Units by default.

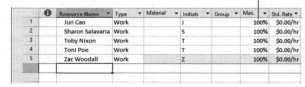

These resources are all individual people. You can also have a resource that represents multiple people. You'll enter such a resource next.

5   In the **Resource Name** field, below the last resource, type **Copyeditors**, and then press Enter.

> **TIP** If you find you need to add a new resource to your list and you want to add the new resource at a point other than at the end of the list, here's how. Select the resource name that you want to appear directly below the new resource. On the Resource tab, in the Insert group, click Add Resources and then select the resource type you want.

What is the best way to enter resource names?

In Project, work resource names can refer to specific people (Sharon Salavaria) or to specific job titles, such as Publisher or Contract Specialist. Use whatever naming convention makes the most sense to you and to those who will see your plan. The important questions are these: who will see these resource names, and how will they identify the resources? The resource names you choose will appear both in Project and in any resource information shared from Project. Here are two examples. In the default Gantt Chart view, the name of each resource appears next to the bars of the tasks to which that resource is assigned. In the Resource Overview report, the name of each resource appears on the axis of the Resource Stats and Work Status charts, as well as in the Resource Status table.

A resource might refer to somebody who is already on staff or to a position to be filled later. If you have not yet filled all the resource positions required, you might not have the names of specific people to enter. In that case, use descriptive placeholder names or job titles when setting up resources in Project.

Entering resources' maximum capacity

The Max. Units field represents the maximum capacity of a resource to work on the tasks assigned to that resource. Specifying that a resource has 100% *maximum units* means that 100 percent of that resource's working time is available to work on assigned tasks in the plan. Project will alert you with an indicator and red formatting if you assign the resource to more tasks than the resource can accomplish at 100 percent maximum units (in other words, if the resource becomes *overallocated*). 100% is the default Max. Units value for new resources.

For a resource that represents not a specific person but a category of interchangeable people with a common skill set, you can enter a larger maximum units value to indicate the number of available people. Entering a maximum units value such as 800% for such a resource means you can expect that eight individual people who all belong to that resource category will be available to work full-time every workday.

For a resource that has a working schedule that is less than full-time, you can enter a smaller maximum units value. Entering a maximum units value such as 75% for such a resource means you can expect that resource's capacity to be three quarters of a full-time resource. For a 40-hour work week, this equals 30 hours of capacity. Note that such a part-time working capacity might apply to a part-time worker or to a full-time worker who is allocated to a specific project only part-time.

The scenario: At Lucerne Publishing, you need to change the default 100% maximum units value for some resources. You learned that the equivalent of four copyeditors will be allocated to the new book launch. You also have one resource in the plan, Sharon Salavaria, who works for Lucerne half-time.

In this exercise, you adjust the Max. Units values for one resource that represents multiple people and for another resource whose capacity to work in this plan is less than full-time.

1   Click the **Max. Units** field for the *Copyeditors* resource.

2   Type or select **400%**, and then press Enter.

> **TIP** When you click a numeric value in a field like Max. Units, up and down arrows appear. You can click these to display the number you want, or simply type the number in the field.

Next you'll update the Max. Units value for Sharon Salavaria to indicate that she works half time.

3   Click the **Max. Units** field for *Sharon Salavaria*, type or select **50%**, and then press Enter.

❶	Resource Name	Type	Material	Initials	Group	Max.	Std. Rate
1	Jun Cao	Work		J		100%	$0.00/hr
2	Sharon Salavaria	Work		S		50%	$0.00/hr
3	Toby Nixon	Work		T		100%	$0.00/hr
4	Toni Poe	Work		T		100%	$0.00/hr
5	Zac Woodall	Work		Z		100%	$0.00/hr
6	Copyeditors	Work		C		400%	$0.00/hr

TIP If you prefer, you can enter maximum units as partial or whole numbers (such as .5, 1, 4) rather than as percentages (such as 50%, 100%, 400%). To use this format, on the File tab, click Options. In the Project Options dialog box, click on the Schedule tab. Under the Schedule heading, in the Show Assignment Units As A box, click Decimal.

With these changes to Max. Units, Project will identify these resources as being overallocated when their assigned work exceeds their capacities. You will work with resource overallocation in Chapter 11.

Entering resource pay rates

Almost all projects have some financial aspect, and cost limits the scope of many projects. Tracking and managing cost information in Project allows the project manager to answer such important questions as

- What is the expected total cost of the project based on task durations and resource assignments?

- Is the organization using expensive resources to do work that less expensive resources could do?

- How much money will a specific type of resource or task cost over the life of the project?

- Is the organization spending money at a rate that it can sustain for the planned duration of the project?

In Project, you can enter standard rates and costs per use for work and material resources, as well as overtime rates for work resources. Recall that in Project there are three types of resources: work, material, and cost. Cost resources do not use pay rates and are described later in this chapter.

When a work resource has a standard pay rate entered and is assigned to a task, Project calculates the cost of the assignment. Project does so by multiplying the assignment's work value by the resource's pay rate—both using a common increment of time (such as hours). You can then see the cost per resource, cost per assignment, and cost per task (as well as costs rolled up to summary tasks and the entire plan). You will assign resources to tasks in Chapter 6, "Assigning resources to tasks."

Project handles overtime expenses differently. Project will apply the overtime pay rate only when you specifically record overtime hours for an assignment. You will find more information about working with overtime in Chapter 16, "Getting your project back on track." Project does not automatically calculate overtime hours and associated costs because there's too great a chance that it would apply overtime when you did not intend it. In the scenario for the new book's launch, Jun Cao's working schedule provides a good example. In the next section, you will set up a working schedule of 10 hours per day, four days per week for Jun (a "four-by-ten" work schedule). This is still a regular 40-hour workweek, even though two hours per day could be mistaken for overtime with the normal assumption of an eight-hour day.

In addition to or instead of cost rates, a resource can include a set fee that Project accrues to each task to which the resource is assigned. This is called a *cost per use*. Unlike cost rates, the cost per use does not vary with the task's duration or amount of work the resource performs on the task. You specify the cost per use in the Cost/Use field in the Resource Sheet view.

The scenario: At Lucerne Publishing, you received the pay rates for the work resources involved in the new book launch from your payroll department. These pay rates are a mix of hourly and weekly rates. You need to enter these pay rates in the new book launch's plan.

In this exercise, you enter standard and overtime pay rates for work resources.

1   In the Resource Sheet, click the **Std. Rate** field for *Jun Cao*.

2   Type **42** and press Enter.

Jun's standard hourly rate of $42 appears in the Std. Rate column. Note that the default standard rate is hourly, so you did not need to specify cost per hour.

3   In the **Std. Rate** field for *Sharon Salavaria*, type **1100/w** and press Enter.

Sharon's weekly pay rate appears in the Std. Rate column. (You might need to widen the column to fully see the pay rates, as shown here.)

	ⓘ	Resource Name ▾	Type ▾	Material ▾	Initials ▾	Group ▾	Max. ▾	Std. Rate ▾	Ovt. ▾
1		Jun Cao	Work		J		100%	$42.00/hr	$0.00/hr
2		Sharon Salavaria	Work		S		50%	$1,100.00/wk	$0.00/hr
3		Toby Nixon	Work		T		100%	$0.00/hr	$0.00/hr
4		Toni Poe	Work		T		100%	$0.00/hr	$0.00/hr
5		Zac Woodall	Work		Z		100%	$0.00/hr	$0.00/hr
6		Copyeditors	Work		C		400%	$0.00/hr	$0.00/hr

4   Enter the following standard pay rates for the given resources:

Resource Name	Standard Rate
Toby Nixon	2700/w
Toni Poe	Leave at 0 (Toni is the book author, and you're not tracking her rate-based costs in this plan.)
Zac Woodall	55
Copyeditors	45

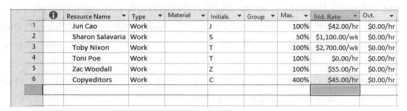

	ⓘ	Resource Name ▾	Type ▾	Material ▾	Initials ▾	Group ▾	Max. ▾	Std. Rate ▾	Ovt. ▾
1		Jun Cao	Work		J		100%	$42.00/hr	$0.00/hr
2		Sharon Salavaria	Work		S		50%	$1,100.00/wk	$0.00/hr
3		Toby Nixon	Work		T		100%	$2,700.00/wk	$0.00/hr
4		Toni Poe	Work		T		100%	$0.00/hr	$0.00/hr
5		Zac Woodall	Work		Z		100%	$55.00/hr	$0.00/hr
6		Copyeditors	Work		C		400%	$45.00/hr	$0.00/hr

TIP You might need to widen some columns to see the full column headings and values as shown here.

As you can see, you can enter pay rates with a variety of time bases—hourly (the default), daily, weekly, and so on. In fact, you can enter pay rates in all the increments of time for which you can enter task durations—from minutes to years.

Next you will enter an overtime pay rate for one of the resources.

5   In the field for the overtime rate (labeled **Ovt. Rate**) for *Jun Cao*, type **63**, and then press Enter.

TIP If you work with a large number of resources who have the same standard or overtime pay rates, you can set up Project to apply these pay rates automatically whenever you add a new resource. To do this, on the File tab, click Options. In the Project Options dialog box, click Advanced. Under the heading General Options For This Project, select the Automatically Add New Resources And Tasks check box and then enter the default pay rates you want.

5

Project management focus: Getting resource cost information

Work resources can account for the majority of costs in many projects. To take full advantage of the extensive cost-management features in Project, the project manager ideally should know the costs associated with each work resource. For people resources, it might be difficult to obtain such information. In many organizations, only senior management and human resource specialists know the pay rates of all resources working on a project, and they might consider this information confidential. Depending on your organizational policies and project priorities, you might not be able to track resource pay rates. If you cannot track resource cost information and your project is constrained by cost, your effectiveness as a project manager might be reduced, and the sponsors of your projects should understand this limitation.

If you do include cost details in your plan and this is considered sensitive information, consider requiring a password to open such plans. To set a password, click the File tab and then click Save As. Select the location you want, and then click Browse. In the Save As dialog box, click Tools and then click General Options.

Another strategy to consider is to use averaged burdened rates for people resources. A *burdened rate* is a pay rate plus overhead costs per worker. An averaged burdened rate describes everyone in general, but no one in particular.

Adjusting working time in a resource calendar

Project uses different types of calendars for different purposes. In Chapter 3, "Starting a new plan," you modified the *project calendar* to specify nonworking days for the entire project. In this section, your focus is the resource calendar. A *resource calendar* controls the working and nonworking times of a specific resource. Project uses a resource calendar to determine when work for a resource can be scheduled. Resource calendars apply only to work resources (people and equipment), not to material or cost resources.

When you initially create resources in a plan, Project creates a resource calendar for each work resource. The initial working-time settings for resource calendars exactly match those of the project calendar, which by default is the *Standard base calendar*. The Standard base calendar is built into Project and accommodates a default work schedule from 8 A.M. to 5 P.M., Monday through Friday, with an hour off for lunch each day. If all the working times of your resources match the working time of the project calendar, you do not need to edit any resource calendars. However, chances are that some of your resources will need exceptions to the working time in the project calendar—such as:

- A flex-time work schedule

- Vacation time

- Other times when a resource is not available to work on the project, such as time spent in training or attending a conference

TIP If you have a resource who is available to work on your project only part-time, you might be tempted to set the working time of the resource in your project to reflect a part-time schedule, such as 8 A.M. to 12 P.M. daily. However, a better approach is to adjust the availability of the resource as recorded in the Max. Units field to 50%, as you did in the previous exercise for the resource named Sharon Salavaria. Changing the unit availability of the resource keeps the focus on the capacity of the resource to work on the project rather than on the specific times of the day when that work might occur. You can set the maximum units for a resource in the Resource Sheet view.

Changes that you make to the project calendar are reflected automatically in resource calendars derived from the same project calendar. For example, in Chapter 3, you specified a nonworking day for a staff morale event, and Project rescheduled all work to skip that day. Note, however, that once you create a resource calendar exception, that exception is not affected by later changes to the project calendar.

The scenario: At Lucerne Publishing, you have a couple of working-time updates to make in the new book launch's plan. Toby Nixon has told you he'll be away at a conference, and Jun Cao works a full-time but nonstandard schedule of 10 hours per day, four days per week. You need to update their resource calendars accordingly.

In this exercise, you specify the working and nonworking times for work resources.

1 On the **Project** tab, in the **Properties** group, click **Change Working Time**.

   The Change Working Time dialog box appears.

2 In the **For calendar** box, click *Toby Nixon*.

   Toby Nixon's resource calendar appears in the Change Working Time dialog box. Toby has told you he will not be available to work on Friday, January 23 because he plans to attend a book-industry conference.

3   On the **Exceptions** tab in the Change Working Time dialog box, click in the first row directly below the **Name** column heading and type Toby attending a conference.

The description for the calendar exception is a handy reminder for you and others who might view the plan later.

4   Click in the **Start** field, and type or select 1/23/15.

5   To see the updated calendar preview in the dialog box, click in the **Finish** field.

TIP Alternatively, in the calendar in the Change Working Time dialog box you can first select the date or date range for which you want to create an exception, and then enter the exception name. Project will insert the Start and Finish dates automatically based on your selection; after it does that, press the Enter key.

Every work resource calendar is based on the project calendar; the default project calendar is the Standard base calendar.

Project will not schedule work for Toby on this January 23. Note also that January 22 is a nonworking day. That day is the staff morale event calendar exception in the project calendar you created in Chapter 3.

NOTE To set up a partial working-time exception for a resource, such as a portion of a day when a resource cannot work, click Details. In the Details dialog box, you can also create recurring exceptions to the resource's availability.

To conclude this exercise, you will set up a "4 by 10" work schedule (that is, 4 days per week, 10 hours per day) for a resource.

6   In the **For calendar** box, click *Jun Cao*.

7   When prompted to save the resource calendar changes you made for Toby Nixon, click **Yes**.

8   Click the **Work Weeks** tab in the Change Working Time dialog box.

9   Click **[Default]** directly under the **Name** column heading, and then click **Details**.

Next you will modify the default working week days and times for Jun Cao.

10 Under **Selected Day(s)**, select **Monday** through **Thursday**.

These are the weekdays Jun can normally work.

11 Click **Set day(s) to these specific working times**.

Next you'll modify Jun's regular daily schedule for the days she normally works.

12 In row 2, in the **To** column click **5:00 PM** and replace it with 7:00 PM, and then press Enter.

Finally, you will mark Friday as a nonworking day for Jun Cao.

13 Click **Friday**.

14 Click **Set days to nonworking time**.

Now Project can schedule work for Jun as late as 7 P.M. every Monday through Thursday, but it will not schedule work for her on Fridays.

15   Click **OK** to close the Details dialog box.

You can see in the calendar in the Change Working Time dialog box that Fridays (as well as Saturdays and Sundays) are marked as nonworking days for Jun Cao.

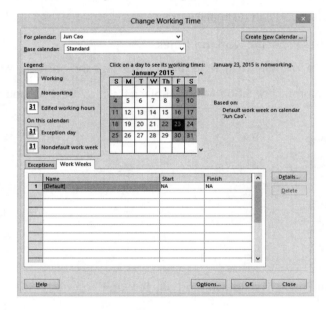

16   Click **OK** to close the Change Working Time dialog box.

Because you have not yet assigned these resources to tasks, you don't see the scheduling effect of their nonworking time settings. You will assign resources to tasks in Chapter 6.

TIP If you find that you must edit several resource calendars in a similar way (to handle a night shift, for example), it might be easier to assign a different base calendar to a resource or collection of resources. This is more efficient than editing individual resource calendars, and you can use the new base calendar to make projectwide adjustments to a single base calendar if needed. For example, if your project includes a day shift and a night shift, you can apply the Night Shift base calendar to resources who work the night shift. You change a base calendar in the Change Working Time dialog box. For collections of resources, you can select a specific base calendar directly in the Base Calendar column on the Entry table in the Resource Sheet view.

Setting up cost resources

Another type of resource you can use in Project is the *cost resource*. You can use a cost resource to represent a financial cost associated with a task in a plan. While work resources (people and equipment) can have associated costs (hourly rates and fixed costs per assignment), the sole purpose of a cost resource is to associate a particular type of cost with one or more tasks. Common types of cost resources might include categories of expenses you want to track in a plan for accounting or financial reporting purposes, such as travel, entertainment, or training.

Cost resources do no work and have no effect on the scheduling of a task. The Max. Units, Standard and Overtime pay rates, and Cost/Use fields do not apply to cost resources. After you assign a cost resource to a task and specify the cost amount per task, you can then see the cumulative costs for that type of cost resource, such as total travel costs in a project.

The way in which cost resources generate cost values differs from that of work resources. When you assign a work resource to a task, the work resource can generate a cost based on a pay rate (such as $40 per hour for the length of the assignment), a flat per-use cost (such as $100 per assignment), or both. You set up such pay rates and cost-per-use amounts once for the work resource, as you did in the section "Entering resource pay rates" earlier in this chapter. However, you enter the cost value of a cost resource only when you assign it to a task. You do this in the Cost field of the Assign Resources dialog box or in the Cost field of the Task form with the Cost detail shown. In fact, you'll do so in "Assigning cost resources to tasks" in Chapter 6.

The scenario: At Lucerne Publishing, the publisher maintains a profit and loss (P&L) sheet for every book it publishes. Travel is a major expense incurred in a book launch. Your finance department has asked you to track travel expenses in the plan. You'll do so via a cost resource.

In this exercise, you'll set up a cost resource.

1   In the Resource Sheet view, click the next empty cell in the **Resource Name** column.

2   Type Travel and press the Tab key.

3   In the **Type** field, click **Cost**.

	ⓘ	Resource Name ▾	Type ▾	Material ▾	Initials ▾	Group ▾	Max. ▾	Std. Rate ▾	Ovt. ▾	Cost/Use ▾
1		Jun Cao	Work		J		100%	$42.00/hr	$63.00/hr	$0.00
2		Sharon Salavaria	Work		S		50%	$1,100.00/wk	$0.00/hr	$0.00
3		Toby Nixon	Work		T		100%	$2,700.00/wk	$0.00/hr	$0.00
4		Toni Poe	Work		T		100%	$0.00/hr	$0.00/hr	$0.00
5		Zac Woodall	Work		Z		100%	$55.00/hr	$0.00/hr	$0.00
6		Copyeditors	Work		C		400%	$45.00/hr	$0.00/hr	$0.00
7		Travel	Cost ▾		T					

In Chapter 6, you will assign this cost resource to a task.

Documenting resources with notes

You might recall from Chapter 4, "Building a task list," that you can record additional information about a task, resource, or assignment in a *note*. For example, if a resource has flexible skills that can help the project, it is a good idea to record this in a note. That way, the note resides in the plan and can be easily viewed or printed.

In Chapter 4, you entered a task note by clicking the Notes button on the Task tab of the Properties group. You can enter resource notes in a similar way (by clicking the Notes button on the Resource tab of the Properties group), but in this exercise, you'll use a different method. You'll use the Resource form, which allows you to view and edit notes for multiple resources more quickly.

The scenario: At Lucerne Publishing, you collected some resource details that would be valuable to record in the plan. For one resource, you want to record some relevant work history, and for another resource, you have a clarifying note about her pay rate.

In this exercise, you'll enter notes in the Resource Form view.

1   In the **Resource Name** column, click *Toby Nixon*.

2   On the **Resource** tab, in the **Properties** group, click the **Details** button.

TIP You can also click Details, Resource Form on the View tab of the Split View group.

The Resource Form view appears below the Resource Sheet view

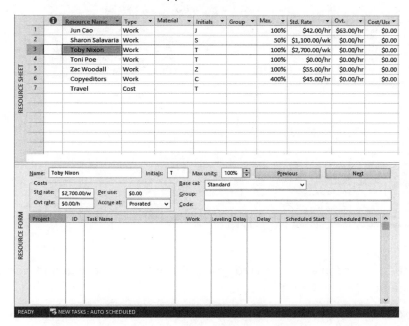

In this type of split view, details about the selected item in the upper view (a resource, in this case) appear in the lower view. You can quickly change the selected resource name in the upper view by clicking directly on a name, using the up arrow or down arrow keys, or clicking Previous or Next in the Resource Form view.

The Resource Form view can display one of several details; initially, it displays the Schedule details. Next you'll switch it to display the Notes details.

3   Click anywhere in the Resource Form view.

With the focus now on the Resource Form, the contextual label of the Format tab changes to Resource Form Tools.

4   On the **Format** tab, in the **Details** group, click **Notes**.

TIP You can also right-click in the gray background area of the Resource Form view and, in the shortcut menu that appears, click Notes.

The Notes details appear in the Resource Form view.

5　In the **Notes** box, type Toby worked on launch campaigns for Toni Poe's previous two books.

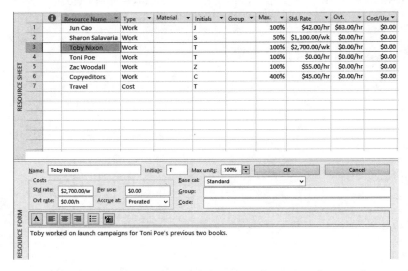

Notice that as soon as you started typing the note, the Previous and Next buttons changed to OK and Cancel.

6　Click **OK**.

In the Resource Sheet view, a note icon appears in the Indicators column.

7　Point to the note icon that appears next to Toby's name in the Resource Sheet view.

The note appears in a ScreenTip. For notes that are too long to appear in a ScreenTip, you can double-click the note icon to display the full text of the note. You can also see more of long notes in the Resource Form view or in the Resource Information dialog box.

To conclude this exercise, you'll add a note for one more resource.

8   In the Resource Form view, click **Previous** to shift the focus to *Sharon Salavaria* and display her details.

    TIP You can also click on Sharon's name in the Resource Sheet view above the Resource Form view.

9   In the **Notes** box, type **Sharon's standard pay rate is adjusted for her half-time work schedule.** Then click **OK**.

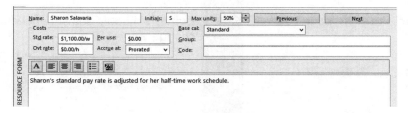

Finally, you'll hide the Resource Form view.

10   On the **Resource** tab, in the **Properties** group, click the **Details** button. The Resource Form view is hidden, leaving the Resource Sheet view displayed.

❌ CLEAN UP Close the Simple Resources file.

Key points

- Recording resource information in your plan helps you better control who does what work, when they do it, and at what cost.

- Work resources (people and equipment) perform the work in a project.

- Cost resources account for the types of expenses that you might want to track across a project.

Chapter at a glance

People

Assign work resources to tasks, page 104.

Control

Control schedule adjustment when resources change, page 112.

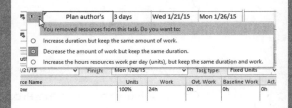

Cost

Assign cost resources to tasks, page 116.

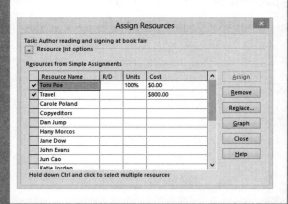

Review

Check the plan's essential details, such as duration and costs, page 118.

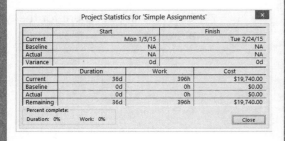

Assigning resources to tasks

IN THIS CHAPTER, YOU WILL LEARN HOW TO

- Assign work resources to tasks.

- Control how Project schedules additional resource assignments.

- Assign cost resources to tasks.

- Check on key schedule indicators for duration, cost, and work.

In Chapter 4, "Building a task list," and Chapter 5, "Setting up resources," you created tasks and resources. You are now ready to assign resources to tasks. An *assignment* is the matching of a *resource* to a *task* to do *work*. From the perspective of a task, you might call the process of assigning a resource a *task assignment*; from the perspective of a resource, you might call it a *resource assignment*. It is the same thing in either case: a task plus a resource equals an assignment.

> **IMPORTANT** When we talk about resources throughout this chapter, we are talking about work resources (people and equipment) unless we specify material or cost resources. For a refresher on resource types, see Chapter 5.

You do not have to assign resources to tasks in Microsoft Project 2013; you could work only with tasks. However, there are several good reasons for assigning resources in your plan. When you assign resources to tasks, you can answer questions such as

- Who should be working on what tasks and when?

- Do you have the correct number of resources to accomplish the scope of work that your project requires?

- Are you expecting a resource to work on a task at a time when that resource will not be available to work (for example, when someone will be on vacation)?

- Have you assigned a resource to so many tasks that you have exceeded the capacity of the resource to work—in other words, have you *overallocated* the resource?

In this chapter, you assign *work resources* to tasks, and you determine when resource assignments should affect task duration and when they should not. You then assign a *cost resource* and see what effect it has on a task.

PRACTICE FILES Before you can complete the exercises in this chapter, you need to copy the book's practice files to your computer. A complete list of practice files is provided in "Download the practice files" at the beginning of this book. For each exercise that has a practice file, simply browse to where you saved the book's practice file folder.

IMPORTANT If you are running Project Professional with Project Web App/Project Server, take care not to save any of the practice files you work with in this book to Project Web App (PWA). For more information, see Appendix C, "Collaborating: Project, SharePoint, and PWA."

Assigning work resources to tasks

By assigning a work resource to a task, you can track the progress of the resource's work on the task. If you enter resource pay rates, Project also calculates resource and task costs for you.

Assigning work resources to tasks enables Project's scheduling engine to calculate with all three variables of the so-called *scheduling formula*: work, duration, and assignment units. In fact, when you assign a work resource to a task with a duration greater than zero, Project then calculates the resulting work value following the scheduling formula. The scheduling formula is described in detail later in the chapter, following the hands-on activity.

You might recall from Chapter 5 that the capacity of a resource to work is measured in units (a level-of-effort measurement) and recorded in the Max. Units field. The specific assignment of a work resource to a task involves an assignment units value, normally expressed as a percentage. Unless you specify otherwise, Project assigns 100 percent of the units for the resource to the task—that is, Project assumes that all the resource's work time can be allotted to the task. If the resource has less than 100 percent maximum units, Project assigns the resource's Max. Units value.

The scenario: At Lucerne Publishing, you are ready to make the initial resource assignments in the new book launch plan. Because you previously accounted for the pay rates of work resources, you also want to see the initial cost and duration calculations of the plan for later comparison.

In this exercise, you assign work resources to tasks.

SET UP You need the Simple Assignments_Start file located in your Chapter06 practice file folder to complete this exercise. Open the Simple Assignments_Start file, and save it as Simple Assignments.

Before making any resource assignments, you'll check the plan's current duration and cost values for later comparison.

1   On the **Project** tab, in the **Properties** group, click **Project Information**, and then click **Statistics**.

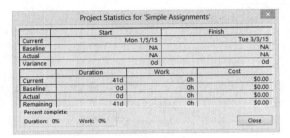

Note the current duration of 41 days and zero cost. After you assign work and cost resources, you'll check these values again.

2   Click **Close**.

Next you'll make your first resource assignment.

3   On the **Resource** tab, in the **Assignments** group, click **Assign Resources**.

The Assign Resources dialog box appears, in which you see the resource names you entered in Chapter 5, plus additional resources.

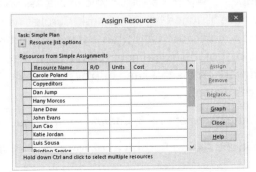

Except for assigned resources, which always appear at the top of the list, resources are sorted alphabetically in the Assign Resources dialog box.

4   In the **Task Name** column in the Gantt Chart view, click the name of task 2, *Assign launch team members*.

5   In the **Resource Name** column in the **Assign Resources** dialog box, click *Carole Poland*, and then click **Assign**.

The resource assigned to the selected task has a check mark next to its name in the Assign Resources dialog box.

The name of the assigned resource appears next to the Gantt bar.

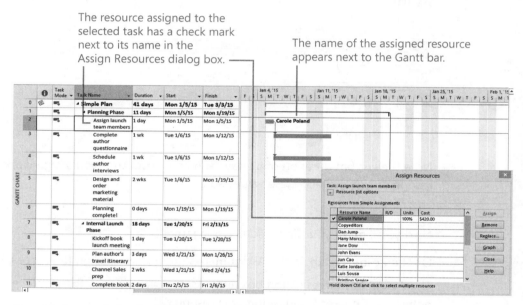

A cost value and check mark appears next to Carole's name in the Assign Resources dialog box, indicating that you have assigned her to the task. Carole's name also appears next to the task 2 Gantt bar. Because Carole has a standard cost rate recorded, Project calculates the cost of the assignment (Carole's standard pay rate times her scheduled amount of work on the task) and displays that value, $420, in the Cost field of the Assign Resources dialog box.

6   In the **Task Name** column, click the name of task 3, *Complete author questionnaire*.

7   In the **Resource Name** column in the **Assign Resources** dialog box, click *Toni Poe*, and then click **Assign**.

The names of assigned resources appear at the top of the list.

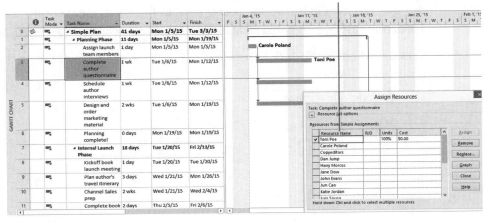

TIP To remove or unassign a resource from a selected task, in the Assign Resources dialog box, click the resource name and then click Remove.

Next you'll take a closer look at the details of task 3. You'll use a handy view called the Task Form.

8   On the **View** tab, in the **Split View** group, select the **Details** check box.

Project splits the window into two panes. In the upper pane is the Gantt Chart view, and below it is the Task Form view.

The names of the view or views displayed appear here.

If you completed Chapter 5, you might recognize that the Task Form is similar to the Resource Form but shows different details. In this type of split view, the details about the selected item in the upper view (a task, in this case) appear in the lower view. The Task Form displays one of several details. Next you'll change the displayed details.

9   Click anywhere in the **Task Form** view and then, on the **Format** tab, in the **Details** group, click **Work**.

The Work details appear.

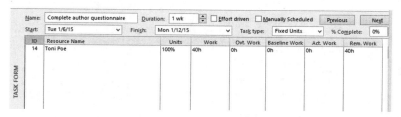

Now in the Task Form view, you can see the essential scheduling values for this task: 1 week duration, 40 hours of work, and 100% assignment units. Because the Task Form is a handy way to see a task's duration, units, and work values, leave it displayed for now.

10   Using the **Assign Resources** dialog box, assign the following resources to tasks. As you do so, note the **Duration**, **Units**, and **Work** values in the **Task Form** view.

For this task	Assign this resource
4, Schedule author interviews	Jun Cao
5, Design and order marketing material	Toby Nixon

When you are finished, your screen should look similar to the following illustration:

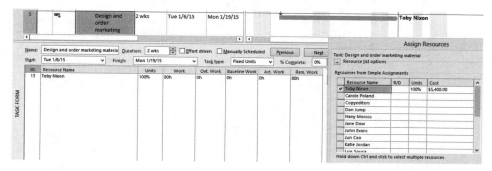

TIP If you accidentally assign the wrong resource, you can quickly undo the assignment. On the Quick Access toolbar, click Undo. Or press Ctrl + Z.

Next you will assign two resources to a single task.

11 In the **Task Name** column, click the name of task 8, *Kickoff book launch meeting*.

12 In the Assign Resources dialog box, select the names of *Sharon Salavaria* and *Toby Nixon*, and then click **Assign**.

> **TIP** To select nonadjacent resource names, select the first name, hold down the Ctrl key, and then select additional names. This technique also works with tasks and other items in lists.

Sharon and Toby are assigned to the task. You can also see their names next to the task 8 Gantt bar.

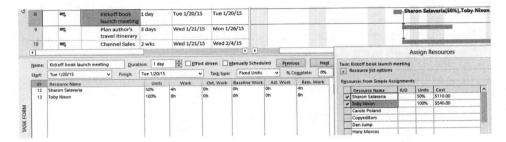

13 In the Assign Resources dialog box, click **Close**.

Recall from Chapter 5 that Sharon has a 50% Max. Units value to account for her half-time availability. As a result, Project assigned her at 50% units.

To conclude this exercise, you'll use a different means of assigning resources.

14 If the **Resource Names** column is not already visible, in the Gantt Chart view, drag the vertical divider bar to the right.

15 Click in the **Resource Names** column for task 9, *Plan author's travel itinerary*, and then click the arrow that appears.

A list of resource names appears.

Drag this vertical divider bar to see more or
less of the table portion of the Gantt Chart view.

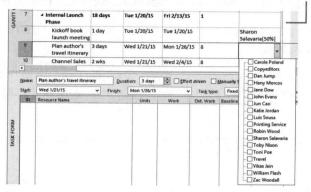

16   In the list of resource names, select the check boxes for *Jane Dow* and *Zac Woodall*,
      and then press the Enter key.

      Jane and Zac are assigned to task 9.

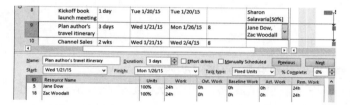

17   Click in the **Resource Names** column for task 10, *Channel Sales prep*, and then click
      the arrow that appears. In the list of resource names that appears, select *Zac Woodall*
      and then press the Enter key.

      Zac is assigned to task 10.

18   Drag the vertical divider bar to the right edge of the **Finish** column.

In this exercise, you assigned resources using the Assign Resources dialog box and the
Resource Names column in the Gantt Chart view. In addition, you can assign resources in
the Task Form view and on the Resources tab of the Task Information dialog box, among
other places. As you use Project, you'll likely develop your own preference for the way you
assign resources.

The scheduling formula: duration, units, and work

After you create a task but before you assign a resource to it, the task has duration but no work associated with it. Why no work? Work represents the amount of effort a resource or resources will spend to complete a task. For example, if you have one person working full-time, the amount of time measured as work is the same as the amount of time measured as duration. In general, the amount of work will match the duration unless you assign more than one resource to a task or the one resource you assign is not working full-time.

Project calculates work using what is sometimes called the *scheduling formula*:

> *Duration × Assignment Units = Work*

Let's look at a specific example and find these values in the Task Form. The duration of task 3 is one week, or five working days. For the new book launch project, five days equals 40 hours. When you assigned Toni Poe to task 3, Project applied 100 percent of Toni's working time to this task. The scheduling formula for task 3 looks like this:

> *40 hours (the same as one week) task duration × 100% assignment units = 40 hours of work*

In other words, with Toni assigned to task 3 at 100% units, the task should require 40 hours of work.

Here's a more complex example. You assigned two resources, Jane Dow and Zac Woodall, to task 9, each at 100% assignment units. The scheduling formula for task 9 looks like this:

> *24 hours (the same as three days) task duration × 200% assignment units = 48 hours of work*

The 48 hours of work is the sum of Jane's 24 hours of work plus Zac's 24 hours of work. In other words, as currently scheduled, both resources will work full-time on the task in parallel for its three-day duration.

Controlling work when adding or removing resource assignments

As you saw previously, you define the amount of work that a task represents when you initially assign a resource or resources to it. When tasks are automatically (as opposed to manually) scheduled, Project gives you an option to control how it should calculate work on a task when you assign additional resources to the task or unassign resources from the task. This option is called *effort-driven tasks*, and it works like this: The work of a task remains constant as you assign or unassign resources. As more resources are assigned to a task, the duration decreases, but the total work remains the same and is distributed among the assigned resources. You have flexibility in how you apply effort-driven scheduling.

By default, effort-driven scheduling is disabled for all tasks you create in Project. You can turn on effort-driven scheduling for an entire plan or just specific tasks. You can also use the options in an Actions list to control how Project should recalculate work on a task immediately after making a resource assignment. (You'll do this below.) Effort-driven scheduling applies only when you assign additional resources or remove resources from automatically scheduled tasks.

The scenario: At Lucerne Publishing, some time has passed since you made the initial resource assignments for the new book launch plan. You received some feedback from the assigned resources that require some adjustments to assignments. As you make these adjustments, you will control how the revised assignments should affect the tasks.

In this exercise, you add and remove resource assignments on tasks and tell Project how it should adjust the tasks.

1   In the Gantt Chart view, click the name of task 5, *Design and order marketing material*.

Currently, Toby is assigned to this task. A quick check of the scheduling formula looks like this:

80 hours (the same as 10 days, or two weeks) task duration × 100% of Toby's assignment units = 80 hours of work

Toby needs some help with this task, so you'll add a resource.

2   On the **Resources** tab, in the **Assignments** group, click **Assign Resources**.

3   In the **Resource Name** column in the **Assign Resources** dialog box, click *Zac Woodall*, and then click **Assign**.

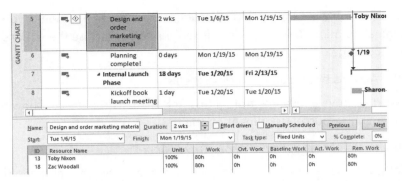

Zac is added to the task, and Project updates the scheduling formula values:

80 hours (the same as 10 days, or two weeks) task duration × 200% (that is, the sum of Toby's and Zac's assignment units) = 160 hours work.

Next you will use a feature called the Actions list to control how Project schedules the work on a task when adding or removing resources. Note the small green triangle in the upper-left corner of the name of task 5. This is a graphical indicator that an action is now available. Until you perform another action, you can use the Actions list to choose how you want Project to handle the additional resource assignment.

4   Click the name of task 5, and then click the **Actions** button that appears just to the left of the task name.

Look over the options on the list that appears.

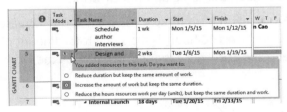

You can use these options to choose the scheduling result that you want. You can adjust the task's duration, the resources' work, or the assignment units.

TIP You will see other Actions indicators while using Project. They generally appear when you might otherwise ask yourself, "Hmm, why did Project just do that?" (such as when a task's duration changes after you assign an additional resource). The Actions list gives you the chance to change how Project responds to your actions.

For this task, you want the additional assignment to mean additional work done in the original duration. This is the default setting, so you'll close the Actions list without making a change.

5   Click the **Actions** button again to close the list.

Next you'll remove a resource from a task and then instruct Project how to schedule the remaining resource assignment on the task.

6   Click the name of task 9, *Plan author's travel itinerary.*

Currently, both Jane and Zac are assigned to the task. Jane has told you she needs to complete the planned work alone, but over a longer time period. This is acceptable to you, so you'll unassign Zac.

7   In the **Resource Name** column in the **Assign Resources** dialog box, click *Zac Woodall*, and then click **Remove**.

Project unassigns Zac from the task.

Next you'll adjust how Project should handle the change in assignments.

8   Click the **Actions** button that appears just to the left of the task name.

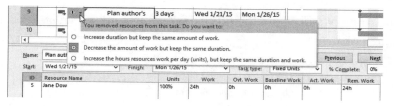

9   Click **Increase duration, but keep the same amount of work**.

Project increases the task's duration from three to six days, and it increases Jane's work total from 24 to 48 hours. This 48 hours is the same total amount of work on the task when both Jane and Zac were assigned, but now all the work belongs to Jane.

So far, you've been adjusting duration and work values as you add or remove resources from tasks. You can also change the default setting for a task such that as you add resources to the task, its duration is decreased. You'll do so next.

10   In the Gantt Chart view, click the name of task 10, *Channel Sales prep.*

Currently, just Zac is assigned to this task, and it has a two-week duration.

11   In the **Task Form**, click **Effort driven**, and then click **OK** in the upper-right corner of the **Task Form**.

There is no change to the duration, units, or work values for this task, but watch what happens when you assign an additional resource.

12   In the Gantt Chart view, click the name of task 10, and then, in the **Assign Resources** dialog box, click *Hany Morcos*, and then click **Assign**.

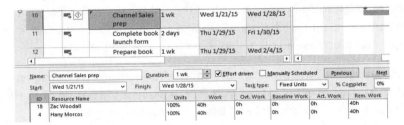

The task 10 duration is reduced from two weeks to one week. The total work on the task remains 80 hours, but now it is split evenly between Zac and Hany. This is the scheduling result you wanted. If it wasn't, you could use the Actions list to change how Project responds to the additional resource assignment.

TIP Recall that effort-driven scheduling is disabled by default. To change the default setting for all new tasks in a plan, do the following. On the File tab, click Options. In the Project Options dialog box, click Schedule and then under Scheduling Options For This Project, select the New Tasks Are Effort Driven check box. To control effort-driven scheduling for a specific task or tasks, first select the task or tasks. Then, on the Task tab, in the Properties group, click Information, and on the Advanced tab of the Task Information dialog box, select or clear the Effort Driven check box.

The order of your actions matters when effort-driven scheduling is enabled. If you initially assign two resources to a task with a duration of three days (equal to 24 hours), Project schedules each resource to work 24 hours, for a total of 48 hours of work on the task. However, you might initially assign one resource to a task with a duration of 24 hours and later add a second resource. In this case, effort-driven scheduling will cause Project to schedule each resource to work 12 hours in parallel, keeping the total of 24 hours of work on the task. Remember that when it's turned on, effort-driven scheduling adjusts the task duration only if you add or remove resources from a task.

Project management focus: When should effort-driven scheduling apply?

You should consider the extent to which effort-driven scheduling should apply to the tasks in your projects. For example, if one resource should take 10 hours to complete a task, could 10 resources complete the task in 1 hour? How about 20 resources in 30 minutes? Probably not—the resources would likely get in each other's way and require additional coordination to complete the task. If the task is very complicated, it might require significant ramp-up time before a resource can contribute fully. Overall productivity might even decrease if you assign more resources to the task.

No single rule exists about when you should apply effort-driven scheduling and when you should not. As the project manager, you should analyze the nature of the work required for each task in your project and use your best judgment.

Assigning cost resources to tasks

Recall from Chapter 5 that *cost resources* are used to represent a financial cost associated with a task in a project. Cost resources do not incur assignment units, so they do no work and have no effect on the scheduling of a task. Cost resources might include categories of expenses you want to budget and track for accounting or financial reporting purposes. Broadly speaking, the costs that tasks can incur can include:

- Work resource costs, such as a person's standard pay rate times the amount of work they perform on the task.

- Cost resource costs, which are a fixed dollar amount you enter when assigning the cost resource to a task. The amount is not affected by changes in duration or any other schedule changes to the task, although you can edit the amount at any time. You can also see cumulative costs resulting from assigning the same cost resource to multiple tasks.

The costs derived from cost-resource assignments represent planned costs. (Indeed, you should consider all costs that Project has calculated so far in the schedule to be planned costs, such as those resulting from work-resource assignments to tasks.) Later, you can enter actual costs if you want to compare them with the budget.

The scenario: At Lucerne Publishing, you want to enter planned travel costs for certain tasks for the plan for the new book launch.

In this exercise, you assign a work resource and a cost resource to a task.

1   Click the name of task 17, *Author reading and signing at book fair*.

This task requires air travel by the author, and you allocated $800 in anticipation of this expense.

Currently, task 17 has no assigned resource and no cost. First, you'll assign the author to the task.

2   In the **Resource Name** column in the **Assign Resources** dialog box, click *Toni Poe*, and then click **Assign**.

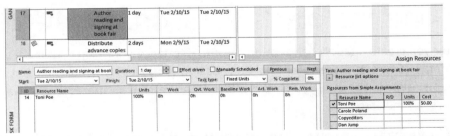

Project assigns Toni Poe, a work resource, to the task. As you can see in the Cost field of the Assign Resources dialog box, this assignment has no cost. That's because this work resource, Toni Poe, has no cost rate or per-use cost. So even though the assignment generated work, there's no cost associated with it. Next you'll assign the cost resource.

3   In the **Assign Resources** dialog box, select the **Cost** field for the **Travel** cost resource, type **800**, and then click **Assign**.

Project assigns the cost resource to the task.

4   To see both assigned resources, scroll up the **Resource** list in the **Assign Resources** dialog box.

You can see the cost incurred by this assignment in the Cost column of the Assign Resources dialog box. The travel cost value will remain the same regardless of any changes made to the scheduling of the task, such as work resources being assigned or unassigned, or the task's duration changing.

5   In the **Assign Resources** dialog box, click **Close.**

Note the task has the same duration of one day and Toni Poe has the same units and work values as before. Assigning the cost resource affected only the cost incurred by this task.

Checking the plan's duration, cost, and work

After you create a task list and assign resources to tasks, your plan contains a large number of details. Some of these details will be critical to the success of your plan, but they might not be visible in the view you have displayed. This section illustrates several ways of seeing a plan's key indicators.

There are many ways you can see key indicators of a plan in Project, which you'll explore next. These indicators can help answer such questions as the following:

- Who is assigned to do what work in the plan?

- How long will it take to complete the project?

- How much will it cost?

For many projects, the answers to these questions are likely to change as time passes. For this reason, it's a good practice to quickly be able to show current project status. This can inform you, as the project manager, of the resources performing the work, as well as the project's sponsors and other stakeholders.

The scenario: At Lucerne Publishing, you established a weekly status reporting cadence for those directly working on the new book launch project. In addition, you've been asked to supply monthly updates on a few key indicators of overall project health more broadly to the organization. You're ready to explore some of the project status features in Project and evaluate them for your regular status reporting routine.

In this exercise, you explore various project status-reporting features, including views and reports.

1   To begin, you will show the Timeline view. On the **View** tab, in the **Split View** group, select the **Timeline** check box.

As you might recall from Chapter 4, you can see the plan's start and finish dates at either end of the timeline. Note the current finish date: 2/24/15.

The timeline does not tell you the plan's specific duration; however, that's visible in the project summary task in the Gantt Chart view. Recall from Chapter 4 that the project summary task is hidden by default, but you previously displayed it. It is identified as task 0 at the top of the Entry table in the Gantt Chart view.

2   If necessary, scroll the Gantt Chart view up so that task 0 *Simple Plan* is visible.

Note the duration value of the project summary task: 36 days. You can also see the plan's start and finish dates here too.

At the start of this chapter, the plan's duration was 41 days. This shorter duration you see now is the result of assignment changes you made earlier.

Both the Timeline view and the project summary task in the Gantt Chart view are good options for quickly seeing the project's overall duration and finish date; you can incorporate these views into your status reporting needs. Next you'll look at project costs.

3   On the **View** tab, in the **Data** group, click **Tables**, and then click **Cost**.

The Cost table appears, replacing the Entry table.

	Task Name	Fixed Cost	Fixed Cost Accrual	Total Cost	Baseline	Variance	W
0	◢ Simple Plan	$0.00	Prorated	$19,740.00	$0.00	$19,740.00	
1	◢ Planning Phase	$0.00	Prorated	$11,900.00	$0.00	$11,900.00	
2	Assign launch team members	$0.00	Prorated	$420.00	$0.00	$420.00	
3	Complete author questionnaire	$0.00	Prorated	$0.00	$0.00	$0.00	ni F

The Cost table includes various cost values for each subtask. These subtask cost values roll up to their summary tasks, and ultimately all cost values roll up to the project summary task.

Note the project summary task's total cost value: $19,740. This cost value is the sum of the work-resource assignments plus the one cost resource assignment you previously made.

Next you will look at some assignment values via a report.

4   On the **Report** tab, in the **View Reports** group, click **Resources** and then click **Resource Overview**.

The Resource Overview report appears.

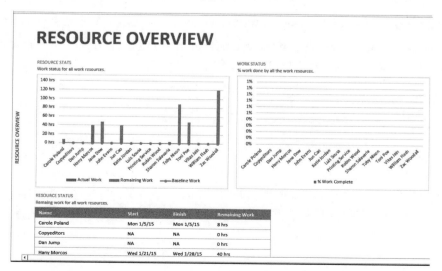

In this report, you can see two charts and one table that contain resource-assignment details. You might need to vertically scroll the report down to see all of its content.

In the Resource Stats chart in the upper left, note the assigned work values for each resource. Currently, the chart contains only remaining work values because you have not yet saved a baseline or reported any actual work. You will do so in Chapter 8, "Tracking progress."

The Resource Status table at the bottom of the report is an excellent summary of each resource's earliest start dates and latest finish dates of their assignments, as well as remaining work.

RESOURCE STATUS
Remaining work for all work resources.

Name	Start	Finish	Remaining Work
Carole Poland	Mon 1/5/15	Mon 1/5/15	8 hrs
Copyeditors	NA	NA	0 hrs
Dan Jump	NA	NA	0 hrs
Hany Morcos	Wed 1/21/15	Wed 1/28/15	40 hrs
Jane Dow	Wed 1/21/15	Thu 1/29/15	48 hrs
John Evans	NA	NA	0 hrs
Jun Cao	Mon 1/5/15	Mon 1/12/15	40 hrs
Katie Jordan	NA	NA	0 hrs
Luis Sousa	NA	NA	0 hrs
Printing Service	NA	NA	0 hrs
Robin Wood	NA	NA	0 hrs
Sharon Salavaria	Tue 1/20/15	Tue 1/20/15	4 hrs
Toby Nixon	Tue 1/6/15	Tue 1/20/15	88 hrs
Toni Poe	Tue 1/6/15	Tue 2/10/15	48 hrs
Vikas Jain	NA	NA	0 hrs
William Flash	NA	NA	0 hrs
Zac Woodall	Tue 1/6/15	Wed 1/28/15	120 hrs

RESOURCE OVERVIEW

Later when you begin to track progress in the plan, this report will be an excellent means of sharing resource and work status.

To conclude this exercise, you'll revisit the project's overall duration and cost values in the Project Statistics dialog box.

5   On the **Project** tab, in the **Properties** group, click **Project Information**, and then click **Statistics**.

Project Statistics for 'Simple Assignments'			
	Start		Finish
Current	Mon 1/5/15		Tue 2/24/15
Baseline	NA		NA
Actual	NA		NA
Variance	0d		0d
	Duration	Work	Cost
Current	36d	396h	$19,740.00
Baseline	0d	0h	$0.00
Actual	0d	0h	$0.00
Remaining	36d	396h	$19,740.00
Percent complete:			
Duration: 0% Work: 0%			Close

Here, again, you see the shorter duration and changed cost and work values.

6   Click **Close**.

✖ CLEAN UP Close the Simple Assignments file.

Key points

- In Project, a task normally has work associated with it after a work resource (which can be people or equipment) has been assigned to the task.

- You must assign resources to tasks before you can track the progress or cost of resources.

- Project follows the scheduling formula Duration × Assignment Units = Work.

- Effort-driven scheduling determines whether work remains constant when you assign additional resources to tasks. Effort-driven scheduling is turned off by default.

- The easiest way to understand effort-driven scheduling is to ask yourself this question: If one person can do this task in 10 days, could two people do it in 5 days? If so, effort-driven scheduling should be applied to the task.

- Actions lists appear after you perform certain actions in Project, such as assigning additional resources to a task. You can use Actions lists to quickly change the effect of your action to something other than the default effect.

- By assigning cost resources, you can associate financial costs with a task other than costs derived from work or material resources.

- Use the Project Statistics dialog box to see key indicators such as a plan's start and finish dates, duration, and cost.

6

Chapter at a glance

Customize

Change the appearance of views, page 126.

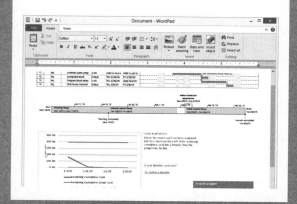

Modify

Customize the appearance of reports, page 136.

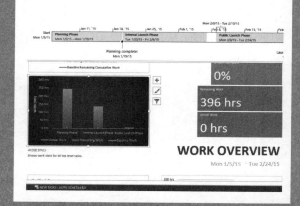

Copy

Take a snapshot copy of views and reports, page 139.

Print

Set print options to get the output you want, page 144.

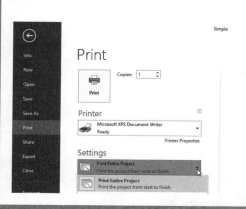

Formatting and sharing your plan

7

IN THIS CHAPTER, YOU WILL LEARN HOW TO

- Customize a Gantt chart view.

- Customize the Timeline view.

- Customize a report.

- Copy snapshots of views and reports to another application.

- Print views and reports.

Project provides a number of ways to change how your data appears when you need to copy or print a plan.

In some respects, a Microsoft Project 2013 plan is really a database of information, not unlike a Microsoft Access database file. You don't normally see all the data in a plan at one time. Instead, you focus on the aspect of the plan you're currently interested in viewing. Views and reports are the most common ways to observe or print a plan's data. In both cases, you can substantially format the data to meet your needs.

In previous chapters, you used views to capture and visualize schedule details. Another means of visualizing your schedule is the Reports feature. Project 2013 has greatly enhanced reports. You can create graphical reports within Project rather than exporting the Project data to another program. You can include colorful charts and images as well as tables in your reports. Project includes many reports you can use as-is or customize, or you can create your own unique report. You can print reports or copy them to other applications.

TIP This chapter introduces you to some of the simpler view and report formatting features in Project. You'll find more material about formatting, printing, and sharing your plans in Chapter 13, "Organizing project details," Chapter 17, "Applying advanced formatting and printing," Chapter 18, "Advanced report formatting," and Appendix C, "Collaborating: Project, SharePoint, and PWA."

Customizing a Gantt chart view

The Gantt chart became a standard way of visualizing schedules when, in the early 20th century, American engineer Henry Gantt developed a bar chart showing the use of resources over time. For many people, a Gantt chart is synonymous with a project's schedule or plan and is a popular and widely understood representation of schedule information throughout the project management world. In Project, the default view is dominated by a Gantt chart. You are likely to spend a lot of your time in this view when working in Project.

TIP By default, when you create a new plan Project displays a split view named Gantt with Timeline. However, you can change this setting to display any view you want as the default view for a new plan. On the File tab, click Options. In the Project Options dialog box, click General. In the Default View box, click the view you want. The next time you create a new plan, the view you have chosen will appear.

A Gantt chart view consists of two parts: a table on the left and a bar chart on the right. The bar chart includes a timescale band across the top that denotes units of time. The bars on the chart graphically represent the tasks in the table in terms of start and finish dates, duration, and status (for example, whether work on the task has started or not). On a Gantt chart, tasks, summary tasks, and milestones all appear as Gantt bars or symbols, and each type of bar has its own format. Whenever you work with Gantt bars, keep in mind that they represent tasks in a plan. Other elements on the chart, such as link lines, represent relationships between tasks. You can change the formatting of almost any element on a Gantt chart.

The default formatting applied to a Gantt chart view works well for onscreen viewing, sharing with other programs, and printing. However, you can change the formatting of almost any element on a Gantt chart. There are three distinct ways to format Gantt bars:

- Quickly apply predefined color combinations from the Gantt Chart Style group, which you can see on the Format tab when a Gantt chart is displayed.

- Apply highly customized formatting to Gantt bars in the Bar Styles dialog box, which you can open by clicking the Format tab when a Gantt chart is displayed, and then, in the Bar Styles group, clicking Format, Bar Styles. In this case, the formatting changes you make to a particular type of Gantt bar (a summary task, for example) apply to all such Gantt bars in the Gantt chart.

- Format individual Gantt bars directly. The direct formatting changes you make have no effect on other bars in the Gantt chart. You can double-click a Gantt bar to view its formatting options, or, on the Format tab in the Bar Styles group, click Format, Bar. For more information, see Chapter 17.

The scenario: At Lucerne Publishing, you are almost done with planning the new book launch project and the team is about to commence work. The plan you developed is getting broader exposure inside Lucerne Publishing, and you want to format the plan to highlight a key milestone. You also want a few other details from the plan to visually stand out.

In this exercise, you change the formatting of different elements in a Gantt chart view.

 SET UP You need the Simple Formatting_Start file located in your Chapter07 practice file folder to complete this exercise. Open the Simple Formatting_Start file, and save it as Simple Formatting.

To begin, you will view the Gantt bar for a manually scheduled task. Then you will adjust the colors of the Gantt bars and milestones in the chart portion of the Gantt Chart view, and see how a manually scheduled task's Gantt bar is formatted.

1   In the **Task Name** column, click the name of task 9, *Prepare book P&L statement.*

2   On the **Task** tab, in the **Editing** group, click **Scroll to Task**.

   TIP You can accomplish the same thing by right-clicking the task name and, in the shortcut menu that appears, clicking Scroll To Task.

Project scrolls the chart portion of the Gantt Chart view to display the Gantt bar for a manually scheduled task that was previously added to the book launch plan. As you can see, the Gantt bar of this manually scheduled task does not look like the Gantt bars of the automatically scheduled tasks.

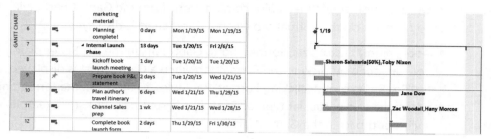

Keep an eye on this Gantt bar as you apply a different Gantt chart style to the plan.

3   On the **Format** tab, in the **Gantt Chart Style** group, click the **More button** to display the predefined color styles.

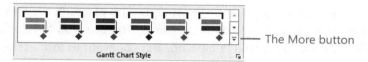

The More button

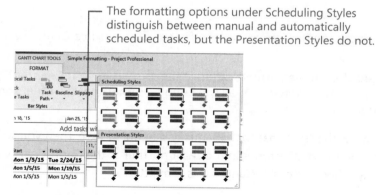

The formatting options under Scheduling Styles distinguish between manual and automatically scheduled tasks, but the Presentation Styles do not.

The Gantt Chart styles are divided into two groups:

- Scheduling Styles distinguish between manually and automatically scheduled tasks.

- Presentation Styles do not make that distinction.

4 Under **Presentation Styles**, click the orange color scheme.

Project applies this style to the Gantt bars in the plan.

		marketing material			
6		Planning complete!	0 days	Mon 1/19/15	Mon 1/19/15
7		◢ Internal Launch Phase	13 days	Tue 1/20/15	Fri 2/6/15
8		Kickoff book launch meeting	1 day	Tue 1/20/15	Tue 1/20/15
9		Prepare book P&L statement	2 days	Tue 1/20/15	Wed 1/21/15
10		Plan author's travel itinerary	6 days	Wed 1/21/15	Thu 1/29/15
11		Channel Sales prep	1 wk	Wed 1/21/15	Wed 1/28/15
12		Complete book launch form	2 days	Thu 1/29/15	Fri 1/30/15

The Gantt bar of task 9, the manually scheduled task, is no longer visually distinct from the automatically scheduled tasks.

Applying a presentation style to the Gantt Chart view is an option you can use when you don't want to distinguish between manual and automatically scheduled tasks— when showing the Gantt chart to an audience for whom you do not want to make this distinction, for example.

Your next step in this exercise is to reformat a task name so that it will visually stand out.

5 In the **Task Name** column, right-click the name of task 6, *Planning Complete!*

This is a milestone task that describes the end of the first phase of the new book launch at Lucerne Publishing. You'd like to highlight this task name.

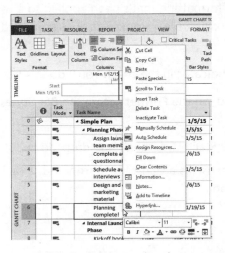

In addition to the regular shortcut menu, note the Mini Toolbar.

6   On the Mini Toolbar, click the arrow next to the **Background Color** button, and under **Standard Colors**, click yellow.

>   **TIP** You can also click the Task tab, and in the Font group, click Background Color.

Background Color button.

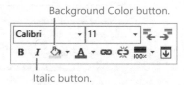

Italic button.

Project applies the yellow background color to the task name's cell.

7   On the Mini Toolbar, click the **Italic** button.

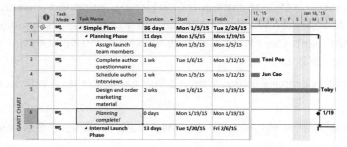

Now the milestone task name stands out.

>   **TIP** You can quickly remove all text formatting that's been applied to a value in a cell. On the Task tab, in the Editing group, click Clear (looks like an eraser), and then click Clear Formatting.

You can also format the milestone indicator in the chart. You'll do this next.

8   With the name of task 6 still selected, on the **Format** tab, in the **Bar Styles** group, click **Format**, and then click **Bar**.

9   In the **Format Bar** dialog box, under **Start**, click the **Shape** drop-down list.

Project displays the symbols you can use as a Gantt bar starting edge or, in this case for a milestone, as a milestone symbol.

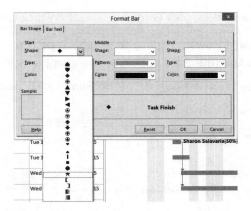

10   Click the star symbol, and then click **OK**.

Project uses the star symbol as the milestone symbol for this task.

	🔒	Task Mode ▾	Task Name ▾	Duration ▾	Start ▾	Finish ▾	11, '15 M T W T F	S S	Jan 18, '15 M T W
0	📝	🏷	◢ **Simple Plan**	**36 days**	**Mon 1/5/15**	**Tue 2/24/15**			
1		🏷	◢ **Planning Phase**	**11 days**	**Mon 1/5/15**	**Mon 1/19/15**			
2		🏷	Assign launch team members	1 day	Mon 1/5/15	Mon 1/5/15			
3		🏷	Complete author questionnaire	1 wk	Tue 1/6/15	Mon 1/12/15	▬ Toni Poe		
4		🏷	Schedule author interviews	1 wk	Mon 1/5/15	Mon 1/12/15	▬ Jun Cao		
5		🏷	Design and order marketing material	2 wks	Tue 1/6/15	Mon 1/19/15			Toby
6		🏷	*Planning complete!*	0 days	Mon 1/19/15	Mon 1/19/15		★ 1/19	
7		🏷	◢ **Internal Launch Phase**	**13 days**	**Tue 1/20/15**	**Fri 2/6/15**			

This milestone symbol has been formatted with a custom shape.

TIP In this exercise, you used the Bar command to format a single item on the Gantt Chart view. You can also customize entire categories of Gantt bars, such as all milestones, via the Bar Styles command. For more information, see Chapter 17.

As you might have noticed already, Project automatically draws horizontal lines in the chart portion of a Gantt chart view for just the selected task. These lines help you visually track from the task's name and other information on the left side of the view to its Gantt bar or symbol on the right. To conclude this exercise, you will add horizontal gridlines for all tasks in the Gantt Chart view.

11   On the **Format** tab, in the **Format** group, click **Gridlines**, and then click **Gridlines**.

12   Under **Lines to change**, leave **Gantt Rows** selected, and in the **Type** box under **Normal**, select the small dashed line (the third option down), and then click **OK**.

Project draws dashed lines across the chart portion of the Gantt Chart view.

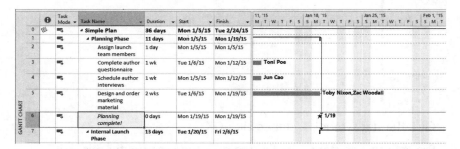

With these dashed lines displayed, the solid horizontal lines Project draws for the selected task are still clearly visible.

Drawing on a Gantt chart

Project includes a Drawing tool with which you can draw objects directly on the chart portion of a Gantt chart. For example, if you would like to note a particular event or graphically call out a specific item, you can draw objects—such as text boxes, arrows, and other items—directly on a Gantt chart.

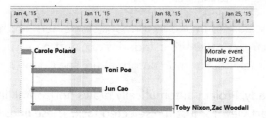

You can also link a drawn object to either end of a Gantt bar or to a specific date on the timescale. Here's how to choose the type of link you need:

- Link objects to a Gantt bar when the object is specific to the task that the Gantt bar represents. The object will move with the Gantt bar if the task is rescheduled.

> - Link objects to a date when the information the object refers to is date-sensitive. The object will remain in the same position relative to the timescale no matter which part of the timescale is displayed.
>
> If you want to draw on a Gantt chart, follow these instructions: On the Format tab, in the Drawings group, click Drawing. Select the drawing shape you want, and then draw it anywhere you like in the chart portion of a Gantt chart view.
>
> To set the type of link you want applied to the drawn object, do this: On the Format tab, in the Drawings Group, click Drawing and then click Properties. Click the Size & Position tab, and then select the options you want.

Customizing a Timeline view

A Timeline view is best suited to display key tasks from your plan in a simple and compact format. This view is especially well suited for conveying quick summaries of plans. The Timeline view is a handy way of sharing project information.

The scenario: At Lucerne Publishing, you know from past experience that some of the stakeholders of the new book launch project will find your Gantt chart view to be more detailed than they like. To help such stakeholders see the key details you want to convey, you decide to build a Timeline view. Later in this chapter, you will copy the Timeline view to another application as a quick "project at a glance" image.

In this exercise, you populate a Timeline view with specific tasks and adjust some display details.

1 Click anywhere in the Timeline view.

Project shifts focus to the Timeline view and displays the Timeline Tools contextual label above the Format tab.

2 On the **Format** tab, in the **Insert** group, click **Existing Tasks**.

The Add Tasks To Timeline dialog box appears.

This dialog box contains an outline of the summary and subtasks in the plan.

3   Select the boxes for the following task names:

■ **Planning Phase**

■ **Planning complete!**

■ **Internal Launch Phase**

■ **Public Launch Phase**

■ **Author travel and appearances**

Use this dialog box to indicate tasks
you want to include in the Timeline view.

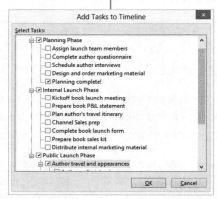

These tasks are summary tasks and a milestone task you will add to the Timeline view.

4   Click **OK**.

Project adds the summary tasks and milestone to the Timeline view. If necessary, adjust the horizontal divider bar between the Timeline and Gantt chart views so that you can see more of the Timeline view.

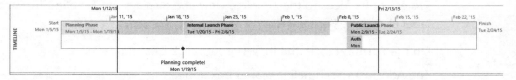

Next you'll adjust the formatting of the *Author travel and appearances* summary task on the Timeline.

5   In the **Timeline** view, click the bar for the *Author travel and appearances* summary task.

Only a portion of the summary task name is visible. Point your mouse pointer over the bar name and Project displays a ScreenTip with the task's full name and other details.

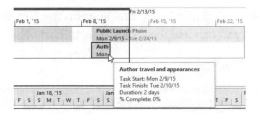

6   On the **Format** tab, in the **Current Selection** group, click **Display as Callout**.

Project displays this summary task as a callout, which for this task has the advantage of making the full task name visible.

Next you'll add the final milestone task to the Timeline, but you'll use a different technique.

7   In the **Task Name** column in the Gantt chart view, click the name of task 24, *Launch complete!*

8   On the **Task** tab, in the **Properties** group, click **Add to Timeline**.

TIP You can also right-click the task name and click Add To Timeline in the shortcut menu that appears.

Project adds this milestone task to the Timeline view.

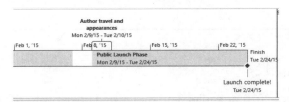

As you can see on the Timeline, Project displays the milestone tasks as callouts and uses the diamond marker that is a visual convention for milestones.

Pan and zoom the Gantt Chart view from the Timeline view

Have you noticed the shading and the vertical and horizontal lines on the Timeline view? This is the pan and zoom control you can use to scroll a Gantt Chart view horizontally or to change its timescale.

Click and drag the top of the pan and zoom control left or right to pan a Gantt Chart view.

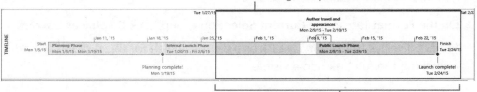

Click and drag these vertical lines of the pan and zoom control left or right to zoom a Gantt Chart view.

The pan and zoom control appears in the Timeline view when the Gantt chart's timeline shows less than the full plan's duration on the screen.

To scroll a Gantt Chart view, click and drag the top line of the pan and zoom control. This is a convenient way to display a specific date range in a Gantt chart.

To change the timescale in a Gantt Chart view, drag the left or right vertical lines on the edge of the pan and zoom control. As you do so, Project adjusts the timescale in the chart portion of a Gantt Chart view so that the time frame that appears in the unshaded portion of the Timeline view is also visible in a Gantt Chart view.

You might find the Timeline view useful not only for creating simplified representations of key details from your plans, but also for navigating a Gantt Chart view. If you want to hide the pan and zoom controls, do this: Click anywhere in the Timeline view, and then on the Format tab, in the Show/Hide group, clear the Pan & Zoom box.

Customizing reports

If you are upgrading from Project 2010 or earlier, you might be familiar with the tabular reports features that were optimized for printing. Reports in Project 2013, however, introduce an entirely new set of features and capabilities.

You can use Project's *reports* to see details of your plans in a variety of ways. A single report can include a dynamic mix of tables, charts, and textual content. Unlike most views in Project, a report is more like a blank canvas onto which you can place whatever elements (such as tables or charts) that focus on the information of most interest to you. Project includes several built-in reports, and you can customize those or create your own for the unique information needs of your project's stakeholders.

Reports are intended for viewing Project details. You don't directly edit your plan in a report as you can in views. However, you can extensively customize what data appears in a report and how it's formatted. Reports are especially well suited for sharing with others via printing or copying.

TIP This section introduces report formatting. For more details about reports, see Chapter 15, "Viewing and reporting project status," and Chapter 18.

The scenario: At Lucerne Publishing, you want to share the Work Overview report with the team. However, you'd like to change the formatting of one element in the report.

In this exercise, you change the formatting of a built-in report.

1   On the **Report** tab, in the **View Reports** group, click **Dashboards** and then click **Work Overview**.

The Work Overview report appears.

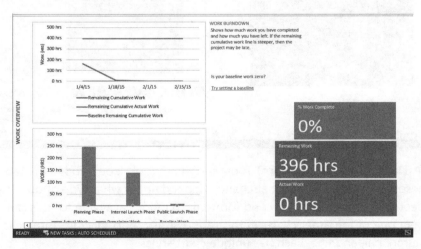

This report includes several charts that describe work over time and per resource. Depending on your screen resolution, you might need to vertically scroll the report to see all of the charts.

On the left side of the report is the Work Stats column chart. You will change the formatting of this chart.

2   Click anywhere in the **Work Stats** column chart.

As soon as you click the chart, the Field List pane appears on the right side of the screen. In Chapter 18, you will use Field List to customize the data that is included in reports. For now, though, your focus is on changing the formatting of the current report.

3   Under **Chart Tools**, click the **Design** tab. Then in the **Chart Styles** group, click the chart style with the black background. (If you hover the mouse pointer over the chart styles, this chart's label, Style 6, will appear in a ToolTip).

Project applies the chart style to the Work Stats chart.

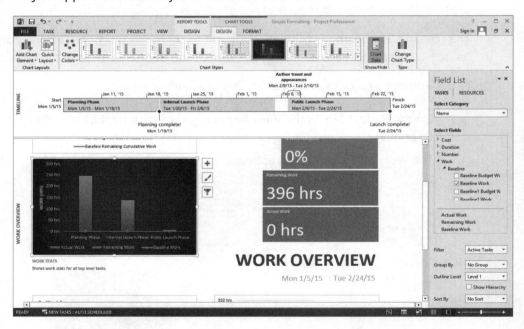

TIP Did you notice the Report Tools and Chart Tools labels above the tab labels? These are contextual tabs that change depending on what type of object you selected. Explore the design and formatting options available for this chart, and then select one of the other charts in this report. This report includes three chart types: column, bar, and line. Each has unique chart styles.

4   On the **View** tab, in the **Task Views** group, click **Gantt Chart**.

The Gantt Chart view replaces the Work Overview report.

Copying views and reports

You might frequently need to share details of your plans with colleagues who do not have Project or who might prefer a simple schedule snapshot. You can quickly copy most views and reports from Project. Copied views and reports can then be pasted into e-mail messages, presentations, and other documents. Views that cannot be directly copied from Project include the Team Planner, Form views (such as the Task Form), and the Relationship diagram.

TIP If you find you need a visual snapshot of a view or report that cannot be directly copied from Project, use a screen capture utility such as the Windows Snipping Tool.

Both Gantt charts and Timeline views are well suited for sharing schedule details. The Timeline is a concise "project at a glance" view, and the Gantt chart is a widely used format of schedules.

Reports are also well suited for sharing with other project stakeholders. Shared reports can be especially effective in conveying Project information you might otherwise need to copy to a spreadsheet application like Microsoft Excel for further formatting, such as tabular data and charts.

The scenario: At Lucerne Publishing, you have a two-pronged approach to sharing the new book launch plan with stakeholders. The first strategy involves taking snapshots of key views and reports from the plan and sharing those via e-mail and Microsoft Word documents. That is the focus of the following exercise. In the next section, you'll focus on your second communication strategy: printing the plan.

In this exercise, you copy the Gantt chart, Timeline view, and a report to another application.

1   In the **Task Name** column, click the name of task 7, *Internal Launch Phase*.

2   On the **Task** tab, in the **Editing** group, click **Scroll to Task**.

The Gantt bars for the Internal Launch Phase summary task and its subtasks are displayed. This is close to the image you'd like to copy.

	ⓘ	Task Mode	Task Name	Duration	Start	Finish
6		⬛	*Planning complete!*	0 days	Mon 1/19/15	Mon 1/19/15
7		⬛	⊿ Internal Launch Phase	13 days	Tue 1/20/15	Fri 2/6/15
8		⬛	Kickoff book launch meeting	1 day	Tue 1/20/15	Tue 1/20/15
9		📌	Prepare book P&L statement	2 days	Tue 1/20/15	Wed 1/21/15
10		⬛	Plan author's travel itinerary	6 days	Wed 1/21/15	Thu 1/29/15
11		⬛	Channel Sales prep	1 wk	Wed 1/21/15	Wed 1/28/15
12		⬛	Complete book launch form	2 days	Thu 1/29/15	Fri 1/30/15
13		⬛	Prepare book sales kit	1 wk	Thu 1/29/15	Wed 2/4/15
14		⬛	Distribute internal marketing material	2 days	Thu 2/5/15	Fri 2/6/15

3   In the Gantt Chart view, select the names of tasks 7 through 14.

These are the *Internal Launch Phase* summary task and its subtasks.

4   On the **Task** tab, in the **Clipboard** group, click the arrow next to **Copy**, and then click **Copy Picture**.

The Copy Picture dialog box appears.

In this dialog box, you can control how Project copies details from the plan to the Clipboard or saves it to a file. The first two options under Render Image control the size and resolution of the Gantt chart image you copy; the third allows you to save the copied image as a Graphics Interchange Format (GIF) image file. The Copy and Timescale options let you fine-tune what you want to copy.

For this exercise, you want to copy the selected rows for screen-resolution quality and leave the timescale as shown on the screen.

5   Click **OK**.

Project copies a graphic image of the Gantt chart for just the selected rows to the Windows Clipboard.

6 Do one of the following:

- If you are running Windows 7 or earlier, do this: on the **Start** menu, click **All Programs**, and in the **Accessories** program group, click **WordPad**.

- If you are running Windows 8, do this: from the Start screen, type wordpad, and in the Apps results list, click or tap **WordPad**.

WordPad opens and creates a new document.

7 In WordPad, click **Paste**.

WordPad pastes the graphic image of the Gantt Chart view into the new document.

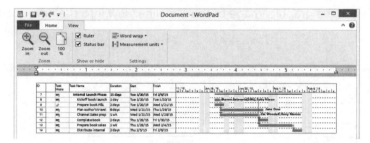

The Gantt Chart view is a standard format for presenting schedules, and it can show quite a bit of schedule detail.

8 Switch back to Project.

You copy most other views in Project in a similar way as you just did with the Gantt Chart view. The Timeline view, however, has unique options for copying, and you'll explore these next.

9 Click anywhere in the Timeline view.

With the focus now on the Timeline, the contextual label of the Format tab changes to Timeline Tools.

10 On the **Format** tab, in the **Copy** group, click **Copy Timeline**.

The Copy Timeline options appear.

TIP Feel free to experiment with the Copy Timeline options and paste the results into whatever applications are relevant for you. For this exercise, you'll paste the results into WordPad, a rich-text editor included with Windows.

11   Click **Full Size**.

Project copies a graphic image of the timeline to the Clipboard.

12   Switch back to WordPad and then press the Enter key to add some space below the Gantt chart image.

13   In WordPad, on the **Home** tab, in the **Clipboard** group, click **Paste**.

WordPad pastes the graphic image of the Timeline view into the new document.

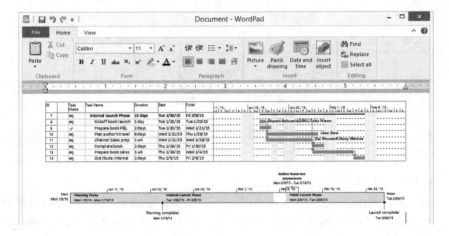

14   Switch back to Project.

So far you've worked with the Timeline in its detailed format. To give you more room on the screen, you'll switch the Timeline to its less detailed format.

15   Click anywhere in the Timeline view, and then on the **Format** tab, in the **Show/Hide** group, click **Detailed Timeline**.

Project toggles the Timeline to its less detailed format. Next you will copy and paste a report.

16   On the **Report** tab, in the **View Reports** group, click **Dashboards** and then click **Work Overview**.

The same Work Overview report you customized earlier appears.

17   Click anywhere in the **Work Overview** report and then, under **Report Tools**, click the **Design** tab. In the **Report** group, click **Copy Report**.

Project copies a graphic image of the report to the Clipboard.

TIP To copy just one chart from the report, right-click on the outer edge of the chart you want and, in the shortcut menu that appears, click Copy.

18   Switch back to WordPad, and then press the Enter key to add some space below the Timeline image.

19   In WordPad, click **Paste**.

WordPad pastes the graphic image of the report into the new document.

You now have in your document copies of the Gantt chart and Timeline views, as well as the Work Overview report.

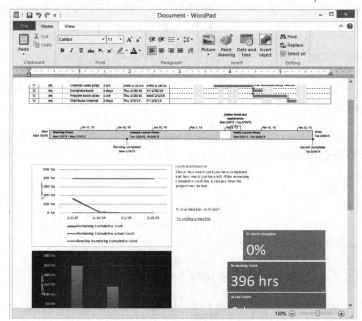

20   Close WordPad without saving the document, and return to Project.

21   On the **View** tab, in the **Task Views** group, click **Gantt Chart**.

The Gantt chart view replaces the Work Overview report.

Printing views and reports

By printing views and reports, you can put on paper just about anything you see on your screen. For a plan with many tasks, what you can see on your screen at one time might be a relatively small portion of the full plan. When using standard letter-sized paper, you might need several sheets to print the full plan. For example, a Gantt Chart view of a six-month project with 100 or so tasks can require 12 or more letter-size pages to print in its entirety. Printing out of Project can use quite a bit of paper; in fact, some heavy-duty Project users make poster-size printouts of their plans using plotters. Whether you use a printer or plotter, it's a good idea to preview the views and reports you intend to print.

You have several options when printing from Project, such as printing a specific date range in a Gantt Chart view. (You'll do this next.) You can also control what will print in a view prior to printing by filtering or collapsing tasks, or displaying only summary tasks. (You'll explore such options in Chapter 13.)

Compared to views, reports can be a more compact way to print information about your plan. Reports use commonly understood formats, such as table and charts, to organize and present information.

The scenario: At Lucerne Publishing, you've shared online snapshots of views and reports of the new book launch plan with a broad audience of stakeholders. Next you will print views and reports from the plan to post to the wall space the team has set aside for this project's key planning documents. Once these schedule details are printed and hung on the wall, you'll encourage the team to mark up the plan with feedback or clarifications by hand.

In this exercise, you will see the Print Preview of the Gantt Chart view, as well as a report.

1   On the **File** tab, click **Print**.

The Print Preview appears in the Backstage view with the Gantt Chart in the preview.

Here you can see the legend for the Gantt Chart view. You can control how it is displayed using the Page Setup dialog box.

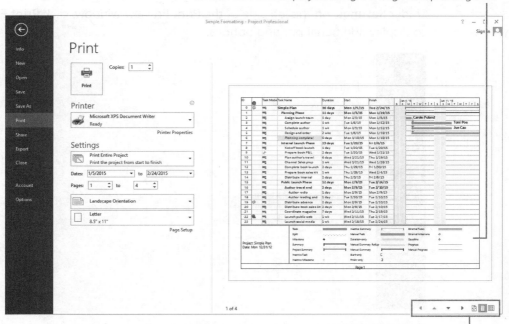

Use these buttons to navigate in the Print Preview.

The Print Preview has several options to explore. You will start with the page navigation buttons in the lower-right corner of the screen. To observe the broader view of the output, you'll switch to a multipage view.

2   Click the **Multiple Pages** button.

Multiple pages button

The full Gantt chart appears in the Print Preview. Assuming that you have a letter-size sheet as your paper size, you should see the Gantt chart spread across several sheets—what you see in the Print Preview might vary, depending on your specific printer. This is more information than you need to communicate right now, so you'll adjust the Print Preview to include just the portion of the Gantt chart that covers the month of January.

NOTE If you have a plotter selected as your default printer or have a different page size selected for your default printer, what you see in the Print Preview windows might differ from what's shown in this exercise. The next several steps will assume that you see the Gantt Chart view split across four sheets.

3   Under **Settings**, on the left side of the Print Preview window, click **Print Entire Project** to display additional printing options.

These options let you customize what details will be printed.

4   Click **Print Specific Dates**.

Notice the two date fields directly below the Print Specific Dates setting. In the first date field, *1/5/2015* should already be displayed. This is the project start date.

5   In the **To** date field, type or select **1/31/2015**.

Project adjusts the timescale in the chart portion of the Gantt Chart view to match this time frame.

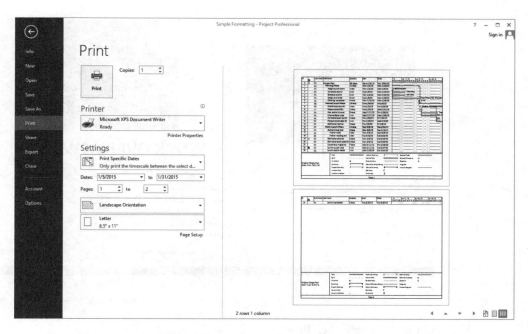

6   Click the **Back** button to close the Backstage view.

To conclude this exercise, you will work with a report.

7   On the **Report** tab, in the **View Reports** group, click **Dashboards** and then click **Work Overview**.

The Work Overview report appears. Next you'll review some of the Page Setup options for reports.

8   Under **Report Tools**, click the **Design** tab, and in the **Page Setup** group, click **Page Breaks**.

The dashed lines you see in the report tell you how it will print across pages based on the current page settings. The options you see in the Page Setup group, such as margins and paper size, can be useful as you design your report.

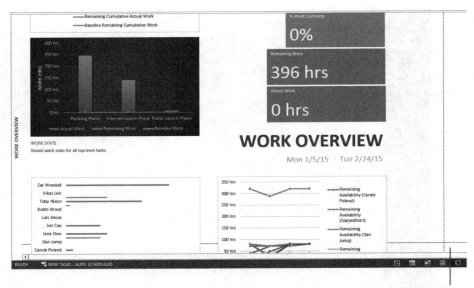

These dashed lines indicate page breaks when printing.

9   On the **File** tab, click **Print**.

The Print Preview appears in the Backstage view.

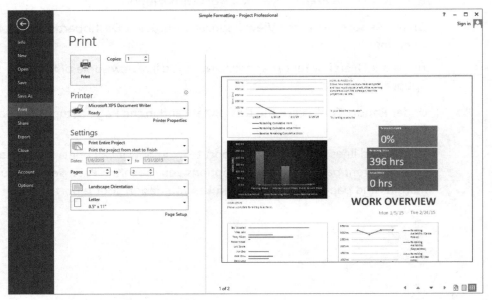

10   Click the **Multiple Pages** button.

The full Work Overview report appears in the Print Preview.

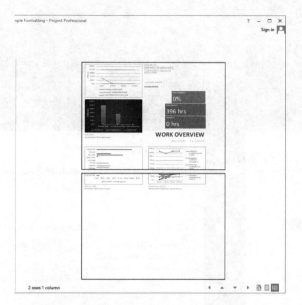

Here you can see how the report's pages will print.

11   Click the **Back** button to close the Backstage view.

❌ CLEAN UP Close the Simple Formatting file.

Key points

- Use the predefined Gantt Chart styles to quickly format a Gantt chart view.

- You can format individual Gantt bars or whole categories of Gantt bars by doing the following: on the Format tab, in the Bar Styles group, click either Bar or Bar Styles.

- Add select tasks to the Timeline view when you need to show a simplified graphical representation of a plan.

- Use the Copy Picture feature (accessed by clicking the Task tab in the Clipboard group) to create a graphic image snapshot of the active view and copy it to the Clipboard. For the Timeline view, use the Copy Timeline feature (accessed by clicking the Format tab in the Copy group).

- Reports are combinations of tabular data and charts that focus on key aspects of a plan. You can customize elements in a report.

Chapter at a glance

Baseline

Capture a snapshot of the current plan, page 153.

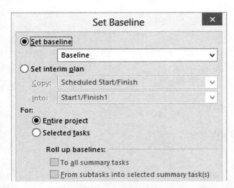

Update

Track progress as scheduled, page 156.

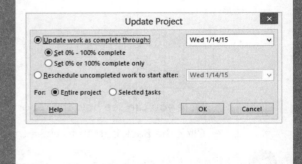

Progress

Record progress in percentage values, page 157.

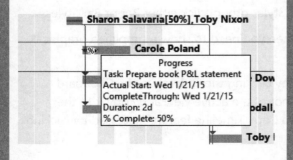

Actuals

Record actual dates and durations, page 160.

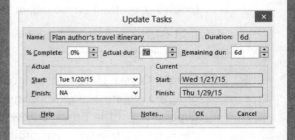

Tracking progress

8

IN THIS CHAPTER, YOU WILL LEARN HOW TO

- Save current schedule values in a plan as a baseline.

- Record progress on tasks through a specific date.

- Record tasks' percentage of completion.

- Enter actual work and duration values for tasks.

Until now, you have focused on project *planning*—developing and communicating the details of a plan before actual work begins. When work begins, so does the next phase of project management: *tracking* progress. Tracking means recording details such as who did what work, when the work was done, and at what cost. These details are often called *actuals*.

Tracking actuals is essential to properly managing a project, as opposed to just planning it. The project manager must know how well the team is performing and when to take corrective action. By properly tracking project performance and comparing it with the original plan (as saved in a *baseline*) you are able to answer such questions as the following:

- Are tasks starting and finishing as planned? If not, what will be the impact on the project's finish date?

- Are *resources* spending more or less time than planned to complete tasks?

- Are higher-than-anticipated task costs driving up the overall cost of the project?

- When planning similar projects in the future, will you be able to determine how good your (or the team's) estimating skills were in prior projects?

TIP As you enter actuals such as duration, start, or finish values, you might observe that the scheduled duration, start, or finish values in your plan change. Such changes are the result of Project dynamically recalculating the plan; we'll point this out as it occurs in the exercises that follow.

Project supports several ways to track progress. Your choice of a tracking method should depend on the level of detail or control required by you, your project sponsor, and other stakeholders. Tracking the fine details of a project requires additional work from you and, possibly, from the resources working on the project. Therefore, before you begin tracking progress, you should determine the level of detail you need.

The different levels of tracking detail include the following:

- Record project work as scheduled. This level works best if everything in the project occurs exactly as planned.

- Record each task's percentage of completion, either at precise values or at preset increments such as 25, 50, 75, or 100 percent.

- Record the actual start date, actual finish date, actual work, and actual and remaining duration for each task or assignment.

- Track assignment-level work by time period. This is the most detailed level of tracking. Here, you record actual work values per day, week, or other interval.

Because different portions of a project might have different tracking needs, you might need to apply a combination of these approaches within a single plan. For example, you might want to track high-risk tasks more closely than low-risk ones. In this chapter, you will perform the first three actions in the preceding list; the fourth (tracking assignment-level work by time period) is addressed in Chapter 14, "Tracking progress on tasks and assignments."

PRACTICE FILES Before you can complete the exercises in this chapter, you need to copy the book's practice files to your computer. A complete list of practice files is provided in "Download the practice files" at the beginning of this book. For each exercise that has a practice file, simply browse to where you saved the book's practice file folder.

IMPORTANT If you are running Project Professional with Project Web App/Project Server, take care not to save any of the practice files you work with in this book to Project Web App (PWA). For more information, see Appendix C, "Collaborating: Project, SharePoint, and PWA."

Saving a baseline of your plan

After developing a plan, one of your most important activities as a project manager is to record actuals and evaluate project performance. As you record actuals or update your plan, the original plan will likely change. This makes it difficult to keep track of the plan in its original state.

To judge project performance properly, you'll find it helpful to compare the performance with your original plan. This original plan is called the baseline plan, or just the *baseline.* A baseline is a collection of important schedule, cost, and work values, including some values distributed over time (called *timephased* values).

TIP In Chapter 14, you will work with timephased values.

When you save a baseline, Project takes a snapshot of the existing values and saves it in your plan for future comparison. You should save the baseline when

- You have developed the plan as fully as possible. (However, this does not mean that you cannot add tasks, resources, or assignments to the plan after work has started—this is often unavoidable.)

- You have not yet started entering actual values, such as a task's percentage of completion.

The specific values saved in a baseline include several task, resource, and assignment fields, as well as timephased fields.

Task Fields	Resource Fields	Assignment Fields
Start	Work and timephased work	Start
Finish	Cost and timephased cost	Finish
Duration		Work and timephased work
Work and timephased work		Cost and timephased cost

Project supports not just one baseline, but up to 11 baselines in a single plan. The first one is called *Baseline*, and the rest are *Baseline 1* through *Baseline 10*. Saving multiple baselines can be useful for projects with especially long planning phases, in which you might want to compare different sets of baseline values. For example, you might want to save and compare the baseline plans every month as the planning details change. Or you might want to save a new baseline at various points during the execution of the project. You could, for example, save Baseline before work starts, Baseline 1 a month after work starts, Baseline 2

8

two months after work starts, and so on. You can then view the various baselines and compare them to the actual schedule throughout the project's duration.

The scenario: At Lucerne Publishing, the new book launch plan is now fully developed. Actual work on the project will soon begin. To allow a later comparison of actual work and the current schedule with the original plan, you will first save a baseline.

In this exercise, you save the current state of a schedule as a baseline and then view the baseline task values.

SET UP You need the Simple Tracking_Start file located in your Chapter08 practice file folder to complete this exercise. Open the Simple Tracking_Start file, and save it as Simple Tracking.

1   On the **Project** tab, in the **Schedule** group, click **Set Baseline**, and then click **Set Baseline**.

The Set Baseline dialog box appears.

You'll set the baseline for the entire plan by using the default settings of the dialog box.

2   Click **OK**.

Project saves the baseline, even though there's no indication in the Gantt Chart view that anything has changed. You will now see some of the changes caused by saving the baseline.

TIP When working with a plan that includes a saved baseline, you can see when the baseline was saved in the Set Baseline dialog box. The date the baseline was saved appears after the baseline name in the Set Baseline field.

3	On the **Task** tab, in the **View** group click the down arrow below **Gantt Chart**, and then click **Task Sheet**.

The Task Sheet view appears. Because this is a tabular view, it does not include the Gantt chart, so more room is available to see the fields in the Entry table.

Now you'll switch to the Variance table in the Task Sheet view. The Variance table is one of several predefined tables that include baseline values.

4	On the **View** tab, in the **Data** group, click **Tables**.

In the listed tables, note the check mark next to Entry. This means that the Entry table is currently displayed in the Task Sheet view. You'll switch to another table next.

5	Click **Variance**.

TIP You also can right-click the Select All button in the upper-left corner of the active table to switch to a different table.

The Variance table appears. This table includes both the scheduled and baseline start and finish columns, shown side by side for easy comparison.

Select All button

Because no actual work has occurred yet and no changes to the scheduled work have been made, the values in the Start and Baseline Start fields are identical, as are the values in the Finish and Baseline Finish fields. After actual work is recorded or later schedule adjustments are made, the scheduled start and finish values might differ from the baseline values. You would then see the differences displayed in the variance columns.

6	On the **View** tab, in the **Task Views** group, click **Gantt Chart**.

The Gantt Chart view appears.

TIP Project includes views that compare the current schedule to the baseline, but here's one quick way to see baseline values in the Gantt Chart view: on the Format tab, in the Bar Styles group, click Baseline and then click the baseline (Baseline or Baseline1 through Baseline10) that you want to display. Project draws baseline Gantt bars for the baseline you choose.

Now that you've had a look at some baseline fields, it is time to enter some actuals!

Tracking a plan as scheduled through a specific date

The simplest approach to tracking progress is to report that the actual work is proceeding exactly as planned. For example, if the first week of a five-week project has elapsed and all its tasks have started and finished as scheduled, you can quickly record this in the Update Project dialog box.

When you record progress through a specific date, Project calculates the actual duration, the remaining duration, actual costs, and other values up to the date you entered. This approach might be fine even if the actual work and cost values generated by Project won't exactly match what happened in the real world, but are close enough for your schedule-tracking purposes. This is a judgment call that you as a project manager (in consultation with your project sponsors and other stakeholders) can consider.

TIP Another way to indicate that just certain tasks (not the entire plan) have been completed as scheduled is to use the Mark On Track command (Task tab, Schedule group). This command applies only to the selected tasks, and it sets them as complete through the status date (if you set a status date on the Project tab, Status group, Status Date command). Or if you have not set a status date, the command applies through the current date.

The scenario: At Lucerne Publishing, some time has passed since saving the baseline in the new book launch plan. Work has been completed through the first week and a half, as planned. You need to account for the completed work in the plan.

In this exercise, you track the plan as scheduled through a specific date, resulting in Project recording project actuals.

1   On the **Project** tab, in the **Status** group, click **Update Project**.

The Update Project dialog box appears.

2   Make sure the **Update work as complete through** option is selected. In the adjacent date box, type or select **1/14/15**.

3   Click **OK**.

Project records the completion percentage for the tasks that were scheduled to start before January 14. It displays that progress by drawing *progress bars* in the Gantt bars for those tasks.

Check marks appear in the Indicators column for tasks that have been completed.

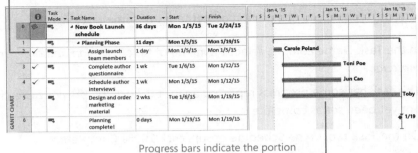

Progress bars indicate the portion of each task that has been completed.

In the chart portion of the Gantt Chart view, the progress bar shows how much of each task has been completed. Because tasks 2, 3, and 4 have been completed, a check mark appears in the Indicators column for those tasks, and the progress bars extend through the full length of those tasks' Gantt bars. Task 5 is only partially completed, however.

8

Entering a task's completion percentage

After work begins on a task, you can quickly record its progress as a percentage. When you enter a completion percentage greater than 0, Project sets the task's actual start date to match its scheduled start date. Project then calculates the actual duration, the remaining duration, actual costs, and other values based on the percentage you enter. For example, if you specify that a four-day task is 25 percent complete, Project calculates that it has had one day of actual duration and three days of remaining duration.

Here are some ways of entering completion percentages:

- Use the 0%, 25%, 50%, 75%, and 100% Complete buttons in the Schedule group of the Task tab.

- Add the percent complete column (labeled % Complete in the interface) to a table in a task view, and enter the value you want.

- Enter any percentage value you want in the Update Tasks dialog box. (To access this dialog box, on the Task tab, in the Schedule group, click the down arrow to the right of Mark On Track, and then click Update Tasks.)

- Use the mouse to set progress on Gantt bars.

The scenario: At Lucerne Publishing, work continues on the new book launch. You have additional progress to record in the plan as percent complete values.

In this exercise, you record completion percentages of some tasks.

1 In the **Task Name** column, select the name of task 5, *Design and order marketing material*.

   This task has some progress reported against it from the previous exercise, but it has not yet been set as complete.

2 On the **Task** tab, in the **Schedule** group, click **100% Complete**.

   Project records the actual work for the task as scheduled and extends a progress bar through the length of the Gantt bar.

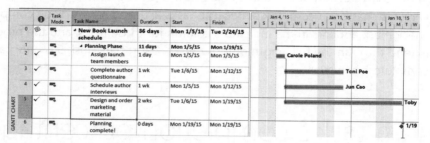

Next you'll record that the completion milestone for the Planning Phase and the first task of the Internal Launch Phase are complete.

3 In the **Task Name** column, select the name of task 6, *Planning complete!*, and while holding down the Ctrl key, select the name of task 8, *Kickoff book launch meeting*.

4 On the **Task** tab, in the **Schedule** group, click **100% Complete**.

Because task 6 is a milestone task with no duration, there is no change in appearance of its symbol in the chart portion of the Gantt Chart view as there is for task 8. You do, however, see the completion check marks for both tasks in the Indicators column.

Next, you'll get a better look at how progress is displayed in a task's Gantt bar. You will enter a completion percentage value for a different task.

5   Click the name of task 9, *Prepare book P&L statement*.

6   On the **Task** tab, in the **Schedule** group, click **50% Complete**.

Project records the actual work for the task as scheduled and then draws a progress bar through part of the Gantt bar.

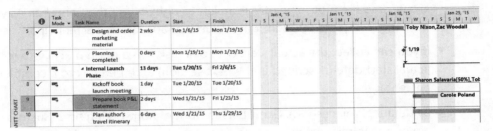

Note that although 50% of the work on task 9 is completed, the progress bar does not span 50% of the width of the Gantt bar. This is because Project measures duration in working time but draws the Gantt bars to extend over nonworking time, which in this case includes Thursday, January 22, the nonworking day.

7   In the chart portion (on the right) in the Gantt Chart view, hold the mouse pointer over the progress bar in task 9's Gantt bar. When the mouse pointer changes to a percent symbol and right arrow, a Progress ScreenTip appears.

Depending on the type of bar or symbol you point to—in this case, the progress bar—a ScreenTip pops up, providing information about that item.

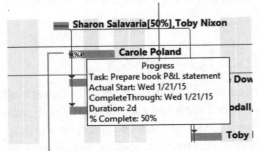

The mouse pointer changes to a percent symbol and arrow when pointing to a progress bar.

8

The Progress ScreenTip informs you of the task's completion percentage and other tracking values.

So far, you have recorded actual work that started and finished on schedule. Although staying on schedule might prove true for some tasks, you often need to record actuals for tasks that lasted longer or shorter than planned, or occurred sooner or later than scheduled. This is the subject of the next topic.

Here are some additional tips and suggestions for entering task completion percentages:

- You can also set the percent complete by pointing to a Gantt bar (or progress bar within a Gantt bar). When the mouse pointer changes to a percent symbol and right arrow, drag the mouse pointer from left to right within the Gantt bar. As you do so, note the "complete through" date value that appears in a ScreenTip.

- If you can collect the actual start date of a task, it is a good practice to record the actual start date (described in the next section) and then record a completion percentage.

- By default, Project shows Gantt bars in front of nonworking time (such as weekends), as you see in this section. However, Project can show nonworking time in front of task bars, visually indicating that no work on the task will occur during the nonworking time. If you prefer this type of presentation, right-click any shaded nonworking time (such as a weekend) in the chart portion of the Gantt Chart view and click Nonworking Time in the shortcut menu. In the Timescale dialog box, click the Non-Working Time tab. Next to Draw, click In Front Of Task Bars.

- Here's a simple tracking technique for projects with a large number of short-duration "to-do list" style tasks that don't require detailed tracking. Use just the 0%, 50%, and 100% complete values. 0% means work on the task has not yet started, 50% means work has started, and 100% means the task is complete. If you just need to know what's in progress and what's done, this is the simplest form of tracking you can apply.

Entering actual values for tasks

A more detailed way to keep your schedule up to date is to record what actually happened for each task in your project. You can record each task's actual start, finish, work, and duration values. For example, when you enter 3 days of actual duration on a task with 5 days of scheduled duration and 40 hours of work, Project calculates the actual work to be 24 hours, the percent complete to be 60%, and the remaining duration to be 2 days.

When you enter various actual values, Project uses the following rules to update the plan:

- When you enter a task's actual start date, Project moves the scheduled start date to match the actual start date.

- When you enter a task's actual finish date, Project moves the scheduled finish date to match the actual finish date and sets the task to 100% complete.

- When you enter a task's actual work value, Project recalculates the task's remaining work value, if any.

- When you enter a task's actual duration, if it is less than the scheduled duration, Project subtracts the actual duration from the scheduled duration to determine the remaining duration.

- When you enter a task's actual duration, if it is equal to the scheduled duration, Project sets the task to 100% complete.

- When you enter a task's actual duration, if it is longer than the scheduled duration, Project adjusts the scheduled duration to match the actual duration and sets the task to 100% complete.

Because your plan is updated with actuals, your plan as scheduled will likely change. The original plan as saved in a baseline is not altered, however.

The scenario: At Lucerne Publishing, a few more days have passed and work on the new book launch has progressed. Resources performing the work have given you actual progress that differs somewhat from the plan, and you want to record these actuals and observe the effect on the overall plan.

In this exercise, you record actual work values for some tasks, as well as actual start dates and durations for other tasks.

1   On the **View** tab, in the **Data** group, click **Tables** and then click **Work**.

The Work table appears.

> **TIP** You can display whichever table is most relevant to the details you are focused on while tracking progress in a plan. Useful tables include the Work table, which focuses on work values, and the Cost table, which focuses on cost values. The Tracking table is a good all-around table when recording or viewing progress.

2   If needed, drag the vertical divider bar to the right to expose the last column in the Work table, **%W. Comp** (% Work Complete).

This table includes both the total scheduled work (labeled Work) and Actual and Remaining work columns. You'll refer to the values in these columns as you update tasks.

In the chart portion of the Gantt Chart view, you can see that task 9 is partially complete. In the Work table, note the actual work value of 8 hours. This 8 hours is the result of setting the task at 50% complete in the previous exercise. The task had 16 hours of work total, so 50% complete equals 8 hours of actual work completed and 8 hours remaining. You want to record that the task is now complete but required more actual work than expected.

3   In the **Actual** field for task 9, *Prepare book P&L statement*, type or select 24, and then press Enter.

Project records that 24 hours of work have been completed on task 9. Because 24 hours is greater than the originally scheduled 16 hours (visible in the tasks' baseline field), Project marks the task as completed and extends the Gantt bar of the task to indicate its longer duration.

Actual work is rolled up from the
subtask to the summary tasks.

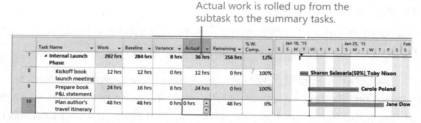

To conclude this exercise, you will enter actual start dates and durations of other tasks in the Internal Launch Phase.

4   In the **Task Name** column, click task 10, *Plan author's travel itinerary*.

This task started one working day ahead of schedule (the Tuesday before its scheduled start date) and took a total of seven days to complete. You will record this information in the Update Tasks dialog box.

5   On the **Task** tab, in the **Schedule** group, click the down arrow to the right of the **Mark on Track** button, and then click **Update Tasks**.

The Update Tasks dialog box appears. This dialog box shows both the actual and scheduled values for the task's duration, start, and finish, as well as its remaining duration. In this box, you can update the actual and remaining values.

6   In the **Start** field in the **Actual** group on the left side of the dialog box, type or select 1/20/15.

7   In the **Actual dur** field, type or select **7d**.

8   Click **OK**.

Project records the actual start date, duration, and scheduled and actual work of the task. These values also roll up to the *Internal Launch Phase* summary task (task 7) and the project summary task (task 0), as indicated by the change highlighting.

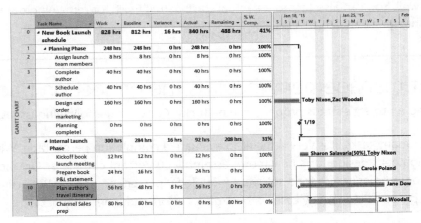

	Task Name	Work	Baseline	Variance	Actual	Remaining	% W. Comp.
0	⊿ New Book Launch schedule	828 hrs	812 hrs	16 hrs	340 hrs	488 hrs	41%
1	⊿ Planning Phase	248 hrs	248 hrs	0 hrs	248 hrs	0 hrs	100%
2	Assign launch team members	8 hrs	8 hrs	0 hrs	8 hrs	0 hrs	100%
3	Complete author	40 hrs	40 hrs	0 hrs	40 hrs	0 hrs	100%
4	Schedule author	40 hrs	40 hrs	0 hrs	40 hrs	0 hrs	100%
5	Design and order marketing	160 hrs	160 hrs	0 hrs	160 hrs	0 hrs	100%
6	Planning complete!	0 hrs	0 hrs	0 hrs	0 hrs	0 hrs	100%
7	⊿ Internal Launch Phase	300 hrs	284 hrs	16 hrs	92 hrs	208 hrs	31%
8	Kickoff book launch meeting	12 hrs	12 hrs	0 hrs	12 hrs	0 hrs	100%
9	Prepare book P&L statement	24 hrs	16 hrs	8 hrs	24 hrs	0 hrs	100%
10	Plan author's travel itinerary	56 hrs	48 hrs	8 hrs	56 hrs	0 hrs	100%
11	Channel Sales prep	80 hrs	80 hrs	0 hrs	0 hrs	80 hrs	0%

To conclude this exercise, you will record that task 11 started on time but took longer than planned to complete.

9   In the **Task Name** column, click task 11, *Channel Sales prep*.

10   On the **Task** tab, in the **Schedule** group, click the down arrow to the right of the **Mark on Track** button, and then click **Update Tasks**.

The Update Tasks dialog box appears.

11   In the **Actual dur** field, type **7d**, and then click **OK**.

Project records the actual duration of the task. Remember that an actual duration value of "7d" means seven working days, not seven calendar days.

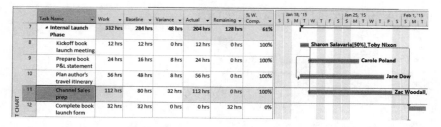

Task Name	Work	Baseline	Variance	Actual	Remaining	% W. Comp.		
7	▲ Internal Launch Phase	332 hrs	284 hrs	48 hrs	204 hrs	128 hrs	61%	
8	Kickoff book launch meeting	12 hrs	12 hrs	0 hrs	12 hrs	0 hrs	100%	
9	Prepare book P&L statement	24 hrs	16 hrs	8 hrs	24 hrs	0 hrs	100%	
10	Plan author's travel itinerary	56 hrs	48 hrs	8 hrs	56 hrs	0 hrs	100%	
11	Channel Sales prep	112 hrs	80 hrs	32 hrs	112 hrs	0 hrs	100%	
12	Complete book launch form	32 hrs	32 hrs	0 hrs	0 hrs	32 hrs	0%	

Because you did not specify an actual start date, Project assumes that the task started as scheduled. However, the actual duration you entered causes Project to calculate an actual finish date that is later than the originally scheduled finish date. Likewise, the actual work value (112 hours) is larger than the originally scheduled work (80 hours).

TIP You can apply all the tracking methods shown in this chapter to manually scheduled tasks as well. You can also record an actual start, actual finish, or remaining duration value for a manually scheduled task.

Project management focus: Is the project on track?

Evaluating a project's status properly can be tricky. Consider the following issues:

- For many tasks, it is very difficult to evaluate a completion percentage. When is an engineer's design for a new motor assembly 50 percent complete? Or when is a programmer's code for a software module 50 percent complete? Reporting work in progress is, in many cases, a best-guess effort and inherently risky.

- The elapsed portion of a task's duration is not always equal to the amount of work accomplished. For example, a task might require relatively little effort initially, but it might require more work as time passes. (This is referred to as a *back-loaded task*.) When 50 percent of its duration elapses, far less than 50 percent of its total work will be completed. In fact, Project tracks both values: % Complete tracks the percentage of the task's *duration* that has been completed, while % Work Complete tracks the percentage of the task's *work* that has been completed.

- The resources assigned to a task might have different criteria for what constitutes the task's completion than the criteria determined by the project manager or the resources assigned to successor tasks. In other words, the team lacks a common definition of "done."

Good project planning and communication can help you avoid or mitigate these and other problems that arise in project execution. For example, developing proper task durations and status-reporting periods should help you identify tasks that have varied substantially from baseline early enough to make adjustments. Having well-documented and well-communicated task-completion criteria should help prevent downstream surprises. Nevertheless, large, complex projects will almost always vary from the baseline.

❌ **CLEAN UP** Close the Simple Tracking file.

Key points

- Before tracking actual work in a plan, you should set a baseline. This provides you with a snapshot of your initial plan.

- After recording progress in your plan, you can then compare the plan as currently scheduled with its baseline. This is one way to tell whether your project is on track.

- When recording progress in a plan, you have a range of options, including tracking progress as scheduled, by percent complete, or by actual work, start, finish, or duration values.

8

Advanced Scheduling Techniques

9 Advanced task scheduling   168

10 Fine-tuning task details   198

11 Fine-tuning resource and assignment details   216

12 Fine-tuning the Project plan   248

13 Organizing project details   274

14 Tracking progress on tasks and assignments   298

15 Viewing and reporting project status   322

16 Getting your project back on track   342

Chapter at a glance

Relate

Change how tasks are related to each other, page 170.

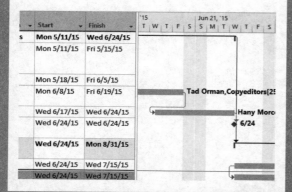

Constrain

Apply constraints to control when tasks can be scheduled, page 179.

Interrupt

Interrupt work on a task, page 185.

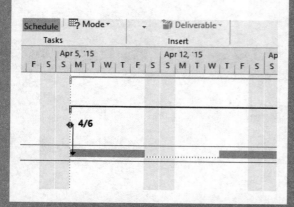

Control

Fine-tune how Project responds to schedule changes, page 191.

Advanced task scheduling

IN THIS CHAPTER, YOU WILL LEARN HOW TO

- Visually highlight a task's predecessors and successors.

- Adjust task links for more control over how tasks are related.

- Apply a constraint to a task.

- Split a task to record an interruption in work.

- Create a calendar and apply it to a task.

- Change a task type to control how Project schedules tasks.

In Part 3, "Advanced scheduling techniques," you'll complete a full project life cycle (planning, tracking progress, and responding to variance) as you did in Part 2, "Simple scheduling basics." In Part 3, however, you dive deeper into the Microsoft Project 2013 feature set to handle more complex needs. This chapter and the next one introduce you to a broad feature set that focuses on a deeper level of task management. This chapter focuses on core task scheduling features, including task links, constraints, and task types.

PRACTICE FILES Before you can complete the exercises in this chapter, you need to copy the book's practice files to your computer. A complete list of practice files is provided in "Download the practice files" at the beginning of this book. For each exercise that has a practice file, simply browse to where you saved the book's practice file folder.

IMPORTANT If you are running Project Professional with Project Web App/Project Server, take care not to save any of the practice files you work with in this book to Project Web App (PWA). For more information, see Appendix C, "Collaborating: Project, SharePoint, and PWA."

See task relationships with Task Path

When fine-tuning task relationships, you need to keep track of the predecessor tasks that affect the scheduling of their successor tasks. In complex plans, visually identifying predecessor and successor relationships is not always easy. This is especially true when a task has multiple predecessors or successors.

Project 2013 introduces a feature called Task Path that applies color formatting to the Gantt bars of the selected task's predecessor and successor tasks. Task Path can also distinguish a task's driving predecessor (the predecessor that directly determines, or drives, the start date of the task) from that task's other predecessors. (Predecessor tasks that can slip without rescheduling their successor tasks are said to have *slack*, described in detail in Chapter 10, "Fine-tuning task details.") The Task Path feature can also do the same for driving successor tasks.

The scenario: At Lucerne Publishing, at an upcoming team meeting you'd like to demonstrate some of the more complex task dependencies in a new children's book plan.

In this exercise, you use the Task Path feature to see predecessor and successor tasks.

➡️ SET UP You need the Advanced Tasks_Start file located in your Chapter09 practice file folder to complete this exercise. Open the Advanced Tasks_Start file, and save it as Advanced Tasks.

1   Vertically scroll the task list until task 16, *Proofread and index*, is near the top.

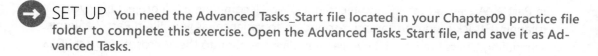

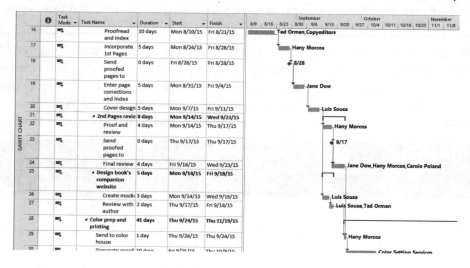

Now you'll more easily see the results of your next actions.

2 Click the name of task 29, *Send to color house*.

You'd like to identify this task's predecessor and successor tasks.

3 On the **Format** tab, in **Bar Styles** group, click **Task Path** and then click **Predecessors**.

Project applies a gold highlight formatting to the Gantt bars of task 29's predecessor tasks.

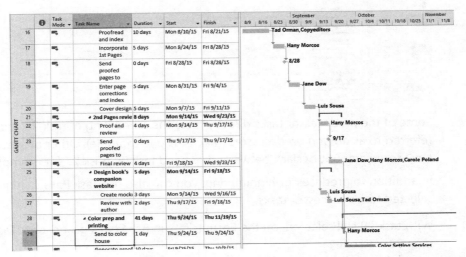

As you can see in the view, task 29 has a chain of predecessor tasks. Next you'll take a closer look at the predecessor tasks that directly affect the scheduling of task 29.

4 On the **Format** tab, in the **Bar Styles** group, click **Task Path** and then click **Driving Predecessors**.

Project applies a dark orange highlight formatting to the Gantt bars of this task's driving predecessor tasks.

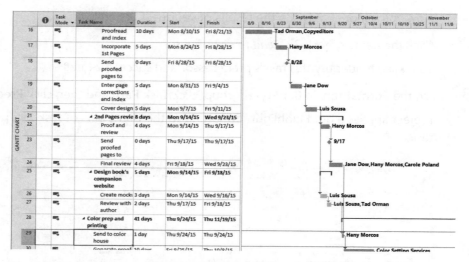

Some of the predecessor tasks directly drive the scheduling of task 29, and are referred to as *driving predecessors* (task 24 is one example). Other predecessor tasks have some amount of slack between them and task 29 (task 27 for example).

In addition to predecessor highlighting, you can also use Task Path to highlight the selected task's successor tasks.

5   With task 29 still selected, on the **Format** tab, in **Bar Styles** group, click **Task Path** and then **Successors**.

Project applies a light purple highlight formatting to the Gantt bars of this task's successor tasks. These are tasks 30 and 31.

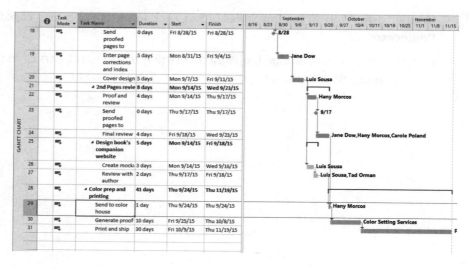

Now the predecessor, driving predecessor, and successor task highlighting is turned on for the selected task. Next you'll see these highlights for another task.

6   Select the name of task 22, *Proof and review*.

Project applies highlight formatting to the Gantt bars of this task's predecessor, driving predecessor, and successor tasks.

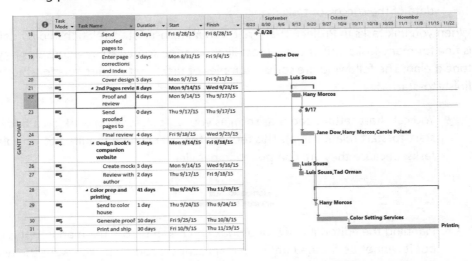

To conclude this exercise, you'll turn off the highlighting and change the zoom level.

7   On the **Format** tab, in the **Bar Styles** group, click **Task Path** and then click **Remove Highlighting**.

8   On the **View** tab, in the **Zoom** group, in the **Timescale** box, click **Days**.

When you're working in a complex project, you can turn on Task Path highlighting to help you quickly visually identify predecessor and successor tasks. The different color highlighting for driving predecessor and successor tasks is especially useful when you're focused on managing the overall duration of a sequence of linked tasks.

Adjusting task link relationships

You might recall from Chapter 4, "Building a task list," that there are four types of task dependencies, or relationships:

- **Finish-to-start (FS)**   The finish date of the predecessor task determines the start date of the successor task.

- **Start-to-start (SS)**   The start date of the predecessor task determines the start date of the successor task.

- **Finish-to-finish (FF)**   The finish date of the predecessor task determines the finish date of the successor task.

- **Start-to-finish (SF)**   The start date of the predecessor task determines the finish date of the successor task.

When you link tasks in Project, they are given a finish-to-start relationship by default. This is fine for many tasks, but you will most likely change some task relationships as you fine-tune a plan. The following are some examples of tasks that require relationships other than finish-to-start:

- You can start setting pages as soon as you start illustration work on a book project (a start-to-start relationship). This reduces the overall time required to complete the two tasks, because they are completed in parallel.

- Planning the editorial work for a book can begin before the manuscript is complete, but it cannot be finished until the manuscript is complete. You want the two tasks to finish at the same time (a finish-to-finish relationship).

Task relationships should reflect the sequence in which work should be performed. After you have established the correct task relationships, you can fine-tune your schedule by entering overlap (called *lead time*) or delay (called *lag time*) between the finish or start dates of predecessor and successor tasks.

When two tasks have a finish-to-start relationship

- Lead time causes the successor task to begin before its predecessor task concludes.

- Lag time causes the successor task to begin sometime after its predecessor task concludes.

The following is an illustration of how lead and lag time affect task relationships. Assume that you initially planned the following three tasks using finish-to-start relationships.

Initially, the tasks are linked with finish-to-start relationships, so the successor task is scheduled to begin when the predecessor task finishes.

Before task 2 can begin, you need to allow an extra day for the copyedited manuscript to be shipped to the author. You do not want to add a day to the duration of task 5 because no real work will occur on that day. Instead, you enter a one-day lag between tasks 1 and 2.

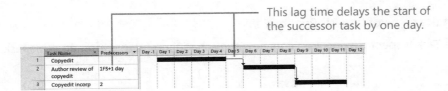

This lag time delays the start of the successor task by one day.

However, task 3 can start as soon as task 2 is halfway completed. To make this happen, enter a 50 percent lead time between tasks 2 and 3.

This lead time schedules the successor task to start before the predecessor task finishes.

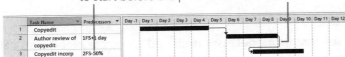

You can enter lead and lag time as units of time, such as two days, or as a percentage of the duration of the predecessor task, such as 50 percent. Lag time is entered in positive units and lead time in negative units (for example, −2d or −50%). You can apply lead or lag time to any type of task relationship: finish-to-start, start-to-start, or any other types.

Places in which you can enter lead or lag time include the Task Information dialog box (Task tab), the Predecessors column in the Entry table, the Task Form (View tab, Split View group, Details command), and the Task Dependency dialog box (viewable by double-clicking a link line between Gantt bars).

The scenario: At Lucerne Publishing, editorial and design work on a new children's book is about to begin. At this stage, you have an initial plan with task names, durations, relationships, and resource assignments. Now you want to fine-tune those task relationships.

In this exercise, you enter lead and lag time and change task relationships between predecessor and successor tasks.

1   On the **Task** tab, in the **Tasks** group, click **Inspect**.

The Task Inspector pane appears. This pane succinctly reveals the scheduling factors that affect the selected task, such as predecessor task relationships, resource calendars, task calendars, or a combination of factors. You can click any item in the Task Inspector that appears in blue to get more details. For example, you can click the assigned resource's name under Calendar to see their resource calendar. You do not need to display the Task Inspector to change task details, but it can be a handy tool in some cases.

2   Select the name of task 31, *Print and ship*.

In the Task Inspector pane, you can view the scheduling factors affecting this task.

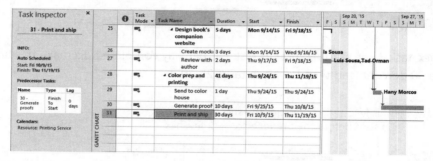

For task 31, you can see that its predecessor is task 30, *Generate proofs*. You can see in the pane that the two tasks have a finish-to-start relationship with zero lag time.

Next, you'll adjust the lag value on the task relationship to account for the transit time of the proofs to the printer. Because you cannot edit this value directly in the Task Inspector, you'll display the Task Information dialog box. First, though, you'll display this task's Gantt bar so that you can more easily observe the effect of adjusting the lag.

3   On the **Task** tab, in the **Editing** group, click **Scroll to Task**.

Next, you'll adjust the lag value between this task and its predecessor.

4   On the **Task** tab, in the **Properties** group, click **Information**.

The Task Information dialog box appears. It contains details about the currently selected task, 31.

5   Click the **Predecessors** tab.

6   In the **Lag** field for predecessor task 30, type **3d**, and then click **OK** to close the **Task Information** dialog box.

Task 31 is now scheduled to start three working days after the end of task 30.

Predecessor details such as lag time appear in the Task Inspector.

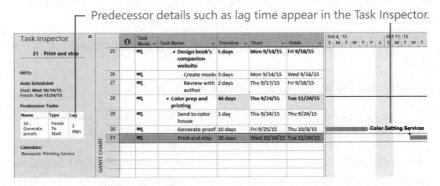

Next, you will adjust the lag time between two other tasks.

7   Click the name of task 10, *Copyedit incorp*.

You'd like to overlap this task with its predecessor; the *Copyedit incorp* task can start before the author review of the copyediting is completed.

8   On the **Task** tab, in the **Editing** group, click **Scroll to Task**.

9   On the **Task** tab, in the **Properties** group, click **Information**, and then click the **Predecessors** tab.

> **TIP** You can use the selected task's shortcut menu for both commands: Scroll To Task and Information. Right-click the task name and, in the shortcut menu, select the command you want.

10   In the **Lag** field for predecessor task 9, type –25%, and then click **OK**.

Entering lag time as a negative value results in lead time.

Task 10 is now scheduled to start at the 25-percent-remaining point of the duration of task 9. Should the duration of task 9 change, Project will reschedule the start of task 10 so that it maintains a 25 percent lead time.

To conclude this exercise, you will change the type of task relationship between two tasks.

11   Double-click the name of task 14, *Interior illustration design*.

> **TIP** Double-clicking a task name is a shortcut way to display the Task Information dialog box.

The Predecessors tab should be visible. Note also that the Task Inspector pane in the background updates to display the scheduling details for task 14, the currently selected task.

12   On the **Predecessors** tab, click in the **Type** column for predecessor task 13. Select **Start-to-Start (SS)**, and click **OK**.

Project changes the task relationship between tasks 13 and 14 to start-to-start.

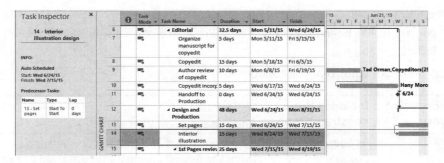

Adjusting relationships between tasks and entering lead or lag times where appropriate are excellent techniques to fine-tune task relationships so that you get the results you want. However, Project cannot automatically make such schedule adjustments for you. As a project manager, you must analyze the sequences and relationships of your tasks and use your best judgment when making such adjustments.

Setting task constraints

Every task that you enter into Project has some type of constraint applied to it. A constraint determines the degree to which that task can be rescheduled. There are three categories of constraints:

- *Flexible constraints*   Project can change the start and finish dates of a task. The default constraint type in Project is that tasks start as soon as possible. This type of flexible constraint is called As Soon As Possible, or ASAP for short. No constraint date is associated with flexible constraints. Project does not display any special indicator in the Indicators column for flexible constraints.

- *Inflexible constraints*   A task must begin or end on a certain date. For example, you can specify that a task must end on November 13, 2015. Inflexible constraints are sometimes called *hard constraints*. When an inflexible constraint has been applied to a task, Project displays a special indicator in the Indicators column. You can point to a constraint indicator, and the constraint details will appear in a ScreenTip.

- *Semi-flexible constraints*   A task has a start or finish date boundary. However, within that boundary, Project has the scheduling flexibility to change the start and finish dates of a task. For example, let's say a task must finish no later than June 19, 2015. However, the task could finish before this date. Semi-flexible constraints are sometimes called *soft constraints* or *moderate constraints*. When a semi-flexible constraint has been applied to a task, Project displays a special indicator in the Indicators column.

In total, there are eight types of task constraints.

This constraint category	Includes these constraint types	And means
Flexible	As Soon As Possible (ASAP)	Project will schedule a task to occur as soon as it can occur. This is the default constraint type applied to all new tasks when scheduling from the project start date. There is no constraint date for an ASAP constraint.
	As Late As Possible (ALAP)	Project will schedule a task to occur as late as it can occur. This is the default constraint type applied to all new tasks when scheduling from the project finish date. There is no constraint date for an ALAP constraint.
Semi-flexible	Start No Earlier Than (SNET)	Project will schedule a task to start on or after the constraint date you specify. Use this constraint type to ensure that a task will not be scheduled to start before a specific date.
	Start No Later Than (SNLT)	Project will schedule a task to start on or before the constraint date you specify. Use this constraint type to ensure that a task will not start after a specific date.
	Finish No Earlier Than (FNET)	Project will schedule a task to finish on or after the constraint date you specify. Use this constraint type to ensure that a task will not finish before a specific date.
	Finish No Later Than (FNLT)	Project will schedule a task to finish on or before the constraint date you specify. Use this constraint type to ensure that a task will not finish after a specific date.
Inflexible	Must Start On (MSO)	Project will schedule a task to start on the constraint date you specify. Use this constraint type to ensure that a task will start on an exact date.
	Must Finish On (MFO)	Project will schedule a task to finish on the constraint date you specify. Use this constraint type to ensure that a task will finish on an exact date.

These three constraint categories have very different effects on the scheduling of tasks:

- **Flexible constraints**, such as As Soon As Possible (ASAP), allow tasks to be scheduled without any limitations other than their predecessor and successor relationships, and the project's start date (for ASAP task constraints) or finish date (for As Late As

Possible, or ALAP, task constraints). No fixed start or end dates are imposed by these constraint types. Use these constraint types whenever possible.

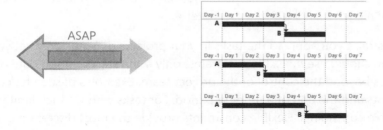

In this example, tasks A and B are linked and task B has an ASAP constraint applied. As the duration of task A shrinks or grows, the start date of task B is automatically adjusted accordingly.

- **Semi-flexible constraints**, such as Start No Earlier Than or Start No Later Than (SNET or SNLT), limit the rescheduling of a task within the date boundary you specify.

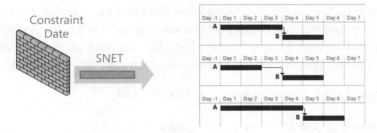

Here, tasks A and B are linked and task B has an SNET constraint set to Day 4 applied. If Task A's duration decreases, the start of Task B is unaffected. However, if Task A's duration extends, Project adjusts Task B's start date automatically.

- **Inflexible constraints**, such as Must Start On (MSO), prevent the rescheduling of a task. Use these constraint types only when absolutely necessary.

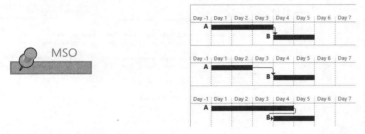

In this example, tasks A and B are linked and task B has an MSO constraint set to Day 4 applied. If task A's duration decreases or increases, the start of task B is unaffected.

9

TIP When working with a manually scheduled task, you cannot change the constraint type or set a constraint date. The reason is that Project does not schedule manually scheduled tasks, so constraints have no effect. For more information about manually scheduled tasks versus automatically scheduled tasks, see Chapter 4.

The type of constraint you apply to the tasks in your projects depends on what you need from Project. You should use inflexible constraints only if the start or finish date of a task is fixed by factors beyond the control of the project team. Examples of such tasks include handoffs to clients and the end of a funding period. For tasks without such limitations, you should use flexible constraints. Flexible constraints provide the most discretion in adjusting start and finish dates, and they allow Project to adjust dates if your plan changes. For example, if you used ASAP constraints and the duration of a predecessor task changes from four days to two days, Project adjusts, or *pulls in*, the start and finish dates of all successor tasks. However, if a successor task had an inflexible constraint applied, Project cannot adjust its start or finish dates.

The scenario: At Lucerne Publishing, a task in the new children's book plan cannot start quite as early as you had expected. Tad Orman, the children's book author, needs to proofread his book at a certain stage in the design process. This work is accounted for in task 16, *Proofread and index*. However, Tad has informed you that because of his travel schedule, he will be unable to start his review before July 17—later than currently scheduled.

In this exercise, you apply a constraint type and date to a task.

1 Select the name of task 16, *Proofread and index*.

2 On the **Task** tab, in the **Editing** group, click **Scroll to Task**.

    TIP To select a task quickly, even a task you can't see in the current view, press Ctrl+G, and in the ID field of the Go To dialog box, enter a task number, and then click OK.

Note the current scheduled start date: 7/15/15. This needs to be adjusted.

3   On the **Task** tab, in the **Properties** group, click **Information**.

4   In the **Task Information** dialog box, click the **Advanced** tab.

5   In the **Constraint Type** box, select **Start No Earlier Than**.

6   In the **Constraint Date** box, type or select **7/17/15**.

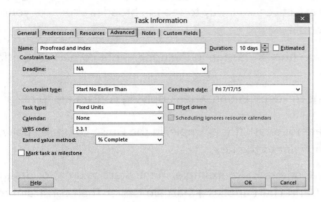

7   Click **OK**.

Project applies a Start No Earlier Than constraint to the task, and a constraint icon appears in the Indicators column. You can point to the icon to see the constraint details in a ScreenTip.

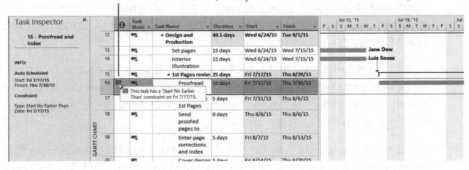

To see a ScreenTip position the mouse pointer on a constraint indicator (or any icon in the Indicators column).

Because this constraint affects the scheduling of the task, the Task Inspector pane now includes the constraint details.

Task 16 is rescheduled to start on July 17 instead of July 15. All tasks that depend on task 16 are also rescheduled. One way to view this rescheduling is by the light blue change highlighting that Project applies to the Start and Finish dates of the successor tasks of task 16. Because the durations of the *1st Pages review* and *Design and Production* summary tasks were also changed by applying the constraint to task 16, the Duration and Finish fields for those summary tasks are also highlighted. Change highlighting remains visible until you perform another editing action or save the file, and it is an effective visual way to see the broader effects of your specific actions in your schedule.

8   Click the **Close** button (the "X" button in the upper-right corner) on the Task Inspector pane.

Here are a few other things to keep in mind when applying constraints to tasks:

- Entering a Finish date for a task (for example, in the Finish column) applies a Finish No Earlier Than constraint to the task.

- Entering a Start date for a task (for example, in the Start column) or dragging a Gantt bar directly on the Gantt chart applies a Start No Earlier Than constraint to the task.

- In many cases, entering a deadline date is a preferable alternative to entering a semi-flexible or inflexible constraint. You will work with deadline dates in Chapter 10.

- Unless you specify a time, Project schedules a constraint date's start or finish time using the Default Start Time or Default End Time value on the Schedule tab of the Project Options dialog box. (To open this dialog box, on the File tab, click Options.) In this project, the default start time is 8 A.M. If you want a constrained task to be scheduled to start at a different time, enter that time along with the start date. For example, if you want to schedule a task to start at 10 A.M. on July 16, enter 7/16/15 10AM in the Start field.

- To remove a constraint, first select the task or tasks and, on the Task tab, in the Properties group, click Information. In the Task Information dialog box, click the Advanced tab. In the Constraint Type box, select As Soon As Possible or (if scheduling from the project finish date) As Late As Possible.

- If you must apply semi-flexible or inflexible constraints to tasks in addition to task relationships, you might create what is called *negative slack*. For example, assume that you have a successor task that has a finish-to-start relationship with its predecessor task. If you enter a Must Start On constraint on the successor task earlier than the finish date of the predecessor task, this results in negative slack and a scheduling conflict. By default, the constraint date applied to the successor task will override the relationship. However, if you prefer, you can set Project to honor relationships over constraints. On the File tab, click Options, and in the Project Options dialog box, click the Schedule tab. Clear the Tasks Will Always Honor Their Constraint Dates check box.

- If you must schedule a project from a finish date rather than a start date, some constraint behaviors change. For example, the As Late As Possible constraint type, rather than As Soon As Possible, becomes the default for new tasks. You should pay close attention to constraints when scheduling from a finish date to make sure that they create the effect you intend.

Interrupting work on a task

When initially planning project tasks, you might know that work on a certain task will be interrupted. Rather than listing a task twice to account for a known interruption in work, you can *split* the task into two or more segments. The following are some reasons why you might want to split a task:

- You anticipate an interruption in a task. For example, the facility where a task must be performed will not be accessible midway through the tasks' completion.

- A task is unexpectedly interrupted. After a task is underway, a resource might have to stop work on the task because another task has taken priority. After the second task is completed, the resource can resume work on the first task.

The scenario: At Lucerne Publishing, you've learned that work on a task in the new children's book plan will be interrupted. You'd like to account for this in the plan by recording the interruption where no work should be scheduled but keep the assigned work values on the task unchanged.

In this exercise, you split a task to account for a planned interruption of work on that task.

1 Select the name of task 3, *Content edit*.

2 On the **Task** tab, in the **Editing** group, click **Scroll to Task**.

You have learned that work on this task will be interrupted for three days starting Monday, April 13.

3 On the **Task** tab, in the **Schedule** group, click **Split Task** (it looks like a broken Gantt bar).

A ScreenTip appears, and the mouse pointer changes.

4   Move the mouse pointer over the Gantt bar of task 3.

This ScreenTip is essential for accurately splitting a task because it contains the date at which you would start the second segment of the task if you dragged the mouse pointer from its current location on the Gantt bar. As you move the mouse pointer along the Gantt bar, you will see the start date in the ScreenTip change.

5   Move (but don't click) the mouse pointer over the Gantt bar of task 3 until the scheduled start date of Monday, April 13, appears in the ScreenTip.

To help you accurately split tasks use this ScreenTip, which will change as you move the Split Task mouse pointer.

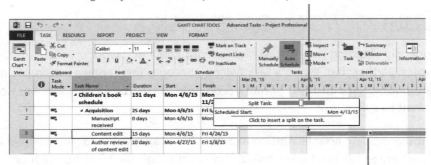

Split Task mouse pointer

6   Click and drag the mouse pointer to the right until the task start date of Thursday, April 16, appears in the ScreenTip, and then release the mouse button.

Project inserts a task split, represented in the Gantt chart as a dotted line, between the two segments of the task.

The split, which indicates an interruption of work on a task, appears as a dotted line connecting the segments of the task.

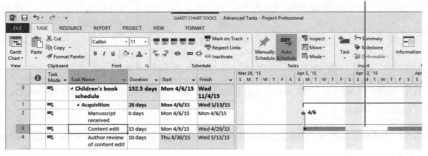

TIP Splitting tasks with the mouse might take a little practice. In step 6, if you didn't split task 3 so that the second segment starts on April 16, just point to the second segment again. When the mouse pointer changes to a four-headed arrow, drag the segment to the correct start date.

Here are a few other things to keep in mind when splitting tasks:

- You can split a task into multiple segments.

- You can drag a segment of a split task either left or right to reschedule the split.

- To rejoin two segments of a split task, drag one segment of the task until it touches the other segment.

- The time of the task split, represented by the dotted line, is not counted in the duration of the task. No work occurs during the split.

- If the duration of a split task changes, the last segment of the task is increased or decreased.

- If a split task is rescheduled (for example, if its start date changes), the entire task is rescheduled, splits and all. The task keeps the same pattern of segments and splits.

- Resource leveling or manually contouring assignments over time can cause tasks to split. You will contour assignments in Chapter 11, "Fine-tuning resource and assignment details," and level resources in Chapter 12, "Fine-tuning the project plan."

- If you do not want to display splits as a dotted line, you can hide the dotted lines. On the Format tab, in the Format group, click Layout. In the Layout dialog box, clear the Show Bar Splits check box.

9

Adjusting working time for individual tasks

There might be times when you want a specific task to occur at times that differ from the working time of the project calendar. Or perhaps you want a task to occur at a time outside of the resource working time, as determined by the resource's calendar. To accomplish this, you apply a *task calendar* to such tasks. As with the project calendar, you specify which base calendar to use as a task calendar. The following are some examples of when you might need a task calendar:

- You are using the Standard base calendar with 8:00 A.M. to 5:00 P.M. normal working hours as your project calendar, and you have a task that must run overnight.

- You have a task that must occur on a specific weekday.

- You have a task that must occur over a weekend.

Unlike resources, Project does not create task calendars as you create tasks. (If you need a refresher on resource calendars, see Chapter 5, "Setting up resources.") When you need a task calendar, you assign a base calendar to the task. This base calendar might be one that is provided with Project or a new base calendar that you create for the task. For example, if you assign the 24 Hours base calendar to a task, Project will schedule that task according to a 24-hour workday rather than the working time specified in the project calendar.

For tasks that have both a task calendar and resource assignments, Project schedules work during the working times that are common between the task calendar and resource calendar(s). If there is no common working time, Project alerts you when you apply the task calendar or assign a resource to the task.

When you apply a task calendar to a task, you can choose to ignore resource calendars for all resources assigned to the task. Doing so causes Project to schedule the resources to work on the task according to the task calendar and not their own resource calendars (for example, to work 24 hours per day).

The scenario: At Lucerne Publishing, you need to record that a task in the new children's book project has a more restrictive working time than the rest of the tasks. The plan includes a task for the handoff of final book proofs to a color-setting services firm, which then prepares the book for commercial printing. However, this firm starts new jobs only on Mondays through Wednesdays.

In this exercise, you create a new base calendar and apply it to a task as a task calendar.

1   On the **Project** tab, in the **Properties** group, click **Change Working Time**.

   The Change Working Time dialog box appears.

2   In the **Change Working Time** dialog box, click **Create New Calendar**.

   The Create New Base Calendar dialog box appears.

3   In the **Name** box, type Monday-Wednesday.

4   Make sure that the **Make a copy of** option is selected and that **Standard** is selected in the drop-down list.

5   Click **OK**.

> **TIP** This plan uses the Standard base calendar as its Project calendar. One benefit of creating a new calendar by copying the Standard base calendar is that all the working-day exceptions from the Standard calendar, such as national holidays you have previously entered, will also appear in the new calendar. Any future changes made to either calendar do not affect the other calendar, however.

Note that *Monday-Wednesday* now appears in the For calendar box.

6   In the **Change Working Time** dialog box, click the **Work Weeks** tab.

Next, you'll enter the working-time details for this new calendar.

7   Make sure that the **Name** value **[Default]** in Row 1 is selected, and then click **Details**.

8   In the **Select day(s)** box, select **Thursday** and **Friday**.

These are the days you want to change to nonworking days for this calendar.

9   Choose **Set days to nonworking time**.

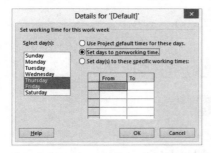

10   Click **OK** to close the **Details** dialog box, and then click **OK** again to close the **Change Working Time** dialog box.

Now that you've created the Monday-Wednesday calendar, you're ready to apply it to a task.

11   Select the name of task 29, *Send to color house*.

Currently, this task is scheduled to start on Thursday, September 3.

12   On the **Task** tab, in the **Properties** group, click **Information**.

The Task Information dialog box appears.

13   Click the **Advanced** tab.

As you can see in the Calendar box, the default for all tasks is None.

14   In the **Calendar** box, select **Monday-Wednesday** from the list of available base calendars.

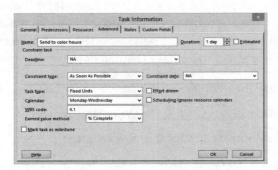

15   Click **OK** to close the dialog box.

Project applies the Monday-Wednesday calendar to task 29. The task calendar causes Project to reschedule the task to the next available working day, which is the following Monday. A calendar icon appears in the Indicators column, reminding you that this task has a task calendar applied to it.

16   Point to the calendar icon.

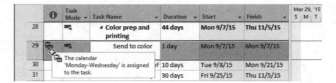

A ScreenTip appears, showing the calendar details. Because of the custom calendar you applied to this task, it will not be scheduled on a Thursday or Friday or over the weekend.

Control task scheduling with task types

You might recall from Chapter 6, "Assigning resources to tasks," that Project uses the following formula, called the *scheduling formula*, to calculate a task's work value:

Duration × Assignment Units = Work

Here, *assignment units* are normally expressed as a percentage. Remember also that a task has work when it has at least one work resource (people or equipment) assigned to it. Each value in the scheduling formula corresponds to a task type. A task type determines which of the three scheduling formula values remains fixed if the other two values change.

The default task type is *fixed units*: If you change a task's duration, Project will recalculate work. Likewise, if you change a task's work, Project will recalculate the duration. In either case, the units value is not affected.

The two other task types are *fixed duration* and *fixed work*. For these task types, Project uses a timephased field called *peak units* when responding to schedule changes.

For a fixed-work task

- You can change the assignment units value and Project will recalculate the duration.

- You can change the duration value and Project will recalculate peak units per time period. The assignment units value is not affected.

TIP You cannot turn off effort-driven scheduling for a fixed-work task. If you need a refresher on effort-driven scheduling, see "Controlling work when adding or removing resource assignments" in Chapter 6.

For a fixed-duration task

- You can change the assignment units value and Project will recalculate work.

- You can change the work value and Project will recalculate peak units per time period. The assignment units value is not affected.

Project also keeps track of the highest peak units value per assignment. This value is stored in the Peak field, which is explained later in the chapter.

9

TIP You cannot change the task type of a manually scheduled task, and the effect of the task type on the scheduling of a task as described here applies only to automatically scheduled tasks. If you need a refresher on manually scheduled tasks, see Chapter 4, "Building a task list."

To view the task type of the selected task, on the Task tab, in the Properties group, click Information. Then, in the Task Information dialog box, click the Advanced tab. You can also view the task type in the Task Form. (When in the Gantt Chart view, you can display the Task Form by clicking Details on the View tab, in the Split View group.) You can change a task type at any time. Note that characterizing a task type as *fixed* does not mean that its duration, assignment units, or work values are unchangeable. You can change any value for any task type.

Which is the right task type to apply to each of your tasks? It depends on how you want Project to schedule that task. The following table summarizes the effects of changing any value for any task type. You read it like a multiplication table.

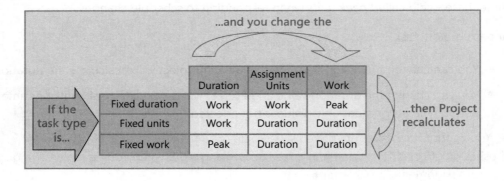

If the task type is...	Duration	Assignment Units	Work
Fixed duration	Work	Work	Peak
Fixed units	Work	Duration	Duration
Fixed work	Peak	Duration	Duration

...and you change the → ...then Project recalculates

Assignment units, peak, peak units, and the scheduling formula

In previous versions of Project, it was possible that a resource's initial assignment units value would change, and this led to unexpected results with regard to the scheduling formula. This behavior changed starting with Project 2010. Project now tracks both the assignment units value and a calculated value called *peak* (or, when viewed in a timescale, *peak units*).

Project uses the assignment units value when initially scheduling or later rescheduling a task, but it uses peak units when reporting a resource's maximum peak units value. Here's one example. If you initially assigned a resource at 100% assignment units to a 1-day, fixed-unit task, Project used that value to initially calculate 8 hours of work. However, if you then recorded 10 hours of actual work on the task, versions of Project prior to 2010 would have recalculated the assignment units to be 120% to keep the scheduling formula accurate. If you then added more work or changed the duration of the task, Project would have scheduled the task using the 120% assignment units value—probably not the result you'd want. Project 2010 and later, however, will record the 120% peak value, and if you subsequently add work or change the duration of the task, Project will use the original assignment units value of 100% rather than the peak value of 120% to reschedule the task.

Scenario: At Lucerne Publishing, you tried adjusting work and assignment details of some tasks in the new children's book plan but didn't get the results you wanted. After learning how to adjust task types, you decide to give that a try.

In this exercise, you change a task type and some scheduling formula values, and you see the resulting effect on the tasks.

1 On the **View** tab, in the **Task Views** group, click **Task Usage**.

The Task Usage view appears.

2 In the **Task Name** column, select the name of task 8, *Copyedit*.

3 On the **Task** tab, in the **Editing** group, click **Scroll to Task**.

Project displays the schedule and assignment details for task 8, *Copyedit*.

The Task Usage view groups the assigned resources below each task and shows you, among other things, each task's duration and work—two of the three variables of the scheduling formula.

4   If necessary, drag the vertical divider bar to the right so that the **Finish** column is visible.

Next, you'll add two columns to the Usage table so that you can see the assignment units (the third variable of the scheduling formula) and the peak values. You don't need to modify this view every time you want to use it, but for our purposes here, this is a good way to illustrate the effect of changing task types and scheduling formula values.

5   Click the **Start** column heading, and then, on the **Format** tab, in the **Columns** group, click **Insert Column**.

A list of fields appears.

6   Click **Assignment Units**.

7   Click the **Start** column heading again, and on the **Format** tab, in the **Columns** group, click **Insert Column**.

8   Click **Peak**.

Project inserts the Assignment Units and Peak columns to the left of the Start column. *Peak* is the resource's maximum units value at any time throughout the assignment's duration.

		Task Mode	Task Name	Work	Duration	Assignmen Units	Peak	Details	T	W	T	F	S	May 24, '15 S	M
6			◢ Editorial	420 hrs	32.5 days			Work	8h	8h	16h	16h			16h
7			◢ Organize manus	40 hrs	5 days			Work	8h	8h					
			Hany Morco	40 hrs		100%	100%	Work	8h	8h					
8			◢ Copyedit	240 hrs	15 days			Work			16h	16h			16h
			Copyeditors	240 hrs		200%	200%	Work			16h	16h			16h
9			◢ Author review	100 hrs	10 days			Work							
			Copyeditors	20 hrs		25%	25%	Work							
			Tad Orman	80 hrs		100%	100%	Work							
10			◢ Copyedit incorp	40 hrs	5 days			Work							
			Hany Morco	40 hrs		100%	100%	Work							

You can see that task 8 has a total work value of 240 hours, a resource assignment units value of 200%, and a duration of 15 days. Next, you will change the task's duration to observe the effects on the other values.

After a discussion between the two copyeditors about who will perform the copyedit, you all agree that the task's duration should increase and the resource's daily work on the task should decrease correspondingly.

9   In the **Duration** field for task 8, type or select 20d, and press the Enter key.

Project changes the task's duration to 20 days and increases the work to 320 hours. Note the change highlighting applied to the Work and Duration values. You increased the duration and wanted the total work to remain the same (it didn't), so you will use the Action button to adjust the results of the new task duration.

10   Click the **Action** button for task 8's **Duration** field.

Review the options on the list that appears.

Because task 8's task type is fixed units (the default task type), the Action's default selection is to increase work as the duration increases. However, you'd like to keep the work value the same and decrease the resource's assigned daily work on the task.

11   On the **Actions** list, click **Decrease the hours resources work per day (units) but keep the same amount of work**.

The assignment units and peak values decreases to 150%, and the total work on the task remains unchanged at 240 hours. On the right side of the usage view, you can see that the work scheduled per day was reduced from 16 to 12 hours per day.

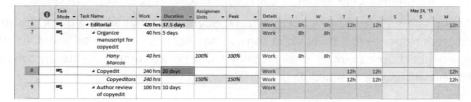

Next, you will change a task type and then adjust the work on another task.

12   Select the name of task 24, *Final review*.

13   On the **Task** tab, in the **Editing** group, click **Scroll to Task**.

Project displays work values for task 24, *Final review* in the timephased grid.

14   On the **Task** tab, in the **Properties** group, click **Information**.

The Task Information dialog box appears.

15   Click the **Advanced** tab.

The selected task describes the final review of the new book's page proofs. As you can see in the Task Type box, this task has the default task type of fixed-units. The task is scheduled for four days. Because it's Lucerne's policy to allow four working days for such reviews, you'll make this a fixed-duration task.

16   In the **Task Type** box, select **Fixed Duration**.

17   Click **OK** to close the **Task Information** dialog box.

Changing the task type does not result in any immediate change to the schedule. Next, you'll add work to the task and observe the effect.

18   In the **Work** field for task 24, *Final review*, type **120h**, and then press Enter.

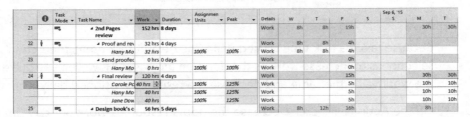

	ℹ	Task Mode	Task Name	Work	Duration	Assignmen Units	Peak	Details	W	T	F	S	Sep 6, '15 S	M	T
21		▬	⊿ 2nd Pages review	152 hrs	8 days			Work	8h	8h	19h			30h	30h
22	⚕	▬	⊿ Proof and rev	32 hrs	4 days			Work	8h	8h	4h				
			Hany Mo	32 hrs		100%	100%	Work	8h	8h	4h				
23		▬	⊿ Send proofec	0 hrs	0 days			Work			0h				
			Hany Mo	0 hrs		100%	100%	Work			0h				
24	⚕	▬	⊿ Final review	120 hrs	4 days			Work			15h			30h	30h
			Carole Pc	40 hrs		100%	125%	Work			5h			10h	10h
			Hany Mo	40 hrs		100%	125%	Work			5h			10h	10h
			Jane Dow	40 hrs		100%	125%	Work			5h			10h	10h
25		▬	⊿ Design book's c	56 hrs	5 days			Work	8h	12h	16h			8h	

Because this is a fixed duration task and you added work, Project adjusted the peak value to 125%; this represents an intentional overallocation. On the right side of the usage view, you can see that the resources assigned to task 24 now have 10 hours of work scheduled per day for most days of their assignments to this task. Their original assignment units values of 100% each remain unaffected, however.

As you fine-tune your plans in Project, you might find times when a quick adjustment to Project's response to a schedule change via the Actions button is sufficient. At other times, you might choose to intentionally change a task type to more consistently control how Project will handle its scheduling.

Task types and effort-driven scheduling

Many people misunderstand task types and effort-driven scheduling and conclude that these two issues are more closely related than they really are. Both settings can affect your schedule. Whereas the effect of a task type applies whenever you edit a task's work, duration, or unit values, effort-driven scheduling affects your schedule only when you're assigning or removing resources from tasks. For more information about effort-driven scheduling, see Chapter 6.

❌ CLEAN UP Close the Advanced Tasks file.

Key points

- Use the Task Path feature to quickly highlight predecessors and successors of the selected task.

- By using a combination of task relationships plus lead and lag time, you can more accurately model when work should be done.

- When entering lead time between a predecessor task and successor task, entering a percentage lead time value offers some flexibility because Project recalculates the lead time value whenever the duration of the predecessor task changes.

- Think through the effects of semi-flexible and inflexible constraints on your schedules, and use them sparingly.

- For tasks that must be completed at times other than the project's normal working time (as specified by the project calendar), you can create a new base calendar and apply it to the task.

- You can interrupt work on a task by splitting it.

9

Chapter at a glance

Deadline

Set a deadline date for a task, page 200.

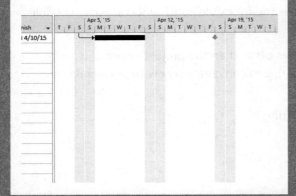

Cost

Record a fixed cost on a task, page 202.

Task Name	Fixed Cost	Fixed Cost Accrual	Total Cost	Base
⊿ **2nd Pages revie**	$0.00	Prorated	**$7,400.00**	
Proof and rev	$0.00	Prorated	$1,550.00	
Send proofec	$0.00	Prorated	$0.00	
Final review	$0.00	Prorated	$5,850.00	
⊿ **Design book's o**	$0.00	**Prorated**	**$2,800.00**	
Create mocki	$0.00	Prorated	$1,680.00	
Review with	$0.00	Prorated	$1,120.00	
⊿ **Color prep and pri**	$0.00	**Prorated**	**$810.00**	
Send to color hc	$0.00	Prorated	$310.00	
Generate proof	$500.00	End	$500.00	
Print and ship	$0.00	Prorated	$0.00	

Repeat

Set up a recurring task, page 204.

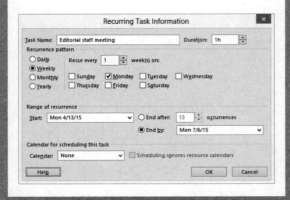

Critical path

See which tasks drive the project's finish date, page 208.

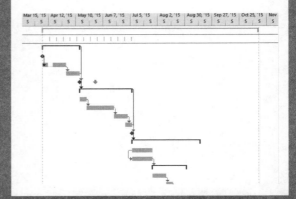

Fine-tuning task details

IN THIS CHAPTER, YOU WILL LEARN HOW TO

- Enter deadlines for tasks.

- Enter a fixed cost for a task.

- Set up a recurring task.

- View the project's critical path.

- Enter a specific duration value for a summary task.

In this chapter, you continue the deep dive into task-management features that you began in the previous chapter. This chapter focuses on specific features you can apply to individual tasks, including deadline dates and fixed costs. In addition, you'll set up a recurring task and view a project's critical path.

PRACTICE FILES Before you can complete the exercises in this chapter, you need to copy the book's practice files to your computer. A complete list of practice files is provided in "Download the practice files" at the beginning of this book. For each exercise that has a practice file, simply browse to where you saved the book's practice file folder.

IMPORTANT If you are running Project Professional with Project Web App/Project Server, take care not to save any of the practice files you work with in this book to Project Web App (PWA). For more information, see Appendix C, "Collaborating: Project, SharePoint, and PWA."

Entering deadline dates

Entering a *deadline date* for a task causes Project to display a deadline indicator on the chart portion of a Gantt chart view. If the task's finish date moves past its deadline date, Project displays a missed deadline indicator in the Indicator field for that task.

The deadline date feature can help you avoid a common mistake made by new Project users: placing semi-flexible or inflexible *constraints* on too many tasks in your plan. Such constraints severely limit your scheduling flexibility.

Yet, if you know that a specific task must be completed by a certain date, why not enter a Must Finish On constraint? This is the reason: Assume that you have a five-day task that you want to see completed by April 17, and today is April 6. If you enter a Must Finish On constraint on the task and set it to April 17, Project will move it out so that it will indeed end on April 17.

Pointing to the constraint indicator will display constraint details.

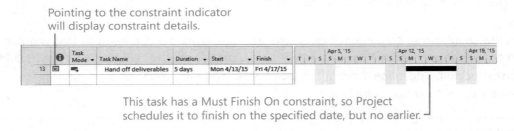

This task has a Must Finish On constraint, so Project schedules it to finish on the specified date, but no earlier.

Even if the task could be completed earlier, Project will not reschedule it to start earlier. In fact, by applying that constraint, you increased the risk for this task. If the task is delayed for even one day for any reason (a required resource is sick, for example), the task will miss its planned finish date.

A better approach to scheduling this task is to use the default As Soon As Possible constraint and then enter a deadline of April 17. A deadline is a date value you enter for a task that indicates the latest date by which you want the task to be completed, but the deadline date itself does not constrain the scheduling of the task.

The deadline indicator appears on the Gantt chart.

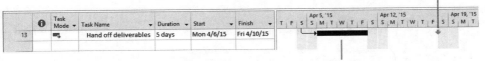

	❶	Task Mode ▾	Task Name ▾	Duration ▾	Start ▾	Finish ▾	T F	S	S M T W T F	S S M T W T F	S S M T
13		🛒	Hand off deliverables	5 days	Mon 4/6/15	Fri 4/10/15					

With an As Soon As Possible constraint applied, the task starts earlier and leaves some time between its finish date and the deadline date.

Now the task has the greatest scheduling flexibility. It might be completed well before its deadline, depending on resource availability, predecessor tasks, and whatever other scheduling issues apply.

The scenario: At Lucerne Publishing, the publisher has expressed concern that the acquisition tasks for the new children's book should not slip past a certain date. You'd like to flag this date without unduly restricting your scheduling flexibility in the plan.

In this exercise, you enter a deadline date for a task.

SET UP You need the Fine Tuning Tasks_Start file located in your Chapter10 practice file folder to complete this exercise. Open the Fine Tuning Tasks_Start file, and save it as Fine Tuning Tasks.

1   In the **Task Name** column, select the name of task 5, *Handoff to Editorial*.

This task is a milestone marking the end of the acquisition phase of the new book project. You want to make sure that the acquisition task concludes by the end of May, so you will enter a deadline date for this milestone.

2   On the **Task** tab, in the **Properties** group, click **Information**.

The Task Information dialog box appears.

3   Click the **Advanced** tab.

4   In the **Deadline** box, type or select 5/29/15, and then click **OK**.

Project displays a deadline indicator in the chart portion of the Gantt Chart view.

10

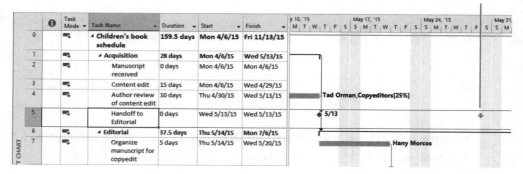
Deadline indicator

You can now see at a glance how close the end of the acquisition phase, as currently scheduled, will come to meeting or missing its deadline. If the scheduled completion of the Acquisition phase moves past May 29, Project will display a missed deadline indicator in the Indicators column.

Entering a deadline date has no effect on the scheduling of a summary task or subtask. However, a deadline date will cause Project to alert you if the scheduled completion of a task exceeds its deadline date—Project will display a red exclamation symbol in the Indicators column.

Here are a few other things relating to the deadline date feature:

- You can add the Deadline field directly to a table. Click any column heading, and then on the Format tab, in the Columns group, click Insert Column. And then select Deadline.

- You can change an existing deadline date by dragging the deadline indicator in the chart portion of a Gantt chart view.

- To remove a deadline from a task, clear the Deadline field on the Advanced tab of the Task Information dialog box.

Entering fixed costs

For projects in which you must track budget or financial costs, you might need to work with several different sources of costs. These include costs associated with resources, as well as costs associated directly with a specific task.

For many projects, financial costs are derived mainly from costs associated with work resources, such as people and equipment, or with material resources. To handle costs of similar types for which you want to track aggregate sums (travel is one example in many projects), Project supports *cost resources*. If you need a refresher on cost resources, see Chapter 5, "Setting up resources."

However, you might occasionally want to associate a cost with a task that is not tied to resources or work and is not something you want to aggregate across the project. Project calls this a *fixed cost*, and it is applied per task. A fixed cost is a specific monetary amount budgeted for a task. It remains the same regardless of any resources assigned to the task. The following are common examples of fixed costs in projects:

- A setup fee, charged in addition to a per-day rental fee, for a piece of equipment
- A building permit

If you assign resources with pay rates, assign cost resources, or add fixed costs to a task, Project adds it all together to determine the task's total cost. If you do not enter resource cost information into a plan (perhaps because you do not know how much your work resources will be paid), you can still gain some control over the project's total cost by entering fixed costs per task.

You can specify when fixed costs should accrue as follows:

- **Start** The entire fixed cost is scheduled for the start of the task. When you track progress, the entire fixed cost of the task is incurred as soon as the task starts.
- **End** The entire fixed cost is scheduled for the end of the task. When you track progress, the entire fixed cost of the task is incurred only after the task is completed.
- **Prorated** (Default accrual method) The fixed cost is distributed evenly over the duration of the task. When you track progress, the project incurs the cost of the task at the rate at which the task is completed. For example, if a task has a $100 fixed cost and is 75 percent complete, the project has incurred $75 against that task.

When you plan a project, the accrual method you choose for fixed costs determines how these costs are scheduled over time. This can be important in anticipating budget and cash-flow needs. By default, Project uses the prorated accrual method for fixed costs, but you can change that to match your organization's cost accounting practices.

The scenario: At Lucerne Publishing, you've learned that the generating of page proofs by the color-setting services firm will cost $500. Lucerne Publishing has a credit account

10

with this firm, but to keep the book's profit and loss (P&L) statement accurate, you'd like to accrue this expense when the color-setting services firm completes the task.

In this exercise, you assign a fixed cost to a task and specify its accrual method.

1   On the **View** tab, in the **Task Views** group, click **Other Views** and then click **Task Sheet**.

The Task Sheet view appears.

2   On the **View** tab, in the **Data** group, click **Tables**, and then click **Cost**.

The Cost table appears, replacing the Entry table.

3   In the **Fixed Cost** field for task 30, *Generate proofs*, type **500**, and press the Tab key.

4   In the **Fixed Cost Accrual** field, select **End**, and press Tab.

	Task Name	Fixed Cost	Fixed Cost Accrual	Total Cost	Baseline	Variance	Actual	Remaining
21	◢ 2nd Pages revie	$0.00	Prorated	$7,400.00	$0.00	$7,400.00	$0.00	$7,400.00
22	Proof and rev	$0.00	Prorated	$1,550.00	$0.00	$1,550.00	$0.00	$1,550.00
23	Send proofec	$0.00	Prorated	$0.00	$0.00	$0.00	$0.00	$0.00
24	Final review	$0.00	Prorated	$5,850.00	$0.00	$5,850.00	$0.00	$5,850.00
25	◢ Design book's c	$0.00	Prorated	$2,800.00	$0.00	$2,800.00	$0.00	$2,800.00
26	Create mocki	$0.00	Prorated	$1,680.00	$0.00	$1,680.00	$0.00	$1,680.00
27	Review with	$0.00	Prorated	$1,120.00	$0.00	$1,120.00	$0.00	$1,120.00
28	◢ Color prep and pri	$0.00	Prorated	$810.00	$0.00	$810.00	$0.00	$810.00
29	Send to color he	$0.00	Prorated	$310.00	$0.00	$310.00	$0.00	$310.00
30	Generate proof	$500.00	End	$500.00	$0.00	$500.00	$0.00	$500.00
31	Print and ship	$0.00	Prorated	$0.00	$0.00	$0.00	$0.00	$0.00

Project will now accrue a $500 cost against the task *Generate proofs* at the task's end date. This fixed cost is independent of the task's duration and of any costs of resources that could be assigned to it.

Setting up a recurring task

Many projects require repetitive tasks, such as attending project status meetings, creating and publishing status reports, or running quality-control inspections. Although it is easy to overlook the scheduling of such events, you should consider accounting for them in your plan. After all, status meetings and similar events that indirectly support the project require time from resources, and such events take time away from your resources' other assignments.

To help account for such events in your plan, create a *recurring task*. As the name suggests, a recurring task is repeated at a specified frequency such as daily, weekly, monthly, or yearly. When you create a recurring task, Project creates a series of tasks with Start No Earlier Than constraints, with effort-driven scheduling turned off, and with no task relationships defined.

The scenario: At Lucerne Publishing, the new children's book project requires a weekly status meeting involving some, but not all, of the resources working on it. You'd like this recurring status meeting to have visibility in the plan.

In this exercise, you create a recurring task that will occur on a weekly basis.

1   On the **View** tab, in the **Task Views** group, click **Gantt Chart**.

The Gantt Chart view appears.

2   Select the name of task 1, *Acquisition*.

You'll insert the recurring task above the first phase of the plan, because it will occur throughout multiple phases of the plan.

3   On the **Task** tab, in the **Insert** group, click the down arrow below the **Task** button and then click **Recurring Task**.

The Recurring Task Information dialog box appears.

4   In the **Task Name** box, type Editorial staff meeting.

5   In the **Duration** box, type 1h.

6   Under **Recurrence pattern**, make sure **Weekly** is selected, and then select the **Monday** check box.

Next, you will specify the date of its first occurrence. By default, it is the project start date. However, you want the weekly status meetings to begin one week later.

7   In the **Start** box, type or select 4/13/15.

Next, you will specify the end date. You'll plan for these staff meetings to continue until the project reaches the Design And Production phase. In the Gantt Chart, you can see that as currently scheduled, that phase starts on July 6, so you'll use that date for now. You can always update the recurring task later as needed.

8   In the **End by** box, type or select 7/6/15.

10

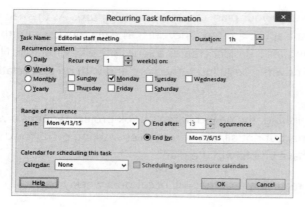

9   Click **OK** to create the recurring task.

Project inserts the recurring task. Initially, the recurring task is expanded. A recurring task icon appears in the Indicators column. Each occurrence of the recurring task is sequentially numbered. (If you want to verify this, widen the Task Name column, or point to the task's name and note the content of the ScreenTip.)

10 To view the first occurrences of the recurring meeting's Gantt bars, on the **Task** tab, in the **Editing** group, click **Scroll To Task**.

This is a recurring task indicator.

Each bar represents a specific occurrence of the recurring task.

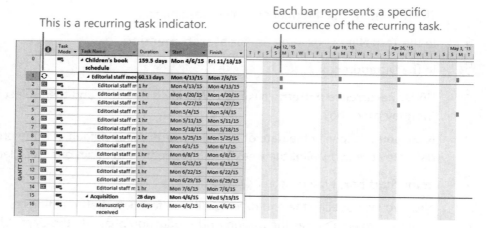

Next, you will assign resources to the recurring task.

11 Verify that task 1, *Editorial staff meeting*, is selected, and then, on the **Resource** tab, in the **Assignments** group, click **Assign Resources**.

12 In the **Assign Resources** dialog box, click **Carole Poland**. Then hold down the Ctrl key while clicking **Hany Morcos** and **Jun Cao**.

13 Click **Assign**, and then click **Close**.

The Assign Resources dialog box closes, and Project assigns the selected resources to each occurrence of the recurring task.

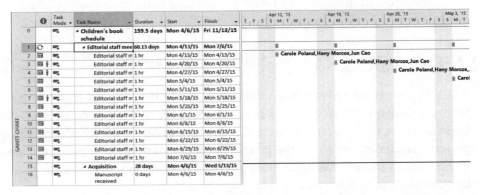

Next you will collapse the recurring task to hide its individual occurrences.

14 Click the expand/collapse arrow next to the recurring task's title, *Editorial staff meeting*.

Here are a few other things to keep in mind when creating recurring tasks:

- By default, Project schedules a recurring task to start at the plan's default start time. (Click **File**, click **Options**, and then click **Schedule**.) In this project, that value is 8 A.M. If you want to schedule a recurring task to start at a different time, enter that time along with the start date in the **Start** box of the **Recurring Task Information** dialog box. For example, if you want the recurring staff meeting to be scheduled for 10 A.M. starting on April 13, you enter 4/13/15 10 AM in the **Start** box.

- As with a summary task, the duration of a recurring task spans the earliest start to latest finish date of the individual occurrences of the recurring task.

- You can set a recurring task to end either after the number of occurrences you specify, or a date. If you schedule a recurring task to end on a specific date, Project suggests the current project end date. If you use this date, be sure to change it manually if the project end date changes later.

10

- If you want to assign the same resources to all occurrences of a recurring task, assign the resources to recurring tasks with the Assign Resources dialog box. Entering resource names in the Resource Name field of the summary recurring task assigns the resources to the summary recurring task only and not to the individual occurrences.

Viewing the project's critical path

A *critical path* is the series of tasks that will push out the project's end date if any of those tasks are delayed. The word *critical* in this context has nothing to do with how important these tasks are to the overall project. It refers only to how their scheduling will affect the project's finish date; however, the project finish date is of great importance in most projects. If you want to shorten the duration of a project to bring in the finish date, you must begin by shortening (also referred to as *crashing*) the critical path.

Over the life of a project, the project's critical path is likely to change from time to time as tasks are completed ahead of or behind schedule. Schedule changes, such as changing task relationships or durations, can also alter the critical path. After a task on the critical path is completed, it is no longer critical because it cannot affect the project finish date. In Chapter 16, "Getting your project back on track," you will work with a variety of techniques to shorten a project's overall duration.

A key to understanding the critical path is to understand *slack*, also known as *float*. There are two types of slack: free and total. Free slack is the amount of time a task can be delayed before it delays another task. Total slack is the amount of time a task can be delayed before it delays the completion of the project.

A task is on the critical path if its total slack is less than a certain amount of time—by default, if it is zero slack. In contrast, noncritical tasks have slack, meaning they can start or finish earlier or later within their slack time without affecting the completion date of a project.

TIP The Task Path feature introduced in Chapter 9, "Advanced task scheduling," distinguishes between the selected task's predecessor and successor relationships. The critical path, in contrast, applies to whatever sequence of linked tasks in a plan that drive the plan's finish date.

The scenario: At Lucerne Publishing, you frequently get asked when the new children's book project will be completed. You can quickly see the project's overall duration and finish date in Project, but occasionally you need to show a project stakeholder the project's critical path because that sequence of tasks drives the project's duration. One way to see the critical path is to switch to the Detail Gantt view.

In this exercise, you view the project's critical path.

1   On the **View** tab, in the **Task Views** group, click the down arrow below the **Gantt Chart** button and then click **More Views**.

2   In the **More Views** dialog box, select **Detail Gantt**, and then click **Apply**.

The plan appears in the Detail Gantt view.

3   On the **View** tab, in the **Zoom** group, click **Entire Project**.

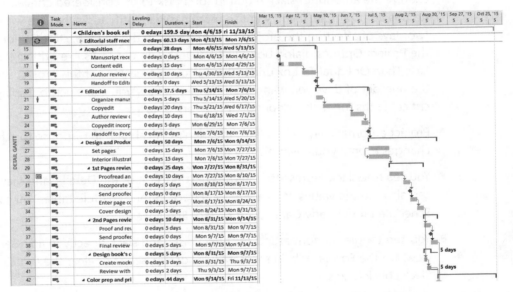

Because of the highly sequential nature of the task relationships in this plan, almost all the tasks are on the critical path, and in the Detail Gantt view, their Gantt bars are formatted in red.

Notice the Gantt bar of task 41, *Review with author*. The blue bar represents the duration of the task. The thin teal line and the number next to it represent free slack for this task. As you can see, this particular task has some slack and is therefore a noncritical task.

TIP Remember that the term *critical* in this sense has nothing to do with the task's importance, but only with how much or little total slack is associated with the task and, ultimately, what effect the task has on the project's finish date.

4   On the **View** tab, in the **Task Views** group, click the down arrow below the **Gantt Chart** button and then click **Gantt Chart**.

Working with the critical path is the most important way to manage a project's overall duration. In later chapters, you will make adjustments that might extend the project's duration. Checking the project's critical path and, when necessary, shortening the overall project duration are important project-management skills.

Here are a few other things to keep in mind when working with the critical path:

- By default, Project defines a task as critical if it has zero slack. However, you can change the amount of slack required for a task to be considered critical. You might do this, for example, if you want to more easily identify tasks that are within one or two days of affecting the project's finish date. On the File tab, click Options, and in the Project Options dialog box, click Advanced. In the Tasks Are Critical If Slack Is Less Than Or Equal To box under the Calculation options of this project section, enter the number of days you want. In the same section, you can elect to display multiple critical paths for each independent network of tasks.

- Project automatically recalculates the plan's critical path in response to schedule changes even if you never display it.

- You see free slack represented in the chart portion of the Detail Gantt view, and you can also see the values of free and total slack in the Schedule table. You can apply the Schedule table to any Gantt chart or Task Sheet view.

- You can toggle the formatting of critical tasks and slack directly in any Gantt chart view. On the Format tab, in the Bar Styles group, select or clear the Critical Tasks and Slack check boxes.

- Here's another way you can identify the tasks on the critical path. On the Format tab, in the Data group, select Critical in the Highlight or Filter boxes.

TIP To learn more about the critical path, click the Help button (which looks like a question mark) in the upper-right corner of the Project window, and in the Search box, type **critical path**.

Scheduling summary tasks manually

In Chapter 4, "Building a task list," you worked with *summary tasks* and subtasks. Recall that the default behavior of Project is to automatically calculate a summary task's duration as the span of time between the earliest start and latest finish dates of its subtasks. For this reason, Project sets summary tasks as automatically scheduled—their durations are automatically determined by their subtasks, regardless of whether those subtasks are manually or automatically scheduled (or are a mix of both).

There might be times, however, when you want to directly enter a duration value for a summary task that is independent of its calculated duration as determined by its subtasks. For example, a summary task might represent a phase of work for which you want to allocate 60 working days and compare that duration with the calculated duration determined by the subtasks (their durations, task relationships, and other factors). This is especially true during the initial planning of a plan, when you might need to account for the gap between how long you'd like a phase of work to take and its duration as determined by its subtasks.

Fortunately, you can enter any duration you want for a summary task. When you do so, Project switches the summary task from automatic to manually scheduled and reflects both the automatically calculated and manually entered durations as separate parts of the summary task's Gantt bar. If the summary task is a predecessor of another task, Project will reschedule the successor task based on the manual, not automatic, duration.

Setting a manual duration for a summary task is a good way to apply a top-down focus to a plan. You can, for example, introduce some slack or buffer to a phase of work by entering a manual duration for the summary task that is longer than its calculated duration. Conversely, you can enter a desired manual duration that is shorter than the scheduled duration of a summary task.

The scenario: At Lucerne Publishing, the publisher has challenged the team to aim for a 30-working-day duration for the Editorial phase of the new children's book project. The publisher is not focused on a specific completion date here, so applying a deadline date is not your best option. Instead, you'll record a manual duration on the Editorial summary task and later compare that duration with the automatically scheduled duration provided by Project.

10

In this exercise, you enter manual durations for some summary tasks.

1 On the **View** tab, in the **Data** group, click **Outline**, and then click **Level 1**.

Project hides all subtasks and nested summary tasks, letting you more easily focus on the top-level tasks in the plan.

2 On the **View** tab, in the **Zoom** group, click **Entire Project**.

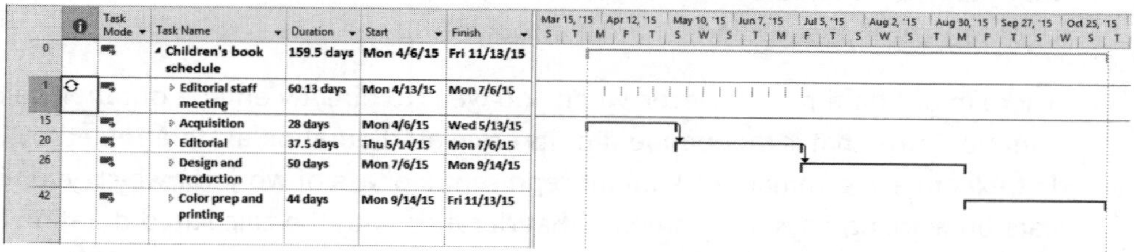

Task Mode
Task Name
Duration
Start
Finish
0 Children's book schedule 159.5 days Mon 4/6/15 Fri 11/13/15
1 Editorial staff meeting 60.13 days Mon 4/13/15 Mon 7/6/15
15 Acquisition 28 days Mon 4/6/15 Wed 5/13/15
20 Editorial 37.5 days Thu 5/14/15 Mon 7/6/15
26 Design and Production 50 days Mon 7/6/15 Mon 9/14/15
42 Color prep and printing 44 days Mon 9/14/15 Fri 11/13/15
Mar 15, '15 Apr 12, '15 May 10, '15 Jun 7, '15 Jul 5, '15 Aug 2, '15 Aug 30, '15 Sep 27, '15 Oct 25, '15

Note that the expand/collapse triangles next to the summary task names changed direction and color, indicating that the subtasks are hidden. In this view, you can more easily see and compare the durations of the individual summary tasks.

Next, you'll enter some manual durations. You'll begin with the Editorial phase, which you'd like to see completed within 30 working days.

3 Click the expand/collapse arrow next to the name of task 20, the *Editorial* summary task.

With the summary task's subtasks now displayed, you'll more easily see the effect of entering a manual duration for the summary task.

4 In the **Duration** field for the summary task 20, *Editorial*, type **30d** and press Enter.

A manually scheduled summary task displays two bars to account for both the manual and automatic durations.

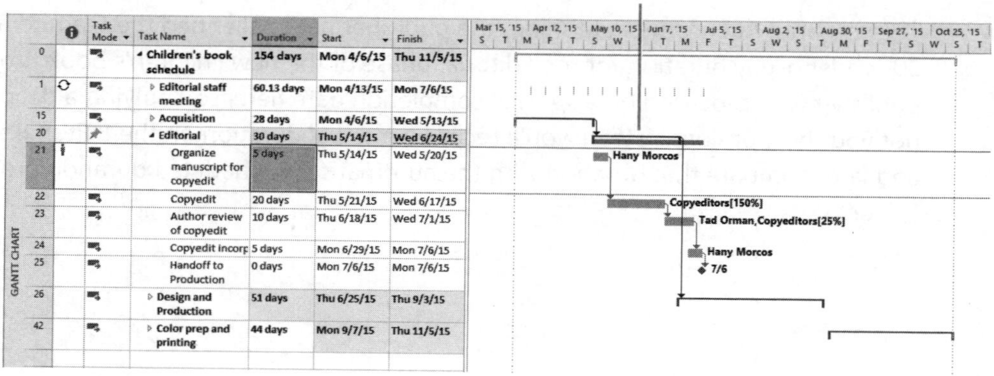

GANTT CHART
Task Mode
Task Name
Duration
Start
Finish
0 Children's book schedule 154 days Mon 4/6/15 Thu 11/5/15
1 Editorial staff meeting 60.13 days Mon 4/13/15 Mon 7/6/15
15 Acquisition 28 days Mon 4/6/15 Wed 5/13/15
20 Editorial 30 days Thu 5/14/15 Wed 6/24/15
21 Organize manuscript for copyedit 5 days Thu 5/14/15 Wed 5/20/15
22 Copyedit 20 days Thu 5/21/15 Wed 6/17/15
23 Author review of copyedit 10 days Thu 6/18/15 Wed 7/1/15
24 Copyedit incorp 5 days Mon 6/29/15 Mon 7/6/15
25 Handoff to Production 0 days Mon 7/6/15 Mon 7/6/15
26 Design and Production 51 days Thu 6/25/15 Thu 9/3/15
42 Color prep and printing 44 days Mon 9/7/15 Thu 11/5/15
Hany Morcos
Copyeditors[150%]
Tad Orman,Copyeditors[25%]
Hany Morcos
7/6

Project records your manually entered duration and makes some adjustments to the schedule:

- The summary task is switched from automatically scheduled (the default for summary tasks) to manually scheduled. Note the pin icon in the Task Mode column that reflects the task's scheduling status.

- Project drew two bars for the summary task. The upper bar represents the manual duration, and the lower bar represents the automatically scheduled duration.

- Project draws a red squiggly line under the new finish date to flag this as a potential scheduling conflict.

- Project rescheduled the successor tasks throughout the schedule based on task 20's manually entered duration.

Note that some of the subtasks now extend beyond the scheduled finish date of their summary task. This additional time represents the amount by which the plan currently exceeds the desired 30-day duration of the Editorial phase of work.

Looking at the updated schedule, you decide you'd next like to allow a bit more time for the color prep and printing. To do so, you'll enter a manual duration on a summary task that is greater than its scheduled duration.

5   Click the expand/collapse arrow next to the name of task 42, the *Color prep and printing* summary task.

6   In the **Duration** field for task 42, type 50d and press Enter.

Project records your manually entered duration, switches the summary task to manually scheduled, and redraws the Gantt bar.

10

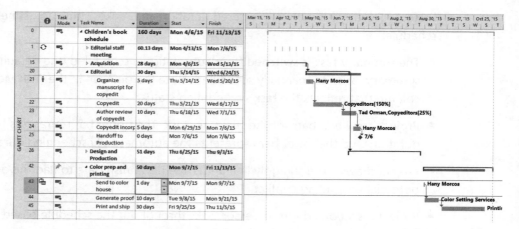

	ⓘ	Task Mode	Task Name	Duration	Start	Finish
0		🔒	⊿ Children's book schedule	160 days	Mon 4/6/15	Fri 11/13/15
1	↻	🔒	▷ Editorial staff meeting	60.13 days	Mon 4/13/15	Mon 7/6/15
15		🔒	▷ Acquisition	28 days	Mon 4/6/15	Wed 5/13/15
20		✐	⊿ Editorial	30 days	Thu 5/14/15	Wed 6/24/15
21	⫶	🔒	Organize manuscript for copyedit	5 days	Thu 5/14/15	Wed 5/20/15
22		🔒	Copyedit	20 days	Thu 5/21/15	Wed 6/17/15
23		🔒	Author review of copyedit	10 days	Thu 6/18/15	Wed 7/1/15
24		🔒	Copyedit incorp	5 days	Mon 6/29/15	Mon 7/6/15
25		🔒	Handoff to Production	0 days	Mon 7/6/15	Mon 7/6/15
26		🔒	▷ Design and Production	51 days	Thu 6/25/15	Thu 9/3/15
42		✐	⊿ Color prep and printing	50 days	Mon 9/7/15	Fri 11/13/15
43	📋	🔒	Send to color house	1 day	Mon 9/7/15	Mon 9/7/15
44		🔒	Generate proof	10 days	Tue 9/8/15	Mon 9/21/15
45		🔒	Print and ship	30 days	Fri 9/25/15	Thu 11/5/15

Here, you can see that the finish date of summary task 42 now extends beyond the finish dates of its subtasks by several days. These additional days represent the difference between the scheduled duration of the summary task 42 and the manual duration you entered. This time is effectively a buffer you've added to the summary task.

TIP When you enter a manual duration on a summary task, you might find it helpful to compare the manual duration and new finish date with the automatically scheduled duration and finish dates as determined by the subtasks of the summary task. To see the automatically scheduled values, you can add the Scheduled Duration, Scheduled Start, and Scheduled Finish fields to a table. You can also point at the summary task's Gantt bars in the chart portion of a Gantt chart view. The ScreenTip that appears includes these and other values.

To conclude this exercise, you'll adjust the display settings to see all subtasks.

7   On the **View** tab, in the **Data** group, click **Outline**, and then click **All Subtasks**. Project expands the task list to show all subtasks.

❌ CLEAN UP   Close the Fine Tuning Tasks file.

Key points

- You can often set a deadline date for a task instead of applying a hard constraint, such as Must Finish On (MFO).

- You can record any fixed cost value you want per task, and the fixed cost is not affected by resource costs.

- The critical path indicates the series of tasks that determine the project's finish date. Project automatically recalculates the critical path, which can change as the details of your plan change.

- Set up a recurring task for activities, such as status meetings, that occur at regular intervals.

- You can enter a manual duration on a summary task in addition to its automatically scheduled duration.

10

Chapter at a glance

Availability

Change resource availability over time, page 218.

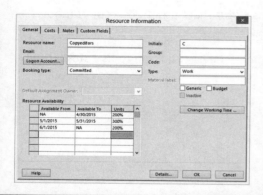

Delay

Control when a resource starts work on an assignment, page 226.

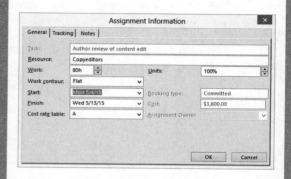

Material

Assign material resources to track consumables, page 236.

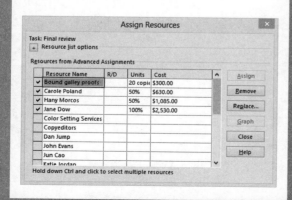

Adjust

Quickly assign and adjust resource assignments in the Team Planner view, page 241.

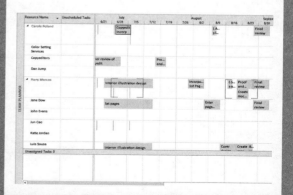

Fine-tuning resource and assignment details

IN THIS CHAPTER, YOU WILL LEARN HOW TO

- Set resource availability to change over time.

- Set up different pay rates for resources.

- Set up pay rates that will change over time for a resource.

- Set up a material resource.

- Delay the start of a resource assignment.

- Control how a resource's work on a task is distributed over time by using work contours.

- Apply different cost rates for a resource to account for different kinds of work performed by the resource.

- Assign a material resource to a task.

- View resources' capacities to do work.

- Adjust resource assignments in the Team Planner view (Project Professional only).

Because *work resources* (people and equipment) are often the most expensive part of a project, understanding how to make the best use of resources' time is an important project-planning skill. In this chapter, you use a variety of advanced Microsoft Project 2013 features relating to resources—their availability, assignments to tasks, and resulting costs. Project Professional users also use the Team Planner view to manage assignments.

PRACTICE FILES Before you can complete the exercises in this chapter, you need to copy the book's practice files to your computer. A complete list of practice files is provided in "Download the practice files" at the beginning of this book. For each exercise that has a practice file, simply browse to where you saved the book's practice file folder.

Setting up resource availability to apply at different times

One of the values that Project stores for each work resource is the resource's maximum units value. This is the maximum capacity of a resource to accomplish tasks. A resource's working-time settings (recorded in the individual resource's *calendar*) determine when work assigned to a resource can be scheduled. However, the resource's capacity to work (the resource's maximum units value) determines the extent to which the resource can work within those hours without becoming *overallocated*. A resource's maximum units value does not prevent a resource from becoming overallocated, but Project will indicate when the resource's assignments exceed the resource's maximum units capacity. You can specify that different maximum units values be applied at different time periods for a resource.

TIP If you need a refresher on resource capacity or resource calendars, see Chapter 5, "Setting up resources."

Setting a resource's availability over time enables you to control exactly what a resource's maximum units value is at any time. For example, you might have two copyeditors available for the first eight weeks of a project, three for the next six weeks, and then two for the remainder of the project. Or you might have a compositor who is normally available at 100 percent capacity reduced to just 50 percent capacity for six weeks, and then return to full capacity.

The scenario: At Lucerne Publishing, you secured additional copyediting capacity for a portion of the duration of new children's book plan. You need to record this in the plan.

In this exercise, you customize a resource's availability over time.

SET UP You need the Advanced Resources_Start file located in your Chapter11 practice file folder to complete this exercise. Open the Advanced Resources_Start file, and save it as Advanced Resources.

1   On the **View** tab, in the **Resource Views** group, click **Resource Sheet**.

The Resource Sheet view appears.

	ⓘ	Resource Name	Type	Material	Initials	Group	Max.	Std. Rate	Ovt.	Cost/Use	Accrue	Base
1	◈	Carole Poland	Work		C		100%	$2,100.00/wk	$0.00/hr	$0.00	Prorated	Standard
2		Color Setting Ser	Work		C		100%	$0.00/hr	$0.00/hr	$0.00	Prorated	Standard
3		Copyeditors	Work		C		200%	$45.00/hr	$0.00/hr	$0.00	Prorated	Standard
4		Dan Jump	Work		D		50%	$75.50/hr	$0.00/hr	$0.00	Prorated	Standard
5	◈	Hany Morcos	Work		H		100%	$1,550.00/wk	$0.00/hr	$0.00	Prorated	Standard
6		Jane Dow	Work		J		100%	$55.00/hr	$0.00/hr	$0.00	Prorated	Standard
7		John Evans	Work		J		100%	$2,780.00/wk	$0.00/hr	$0.00	Prorated	Standard
8		Jun Cao	Work		J		100%	$42.00/hr	$63.00/hr	$0.00	Prorated	Standard
9		Katie Jordan	Work		K		100%	$48.00/hr	$0.00/hr	$0.00	Prorated	Standard
10		Luis Sousa	Work		L		100%	$70.00/hr	$0.00/hr	$0.00	Prorated	Standard
11		Printing Service	Work		P		100%	$0.00/hr	$0.00/hr	$0.00	Prorated	Standard
12		Robin Wood	Work		R		100%	$44.00/hr	$0.00/hr	$0.00	Prorated	Standard
13	🗒	Sharon Salavaria	Work		S		50%	$1,100.00/wk	$0.00/hr	$0.00	Prorated	Standard
14		Tad Orman	Work		T		100%	$0.00/hr	$0.00/hr	$0.00	Prorated	Standard
15		Toby Nixon	Work		T		100%	$2,700.00/wk	$0.00/hr	$0.00	Prorated	Standard
16		Travel	Cost		T						Prorated	
17		Vikas Jain	Work		V		100%	$22.00/hr	$0.00/hr	$0.00	Prorated	Standard
18		William Flash	Work		W		100%	$0.00/hr	$0.00/hr	$0.00	Prorated	Standard
19		Zac Woodall	Work		Z		100%	$55.00/hr	$0.00/hr	$0.00	Prorated	Standard

As you might recall from Chapter 5, this is one view where you can see and edit resources' maximum units values. The maximum units values displayed here normally apply to the full duration of the project. Next, you will customize a resource's maximum units value to vary at different times during this project.

2   In the **Resource Name** column, click the name of resource 3, *Copyeditors*.

The *Copyeditors* resource is not one specific person; it describes a job category that multiple people might occupy at various times throughout the duration of the project. Unlike individually named resources like Hany Morcos or Color Setting Services, the copyeditors are interchangeable. As a project manager, you are more concerned about the specific skill set of whoever might be in this job role than you are about who the specific person is.

3   On the **Resource** tab, in the **Properties** group, click **Information**.

TIP Another way to display the Resource Information dialog box is to right-click the Resource Name value and, in the shortcut menu that appears, click Information.

The Resource Information dialog box appears. If the General tab is not visible, click it.

11

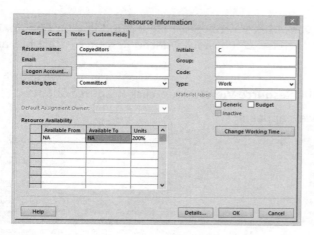

You expect to have two copyeditors available to work on this project from the start of the project through the month of April, three for the month of May, and then back to two for the remainder of the project.

4 Under **Resource Availability**, in the first row of the **Available From** column, leave **NA** (for Not Applicable).

5 In the **Available To** cell in the first row, type or select 4/30/15.

6 In the **Units** cell in the first row, leave the 200% value.

7 In the **Available From** cell in the second row, type or select 5/1/15.

8 In the **Available To** cell in the second row, type or select 5/31/15.

9 In the **Units** cell in the second row, type or select 300%.

10 In the **Available From** cell in the third row, type or select 6/1/15.

11 Leave the **Available To** cell in the third row blank. (Project will insert NA for you after you complete the next step.)

12 In the **Units** cell in the third row, type or select 200%, and then press the Enter key.

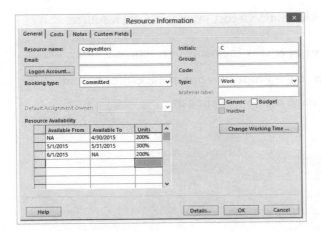

For the month of May, you can schedule up to three copyeditors without overallocating them. Before and after this period, you have just two copyeditors to schedule.

13   Click **OK** to close the **Resource Information** dialog box.

In the Resource Sheet view, the Max. Units field for the Copyeditors resource will display 300% only when the current date is within the May 1 through 31 date range in the year 2015. The current date is based on your computer's system clock or set in the Project Information dialog box. (To see this dialog box, on the Project tab, in the Properties group, click Project Information.) At other times, it will display 200%

Entering multiple pay rates for a resource

Some work resources might perform different tasks with different pay rates. For example, in the new children's book project, the project editor could also serve as a content editor. Because the pay rates for project editor and content editor are different, you can set up two pay rates for the resource. Then, after you assign the resource to tasks, you specify which pay rate should apply. Each resource can have up to five different pay rates, each recorded in a cost rate table.

The scenario: At Lucerne Publishing, you anticipate assigning work that pays a different rate to one of the resources. You need to record this second pay rate for the resource.

In this exercise, you create an additional cost rate table for a resource.

1   In the **Resource Sheet** view, click the name of resource 5, *Hany Morcos*.

2   On the **Resource** tab, in the **Properties** group, click **Information**.

The Resource Information dialog box appears.

3   Click the **Costs** tab.

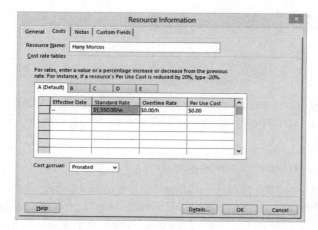

You see Hany's default pay rate of $1,550 per week on rate table A. Each tab (labeled A, B, and so on) corresponds to one of the five pay rates that a resource can have.

4   Under **Cost rate tables**, click the **B** tab.

5   Select the default entry of **$0.00/h** in the field directly below the column heading **Standard Rate**, and then type **45/h**.

6   In the **Overtime Rate** field in the same row, type **60/h**, and then press Enter.

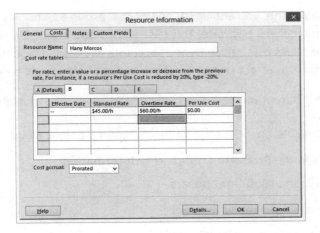

7   Click **OK** to close the **Resource Information** dialog box.

Notice that on the Resource Sheet, Hany's standard pay rate is still $1,550 per week. (This is recorded in the Std. Rate column.) This matches the value in rate table A, the default rate table. This rate will be used for all of Hany's task assignments unless you specify a different rate. You will do so later in this chapter.

Setting up resource pay rates to apply at different times

Resources can have both standard and overtime pay rates. By default, Project uses these rates for the duration of the project. However, you can change a resource's pay rates to be effective as of the date you choose. For example, you could initially set up a resource on January 1 with a standard rate of $40 per hour, planning to raise the resource's standard rate to $55 per hour on July 1.

Project uses pay rates when calculating resource costs based on when the resource's work is scheduled. You can assign up to 25 pay rates to be applied at different times to each of a resource's five cost rate tables. Project is flexible with the additional pay rate formats you enter. You can enter a pay rate as a specific dollar value or as a percentage increase or decrease of the previous pay rate.

The scenario: At Lucerne Publishing, you anticipate one of the resources working on the new children's book plan to receive a pay raise. This raise will go into effect during the book plan's duration. To keep the plan's cost calculations as accurate as possible, you need to record when this raise will go into effect and by what percentage value it will be raised.

In this exercise, you enter a different pay rate for a resource to be applied at a later date.

1 In the **Resource Name** column, select the name of resource 6, *Jane Dow*.

2 On the **Resource** tab, in the **Properties** group, click **Information**.

   The Resource Information dialog box appears.

3 Click the **Costs** tab if it is not already selected.

   You'll enter a pay rate increase in cost rate table A.

4 In the **Effective Date** cell in the second row of cost rate table **A**, type or select 6/1/15.

5 In the **Standard Rate** cell in the second row, type **15%**, and then press Enter.

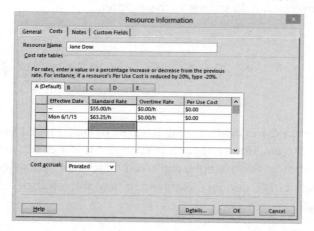

Note that Project calculates the 15% increase to produce a rate of $63.25 per hour. The previous rate of $55 per hour plus 15% equals $63.25 per hour. You can enter a specific value or a percentage increase or decrease from the previous rate.

TIP In addition to or instead of cost rates, a resource can include a set fee that Project accrues to each task to which the resource is assigned. This is called a *cost per use*. Unlike cost rates, the cost per use does not vary with the task's duration or amount of work the resource performs on the task. You specify the cost per use in the Cost/Use field in the Resource Sheet view or in the Per Use Cost field in the Resource Information dialog box.

6   Click **OK** to close the **Resource Information** dialog box.

In the Resource Sheet view, note that Jane Dow's initial rate, $55 per hour, appears in her Std. Rate field. This field will display $55 per hour until the current date changes to 6/1/15 or later. It will then display her new standard rate of $63.25 per hour.

Setting up material resources

Material resources are consumables that you use up as the project proceeds. On a construction project, material resources might include nails, lumber, and concrete. You work with material resources in Project to track a fixed unit amount or a rate of consumption of the material resource and the associated costs. Unlike work resources, you cannot enter a maximum units value for a cost resource or material resource. Because neither type of resource performs work, the maximum units value doesn't apply. Although Project is not a complete system for tracking inventory, it can help you stay better informed about how quickly you are consuming your material resources, and at what cost.

The scenario: At Lucerne Publishing, galley proofs of the new children's book are the consumable resource that interests you most. These are high-fidelity mock-ups of the new book that are created before the book is commercially printed. Because these galley proofs are relatively expensive to have produced, you'd like to account for their costs in the plan. To do so, you need to create a material resource.

In this exercise, you enter information about a material resource.

1   In the **Resource Sheet**, click the next empty cell in the **Resource Name** column.

2   Type **Bound galley proofs**.

3   In the **Type** field, click the down arrow, select **Material**, and press the Tab key.

11

4   In the **Material Label** field, type copies.

Copies is the unit of measurement you'll use for this material resource. You will see this label again in the section "Assigning material resources to tasks" later in this chapter.

5   In the **Std. Rate** field, type 15 and then press Enter.

This is the per-unit cost of this material resource; put another way, each copy of a bound galley proof costs $15. Later in this chapter, you'll specify the unit quantity of the material resource when you assign it to tasks. Project will then calculate the cost of the material resource assignment as the per-unit cost that you entered above times the number of units on the assignment.

The Material Label field applies only to material resources.

	ⓘ	Resource Name	Type	Material	Initials	Group	Max.	Std. Rate	Ovt.	Cost/Use	Accrue	Base
11		Printing Service	Work		P		100%	$0.00/hr	$0.00/hr	$0.00	Prorated	Standard
12		Robin Wood	Work		R		100%	$44.00/hr	$0.00/hr	$0.00	Prorated	Standard
13	🔖	Sharon Salavaria	Work		S		50%	$1,100.00/wk	$0.00/hr	$0.00	Prorated	Standard
14		Tad Orman	Work		T		100%	$0.00/hr	$0.00/hr	$0.00	Prorated	Standard
15		Toby Nixon	Work		T		100%	$2,700.00/wk	$0.00/hr	$0.00	Prorated	Standard
16		Travel	Cost		T						Prorated	
17		Vikas Jain	Work		V		100%	$22.00/hr	$0.00/hr	$0.00	Prorated	Standard
18		William Flash	Work		W		100%	$0.00/hr	$0.00/hr	$0.00	Prorated	Standard
19		Zac Woodall	Work		Z		100%	$55.00/hr	$0.00/hr	$0.00	Prorated	Standard
20		Bound galley proofs	Material	copies	B			$15.00		$0.00	Prorated	

✖ CLEAN UP **Close the Advanced Resources file.**

So far in this chapter, you've focused on resource details. For the remainder of the chapter, your focus shifts to fine-tuning assignment details.

Delaying the start of assignments

If more than one resource is assigned to a task, you might not want all the resources to start working on the task at the same time. You can delay the start of work for one or more resources assigned to a task.

For example, assume that four resources have been assigned a task. Three of the resources initially work on the task, and the fourth later inspects the quality of the work. The inspector should start work on the task later than the other resources.

The scenario: At Lucerne Publishing, the new children's book plan includes a task to which both a copyeditor and the book author, Tad Orman, are assigned. The intent of this task is that the author will review the edits made to his book manuscript, and shortly afterward, the copyeditor will begin to incorporate the author's feedback. Right now, both resources are assigned work throughout the duration of the task, but you'd like to delay the start of the copyeditor's work by two working days.

In this exercise, you delay the start of a resource assignment on a task.

→ SET UP You need the Advanced Assignments_Start file located in your Chapter11 practice file folder to complete this exercise. Open the Advanced Assignments_Start file, and save it as Advanced Assignments.

1   On the **View** tab, in the **Task Views** group, click **Task Usage**.

As you might recall from Chapter 9, "Advanced task scheduling," the Task Usage view groups the assigned resources below each task.

2   In the **Task Name** column, below task 18, *Author review of content edit*, click the assigned resource *Copyeditors*.

3   On the **Task** tab, in the **Editing** group, click **Scroll to Task**.

		Task Mode	Task Name	Work	Duration	Start	Finish	Details	T	W	T	F	S	May 3, '15 S	M	T	W
0		▭	▲ Children's book schedule	1,859 hrs	160 days?	Mon 4/6/15	Fri 11/13/15	Work	8h	8h	16h	16h			19h	16h	16h
1	⟳	▭	▷ Editorial staff meeting	39 hrs	60.13 days	Mon 4/13/15	Mon 7/6/15	Work							3h		
15		▭	▲ Acquisition	280 hrs	28 days	Mon 4/6/15	Wed 5/13/15	Work	8h	8h	16h	16h			16h	16h	16h
16		▭	Manuscript received	0 hrs	0 days	Mon 4/6/15	Mon 4/6/15	Work									
17	👤	▭	▲ Content edit	120 hrs	15 days	Mon 4/6/15	Wed 4/29/15	Work	8h	8h							
	🏃		Carole Poland	120 hrs		Mon 4/6/15	Wed 4/29/15	Work	8h	8h							
18		▭	▲ Author review of content edit	160 hrs	10 days	Thu 4/30/15	Wed 5/13/15	Work			16h	16h			16h	16h	16h
			Copyeditors	80 hrs		Thu 4/30/15	Wed 5/13/15	Work			8h	8h			8h	8h	8h
			Tad Orman	80 hrs		Thu 4/30/15	Wed 5/13/15	Work			8h	8h			8h	8h	8h
19		▭	▲ Handoff to Editorial	0 hrs	0 days	Wed 5/13/15	Wed 5/13/15	Work									
			Carole Poland	0 hrs		Wed 5/13/15	Wed 5/13/15	Work									

As you can see, this task currently has two resources assigned to it: a copyeditor and the new book's author, Tad Orman.

Next you'll delay the copyeditor's assignment in the Task Usage view.

4   On the **Format** tab, in the **Assignment** group, click **Information**.

The Assignment Information dialog box appears.

11

5 Click the **General** tab if it is not already selected, and then in the **Start** box, type or select 5/4/15.

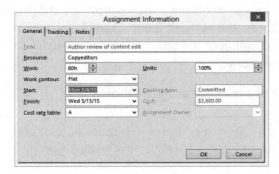

6 Click **OK** to close the **Assignment Information** dialog box.

Project adjusts the copyeditor's assignment on this task so that he works no hours on Thursday or Friday.

The duration of this task has increased because the work is over a longer period of time.

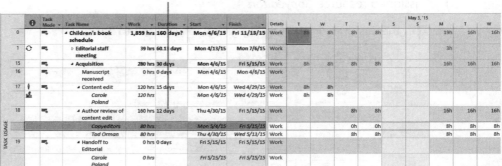

Now, in the timephased portion of the view, you can see that zero hours of work are scheduled for the copyeditor on Thursday and Friday, April 30 and May 1. The other resource assigned to the task is not affected. Note that the total work of this task did not change, but its duration did—the finish date moved out two working days.

TIP If you want an assignment to start at a specific time as well as on a specific date, you can specify the time in the Start box. For example, if you want the copyeditor's assignment to start at 1 P.M. on April 30, type **4/30/15 1:00 PM**. Otherwise, Project uses the default start time. To change the default start time, on the File tab, click Options. In the Project Options dialog box, click the Schedule tab, and in the Default Start Time field, enter the value that you want.

Applying contours to assignments

In the Resource Usage and Task Usage views, you can see exactly how each resource's assigned work is distributed over time. In addition to viewing assignment details, you can change the amount of time a resource works on a task in any given time period. There are various ways to do this:

- Apply a predefined work contour to an assignment. Predefined *contours* generally describe how work is distributed over time in terms of graphical patterns. For example, the Bell predefined contour distributes less work to the beginning and end of the assignment and distributes more work toward the middle. If you were to graph the work over time, the graph's shape would resemble a bell.

- Edit the assignment details directly. For example, in the Resource Usage or Task Usage view, you can change the assignment values directly in the timescaled grid.

How you contour or edit an assignment depends on what you need to accomplish. Predefined contours work best for assignments in which you can predict a likely pattern of effort—for example, a task that requires gradual ramp-up time might benefit from a back-loaded contour to reflect the likelihood that the resource will work the most toward the end of the assignment.

The scenario: At Lucerne Publishing, you've been reviewing assignments in the new children's book plan with the assigned resources. One of these resources tells you that she knows from past experience that the daily work pattern she expects on one of her tasks doesn't match the work pattern on the task as it is currently scheduled. You want to update the plan to more accurately model the expected work contour on this assignment. You also have another assignment that requires an adjustment.

11

In this exercise, you apply a predefined work contour to an assignment and manually edit another assignment.

1 In the **Task Name** column, below task 38, *Final review*, click the assigned resource *Carole Poland*.

2 On the **Task** tab, in the **Editing** group, click **Scroll to Task**.

	ⓘ	Task Mode ▾	Task Name ▾	Work ▾	Duration ▾	Start ▾	Finish ▾	Details	W	T	F	S	Aug 30, '15 S	M	T	W	T
35		■	◢ 2nd Pages review	120 hrs	10 days	Fri 8/21/15	Thu 9/3/15	Work	8h	8h	16h			16h	16h	16h	16h
36	ⓘ	■	◢ Proof and review	40 hrs	5 days	Fri 8/21/15	Thu 8/27/15	Work	8h	8h							
			Hany Morcos	40 hrs		Fri 8/21/15	Thu 8/27/15	Work	8h	8h							
37		■	◢ Send proofed pages to Production	0 hrs	0 days	Thu 8/27/15	Thu 8/27/15	Work		0h							
			Hany Morcos	0 hrs		Thu 8/27/15	Thu 8/27/15	Work		0h							
38		■	◢ Final review	80 hrs	5 days	Fri 8/28/15	Thu 9/3/15	Work			16h			16h	16h	16h	16h
			Carole Poland	20 hrs		Fri 8/28/15	Thu 9/3/15	Work			4h			4h	4h	4h	4h
			Hany Morcos	20 hrs		Fri 8/28/15	Thu 9/3/15	Work			4h			4h	4h	4h	4h
			Jane Dow	40 hrs		Fri 8/28/15	Thu 9/3/15	Work			8h			8h	8h	8h	8h

As you can see in the timescaled data at the right, two resources are scheduled to work on this task four hours per day (that is, 50 percent of their available working time) and a third resource is scheduled to work full time on this task. All these assignments have a flat *contour*—that is, work is distributed evenly over time. This is the default work contour type that Project uses when scheduling work.

You want to change Carole Poland's assignment on this task so that she starts with a brief daily assignment and increases her work time as the task progresses. To accomplish this, you will apply a back-loaded contour to the assignment. Note that task 38, *Final review* is a fixed-duration task type, not the default fixed-units task type. This task type keeps the task's duration fixed as you adjust its assignments.

TIP If you need a refresher on task types, see "Control task scheduling with task types" in Chapter 9, "Advanced task scheduling."

3 On the **Format** tab, in the **Assignment** group, click **Information**.

The Assignment Information dialog box appears. Click the General tab if it is not already selected.

4 Click the down arrow to display the options in the **Work Contour** box.

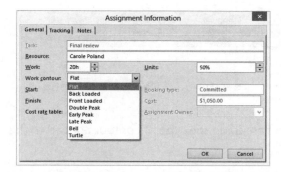

These are all predefined work contours, and some of the names of the contours are graphical representations of a resource's work over time with that contour applied.

5   Select **Back Loaded**, and then click **OK** to close the **Assignment Information** dialog box.

Project applies the contour to this resource's assignment and reschedules her work on the task.

The contour indicator matches the type of contour applied—back-loaded in this case.

		Task Mode	Task Name	Work	Duration	Start	Finish	Details	W	T	F	S	Aug 30, '15 S	M	T	W	T
35			▲ 2nd Pages review	112 hrs	10 days	Fri 8/21/15	Thu 9/3/15	Work	8h	8h	12.5h			13.5h	14.5h	15.5h	16h
36			▲ Proof and review	40 hrs	5 days	Fri 8/21/15	Thu 8/27/15	Work	8h	8h							
			Hany Morcos	40 hrs		Fri 8/21/15	Thu 8/27/15	Work	8h	8h							
37			▲ Send proofed pages to Production	0 hrs	0 days	Thu 8/27/15	Thu 8/27/15	Work		0h							
			Hany Morcos	0 hrs		Thu 8/27/15	Thu 8/27/15	Work		0h							
38			▲ Final review	72 hrs	5 days	Fri 8/28/15	Thu 9/3/15	Work			12.5h			13.5h	14.5h	15.5h	16h
			Carole Poland	12 hrs		Fri 8/28/15	Thu 9/3/15	Work			0.5h			1.5h	2.5h	3.5h	4h
			Hany Morcos	20 hrs		Fri 8/28/15	Thu 9/3/15	Work			4h			4h	4h	4h	4h
			Jane Dow	40 hrs		Fri 8/28/15	Thu 9/3/15	Work			8h			8h	8h	8h	8h

The back-loaded contour causes Project to assign very little work to the resource initially and then add more work each day.

You see that in each successive day of the task's duration, Carole Poland is assigned slightly more time to work on the assignment. You also see a contour indicator in the Indicators column displaying the type of contour that is applied to the assignment.

6   In the Indicators column, point to the contour indicator.

11

38		▲ Final review	72 hrs	5 days	Fri 8/28/15	Thu 9/3/15
		Carole	12 hrs		Fri 8/28/15	Thu 9/3/15
		⬚ This assignment dynamically schedules work using a back loaded pattern.	20 hrs		Fri 8/28/15	Thu 9/3/15
		Jane Dow	40 hrs		Fri 8/28/15	Thu 9/3/15
39		▲ Design book's companion website	80 hrs	5 days	Fri 8/21/15	Thu 8/27/15

Project displays a ScreenTip describing the type of contour applied to this assignment.

TIP Applying a contour to a fixed-duration task will cause Project to recalculate the resource's work value so that the resource works less in the same time period. For example, Carole's total work on task 38 was reduced from 20 to 12 hours when you applied the contour. Depending on the task type, applying a contour to this assignment might cause the overall duration of the task to be extended. Task 38 is a fixed-duration task, so applying the contour did not change the task's duration. For a fixed-work or fixed-unit task, however, it would. If you do not want a contour to extend a task's duration, change the task type (on the Advanced tab of the Task Information dialog box) to Fixed Duration before applying the contour.

Next, you will directly edit the assigned work values of another task.

7   In the **Task Name** column, below task 38, *Final review*, click the assigned resource *Hany Morcos*.

Note that Hany is currently assigned four hours per day for each day of the assignment's duration. Why four hours? Hany normally has eight working hours per day on these particular days (as determined by her resource calendar). She was assigned to this task at 50 percent assignment units, however, so the resulting scheduled work is only four hours per day.

You want to increase Hany's work on the last two days of this task so that she will work full time on it. To accomplish this, you will manually edit her assigned work values.

8   In the timescaled grid in the right pane of the Task Usage view, select Hany Morcos's four-hour assignment for Wednesday, September 2.

TIP Point to each day label in the timescale (M, T, W, and so on) and that day's date value will appear in a ScreenTip.

9   Type **8h**, and then press the Tab key.

10   In Hany's assignment for Thursday, type **8h**, and then press Enter.

	ⓘ	Task Mode ▾	Task Name ▾	Work ▾	Duration ▾	Start ▾	Finish ▾	Details	T	F	S	S	M	T	W	T	F
35		⬆	⊿ 2nd Pages review	120 hrs	10 days	Fri 8/21/15	Thu 9/3/15	Work	8h	12.5h			13.5h	14.5h	19.5h	20h	
36	ⓘ	⬆	⊿ Proof and review	40 hrs	5 days	Fri 8/21/15	Thu 8/27/15	Work	8h								
			Hany Morcos	40 hrs		Fri 8/21/15	Thu 8/27/15	Work	8h								
37		⬆	⊿ Send proofed pages to Production	0 hrs	0 days	Thu 8/27/15	Thu 8/27/15	Work	0h								
			Hany Morcos	0 hrs		Thu 8/27/15	Thu 8/27/15	Work	0h								
38		⬆	⊿ Final review	80 hrs	5 days	Fri 8/28/15	Thu 9/3/15	Work		12.5h			13.5h	14.5h	19.5h	20h	
	⏹		Carole Poland	12 hrs		Fri 8/28/15	Thu 9/3/15	Work		0.5h			1.5h	2.5h	3.5h	4h	
	⏹		Hany Morcos	28 hrs		Fri 8/28/15	Thu 9/3/15	Work		4h			4h	4h	8h	8h	
			Jane Dow	40 hrs		Fri 8/28/15	Thu 9/3/15	Work		8h			8h	8h	8h	8h	

Aug 30, '15

Hany is now assigned eight hours per day on Wednesday and Thursday. Project displays a contour indicator in the Indicators column showing that a manually edited contour has been applied to the assignment.

TIP If you want to document details about contouring an assignment or anything pertaining to an assignment, you can record the details in an assignment note. In the Task Usage or Resource Usage view, select the assignment, and then click the Notes button in the Assignment group on the Format tab. Assignment notes are similar to task and resource notes.

Here are a few more capabilities that you can apply in a usage view:

- In addition to editing work values manually at the resource level as you did before, you can edit work values at the task level. When you change a work value at the task level, Project adjusts the resulting work value per resource in accordance with each resource's units value on that assignment. For example, assume that on a specific day, two resources were assigned four hours each to a task that had a total work value of eight hours. If you then change the total work on the task for that day to 12 hours, Project will increase the work per resource from four to six hours.

- You can split a task in the Gantt Chart view to account for an interruption in the task, as you did in Chapter 9. You can also split a task in the Task Usage view by entering "0" work values in the task's row in the timephased grid for the date range that you want. To preserve the total work on the task, you should add the same amount of work to the end of the task as you subtracted with the split. For example, assume that a task starts on Monday and has eight hours of total work per day for four days. Its work pattern (in hours per day) is 8, 8, 8, and 8. You interrupt work on the task on Tuesday and then add those eight hours to the end of the task (in this case, Friday). The new work pattern would be 8, 0, 8, 8, and 8.

11

- When editing values in the timephased grid, you can work with the cells somewhat like you might work in a Microsoft Excel worksheet—you can drag and drop values and use the AutoFill handle to copy values to the right or downward.

Applying different pay rates to assignments

Recall from "Entering multiple pay rates for a resource" earlier in the chapter that you can set as many as five pay rates per resource, which allows you to apply different pay rates to different assignments for a resource; for example, a different pay rate might depend on the skills required for different assignments. For each assignment, Project initially uses rate table A by default, but you can specify that another rate table should be used.

The scenario: At Lucerne Publishing, Hany is currently assigned to task 36, *Proof and review*, as a content editor rather than her default role of a project editor, but her assignment still reflects her default pay rate as a project editor. You will apply a different pay rate to account for her content editor role on this task. Recall that you set up this second pay rate for Hany in the "Entering multiple pay rates for a resource" section earlier.

In this exercise, you change the cost rate table to be applied to an assignment.

1   In the **Task Name** column, below task 36, *Proof and review*, click the assigned resource *Hany Morcos*.

Next, you'll view the cost of Hany's assignment.

2   On the **View** tab, in the **Data** group, click **Tables** and then click **Cost**.

Project displays the Cost table. Note the current cost of Hany's assignment to this task: $1,550.00.

In the Cost table, you can see the tasks and each assignment's total cost. To see other assignment cost values, such as actual cost or variance, scroll the table to the right.

	Task Name	Fixed Cost	Fixed Cost Accrual	Total Cost	Baseline	Variance	Actual
35	⊿ 2nd Pages revie	$0.00	Prorated	$5,795.00	$0.00	$5,795.00	$0.00
36	⊿ Proof and review	$0.00	Prorated	$1,550.00	$0.00	$1,550.00	$0.00
	Hany Morcos			$1,550.00	$0.00	$1,550.00	$0.00
37	⊿ Send proofed pages to	$0.00	Prorated	$0.00	$0.00	$0.00	$0.00
	Hany Morcos			$0.00	$0.00	$0.00	$0.00
38	⊿ Final review	$0.00	Prorated	$4,245.00	$0.00	$4,245.00	$0.00
	Carole Poland			$630.00	$0.00	$630.00	$0.00
	Hany Morcos			$1,085.00	$0.00	$1,085.00	$0.00
	Jane Dow			$2,530.00	$0.00	$2,530.00	$0.00

3   On the **Format** tab, in the **Assignment** group, click **Information**.

The Assignment Information dialog box appears.

4   Click the **General** tab if it is not already selected.

5   In the **Cost Rate Table** box, type or select **B**, and then click **OK** to close the **Assignment Information** dialog box.

Project applies Hany's cost rate table B to the assignment.

	Task Name	Fixed Cost	Fixed Cost Accrual	Total Cost	Baseline	Variance	Actual
35	⊿ 2nd Pages revie	$0.00	Prorated	$6,045.00	$0.00	$6,045.00	$0.00
36	⊿ Proof and review	$0.00	Prorated	$1,800.00	$0.00	$1,800.00	$0.00
	Hany Morcos			$1,800.00	$0.00	$1,800.00	$0.00
37	⊿ Send proofed pages to	$0.00	Prorated	$0.00	$0.00	$0.00	$0.00
	Hany Morcos			$0.00	$0.00	$0.00	$0.00
38	⊿ Final review	$0.00	Prorated	$4,245.00	$0.00	$4,245.00	$0.00
	Carole Poland			$630.00	$0.00	$630.00	$0.00
	Hany Morcos			$1,085.00	$0.00	$1,085.00	$0.00
	Jane Dow			$2,530.00	$0.00	$2,530.00	$0.00

The new cost of the assignment, $1,800.00, appears in the Total Cost column. The new cost value is also accounted for in the summary tasks and project summary task.

TIP If you frequently change cost rate tables for assignments, you will find it quicker to display the Cost Rate Table field directly in the Resource Usage or Task Usage view. Display the right edge of the table portion of a usage view, click Add New Column, and then select Cost Rate Table.

11

Assigning material resources to tasks

In "Setting up material resources" earlier in this chapter, you created the *material resource* named *Bound galley proofs*. Recall that material resources are used up or "consumed" as a project progresses. Common examples for a construction project include lumber and concrete.

When assigning a material resource, you can handle consumptions and cost in one of two ways:

- Assign a fixed-unit quantity of the material resource to the task. Project will multiply the unit cost of this resource by the number of units assigned to determine the total cost. (You'll use this method in the following exercise.)

- Assign a variable-rate quantity of the material resource to the task. Project will adjust the quantity and cost of the resource as the task's duration changes. This approach is described more in "Variable consumption rates for material resources" later in the section.

The scenario: At Lucerne Publishing, you are interested in tracking the use and cost of the bound galley proofs of the new children's book.

In this exercise, you assign a material resource to a task and enter a fixed-unit quantity of consumption.

1   On the **Task** tab, in the **View** group, click **Gantt Chart**.

2   In the **Task Name** column, click the name of task 38, *Final review*.

    You anticipate that you'll need 20 bound galley proof copies for this review.

3   On the **Task** tab, in the **Editing** group, click **Scroll to Task**.

4   On the **Resource** tab, in the **Assignments** group, click **Assign Resources**.

    The Assign Resources dialog box appears.

5   In the **Assign Resources** dialog box, select the **Units** field for the *Bound galley proofs* resource.

6   Type or select **20**, and then click **Assign**.

    Project assigns the material resource to the task and calculates the $300 cost of the assignment ($15 per copy multiplied by 20 copies).

When you assign a material resource to a task, its label value appears in the Units column.

Because *Bound galley proofs* is a material resource, it cannot do work. Therefore, assigning a material resource does not affect the duration of a task.

7   Click **Close** to close the **Assign Resources** dialog box.

Variable consumption rates for material resources

You just assigned a material resource with a fixed amount, or *fixed consumption rate,* to a task. Another way to use material resources is to assign them with a *variable consumption rate.* The difference between the two rates is as follows:

- A *fixed consumption rate* means that, regardless of the duration of the task to which the material resource is assigned, an absolute quantity of the resource will be used. For example, pouring concrete for a house foundation requires a fixed amount of concrete no matter how long it takes to pour it.

- A *variable consumption rate* means that the quantity of the material resource consumed depends on the duration of the task. When operating a generator, for example, you will consume more fuel in four hours than in two, and you can determine an hourly rate at which you consume the fuel. You enter a variable consumption rate in units per time period; for example, you enter "2/h" to record the consumption of two gallons of fuel per hour. After you enter a variable consumption rate for a material resource's assignment, Project calculates the total quantity of the material resource consumed based on the task's duration.

The advantage of using a variable rate of consumption is that the rate is tied to the task's duration. If the duration changes, the calculated quantity and cost of the material resource will change as well. When you need this level of cost tracking for a material resource, use a variable consumption rate.

Viewing resource capacity

Recall that the amount of time that a resource is able to work on tasks in a project is called its *resource capacity*, and in Project, this is measured in units. By default, such units are presented as a percentage value, with 0% meaning no capacity and 100% meaning the full or maximum capacity of a single resource with a normal working schedule of 40 hours per week. In Project, a resource's maximum capacity to do work is tracked as the resource's maximum units (labeled *Max. Units)* value.

Even experienced project managers have been known to overestimate resource capacity for the people allocated to work on a given project. This can lead to problems during the execution of a project and unhappy resources, especially when the project manager has also underestimated the amount of work required to complete the tasks in the project. There are many legitimate reasons to expect some variability with task work estimates—especially in the initial planning stage of a project. Resource capacity, however, should be easier to estimate more accurately. This section introduces some useful tools in Project that can help you better see and understand resource capacity.

Viewing the working capacity per resource gives you a better understanding of overall capacity for your project. This, in turn, can help inform you and the project's stakeholders about any possible adjustments to the scope of the project to better match that capacity of the team (or vice versa). Normally, you can expect one of the following conditions for resource capacity:

- Planned work is less than the working capacity of the team. You might be able to use some portion of your resources' time for other projects or to do more work in this project.

- Planned work exceeds the working capacity of the team. You might need to reduce the scope of work or secure more resources.

- Planned work is approximately equal to the working capacity of the team.

TIP This way of understanding project scope and resource capacity is explored more in Appendix A, "A short course in project management."

The scenario: At Lucerne Publishing, at this point in the planning for the new children's book project you've set up an initial task list and initial resource details. Now you'll examine resource capacity in detail.

In this exercise, you'll look at individual resource capacity per day and month during the time span in which the project is now scheduled.

1   On the **View** tab, in the **Resource Views** group, click **Resource Usage**.

Project displays the Resource Usage view.

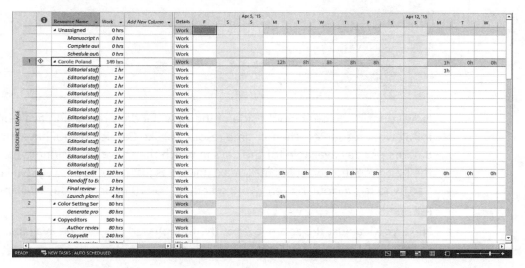

Recall that in this view, the left pane organizes tasks under the resources to which the tasks are assigned. The right pane shows assignment and other values organized on the timeline. Here, our focus is on seeing availability for the resources. To begin, you'll switch the timephased view to show resource availability.

2   On the **Format** tab, in the **Details** group, select the **Remaining Availability** check box.

3   On the **Format** tab, in the **Details** group, clear the **Work** check box.

Project hides the Work details, leaving the Remaining Availability detail visible.

4   Click the **Resource Name** column heading.

5   On the **View** tab, in the **Data** group, click **Outline** and then click **Hide Subtasks**.

#	Resource Name	Work	Add New Column	Details	F	S	S (Apr 5 '15)	M	T	W	T	F	S	S (Apr 12 '15)	M	T	W
	▷ Unassigned	0 hrs		Rem. /	8h			8h	8h	8h	8h	8h				8h	8h	8h
1	▷ Carole Poland	149 hrs		Rem. /	8h			0h	0h	0h	0h	0h				7h	8h	8h
2	▷ Color Setting Ser	80 hrs		Rem. /	16h			16h	16h	16h	16h	16h				16h	16h	16h
3	▷ Copyeditors	360 hrs		Rem. /	16h			16h	16h	16h	16h	16h				16h	16h	16h
4	Dan Jump	0 hrs		Rem. /	4h			4h	4h	4h	4h	4h				4h	4h	4h
5	▷ Hany Morcos	361 hrs		Rem. /	8h			0h	8h	8h	8h	8h				7h	8h	8h
6	▷ Jane Dow	200 hrs		Rem. /	8h			8h	8h	8h	8h	8h				8h	8h	8h
7	John Evans	0 hrs		Rem. /	8h			8h	8h	8h	8h	8h				8h	8h	8h
8	▷ Jun Cao	13 hrs		Rem. /				10h	10h	10h	10h					9h	10h	10h
9	Katie Jordan	0 hrs		Rem. /	8h			8h	8h	8h	8h	8h				8h	8h	8h
10	▷ Luis Sousa	200 hrs		Rem. /	8h			8h	8h	8h	8h	8h				8h	8h	8h
11	▷ Printing Service	240 hrs		Rem. /	8h			8h	8h	8h	8h	8h				8h	8h	8h
12	Robin Wood	0 hrs		Rem. /	8h			8h	8h	8h	8h	8h				8h	8h	8h
13	Sharon Salavaria	0 hrs		Rem. /	4h			4h	4h	4h	4h	4h				4h	4h	4h
14	Tad Orman	256 hrs		Rem. /	8h			8h	8h	8h	8h	8h				8h	8h	8h
15	Toby Nixon	0 hrs		Rem. /	8h			8h	8h	8h	8h	8h				8h	8h	8h
16	Travel			Rem. /														
17	Vikas Jain	0 hrs		Rem. /	8h			8h	8h	8h	8h	8h				8h	8h	8h
18	William Flash	0 hrs		Rem. /	8h			8h	8h	8h	8h	8h				8h	8h	8h
19	Zac Woodall	0 hrs		Rem. /	8h			8h	8h	8h	8h	8h				8h	8h	8h
20	▷ Bound galley pro	20 copies		Rem. /														
				Rem. /														

Now you can see on the right side of the view the daily remaining availability values for all work resources. The full-time resources, like Carole Poland, have the expected 8 hours per day available for the days in which they have no assignments. Dan Jump, the half-time resource with 50% max. units, has just 4 hours per day available. Jun Cao, who has a "four-by-ten" work schedule, has 10 hours per day available four days per week.

Next, you'll adjust the zoom level of the timephased view to see availability per month.

6   On the **View** tab, in the **Zoom** group, click **Months** in the **Timescale** box.

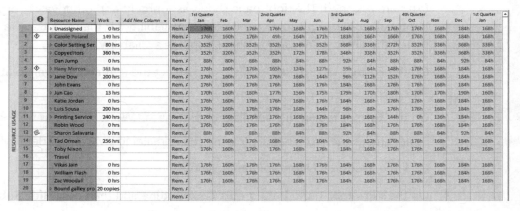

Project shows available hours per resource, per month. Note that some assignment values and resource names are formatted in red and have an alert indicator next to their names. These resources are overallocated: they have been assigned more work than their capacity allows for some portion of time. You'll resolve overallocated resources in Chapter 12, "Fine-tuning the project plan."

TIP In this section, you examined resource capacity in the Resource Usage view. Other Project features that help you see and manage resource capacity include the Resource Graph view (on the View tab, in the Resource Views group, click Other Views and then click Resource Graph) and the two resource-focused reports (on the Report tab, in the View Reports Group, click Resources and then click one of the reports listed).

Adjusting assignments in the Team Planner view

IMPORTANT The Team Planner view is available only in Project Professional, not in Project Standard. If you have Project Standard, skip this section.

The Task and Resource Usage views are powerful views in which you can accomplish intricate goals, like manually contouring resource assignments. If these views present more details than you want, Project Professional includes a simple but powerful view called the Team Planner view.

In the Team Planner view, you see tasks organized by the resource to which they are assigned (like the Resource Usage view) and any unassigned tasks. Both assigned and unassigned tasks might be either:

- **Scheduled tasks** Scheduled for a specific time period and displayed in the Team Planner view at a specific point in time.

- **Unscheduled tasks** Manually scheduled tasks, with or without an assigned resource.

What the Team Planner view enables that the usage views do not is a simple drag-and-drop method of rescheduling or reassigning tasks.

The scenario: At Lucerne Publishing, you have found the Team Planner view to be especially helpful when reviewing assignments with resources working on the new children's book plan. You've identified some assignment issues you need to address, and you will do so in the Team Planner view.

11

In this exercise, you examine resource assignments and address some overallocation problems, as well as assign some unassigned and unscheduled tasks.

1. On the **View** tab, in the **Resource Views** group, click **Team Planner**.

   The Team Planner view appears.

   TIP You can also click the Team Planner view shortcut on the status bar, in the lower-right corner of the Project window

2. In the **Resource Name** column, select *Carole Poland*.

3. On the **Task** tab, in the **Editing** group, click **Scroll to Task**.

   Carole Poland's initial resource assignments come into view.

The Team Planner view includes four sections: assigned but unscheduled tasks...   ...assigned and scheduled tasks...

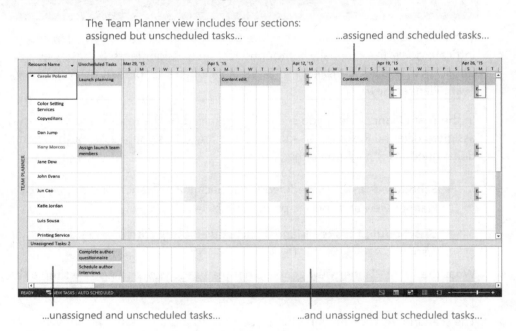

...unassigned and unscheduled tasks...   ...and unassigned but scheduled tasks...

First, you'll schedule the assigned but unscheduled (that is, *manually scheduled*) tasks. Carole has one unscheduled task, as well as several scheduled tasks. In fact, her scheduled tasks have caused her to be overallocated. The red formatting of her name communicates the fact that she is overallocated, and the red boxes Project draws around some of Carole's assignments in April tell you when she is overallocated.

You'd like Carole's unscheduled task, *Launch planning*, to start in the beginning of August, so you'll move it there.

4   Horizontally scroll the view until the week of August 9 is visible in the timescale.

TIP You can also press CTRL+G and in the Date field of the Go To dialog box, type or select 8/9/15 and then click OK.

5   Click and drag Carole's unscheduled task, *Launch planning*, in Carole's row so that the task start date is Monday, August 10.

As on the Gantt Chart, the width of a scheduled task bar corresponds to its duration. Depending on the timescale zoom level, you might not see full task names in some task bars.

6   Point your mouse pointer at the task that you just scheduled.

A ScreenTip appears and contains the essential task details.

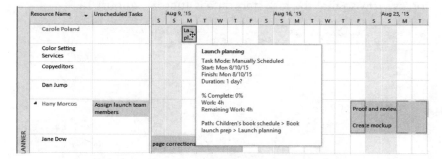

Note that although this task is now scheduled for a specific date and time, it is still a manually scheduled task, and it will remain so until it is switched to *automatic scheduling*.

Next, you'll schedule the unscheduled task assigned to Hany Morcos, and you'll also reassign it to Carole. You'd like this task to be completed in early August as well.

7   Click and drag the name of Hany Morcos's unscheduled task, *Assign launch team members*, to Carole Poland's row so that the task start date is Tuesday, August 11.

Project schedules and reassigns the task.

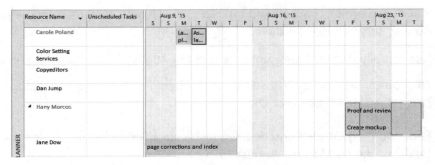

Next, you'll assign the two unassigned and unscheduled tasks. Both of these tasks should be assigned to Hany Morcos.

8   Click and drag the first unassigned task, *Complete author questionnaire*, to Hany Morcos's row so that the task start date is Monday, August 17.

9   Click and drag the remaining unassigned task, *Schedule author interviews*, to Hany Morcos's row so that the task start date is Tuesday, August 18.

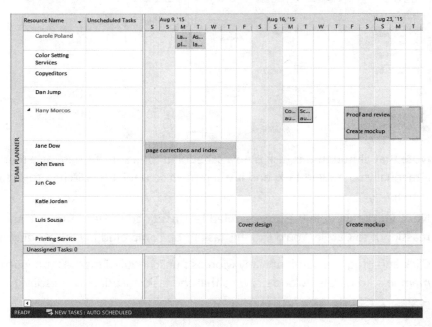

Now both tasks are assigned and scheduled, though they remain manually scheduled tasks.

To conclude this exercise, you'll address some of the resource overallocation problems that are visible in the timescale side of the Team Planner view.

10 On the **View** tab, in the **Zoom** group, click the down arrow next to the **Timescale** box and click **Weeks**.

The timescale adjusts to show more of the plan.

11 Scroll the view horizontally until the week of June 28 is visible in the timescale.

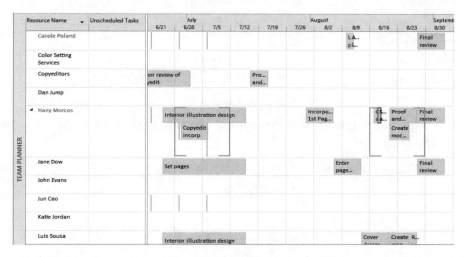

Most of the resource overallocations in the plan are due to the weekly editorial status meeting (represented in this view as the thin vertical lines) overlapping with other tasks. Because each occurrence of the editorial status meeting is only one hour long, you're not concerned with addressing this level of overallocation. You can see a more severe overallocation for Hany Morcos in the week of June 28, however.

Because you need Hany's full attention on the *Interior illustration design* task, you'll reassign the *Copyedit incorp* task to someone else.

12 Right-click Hany's task, *Copyedit incorp*, and in the shortcut menu that appears, click **Reassign To**, and then select *Carole Poland*.

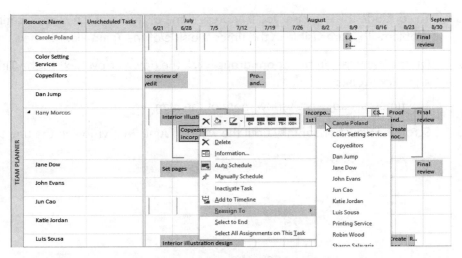

Project reassigns the task but does not change the task's start or finish date or duration.

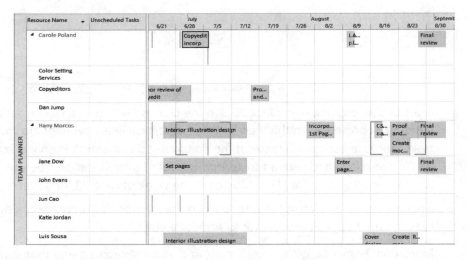

TIP You can also reassign tasks by dragging them from one resource to another. To better control the scheduling of tasks when you reassign them this way, set the timescale to daily (to do this, on the View tab, in the Zoom group, click Days in the Timescale box).

There are still overallocation issues in the plan, but they are minor issues that don't require additional attention.

✖ CLEAN UP Close the Advanced Assignments file.

Key points

- You can account for variable resource availability over time (via a resource's Max. Units value).

- When working with resource costs, you can specify different pay rates for different assignments and apply different pay rates at different times.

- Create material resources to track the cost of items that are consumed during the execution of the project.

- You can change when a resource will start work on an assignment without affecting other resources assigned to the same task.

- Project includes several predefined work contours that you can apply to an assignment.

- When working with resource costs, you can specify different pay rates for different assignments.

- When assigned to a task, material resources can have a fixed or variable consumption rate.

- In a usage view, you can see the remaining availability of work resources at whatever time increment you want.

- The Team Planner view allows easy drag-and-drop adjusting of assignments between resources (Project Professional only).

11

Chapter at a glance

Examine

See how resources are scheduled to work over the duration of a project, page 250.

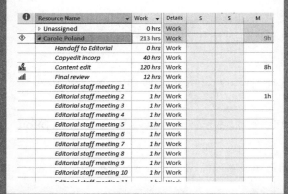

Resolve

Edit resource assignments to manually resolve overallocations, page 255.

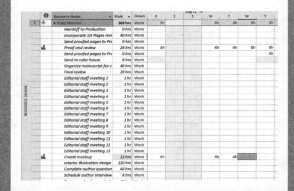

Level

Use resource leveling to resolve resource overallocation problems, page 259.

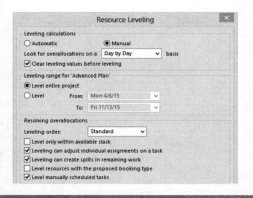

Inactivate

Strike out tasks without removing them from the plan (Project Professional only), page 271.

		Task Mode	Task Name	Duration	Start	Finish
35		🔹	**2nd Pages review**	**10 days**	**Fri 8/21/15**	**Thu 9/3/15**
36		🔹	Proof and review	5 days	Fri 8/21/15	Thu 8/27/15
37		🔹	Send proofed pages to Production	0 days	Thu 8/27/15	Thu 8/27/15
38	📍	🔹	Final review	5 days	Fri 8/28/15	Thu 9/3/15
39		🔹	◢ Design book's companion website	5 days	Fri 8/21/15	Thu 8/27/15
40		🔹	Create mockup	2 days	Fri 8/21/15	Tue 8/25/15
41		🔹	Review with author	2 days	Wed 8/26/15	Thu 8/27/15
42	📌		**◢ Color prep and printing**	**50 days**	**Mon 9/7/15**	**Fri 11/13/15**
43	📋📍	🔹	Send to color	1 day	Mon 9/7/15	Mon 9/7/15

Fine-tuning the Project plan

12

IN THIS CHAPTER, YOU WILL LEARN HOW TO

- Look at how resources are scheduled to work over the duration of a project.

- Edit a resource assignment to resolve a resource overallocation.

- Resolve resource overallocations automatically.

- Check the plan's overall cost and finish date.

- Inactivate tasks so that they remain in the plan but have no effect on the schedule (Project Professional only).

In the previous three chapters, you focused on details about tasks, resources, and assignments. Now, you will examine the results of your previous work on the schedule and dive deeper into resource assignments. In some cases, you'll revisit Project features introduced in previous chapters, but in this chapter your focus is on managing across the entire plan, including overall duration and cost.

PRACTICE FILES Before you can complete the exercises in this chapter, you need to copy the book's practice files to your computer. A complete list of practice files is provided in "Download the practice files" at the beginning of this book. For each exercise that has a practice file, simply browse to where you saved the book's practice file folder.

IMPORTANT If you are running Project Professional with Project Web App/Project Server, take care not to save any of the practice files you work with in this book to Project Web App (PWA). For more information, see Appendix C, "Collaborating: Project, SharePoint, and PWA."

Examining resource allocations over time

In this section, you will focus on resource allocation—how the task assignments you've made affect the workloads of the *work resources* (people and equipment) of a plan. A resource's capacity to work in a given time period is determined by her *maximum units* and *resource calendar*. The relationship between a resource's capacity and her task assignments is called *allocation*. Each work resource is in one of three states of allocation:

- **Underallocated**   The resource's assignments do not fill the resource's maximum capacity to do work. For example, a full-time resource who has only 25 hours of work assigned in a 40-hour workweek is *underallocated*.

- **Fully allocated**   The resource's assignments fill the resource's maximum capacity. For example, a full-time resource who has 40 hours of work assigned in a 40-hour workweek is *fully allocated*.

- **Overallocated**   The resource's assignments exceed the resource's maximum capacity for any period of time. For example, a full-time resource who has 65 hours of work assigned in a 40-hour workweek is *overallocated*.

Project management focus: Evaluating resource allocation

It is tempting to say that fully allocating all resources on every occasion is every project manager's goal, but that would be an oversimplification. Depending on the nature of your project and the resources working on it, some underallocations might be perfectly fine. Overallocation might not always be a problem either, depending on the amount of overallocation. If one resource is overallocated for just a half-hour, Project will flag the overallocation, but such a minor overallocation might not be a problem that you need to solve, depending on the resource involved and the nature of the assignment. Severe overallocation—for example, a resource being assigned twice the work he could possibly accomplish in one week—is always a problem, however, and you should know how to identify it and maintain strategies for addressing it. This chapter helps you identify and remedy resource overallocation.

These states of allocation apply to work resources. *Cost* and *material resources* do not do work; therefore, their assignments are not subject to allocation issues.

In Project, a resource's capacity to work is measured in units; the maximum capacity of a given resource is called *maximum units* (labeled *Max. Units* in Project). Units are measured either as numbers (such as three units) or as a percentage (such as 300% units).

The scenario: At Lucerne Publishing, the new children's book plan is developed to the point that you're ready to closely examine resource assignments and overallocation issues. You'll begin with Carole Poland.

In this exercise, you look at resource allocations and focus on a resource who is overallocated.

→ SET UP You need the Advanced Plan_Start file located in your Chapter12 practice file folder to complete this exercise. Open the Advanced Plan_Start file, and save it as Advanced Plan.

1   On the **View** tab, in the **Resource Views** group, click **Resource Usage**.

The Resource Usage view appears.

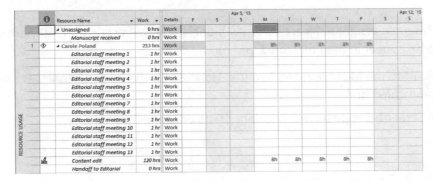

On the left side of the view is a table (the Usage table, by default) that shows assignments grouped per resource, the total work assigned to each resource, and each assignment's work. This information is organized into an *outline* that you can expand or collapse.

The right side of the view contains assignment details (work, by default) arranged on a timescale. You can horizontally scroll the timescale to see different time periods. You can also change the tiers on the timescale to display data in units of weeks, days, hours, and so on.

12

Notice the name in the first row, *Unassigned*. This item lists any tasks to which no specific resources are assigned.

Next, you will collapse the outline in the table to see total work per resource over time.

2   Click the **Resource Name** column heading.

3   On the **View** tab, in the **Data** group, click **Outline** and then click **Hide Subtasks**.

   TIP You also can collapse the outline by pressing Alt+Shift+– (a minus sign).

Project collapses the outline (assignments per resource) in the Resource Usage view.

4   In the **Resource Name** column, click the name *Carole Poland*.

Resource assignments are currently hidden, and the resources' total work values over time appear in the timescaled grid on the right.

5   Point to the **M** column heading (for *Monday*) for the week of April 5 at the top of the timescaled grid.

A ScreenTip appears with the date of the assignment: 4/6/15.

In timescaled views, you can get details about dates by pointing at the timescale.

Such ScreenTips are handy in timescaled views, such as the Resource Usage view or the Gantt Chart view.

Currently, the timescale is set to display weeks and days. You will now change the timescale to see the work data summarized more broadly.

6   On the **View** tab, in the **Zoom** group, in the **Timescale** box, click **Months**.

Project changes the timescaled grid to show scheduled work values per month.

	#	Resource Name	Work	Details	1st Quarter Jan	Feb	Mar	2nd Quarter Apr	May	Jun	3rd Quarter Jul	Aug	Sep	4th Quarter Oct	Nov	Dec
		▷ Unassigned	0 hrs	Work												
⬩	1	▷ Carole Poland	213 hrs	Work				123h	4h	45h	1h	10h	30h			
	2	▷ Color Setting Services	80 hrs	Work									80h			
	3	▷ Copyeditors	300 hrs	Work				0h	192h	88h	20h					
	4	Dan Jump	0 hrs	Work												
⬩	5	▷ Hany Morcos	393 hrs	Work				3h	44h	37h	97h	104h	108h			
⬩	6	▷ Jane Dow	240 hrs	Work						32h	88h	72h	48h			
	7	▷ Jun Cao	13 hrs	Work				3h	4h	5h	1h					
	8	▷ Luis Sousa	200 hrs	Work						32h	88h	80h				
	9	▷ Printing Service	240 hrs	Work									32h	176h	32h	
	10	▷ Tad Orman	296 hrs	Work				8h	72h	80h	80h	16h	40h			
	11	Travel		Work												
	12	Bound galley proofs	0 copies	Work (												
				Work												

Notice that the names and some assignment values of Carole Poland and some other resources appear in red. The red formatting means that these resources are overallocated: at one or more points in the schedule, their assigned tasks exceed their capacity to work.

> **IMPORTANT** If you do not see any overallocated resources, verify in the Resource Leveling dialog box that Day By Day and Manual are selected (on the Resource tab, in the Level group, click the Leveling Options dialog box). If you still don't see overallocated resources, click the Clear Leveling button in the Leveling Options dialog box. If all else fails, reopen the Advance Plan_Start practice file.

As you can see in the timescaled grid, Carole Poland is overallocated in April. She is underallocated for the other months in which she has assignments. Notice that Carole's June work value of 45 hours is formatted in red. Even though 45 hours within a month isn't an overallocation for a full-time resource, at some point in June (perhaps even for just one day), Carole is scheduled to work more hours than she can accommodate.

Next you will change the timescale settings to take a closer look at Carole's overallocations.

7   On the **View** tab, in the **Zoom** group, in the **Timescale** box, click **Days**.

Project adjusts the timescale to its previous setting.

8   Click the expand/collapse arrow next to Carole's name in the **Resource Name** column.

Project expands the Resource Usage view to show Carole's individual assignments.

9   If necessary, scroll the **Resource Usage** view horizontally to the right to see Carole's assignments the week of April 19.

Carole's total work on that Monday, April 20, is 9 hours. This is formatted red, indicating the overallocation.

These two assignments make up the
9 hours of work scheduled on Monday.

	ⓘ	Resource Name	Work	Details	S	Apr 19, '15 S	M	T	W
		▷ Unassigned	0 hrs	Work					
1	◈	◢ Carole Poland	213 hrs	Work			9h	8h	8h
		Handoff to Editorial	0 hrs	Work					
		Copyedit incorp	40 hrs	Work					
	📈	Content edit	120 hrs	Work			8h	8h	8h
	ⅈⅈⅉ	Final review	12 hrs	Work					
		Editorial staff meeting 1	1 hr	Work					
		Editorial staff meeting 2	1 hr	Work			1h		
		Editorial staff meeting 3	1 hr	Work					

Carole has two assignments on April 20: eight hours on the *Content edit* task and the one-hour task *Editorial staff meeting 2* (one instance of a *recurring task*).

These two tasks are scheduled at times that overlap between the hours of 8 A.M. and 9 A.M. (If you want to observe this, adjust the timescale to display hours.) This is a real overallocation: Carole probably cannot complete both tasks simultaneously. However, it is a relatively minor overallocation given the scope of the plan, and you don't need to be too concerned about resolving this level of overallocation. However, there are other, more serious overallocations in the schedule that you will remedy later in this chapter.

10 Click the expand/collapse arrow next to Carole's name in the **Resource Name** column to collapse her assignments.

Here are a few other things to keep in mind when viewing resource allocation:

▪ A quick way to navigate to resource overallocations in the Resource Usage view is to use the Next Overallocation button in the Level group of the Resources tab.

▪ By default, the Resource Usage view displays the Usage table; however, you can display different tables. On the View tab, in the Data group, click Table and then click the table you want displayed.

▪ By default, the Resource Usage view displays work values in the timescaled grid. However, you can display additional assignment values, such as cost and remaining availability. To do this, on the Format tab, in the Details group, click the value that you want displayed.

- Instead of using the Timescale box on the View tab to change the timescale, you can click the Zoom In and Zoom Out buttons on the status bar. However, this method might not produce the exact level of detail that you want.

- To see allocations for each resource graphed against a timescale, you can display the Resource Graph: on the View tab, in the Resource Views group, click Other Views and then click Resource Graph. Use the arrow keys or horizontal scroll bar to switch between resources in this view.

- Project Professional users can use the Team Planner view to see assignments per resource in a simpler format. For more information about the Team Planner view, see Chapter 11, "Fine-tuning resource and assignment details."

Resolving resource overallocations manually

In this section and the next, you will continue to focus on resource allocation—how the task assignments you made affect the workloads of the work resources in the plan. In this section, you will manually edit an assignment to resolve a resource overallocation. In the next section, you will automatically resolve resource overallocations.

Editing an assignment manually is just one way to resolve a resource overallocation. Other solutions include the following:

- Replace the overallocated resource with another resource using the Replace button in the Assign Resources dialog box.

- Reduce the value in the Units field in the Assignment Information or Assign Resources dialog box.

- Assign an additional resource to the task so that both resources share the work.

- Add a leveling delay to an assignment manually.

If the overallocation is not too severe (such as assigning 9 hours of work in a normal 8-hour workday), you can often leave the overallocation in the plan.

The scenario: At Lucerne Publishing, you see more resource overallocations in the new children's book plan. Unlike Carole Poland's minor overallocation you examined earlier, you can see more severe overallocations for Hany Morcos that do require corrective action.

12

In this exercise, you will use the Resource Usage view to examine one overallocated resource's assignments and edit the assignment to eliminate the overallocation.

1   On the **View** tab, in the **Zoom** group, in the **Timescale** box, click **Weeks**.

At the weekly setting, you can more easily spot overallocations that might need to be addressed. Assigned work well over 40 hours per week for a full-time resource could be a serious problem.

	ⓘ	Resource Name	Work	Details	April 3/29	4/5	4/12	4/19	May 4/26	5/3	5/10	5/17	5/24	June 5/31
		▷ Unassigned	0 hrs	Work										
1	◈	▷ Carole Poland	213 hrs	Work		40h	17h	41h	25h	1h	1h	1h	1h	1h
2		▷ Color Setting Services	80 hrs	Work										
3		▷ Copyeditors	300 hrs	Work					0h	40h	40h	32h	80h	69.5h
4		Dan Jump	0 hrs	Work										
5	◈	▷ Hany Morcos	393 hrs	Work		1h	1h	1h	1h	17h	25h	1h	1h	
6	◈	▷ Jane Dow	240 hrs	Work										
7		▷ Jun Cao	13 hrs	Work		1h	1h	1h	1h	1h	1h	1h	1h	
8		▷ Luis Sousa	200 hrs	Work										
9		▷ Printing Service	240 hrs	Work										
10		▷ Tad Orman	296 hrs	Work					16h	40h	24h			6h
11		Travel		Work										
12		Bound galley proofs	0 copies	Work										
				Work										

Note that several names appear in red. These are overallocated resources.

2   Horizontally scroll the usage view to the right to examine the more severe overallocations per week.

You see several cases of minor overallocation, such as 41 hours per week, and some cases of overallocations where the total work is less than 40 hours per week. Note the more severe overallocations that affect Hany Morcos (among others) in August.

	ⓘ	Resource Name	Work	Details	7/5	7/12	7/19	7/26	August 8/2	8/9	8/16	8/23	8/30	September 9/6	9/13	9/20	October 9/27	10/4
		▷ Unassigned	0 hrs	Work														
1	◈	▷ Carole Poland	213 hrs	Work	1h							4.5h	35.5h					
2		▷ Color Setting Services	80 hrs	Work										32h	40h	8h		
3		▷ Copyeditors	300 hrs	Work		8h	12h											
4		Dan Jump	0 hrs	Work														
5	◈	▷ Hany Morcos	393 hrs	Work	41h	24h		8h	32h		16h	52h	16h	48h	40h	8h		
6	◈	▷ Jane Dow	240 hrs	Work	40h	24h			8h	32h		16h	64h					
7		▷ Jun Cao	13 hrs	Work	1h													
8		▷ Luis Sousa	200 hrs	Work	40h	24h			8h	40h	32h							
9		▷ Printing Service	240 hrs	Work											8h	40h	40	
10		▷ Tad Orman	296 hrs	Work		8h	40h	32h			16h		40h					
11		Travel		Work														
12		Bound galley proofs	0 copies	Work														
				Work														

These overallocations are severe enough that they merit more investigation. You'll begin with Hany's overallocations in August

3   Click the expand/collapse arrow next to Hany's name in the **Resource Name** column.

Next, you'd like to get a better look at the tasks that are causing Hany's overallocation this week.

4   On the **View** tab, in the **Zoom** group, in the **Timescale** box, click **Days**.

5   Horizontally scroll the usage view to display Friday, August 21.

> **TIP** You can also press CTRL+G and in the Date field of the Go To dialog box, type or select **8/21/15** and then click OK.

At the daily setting, you can see that Hany is overallocated on Friday, August 21, and Monday and Tuesday, August 24 and 25.

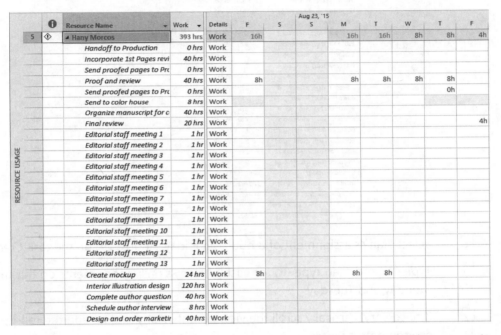

	❶	Resource Name	Work	Details	F	S	Aug 23, '15 S	M	T	W	T	F
5	◈	▲ Hany Morcos	393 hrs	Work	16h			16h	16h	8h	8h	4h
		Handoff to Production	0 hrs	Work								
		Incorporate 1st Pages revi	40 hrs	Work								
		Send proofed pages to Prc	0 hrs	Work								
		Proof and review	40 hrs	Work	8h			8h	8h	8h	8h	
		Send proofed pages to Prc	0 hrs	Work							0h	
		Send to color house	8 hrs	Work								
		Organize manuscript for c	40 hrs	Work								
		Final review	20 hrs	Work								4h
		Editorial staff meeting 1	1 hr	Work								
		Editorial staff meeting 2	1 hr	Work								
		Editorial staff meeting 3	1 hr	Work								
		Editorial staff meeting 4	1 hr	Work								
		Editorial staff meeting 5	1 hr	Work								
		Editorial staff meeting 6	1 hr	Work								
		Editorial staff meeting 7	1 hr	Work								
		Editorial staff meeting 8	1 hr	Work								
		Editorial staff meeting 9	1 hr	Work								
		Editorial staff meeting 10	1 hr	Work								
		Editorial staff meeting 11	1 hr	Work								
		Editorial staff meeting 12	1 hr	Work								
		Editorial staff meeting 13	1 hr	Work								
		Create mockup	24 hrs	Work	8h			8h	8h			
		Interior illustration design	120 hrs	Work								
		Complete author question	40 hrs	Work								
		Schedule author interview	8 hrs	Work								
		Design and order marketir	40 hrs	Work								

You decide to reduce Hany's work on both the *Proof and review* and *Create mockup* tasks.

6   In the timephased grid of the **Resource Usage** view, select Hany's assignment of 8 hours on Friday, August 21, on the task *Proof and review*.

7   Type **4h**, and then press the Tab key multiple times to shift focus to Monday, August 24.

8   With Hany's 8-hour assignment on the same task for Monday, August 24, selected, type **4h** and then press Tab.

9. With Hany's 8-hour assignment on the same task for Tuesday, August 25, selected, type **4h** and then press Tab.

	❶	Resource Name	Work ▾	Details	F	S	Aug 23, '15 S	M	T	W	T	F
5	◈	▲ **Hany Morcos**	**381 hrs**	Work	12h			12h	12h	8h	8h	4h
		Handoff to Production	0 hrs	Work								
		Incorporate 1st Pages revi	40 hrs	Work								
		Send proofed pages to Pro	0 hrs	Work								
	📇	Proof and review	28 hrs	Work	4h			4h	4h	8h	8h	
		Send proofed pages to Pro	0 hrs	Work							0h	
		Send to color house	8 hrs	Work								
		Organize manuscript for c	40 hrs	Work								
		Final review	20 hrs	Work								4h
		Editorial staff meeting 1	1 hr	Work								
		Editorial staff meeting 2	1 hr	Work								
		Editorial staff meeting 3	1 hr	Work								
		Editorial staff meeting 4	1 hr	Work								
		Editorial staff meeting 5	1 hr	Work								
		Editorial staff meeting 6	1 hr	Work								
		Editorial staff meeting 7	1 hr	Work								
		Editorial staff meeting 8	1 hr	Work								
		Editorial staff meeting 9	1 hr	Work								
		Editorial staff meeting 10	1 hr	Work								
		Editorial staff meeting 11	1 hr	Work								
		Editorial staff meeting 12	1 hr	Work								
		Editorial staff meeting 13	1 hr	Work								
		Create mockup	24 hrs	Work	8h			8h	8h			
		Interior illustration design	120 hrs	Work								
		Complete author question	40 hrs	Work								
		Schedule author interview	8 hrs	Work								
		Design and order marketin	40 hrs	Work								

10. Select Hany's assignment of 8 hours on Friday, August 21, on the task *Create mockup*.

11. Type **4h**, and then type **4h** for each of Hany's daily assignments on this task for Monday and Tuesday.

12. If necessary, vertically scroll the view up until Hany's name and the roll-up of her daily assignments is visible.

	Resource Name	Work	Details	F	S	Aug 23, '15 S	M	T	W	T	F
5 ⟡	▲ Hany Morcos	**369 hrs**	Work	8h			8h	8h	8h	8h	4h
	Handoff to Production	0 hrs	Work								
	Incorporate 1st Pages revi	40 hrs	Work								
	Send proofed pages to Prc	0 hrs	Work								
	Proof and review	28 hrs	Work	4h			4h	4h	8h	8h	
	Send proofed pages to Prc	0 hrs	Work							0h	
	Send to color house	8 hrs	Work								
	Organize manuscript for c	40 hrs	Work								
	Final review	20 hrs	Work								4h
	Editorial staff meeting 1	1 hr	Work								
	Editorial staff meeting 2	1 hr	Work								
	Editorial staff meeting 3	1 hr	Work								
	Editorial staff meeting 4	1 hr	Work								
	Editorial staff meeting 5	1 hr	Work								
	Editorial staff meeting 6	1 hr	Work								
	Editorial staff meeting 7	1 hr	Work								
	Editorial staff meeting 8	1 hr	Work								
	Editorial staff meeting 9	1 hr	Work								
	Editorial staff meeting 10	1 hr	Work								
	Editorial staff meeting 11	1 hr	Work								
	Editorial staff meeting 12	1 hr	Work								
	Editorial staff meeting 13	1 hr	Work								
	Create mockup	12 hrs	Work	4h			4h	4h			
	Interior illustration design	120 hrs	Work								
	Complete author question	40 hrs	Work								
	Schedule author interview	8 hrs	Work								
	Design and order marketir	40 hrs	Work								

You addressed her overallocation for the week by reducing her work on the two tasks. Note that by taking this action, you reduced not just Hany's work on these tasks, but the total work in the plan. As a project manager, you have to use your judgment to determine the best course of action in such cases: reduce work, change resource assignments, or spread the work over a longer period of time.

Next, you will look at other resource overallocations in the new children's book plan that you can resolve automatically with resource leveling.

Leveling overallocated resources

In the previous sections, you learned about resource allocation, discovered what causes overallocation, and resolved an overallocation manually. *Resource leveling* is the process of delaying or splitting a resource's work on a task to resolve an overallocation. You can use the options in the Level Resources dialog box to set parameters concerning how you want Project to resolve resource overallocations. Project will attempt to resolve such overallocations when you choose to level resources. Depending on the options you choose, this might involve delaying the start date of an assignment or task or splitting the work on the task.

12

TIP Although the effects of resource leveling on a schedule might be significant, resource leveling does not change who is assigned to tasks nor the total work or assignment unit values of those assignments.

For example, consider the following tasks, all of which have the same full-time resource assigned.

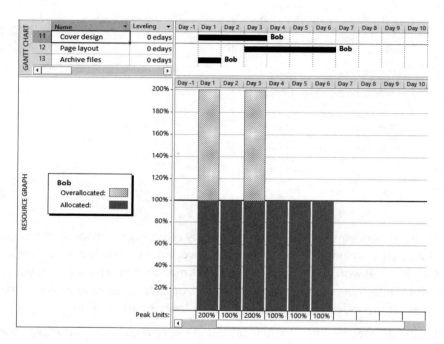

In this split view, the Resource Graph view appears below the Gantt Chart view. On day 1, the resource is overallocated at 200%. On day 2, the resource is fully allocated at 100%. On day 3, he is again overallocated at 200%. After day 3, the resource is fully allocated at 100%.

When you perform resource leveling, Project delays the start dates of the second and third tasks so that the resource is not overallocated.

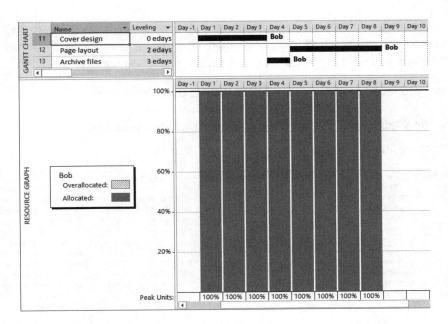

Note that the finish date of the latest scheduled task has moved from day 6 to day 8. This is common with resource leveling, which often pushes out the plan's finish date. There was a total of eight days of work before leveling, but two of those days overlapped, causing the resource to be overallocated on those days. After leveling, all eight days of work are still there, but the resource is no longer overallocated.

Resource leveling is a powerful tool, but it accomplishes only a few basic things: it delays tasks, splits tasks, and delays resource assignments. It does this following a fairly complex set of rules and options that you specify in the Resource Leveling dialog box. (These options are explained in the following exercise.) Resource leveling is a great fine-tuning tool, but it cannot replace your good judgment about resource availability, task durations, relationships, and constraints. Resource leveling will work with all this information as it is entered into your plan, but it might not be possible to fully resolve all resource overallocations within the time frame desired unless you change some of the basic task and resource values in the plan. Additional remedies might include reducing the overall scope of work or adding additional resources.

TIP To learn more about resource leveling, click the Help button (which looks like a question mark) in the upper-right corner of the Project window, and in the Help Search box, type **Level resource assignments**.

The scenario: At Lucerne Publishing, you've examined and manually resolved some resource overallocation issues in the new children's book plan. Now that you understand the basics of resource leveling, you're ready to use Project's resource-leveling feature.

In this exercise, you level resources and view the effects on assignments.

1   On the **View** tab, in the **Resource Views** group, click **Resource Sheet**.

The Resource Sheet view appears.

	ⓘ	Resource Name	Type	Material	Initials	Group	Max.	Std. Rate	Ovt.	Cost/Use	Accrue	Base
1	◈	Carole Poland	Work		C		100%	100.00/wk	$0.00/hr	$0.00	Prorated	Standard
2		Color Setting Ser	Work		C		200%	$0.00/hr	$0.00/hr	$0.00	Prorated	Standard
3		Copyeditors	Work		C		200%	$45.00/hr	$0.00/hr	$0.00	Prorated	Standard
4		Dan Jump	Work		D		50%	$75.50/hr	$0.00/hr	$0.00	Prorated	Standard
5	◈	Hany Morcos	Work		H		100%	550.00/wk	$0.00/hr	$0.00	Prorated	Standard
6	◈	Jane Dow	Work		J		100%	$63.25/hr	$0.00/hr	$0.00	Prorated	Standard
7		Jun Cao	Work		J		100%	$42.00/hr	$63.00/hr	$0.00	Prorated	Standard
8		Luis Sousa	Work		L		100%	$70.00/hr	$0.00/hr	$0.00	Prorated	Standard
9		Printing Service	Work		P		100%	$0.00/hr	$0.00/hr	$0.00	Prorated	Standard
10		Tad Orman	Work		T		100%	$0.00/hr	$0.00/hr	$0.00	Prorated	Standard
11		Travel	Cost		T						Prorated	
12		Bound galley proofs	Material	copies	B			$15.00		$0.00	Prorated	

Note that a few resource names appear in red and display the Overallocated indicator in the Indicators column.

2   On the **Resource** tab, in the **Level** group, click **Leveling Options**.

The Resource Leveling dialog box appears. In the next several steps, you will walk through the options in this dialog box.

3   Under **Leveling calculations**, make sure that **Manual** is selected.

This setting determines whether Project levels resources constantly (Automatic) or only when you tell it to (Manual). Automatic leveling occurs as soon as a resource becomes overallocated.

TIP All settings in the Resource Leveling dialog box apply to all plans that you work with in Project, not only to the active plan. Using automatic leveling might sound tempting, but it will cause frequent adjustments to plans whether you want them or not. For this reason, we recommend you keep this setting on Manual.

4   In the **Look for overallocations on a ... basis** box, make sure that **Day by Day** is selected.

This setting determines the time frame in which Project will look for overallocations. If a resource is overallocated, its name will be formatted in red. If it's overallocated at the level you choose here, Project will also show the Overallocated indicator next to its name.

TIP On most projects, leveling in finer detail than day by day can result in unrealistically precise adjustments to assignments. If you prefer not to see overallocation indicators for day-by-day overallocations, select Week By Week in the Look For Overallocations On A...Basis box and then click OK. Doing so will not level resources, but it will determine when Project displays overallocation indicators next to resource names.

5   Make sure that the **Clear leveling values before leveling** check box is selected.

Sometimes you will need to level resources repeatedly to obtain the results that you want. For example, you might initially attempt to level week by week and then switch to day by day. If the Clear Leveling Values Before Leveling check box is selected, Project removes any existing leveling delays from all tasks and assignments before leveling. For example, if you previously leveled the plan and then added more assignments, you might want to clear this check box before leveling again so that you don't lose the previous leveling results.

6   Under **Leveling range for Advanced Plan,** make sure that **Level entire project** is selected.

Here you choose to level either the entire plan or only assignments that fall within a date range you specify. Leveling within a date range is most useful after you have started tracking actual work and you want to level only the remaining assignments in a plan.

7   In the **Leveling order** box, make sure that **Standard** is selected.

You control the priority that Project uses to determine which tasks it should delay to resolve a resource conflict. The ID Only option delays tasks only according to their ID numbers: numerically higher ID numbers (for example, 10) will be delayed before numerically lower ID numbers (for example, 5). You might want to use this option when your plan has no task relationships or constraints. The Standard option delays tasks according to predecessor relationships, start dates, task constraints, *slack,* priority, and IDs. The Priority, Standard option looks at the task priority value before the other standard criteria. (*Task priority* is a numeric ranking between 0 and 1000

12

that indicates the task's appropriateness for leveling. Tasks with the lowest priority are delayed or split first.)

8   Make sure that the **Level only within available slack** check box is cleared.

   TIP Remember that to *clear* a check box means to remove a check from the check box, and to *select* a check box means to put a check mark in it. You toggle the selection state of a check box by clicking it.

   Clearing this check box allows Project to extend the plan's finish date, if necessary, to resolve resource allocations.

   Selecting this check box would prevent Project from extending the plan's finish date to resolve resource overallocations. Instead, Project would use only the free slack within the existing schedule. Depending on the plan, this might not be adequate to fully resolve resource overallocations.

9   Make sure that the **Leveling can adjust individual assignments on a task** check box is selected.

   This allows Project to add a leveling delay (or split work on assignments if Leveling Can Create Splits In Remaining Work is also selected) independently of any other resources assigned to the same task. This might cause resources to start and finish work on a task at different times.

10   Make sure that the **Leveling can create splits in remaining work** check box is selected.

   This allows Project to split work on a task (or on an assignment if Leveling Can Adjust Individual Assignments On A Task is also selected) as a way of resolving an overallocation.

11   Make sure that the **Level manually scheduled tasks** check box is selected.

   This allows Project to level a manually scheduled task just as it would an automatically scheduled task.

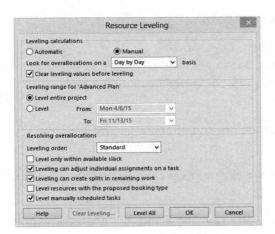

TIP If you are using Project Professional rather than Project Standard, the Resource Leveling dialog box and some other dialog boxes contain additional options relating to Project Server. (In this dialog box, the check box Level Resources With The Proposed Booking Type is a Project Server–related option.) Throughout this book, we won't use Project Server, so you can ignore these options for now. For more information about Project Server, see Appendix C.

Now that you've reviewed the leveling options, you are ready to level the plan.

12   Click **Level All**.

TIP After you set the leveling options that you want in the Resource Leveling dialog box, you can level the plan by clicking the Level All button on the Resource tab in the Level group. You don't need to return to the Resource Leveling dialog box unless you want to change leveling options.

Project levels the overallocated resources.

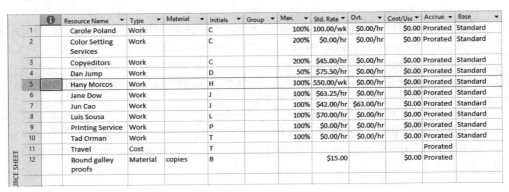

	ⓘ	Resource Name	Type	Material	Initials	Group	Max.	Std. Rate	Ovt.	Cost/Use	Accrue	Base
1		Carole Poland	Work		C		100%	100.00/wk	$0.00/hr	$0.00	Prorated	Standard
2		Color Setting Services	Work		C		200%	$0.00/hr	$0.00/hr	$0.00	Prorated	Standard
3		Copyeditors	Work		C		200%	$45.00/hr	$0.00/hr	$0.00	Prorated	Standard
4		Dan Jump	Work		D		50%	$75.50/hr	$0.00/hr	$0.00	Prorated	Standard
5		Hany Morcos	Work		H		100%	550.00/wk	$0.00/hr	$0.00	Prorated	Standard
6		Jane Dow	Work		J		100%	$63.25/hr	$0.00/hr	$0.00	Prorated	Standard
7		Jun Cao	Work		J		100%	$42.00/hr	$63.00/hr	$0.00	Prorated	Standard
8		Luis Sousa	Work		L		100%	$70.00/hr	$0.00/hr	$0.00	Prorated	Standard
9		Printing Service	Work		P		100%	$0.00/hr	$0.00/hr	$0.00	Prorated	Standard
10		Tad Orman	Work		T		100%	$0.00/hr	$0.00/hr	$0.00	Prorated	Standard
11		Travel	Cost		T						Prorated	
12		Bound galley proofs	Material	copies	B			$15.00		$0.00	Prorated	

Notice that the Overallocated indicators are gone.

TIP When leveling resources with Day By Day selected, you might see the overallocation icons disappear, but some resource names might still appear in red. This means that some resources are still overallocated hour by hour (or minute by minute), but not day by day.

Next, you will look at the plan before and after leveling by using the Leveling Gantt view.

13 On the **View** tab, in the **Task Views** group, click the arrow below **Gantt Chart** and then click **More Views**.

14 In the **More Views** dialog box, click **Leveling Gantt**, and then click **Apply**.

Project switches to the Leveling Gantt view.

15 On the **View** tab, in the **Zoom** group, click **Entire Project**.

This view gives you a better look at some of the tasks that were affected by leveling.

16 Vertically scroll the Leveling Gantt view down to see task 46, the *Book launch prep* summary task.

In the Leveling Gantt view, the bars on the top represent the pre-leveled schedule of the task. The lower bars represent the schedule after leveling.

These are some of the tasks that were more substantially affected by resource leveling. Notice that each task has two bars. The top bar represents the pre-leveled task. You can see a task's pre-leveled start, finish, and duration by pointing to a light tan–colored bar. The bottom bar represents the leveled task as it's now scheduled.

Project was able to resolve the resource overallocations. For this particular plan, leveling did not extend the finish date. The latest scheduled task in the plan (task 45, *Print and ship*) still has some slack because of the manual duration entered on its summary task.

Checking the plan's cost and finish date

Not all plans include cost information, but for those that do, keeping track of project costs can be as important as, or more important than, keeping track of the scheduled finish date. In this section, you examine both the cost and the finish date of the plan.

Two factors to consider when examining project costs are the specific types of costs you want to see and how you can best see them.

The types of costs that you might encounter over the life of a project include the following:

- **Baseline costs** The original planned task, resource, or assignment costs saved as part of a baseline plan.

- **Current (or scheduled) costs** The calculated costs of tasks, resources, and assignments in a plan. As you make adjustments in a plan, such as assigning or removing resources, Project recalculates current costs just as it recalculates task start and finish dates. After you start to incur actual costs (typically by tracking actual work), the current cost equals the actual cost plus the remaining cost per task, resource, or assignment. Current costs are the values you see in the fields labeled Cost or Total Cost.

- **Actual costs** The costs that have been incurred for tasks, resources, or assignments.

- **Remaining costs** The difference between the current or scheduled costs and the actual costs for tasks, resources, or assignments.

You might need to compare these costs (for example, baseline vs. actual) or examine them individually per task, resource, or assignment. Or you might need to examine cost values for summary tasks or for an entire plan. Some common ways to view these types of costs include the following:

- You can see the plan's cost values in the Project Statistics dialog box. (You'll do so later.)

- You can see or print reports that include cash flow, budget, cost overruns for both tasks and resources, and earned value. (To do this, on the Report tab, in the View Reports group, click Costs.)

- You can see task-level, resource-level, or assignment-level cost information in usage views by displaying the Cost table. (To do this, on the View tab, in the Data group, click Tables and then click Cost.)

12

- To see cost details distributed over time in a usage view, do this: On the Format tab, in the Details group, click Add Details and then select the cost values you want.

In addition to cost, the finish date is a critical (often the most critical) measure of a plan. A plan's finish date is a function of its duration and start date. Most projects have a desired, or *soft*, finish date, and many projects have a *must hit*, or *hard*, finish date. When managing projects like these, it is essential that you know the plan's current or scheduled finish.

TIP In the language of project management, a project's finish date is determined by its *critical path*. The critical path is the series of tasks that will push out the project's end date if the tasks are delayed. For this reason, when evaluating the duration of a project, you should focus mainly on the tasks on the critical path, called *critical tasks*. Remember that the word *critical* has nothing to do with how important these tasks are to the overall project. The word refers only to how their scheduling will affect the project's finish date. If you need a refresher on critical paths, see Chapter 10, "Fine-tuning task details."

The scenario: At Lucerne Publishing, you've fine-tuned important parts of the new children's book plan including resource assignments, costs, and task durations. To see the plan's current cost and finish date values, you'll switch to a different view and then see summary values in the Project Information dialog box.

In this exercise, you look at the plan's finish date, overall costs, and individual task costs.

1   On the **View** tab, in the **Task Views** group, click **Other Views**, and then click **Task Sheet**.

Project switches to the Task Sheet view. Next, you will switch to the Cost table.

TIP Wonder where Project got this project summary task name shown for task 0? Project uses the title entered in the Advanced Properties dialog box (on the File tab, in the Info group, Project Information) as the project summary task name. Or, if nobody has entered a distinct title property, Project uses the file name as the project summary task name. If you change the project summary task name once you've displayed it, Project updates the Title property, and vice versa.

2   On the **View** tab, in the **Data** group, click **Tables** and then click **Cost**.

The Cost table appears.

Task Name	Fixed Cost	Fixed Cost Accrual	Total Cost	Baseline	Variance	Actual	Remainir
0 ⁴ Children's Book Sch	$0.00	Prorated	73,707.25	$0.00	$73,707.25	$0.00	73,707.25
1 ▷ Editorial staff mee	$0.00	Prorated	$1,732.25	$0.00	$1,732.25	$0.00	$1,732.25
15 ⁴ Acquisition	$0.00	Prorated	$9,900.00	$0.00	$9,900.00	$0.00	$9,900.00
16 Manuscript rece	$0.00	Prorated	$0.00	$0.00	$0.00	$0.00	$0.00
17 Content edit	$0.00	Prorated	$6,300.00	$0.00	$6,300.00	$0.00	$6,300.00
18 Author review (	$0.00	Prorated	$3,600.00	$0.00	$3,600.00	$0.00	$3,600.00
19 Handoff to Edit	$0.00	Prorated	$0.00	$0.00	$0.00	$0.00	$0.00
20 ⁴ Editorial	$0.00	Prorated	$12,650.00	$0.00	$12,650.00	$0.00	$12,650.00
21 Organize manu:	$0.00	Prorated	$1,550.00	$0.00	$1,550.00	$0.00	$1,550.00
22 Copyedit	$0.00	Prorated	$8,100.00	$0.00	$8,100.00	$0.00	$8,100.00
23 Author review (	$0.00	Prorated	$900.00	$0.00	$900.00	$0.00	$900.00
24 Copyedit incorp	$0.00	Prorated	$2,100.00	$0.00	$2,100.00	$0.00	$2,100.00
25 Handoff to Proc	$0.00	Prorated	$0.00	$0.00	$0.00	$0.00	$0.00
26 ⁴ Design and Produc	$0.00	Prorated	$36,705.00	$0.00	$36,705.00	$0.00	$36,705.00
27 Set pages	$0.00	Prorated	$7,590.00	$0.00	$7,590.00	$0.00	$7,590.00
28 Interior illustrat	$0.00	Prorated	$13,050.00	$0.00	$13,050.00	$0.00	$13,050.00
29 ⁴ 1st Pages reviev	$0.00	Prorated	$7,780.00	$0.00	$7,780.00	$0.00	$7,780.00
30 Proofread an	$0.00	Prorated	$900.00	$0.00	$900.00	$0.00	$900.00
31 Incorporate 1	$0.00	Prorated	$1,550.00	$0.00	$1,550.00	$0.00	$1,550.00
32 Send proofec	$0.00	Prorated	$0.00	$0.00	$0.00	$0.00	$0.00
33 Enter page cc	$0.00	Prorated	$2,530.00	$0.00	$2,530.00	$0.00	$2,530.00
34 Cover design	$0.00	Prorated	$2,800.00	$0.00	$2,800.00	$0.00	$2,800.00
35 ⁴ 2nd Pages revie	$0.00	Prorated	$5,020.00	$0.00	$5,020.00	$0.00	$5,020.00
36 Proof and rev	$0.00	Prorated	$1,085.00	$0.00	$1,085.00	$0.00	$1,085.00
37 Send proofec	$0.00	Prorated	$0.00	$0.00	$0.00	$0.00	$0.00
38 Final review	$0.00	Prorated	$3,935.00	$0.00	$3,935.00	$0.00	$3,935.00
39 ⁴ Design book's c	$0.00	Prorated	$3,265.00	$0.00	$3,265.00	$0.00	$3,265.00

Here, you can see many types of cost values for the overall plan (the total cost of the project summary task 0), project phases (summary tasks), and individual tasks.

At this point in the project life cycle, the plan does not yet include a baseline; therefore, the Baseline column contains only zero values. Similarly, the plan does not yet contain any actual progress, so the Actual column contains only zero values.

Next, you'll check the plan's finish date.

3   On the **Project** tab, in the **Properties** group, click **Project Information**.

The Project Information dialog box appears.

12

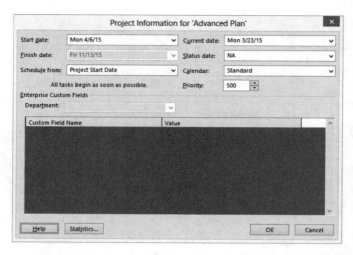

In the Project Information dialog box, you can see the finish date as the plan is currently scheduled. Note that you can edit the start date of the plan here, but not its finish date. Project has calculated this finish date based on the start date plus the overall duration of the plan.

Next, you will look at the duration values for this plan.

4　In the **Project Information** dialog box, click **Statistics**.

The Project Statistics dialog box appears. Here again, you can see the plan's current start and finish dates.

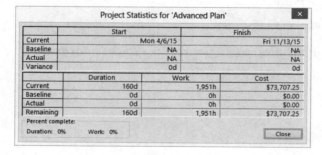

This plan currently has no baseline and actual work reported, so you see *NA* in the Baseline, Actual Start, and Actual Finish fields and zero values in the Actual Duration and Actual Work fields.

Note also that the cost value in the Current row is the same as what you saw in the Task Sheet view.

5　Click **Close** to close the **Project Statistics** dialog box.

Inactivating tasks

You can include tasks in a plan that you might later decide you don't want to have completed, but you also don't want to lose the details about those tasks by deleting them. You might for example develop tasks that pose "what-if" questions that you can't begin to answer until preliminary questions get answered. Or you could design a plan that describes a likely-case scenario for completion but also includes more optimistic and pessimistic sets of tasks as well.

In Project Professional, you can inactivate a single task or multiple tasks. Inactivating tasks can be preferable to deleting tasks, in that it keeps the task information in the plan but removes the scheduling effect of those tasks. A task that drives the start of a successor task, for example, remains visible when inactivated, but it has strikethrough formatting applied in the Gantt Chart and other views, and its link relationship is broken and its successor is rescheduled.

Should you later want to reactivate inactivated tasks, you can easily do so, and Project restores them as active tasks with the same scheduling impact as they previously had.

TIP You can inactivate only tasks that have no progress recorded against them. You cannot inactivate completed tasks or tasks that have any progress recorded.

The scenario: At Lucerne Publishing, you've shared the current cost and schedule details of the new children's book plan with the publisher. She has asked you to identify some activities that could be cut to reduce costs without risking the essential deliverables of the plan. You've identified the activities that could be cut, and to see the result of cutting them while keeping the opportunity to easily restore them, you'll inactivate the tasks in question.

In this exercise, you inactivate a summary task and its subtasks.

1   On the **View** tab, in the **Task Views** group, click the arrow below **Gantt Chart** and then click **Gantt Chart**.

   TIP Are you wondering why you do not just click the Gantt Chart button? Recall that Project includes multiple Gantt Chart views. The Gantt Chart button will display whatever Gantt Chart view you last had displayed—in this case, the Leveling Gantt view. To display the Gantt Chart view at this time, you need to select it from the list of views.

12

2 Select the name of task 39, *Design book's companion website*.

3 On the **Task** tab, in the **Editing** group, click **Scroll to Task**.

This summary task and its subtasks reflect an initial plan to account for the work of designing a website that would promote the new book at its launch. You still think you might want to include this work in the new book plan, but for now, you'd like to inactivate these tasks.

4 On the **Task** tab, in the **Schedule** group, click **Inactivate**.

Project inactivates the summary task and its subtasks.

Inactive tasks are formatted as strikethrough text, and their Gantt bars appear as colorless outlines.

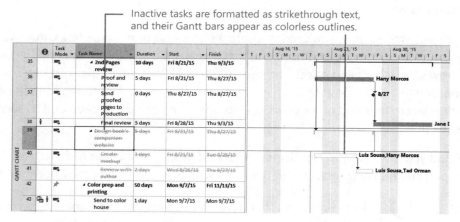

The original task information is still visible, but now it has no impact on the overall plan. Later, if you decide to include these tasks in the plan, you can reactivate them by clicking Inactivate again.

✕ CLEAN UP Close the Advanced Plan file.

Key points

- A work resource's maximum units (Max. Units) value and her working time (as set by the resource calendar) determine when the resource becomes overallocated.

- The Resource Usage view enables you to view the details of assignments that cause resource overallocation.

- You can manually or automatically resolve resource overallocations.

- You can view cost details from the individual assignment level all the way to the entire project level.

- In Project Professional, you can inactivate tasks that are used in "what-if" scenarios or otherwise are no longer needed in the plan but that you don't want to delete permanently.

12

Chapter at a glance

Sort

Sort task or resource data, page 276.

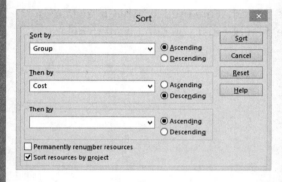

Group

Group tasks or resources, and show summary or "roll-up" values per grouping, page 280.

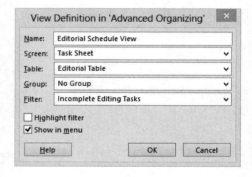

Filter

Create custom filters to show just the data you want, page 285.

Customize

Create your own view with the table, group, and filter definitions you want, page 294.

Organizing project details

13

IN THIS CHAPTER, YOU WILL LEARN HOW TO

- Sort task and resource data.

- Display task and resource data in groups.

- Filter or highlight task and resource data.

- Create a custom table.

- Create a custom view.

After you build a plan in Project, chances are you will need to examine specific aspects of the plan for your own analysis or to share with other *stakeholders*. Although the built-in *views*, *tables*, and *reports* in Microsoft Project 2013 provide many ways to examine a plan, you might need to organize information to suit your own specific needs.

In this chapter, you use some of the tools in Project to control what data appears and how it is organized. Project includes many features that enable you to organize and analyze data that otherwise would require separate tools, such as a spreadsheet application.

PRACTICE FILES Before you can complete the exercises in this chapter, you need to copy the book's practice files to your computer. A complete list of practice files is provided in "Download the practice files" at the beginning of this book. For each exercise that has a practice file, simply browse to where you saved the book's practice file folder.

IMPORTANT If you are running Project Professional with Project Web App/Project Server, take care not to save any of the practice files you work with in this book to Project Web App (PWA). For more information, see Appendix C, "Collaborating: Project, SharePoint, and PWA."

Sorting Project details

Sorting is the simplest way to reorganize task or resource data in Project. You can sort tasks or resources by predefined criteria, or you can create your own sort order with up to three levels of nesting. For example, you can sort resources by resource group (which is the value in the Group field—Design, Editorial, and so on—in our Lucerne Publishing example) and then sort by cost within each resource group.

When you sort data, the sort order applies to the active view regardless of the specific table currently displayed in the view. For example, if you sort the Gantt Chart view by start date while displaying the Entry table and then switch to the Cost table, you'll see the tasks sorted by start date in the Cost table. You can also sort in most views that do not include a table, such as the Resource Graph view.

Like grouping and filtering, which you will work with later in this chapter, sorting does not (with one exception) change the underlying data of your plan; it simply reorders the data you have in the active view. The one exception is the option that Project offers to renumber task or resource IDs after sorting.

It's fine to renumber tasks or resources permanently if that's what you intend to do. For example, when building a resource list, you might enter resource names in the order in which the resources join your project. Later, when the list is complete, you might want to sort them alphabetically by name and permanently renumber them.

In the new children's book plan in our Lucerne Publishing example, each resource is assigned to one of several resource groups. These groups have names such as Design, Editorial, and others that pertain to a book publisher. For your plans, you might use resource groups to represent functional teams, departments, or whatever most logically describes collections of similar resources.

Sorting all resources by resource group enables you to see the costs associated with each resource group more easily. This can help you plan your project's budget. You can also sort resources within each group by cost from most to least expensive.

The scenario: At Lucerne Publishing, you'd like to examine resource costs in the new children's book launch plan in detail. In addition to seeing the cost values per resource based on their pay rates and assigned work, you'd also like to see the cost values organized by the resource groups that map to departments at Lucerne. These include groups like *Editorial* and *Production*.

In this exercise, you sort a resource view by cost.

SET UP You need the Advanced Organizing_Start file located in your Chapter13 practice file folder to complete this exercise. Open the Advanced Organizing_Start file, and save it as Advanced Organizing.

1   On the **View** tab, in the **Resource Views** group, click **Resource Sheet**.

   The Resource Sheet view appears. By default, the Entry table appears in the Resource Sheet view; however, the Entry table includes pay rates but does not display the total cost field per resource. You will switch to the Summary table instead.

2   On the **View** tab, in the **Data** group, click **Tables** and then click **Summary**.

   TIP You can identify the active table by pointing to the Select All button in the upper-left corner of the active table. You also can right-click the Select All button to switch to a different table.

   The Summary table appears.

Select All button

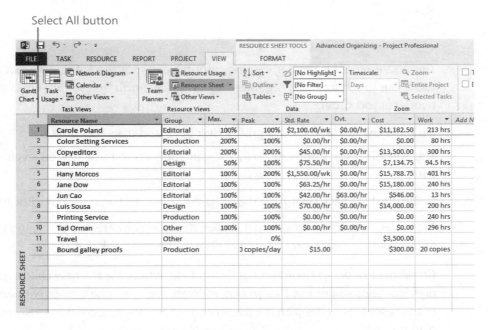

You are now ready to sort the Resource Sheet view.

3   Click the **AutoFilter** arrow in the **Cost** column heading, and in the menu that appears, click **Sort Largest to Smallest**.

> **TIP** If you do not see the AutoFilter arrows in the column headings, try this: on the View tab, in the Data group, in the Filter box, click Display AutoFilter.

The Resource Sheet view is sorted by the Cost column in descending order.

You can quickly sort a table by clicking on the AutoFilter arrow.

	Resource Name	Group	Max.	Peak	Std. Rate	Ovt.	Cost	Work	Add Nev
5	Hany Morcos	Editorial	100%	200%	$1,550.00/wk	$0.00/hr	$15,788.75	401 hrs	
6	Jane Dow	Editorial	100%	100%	$63.25/hr	$0.00/hr	$15,180.00	240 hrs	
8	Luis Sousa	Design	100%	100%	$70.00/hr	$0.00/hr	$14,000.00	200 hrs	
3	Copyeditors	Editorial	200%	200%	$45.00/hr	$0.00/hr	$13,500.00	300 hrs	
1	Carole Poland	Editorial	100%	100%	$2,100.00/wk	$0.00/hr	$11,182.50	213 hrs	
4	Dan Jump	Design	50%	100%	$75.50/hr	$0.00/hr	$7,134.75	94.5 hrs	
11	Travel	Other		0%			$3,500.00		
7	Jun Cao	Editorial	100%	100%	$42.00/hr	$63.00/hr	$546.00	13 hrs	
12	Bound galley proofs	Production		0 copies/day	$15.00		$300.00	20 copies	
2	Color Setting Services	Production	200%	100%	$0.00/hr	$0.00/hr	$0.00	80 hrs	
9	Printing Service	Production	100%	100%	$0.00/hr	$0.00/hr	$0.00	240 hrs	
10	Tad Orman	Other	100%	100%	$0.00/hr	$0.00/hr	$0.00	296 hrs	

This arrangement is fine for viewing resource costs for the entire plan, but perhaps you'd like to see this data organized by resource group. To see this, you'll apply a two-level sort order.

4   On the **View** tab, in the **Data** group, click **Sort**, and then click **Sort By**.

The Sort dialog box appears. In it, you can apply up to three nested levels of sort criteria.

5   Under **Sort By**, click **Group** on the drop-down list, and next to that, click **Ascending**.

> **TIP** When selecting items from a list like this, you can often begin typing the name of the item you want, and when its full name appears, select it.

Group here refers to the Resource Group field, which, for the new children's book plan, contains values like *Design* and *Editorial*; these are the groups with which most of the resources in the plan are associated. These values were previously added to the plan for you.

6   Under **Then By** (in the center of the dialog box), click **Cost** on the drop-down list, and next to that, click **Descending**.

TIP You can sort by any field, not just the fields visible in the active view. However, it's helpful to see the field by which you sort—in this case, the Cost field.

7   Make sure that the **Permanently renumber resources** check box is cleared.

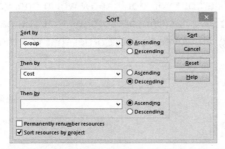

IMPORTANT The Permanently Renumber Resources (or, when in a task view, the Permanently Renumber Tasks) check box in the Sort dialog box is a Project-level (that is, application) setting; if selected, it permanently renumbers resources or tasks in any plan in which you sort. Because you might not want to renumber resources or tasks permanently every time you sort, it's a good idea to keep this check box cleared.

8   Click **Sort**.

Project sorts the Resource Sheet view to display resources by group (*Design, Editorial,* and so on) and then by cost within each group.

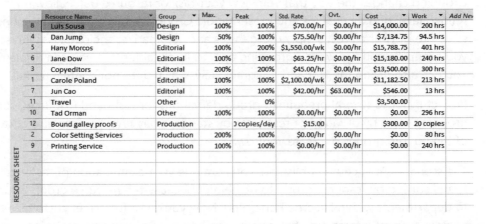

	Resource Name	Group	Max.	Peak	Std. Rate	Ovt.	Cost	Work	Add Nev
8	Luis Sousa	Design	100%	100%	$70.00/hr	$0.00/hr	$14,000.00	200 hrs	
4	Dan Jump	Design	50%	100%	$75.50/hr	$0.00/hr	$7,134.75	94.5 hrs	
5	Hany Morcos	Editorial	100%	200%	$1,550.00/wk	$0.00/hr	$15,788.75	401 hrs	
6	Jane Dow	Editorial	100%	100%	$63.25/hr	$0.00/hr	$15,180.00	240 hrs	
3	Copyeditors	Editorial	200%	200%	$45.00/hr	$0.00/hr	$13,500.00	300 hrs	
1	Carole Poland	Editorial	100%	100%	$2,100.00/wk	$0.00/hr	$11,182.50	213 hrs	
7	Jun Cao	Editorial	100%	100%	$42.00/hr	$63.00/hr	$546.00	13 hrs	
11	Travel	Other		0%			$3,500.00		
10	Tad Orman	Other	100%	100%	$0.00/hr	$0.00/hr	$0.00	296 hrs	
12	Bound galley proofs	Production		0 copies/day	$15.00		$300.00	20 copies	
2	Color Setting Services	Production	200%	100%	$0.00/hr	$0.00/hr	$0.00	80 hrs	
9	Printing Service	Production	100%	100%	$0.00/hr	$0.00/hr	$0.00	240 hrs	

This sort offers an easy way to identify the most expensive resources in each resource group working on the new book project.

To conclude this exercise, you'll re-sort the resource information to return it to its original sort order, which is by ID.

13

9   On the **View** tab, in the **Data** group, click **Sort**, and then click **by ID.**

Project re-sorts the resource list by resource ID.

Reordered ID numbers give you a visual indication that a task or resource view has been sorted. If you see that a sort has been applied but you don't know which one, you can look in the Sort By dialog box. You cannot save custom sort settings that you have specified as you can with grouping and filtering. However, the sort order that you most recently specified will remain in effect until you re-sort the view.

Grouping Project details

As you develop a plan, you can use the views available in Project to view and analyze your data in several ways. One important way to see the data in task and resource views is by grouping. *Grouping* allows you to organize task or resource information (or, when in a usage view, assignment information) according to criteria you choose. For example, rather than viewing the resource list in the Resource Sheet view sorted by ID, you can view resources sorted by cost. Grouping goes a step beyond just sorting, however. Grouping adds summary values, or *roll-ups*, at intervals that you can customize. For example, you can group resources by their cost, with a $1,000 interval between groups.

Grouping changes the way that you view your task or resource data, allowing for a more refined level of data analysis and presentation. Grouping doesn't change the underlying structure of your plan; it simply reorganizes and summarizes the data. As with sorting, when you group data in a view, the grouping applies to all tables that you can display in the view. You can also group the Network Diagram view, which does not contain a table.

Project includes several predefined group definitions for tasks and resources, such as grouping tasks by duration or resources by standard pay rate. You can also customize any of the built-in groups or create your own.

The scenario: At Lucerne Publishing, you continue your examination of resource costs. You found sorting by resource group to be helpful because the resource group values map to departments within Lucerne Publishing. Now you'd like to further customize the view of resource cost information by aggregating it by group. This new grouping is one you anticipate using in the future, so you want to also save it for future use.

In this exercise, you group resources and create a custom grouping definition.

1　On the **View** tab, in the **Data** group, click the down arrow next to the **Group By** box (it initially contains *[No Group]*), and then click **Resource Group**.

TIP　Because the Group column is visible in the Resource Sheet view, you can also click the AutoFilter arrow in the Group column heading, and in the menu that appears, click Group On This Field.

Project reorganizes the resource data into resource groups, adds summary values per group, and presents the data in an expanded outline form.

	Resource Name	Group	Max.	Peak	Std. Rate	Ovt.	Cost	Work	Add New
	◢ **Group: Design**	**Design**	**150%**	**200%**			**$21,134.75**	**294.5 hrs**	
4	Dan Jump	Design	50%	100%	$75.50/hr	$0.00/hr	$7,134.75	94.5 hrs	
8	Luis Sousa	Design	100%	100%	$70.00/hr	$0.00/hr	$14,000.00	200 hrs	
	◢ **Group: Editorial**	**Editorial**	**600%**	**700%**			**$56,197.25**	**1,167 hrs**	
1	Carole Poland	Editorial	100%	100%	$2,100.00/wk	$0.00/hr	$11,182.50	213 hrs	
3	Copyeditors	Editorial	200%	200%	$45.00/hr	$0.00/hr	$13,500.00	300 hrs	
5	Hany Morcos	Editorial	100%	200%	$1,550.00/wk	$0.00/hr	$15,788.75	401 hrs	
6	Jane Dow	Editorial	100%	100%	$63.25/hr	$0.00/hr	$15,180.00	240 hrs	
7	Jun Cao	Editorial	100%	100%	$42.00/hr	$63.00/hr	$546.00	13 hrs	
	◢ **Group: Other**	**Other**	**100%**	**100%**			**$3,500.00**	**296 hrs**	
10	Tad Orman	Other	100%	100%	$0.00/hr	$0.00/hr	$0.00	296 hrs	
11	Travel	Other		0%			$3,500.00		
	◢ **Group: Production**	**Production**	**300%**	**200%**			**$300.00**	**320 hrs**	
2	Color Setting Services	Production	200%	100%	$0.00/hr	$0.00/hr	$0.00	80 hrs	
9	Printing Service	Production	100%	100%	$0.00/hr	$0.00/hr	$0.00	240 hrs	
12	Bound galley proofs	Production		0 copies/day	$15.00		$300.00	20 copies	

This grouping is similar to the sorting that you did in the previous section, but this time you will see summary cost values for each resource group.

Project applies light-colored formatting to the summary data rows. Because the summary data is derived from subordinate data, you cannot edit it directly. Displaying these summary values has no effect on the cost or schedule calculations of the plan.

To give yourself more control over how Project organizes and presents the data, you'll now create a group.

Before you create a custom group and additional customizations throughout this chapter, however, you'll make one change to Project's settings. You'll make this adjustment to prevent this custom group from becoming available in other plans that you might work with that are unrelated to this training material. (You'll switch the adjustment back to the original setting at the end of the chapter.)

2　Click the **File** tab, and then click **Options**.

The Project Options dialog box appears.

3   Click **Advanced**, and under **Display**, clear the **Automatically add new views, tables, filters, and groups to the global** check box.

4   Click **OK** to close the **Project Options** dialog box.

With that housekeeping chore completed, you are ready to create a custom group.

5   On the **View** tab, in the **Data** group, click the down arrow next to the **Group By** box and then click **More Groups**.

The More Groups dialog box appears.

In this dialog box, you can see all of the available predefined groups for tasks (when in a task view) and resources (when in a resource view). Your new group will be most similar to the Resource Group, so you'll start by copying it.

6   Make sure that **Resource Group** is selected, and then click **Copy**.

The Group Definition dialog box appears.

7   In the **Name** box, select the displayed text and then type Resource Groups by Cost.

8   In the **Field Name** column, click the first empty cell below **Group**.

9   Type or select Cost.

10   In the **Order** column for the **Cost** field, select **Descending**.

The resources will be grouped based on the values in the Group field, and then by the Cost field from highest to lowest.

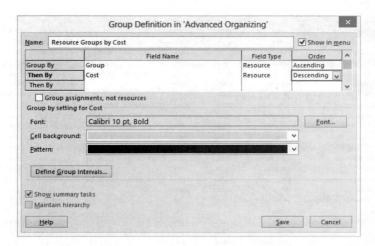

Next, you'll fine-tune the cost intervals at which Project will group the resources.

11   With the **Cost** row still selected, click **Define Group Intervals**.

The Define Group Interval dialog box appears.

12   In the **Group on** box, select **Interval**.

13   In the **Group interval** box, type 1000.

14   Click **OK**.

15   Click **Save** to close the **Group Definition** dialog box.

The new group, *Resource Groups by Cost*, now appears in the More Groups dialog box.

16   Click **Apply**.

Project applies the new group to the Resource Sheet view.

Resource Name	Group	Max.	Peak	Std. Rate	Ovt.	Cost	Work	Add Ne
▲ **Group: Design**	Design	150%	200%			$21,134.75	294.5 hrs	
▲ Cost: $14,000.00 - <$15,000.00	Design	100%	100%			$14,000.00	200 hrs	
8 Luis Sousa	Design	100%	100%	$70.00/hr	$0.00/hr	$14,000.00	200 hrs	
▲ Cost: $7,000.00 - <$8,000.00	Design	50%	100%			$7,134.75	94.5 hrs	
4 Dan Jump	Design	50%	100%	$75.50/hr	$0.00/hr	$7,134.75	94.5 hrs	
▲ **Group: Editorial**	Editorial	600%	700%			$56,197.25	1,167 hrs	
▲ Cost: $15,000.00 - <$16,000.00	Editorial	200%	300%			$30,968.75	641 hrs	
5 Hany Morcos	Editorial	100%	200%	$1,550.00/wk	$0.00/hr	$15,788.75	401 hrs	
6 Jane Dow	Editorial	100%	100%	$63.25/hr	$0.00/hr	$15,180.00	240 hrs	
▲ Cost: $13,000.00 - <$14,000.00	Editorial	200%	200%			$13,500.00	300 hrs	
3 Copyeditors	Editorial	200%	200%	$45.00/hr	$0.00/hr	$13,500.00	300 hrs	
▲ Cost: $11,000.00 - <$12,000.00	Editorial	100%	100%			$11,182.50	213 hrs	
1 Carole Poland	Editorial	100%	100%	$2,100.00/wk	$0.00/hr	$11,182.50	213 hrs	
▲ Cost: $0.00 - <$1,000.00	Editorial	100%	100%			$546.00	13 hrs	
7 Jun Cao	Editorial	100%	100%	$42.00/hr	$63.00/hr	$546.00	13 hrs	
▲ **Group: Other**	Other	100%	100%			$3,500.00	296 hrs	
▲ Cost: $3,000.00 - <$4,000.00	Other		0%			$3,500.00		
11 Travel	Other		0%			$3,500.00		
▲ Cost: $0.00 - <$1,000.00	Other	100%	100%			$0.00	296 hrs	
10 Tad Orman	Other	100%	100%	$0.00/hr	$0.00/hr	$0.00	296 hrs	
▲ **Group: Production**	Production	300%	200%			$300.00	320 hrs	
▲ Cost: $0.00 - <$1,000.00	Production	300%	200%			$300.00	320 hrs	
2 Color Setting Services	Production	200%	100%	$0.00/hr	$0.00/hr	$0.00	80 hrs	
9 Printing Service	Production	100%	100%	$0.00/hr	$0.00/hr	$0.00	240 hrs	
12 Bound galley proofs	Production		0 copies/day	$15.00		$300.00	20 copies	

The resources are grouped by their resource group value (the bands that bind together *Design*, *Editorial*, and so on) and, within each group, by cost values at $1,000 intervals (the light blue bands).

To conclude this exercise, you'll remove the grouping.

17 On the **View** tab, in the **Data** group, click the down arrow next to the **Group By** box, and click **Clear Group**.

Project removes the summary values and outline structure, leaving the original data. Again, displaying or removing a group has no effect on the data in the plan.

TIP All predefined groups and any groups you create are available to you through the Group By box on the View tab. The name of the active group appears in the box. Click the arrow on the Group By box to see other group names. If no group is applied to the current table, the words *No Group* appear in the box.

Filtering Project details

Another useful way to change how you view Project task and resource information is by filtering. As the name suggests, *filtering* hides task or resource data that does not meet the criteria you specify, displaying only the data in which you're interested. Like grouping, filtering does not change the data in your plan; it merely changes what data appears.

There are two ways to use filters. You can either apply an AutoFilter or a predefined filter to a view:

- Use *AutoFilters* for ad hoc filtering in any table in Project. Small AutoFilter arrows appear next to the names of column headings. Click the arrow to display a list of criteria by which you can filter the data. Which criteria you see depends on the type of data contained in the column—for example, AutoFilter criteria in a date column include choices such as Today and This Month, as well as a Custom option, with which you can specify your own criteria. You use AutoFilter in Project in the same way you might use AutoFilter in Microsoft Excel.

- Apply a predefined or custom filter to view only the task or resource information that meets the criteria of the filter. For example, the Critical filter displays only the tasks on the critical path. Some predefined filters, such as the Task Range filter, prompt you to enter specific criteria—for example, a range of task IDs. If a view has a filter applied, the "Filter Applied" message appears on the status bar. Both types of filters hide rows in task or resource sheet views that do not meet the criteria you specify. You might see gaps in the task or resource ID numbers. The "missing" data is only hidden and not deleted. As with sorting and grouping, when you filter data in a view, the filtering applies to all tables you can display in the view. Views that do not include tables, such as the Calendar and Network Diagram views, also support filtering (through the Filter box on the View tab), but not AutoFilters.

A very similar feature is *highlighting*. While applying a filter hides information that does not meet your criteria, applying a highlight applies a yellow format to information that does meet your criteria. Otherwise, the two features are nearly identical—you can apply built-in highlights or create custom highlights, just as with filters. When a highlight is applied, the message "Highlight Filter Applied" appears on the status bar.

13

The scenario: At Lucerne Publishing, you frequently need to look up various editing tasks because editorial work is a major focus area at the publishing house. You can quickly display editing tasks with AutoFilter, and now you'd like to create a custom filter for future use.

In this exercise, you apply a built-in filter and then create a custom filter that meets the criteria you specify.

1   On the **View** tab, in the **Task Views** group, click **Gantt Chart**.

The Gantt Chart view appears. Before you create a filter, you'll quickly see the tasks that you're interested in by applying an AutoFilter.

2   Click the **AutoFilter** arrow in the **Task Name** column heading, point to **Filters**, and then click **Custom**.

The Custom AutoFilter dialog box appears. You'd like to see only the tasks that contain the word *edit*.

3   Under **Name**, select **contains** in the first box.

4   In the adjacent box, type **edit**.

5   Click **OK** to close the **Custom AutoFilter** dialog box.

Project filters the task list to show only the tasks that contain the word *edit* and their summary tasks.

	ⓘ	Task Mode ▾	Task Name ▽	Duration ▾	Start ▾	Finish ▾		F	S	Apr 5, '15 S	M
0		🐾	◢ **Children's Book Schedule**	**158.63 days**	**Mon 4/6/15**	**Thu 11/12/15**					
1	🔄	🐾	▷ **Editorial staff meeting**	60.13 days	Mon 4/13/15	Mon 7/6/15					
15		🐾	◢ **Acquisition**	30.25 days	**Mon 4/6/15**	**Mon 5/18/15**					
17		🐾	Content edit	15 days	Mon 4/6/15	Thu 4/30/15					
18		🐾	Author review of content edit	12 days	Thu 4/30/15	Mon 5/18/15					
19		🐾	Handoff to Editorial	0 days	Mon 5/18/15	Mon 5/18/15					
20		🐾	◢ **Editorial**	29.13 days	**Mon 5/18/15**	**Fri 6/26/15**					
21		🐾	Organize manuscript for copyedit	5.13 days	Mon 5/18/15	Mon 5/25/15					
22		🐾	Copyedit	11.25 days	Mon 5/25/15	Tue 6/9/15					
23		🐾	Author review of copyedit	10 days	Tue 6/9/15	Tue 6/23/15					
24		🐾	Copyedit incorp	5.13 days	Fri 6/19/15	Fri 6/26/15					

READY   AUTOFILTER APPLIED   🐾 NEW TASKS : AUTO SCHEDULED

The status bar indicates when an AutoFilter is applied.

Note that the funnel-shaped filter indicator appears next to the Task Name column label, and the message "AutoFilter Applied" appears on the status bar. These are visual indicators that a custom AutoFilter has been applied to this column.

TIP When an AutoFilter is applied, you can point to the filter indicator, and a summary description of the applied filter appears in a ToolTip. Pointing to the AutoFilter Applied label on the status bar tells you the fields that have been filtered.

Next, you turn off the AutoFilter and create a custom filter.

6   Click the funnel-shaped filter indicator in the **Task Name** column heading, and then click **Clear All Filters**.

Project toggles the AutoFilter off, redisplaying all tasks in the plan. Now you are ready to create a custom filter.

13

7   On the **View** tab, in the **Data** group, click the arrow next to **Filter** and then click **More Filters**.

The More Filters dialog box appears. In this dialog box, you can see all the predefined filters for tasks (when in a task view) and resources (when in a resource view) that are available to you.

8   Click **New**.

The Filter Definition dialog box appears.

9   In the **Name** box, type Incomplete Editing Tasks.

10   In the first row in the **Field Name** column, type or select Name.

11   In the first row in the **Test** column, select **contains**.

12   In the first row in the **Value(s)** column, type edit.

The text value is not case-sensitive. That covers the first criterion for the filter; next, you'll add the second criterion.

13   In the second row in the **And/Or** column, select **And**.

14   In the second row in the **Field Name** column, type or select Actual Finish.

15   In the second row in the **Test** column, select **equals**.

16   In the second row in the **Value(s)** column, type NA.

NA means "not applicable" and is the way that Project marks some fields that do not yet have a value. In other words, any editing task that does not have an actual finish date must be uncompleted.

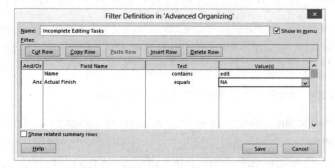

17   Click **Save** to close the **Filter Definition** dialog box.

The new filter appears in the More Filters dialog box.

18   In the list of filters, select **Incomplete Editing Tasks**, and then click **Apply**.

Project applies the new filter to the Gantt Chart view.

The name of the applied filter appears here.

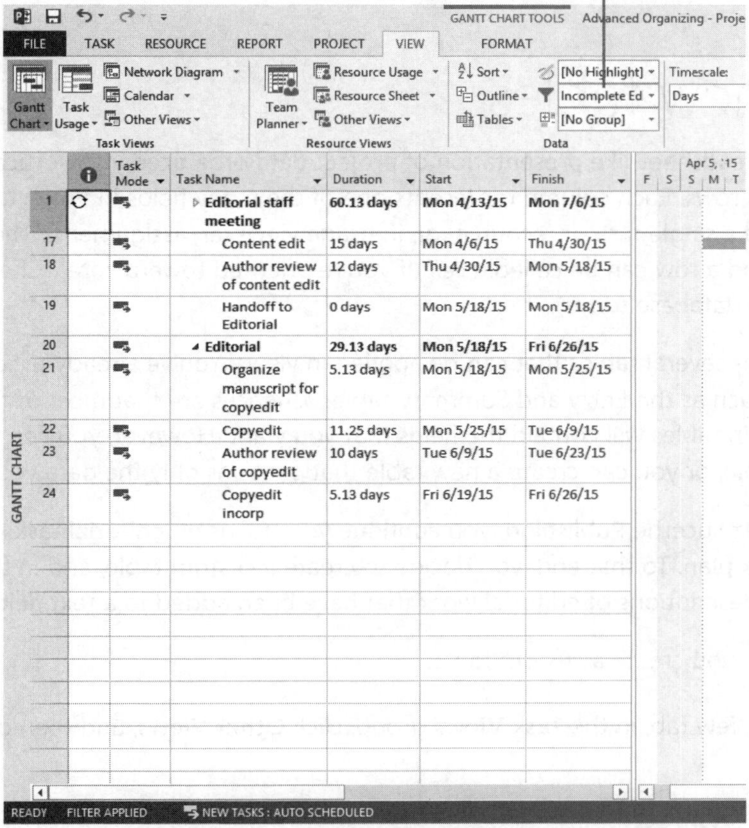

The status bar indicates when a filter is applied.

The tasks are now filtered to show only the uncompleted editing tasks. Because you haven't started tracking actual work yet, all the editing tasks are uncompleted at this time.

TIP When a filter has been applied, you can point to the Filter Applied label on the status bar to see the name of the filter.

To conclude this exercise, you will remove the filter.

13

19   On the **View** tab, in the **Data** group, click the arrow next to **Filter** and then click **Clear Filter**.

Project removes the filter. As always, displaying or removing a filter has no effect on the original data.

Creating new tables

A *table* is a spreadsheet-like presentation of project data organized into vertical columns and horizontal rows. Each column represents one of the many fields in Project, and each row represents a single task or resource (or, in usage views, an assignment). The intersection of a column and a row can be called a *cell* (if you're oriented toward spreadsheets) or a *field* (if you think in database terms).

Project includes several tables that can be applied in views. You've already used some of these tables, such as the Entry and Summary tables. Chances are that most of the time, Project's built-in tables will contain the fields that you want. However, you can modify any predefined table, or you can create a new table that contains only the data you want.

The scenario: At Lucerne Publishing, you continue your focus on editorial tasks in the new children's book plan. To that end, you decide to create a custom table, and in that table expose some descriptions of editorial work that have been added to a text field in the plan.

In this exercise, you create a custom table.

1   On the **View** tab, in the **Task Views** group, click **Other Views**, and then click **Task Sheet**.

Project displays the Task Sheet view.

2   On the **View** tab, in the **Data** group, click **Tables** and then click **More Tables**.

The More Tables dialog box appears. The Entry table should be selected.

In this dialog box, you can see all the available predefined tables for tasks (when in a task view) or resources (when in a resource view).

3   Make sure that **Entry** is selected, and then click **Copy**.

The Table Definition dialog box appears.

4   In the **Name** box, type *Editorial Table*.

Next, you will remove some fields and then add others.

5   In the **Field Name** column, click each of the following field names, and then click the **Delete Row** button after clicking each field name:

Indicators

Task Mode

Predecessors

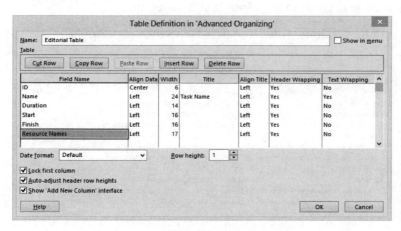

Next, you will add a field to this table definition.

6   In the **Field Name** column, click **Duration**, and then click **Insert Row**.

Project inserts an empty row above *Duration*.

7   In the **Field Name** column, click the arrow in the new row's empty field name, and then select **Editorial Focus (Text9)** from the drop-down list.

The customized text field *Editorial focus* contains some notes about the level of edit required per task. This information was previously customized for you in this plan.

8   In the **Width** column, type or click *20*.

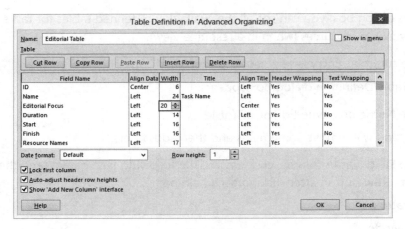

9   Click **OK** to close the **Table Definition** dialog box.

The new table appears in the More Tables dialog box.

10 Make sure that *Editorial Table* is selected, and then click **Apply**.

Project applies the new table to the Task Sheet view.

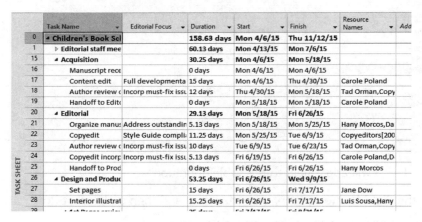

TIP You can add or remove columns quickly in the current table. To add a column, first select the column to the right of the spot where you want to add a new column. Then, on the Format tab, in the Columns group, click Insert Column. Project displays all fields available for the type of table you have displayed (task or resource); select the one that you want to add. To remove a column, right-click the column heading and click Hide Column.

In the next section, you will combine the custom filter with this custom table to create an editorial schedule view for the new book project.

Create custom fields quickly

In this section, you saw a custom field, *Text9*, that had been customized with a title of *Editorial focus* and contained details about editing activities in the new children's book plan. Project supports a wide range of custom fields, and you can add a custom field to any table easily. The rightmost column in a table is labeled *Add New Column*, and you can either click the column heading and select any field you want to add, or you can just start typing in a cell in the *Add New Column* column. When you type in a new column, Project detects the type of data you're typing and adds the correct custom field type. For example, if you type a date value, Project uses one of the custom date fields, such as Date1. If you want, you can later retitle that field to be more meaningful to you.

The custom fields supported by Project include

- Cost (up to 10 cost fields)
- Date (up to 10 date fields)
- Duration (up to 10 duration fields)
- Finish (up to 10 finish date fields)
- Flag (up to 20 "Yes" or "No" fields)
- Number (up to 20 number fields)
- Outline code (up to 10 outline codes)
- Start (up to 10 start date fields)
- Text (up to 30 text fields)

TIP The Finish and Start custom fields are available for your use; however, if you save an interim plan (introduced in Chapter 14, "Tracking progress on tasks and assignments"), the interim plan will use these fields as well and could overwrite your custom Finish and Start values.

In fact, Project supports the preceding custom fields for tasks and for resources as different sets of fields. For example, you can customize the Text1 custom field in a task view and also customize the Text1 field (a different custom field) in a resource view.

These custom fields are a great way to store additional information about tasks or resources in your plans. Normally, none of these custom fields have any impact on the scheduling of tasks or resources.

13

Creating new views

Nearly all work you perform in Project occurs in a *view*. A view might contain elements such as tables, groups, and filters. You can combine these with other elements (such as a timescaled grid in a usage view) or with graphic elements (such as the graphic representation of tasks in the chart portion of the Gantt Chart view).

Project includes dozens of views that organize information for specific purposes. You might find that you need to see your plan's information in some way that is not available in the predefined views. If Project's available views do not meet your needs, you can edit an existing view or create your own view.

The scenario: At Lucerne Publishing, you have made good use of the custom filter and table you created previously to help you focus on editorial tasks in the new children's book plan. Now you'd like to combine these customizations into a custom view that you can easily switch to whenever you like.

In this exercise, you create a new view that combines the custom filter and custom table that you created in the previous sections.

1   On the **View** tab, in the **Task Views** group, click **Other Views**, and then click **More Views**.

    The More Views dialog box appears.

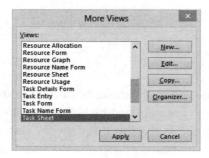

    In this dialog box, you can see all the predefined views available to you.

2   Click **New**.

    The Define New View dialog box appears. Most views occupy a single pane, but a view can consist of two separate panes. In fact, the default view in Project is really a two-pane view: the Gantt Chart and the Timeline.

3　Make sure **Single View** is selected, and then click **OK**.

The View Definition dialog box appears.

4　In the **Name** box, type Editorial Schedule View.

5　In the **Screen** box, select **Task Sheet** from the drop-down list.

In the Screen list box, you can see all the types of views supported by Project. Many of these views consist of a table (such as Resource Sheet), a table plus a chart (such as Gantt Chart), or a form (such as Task Form). Other views are purely diagrammatic, such as the Network Diagram and Timeline views.

6　In the **Table** box, select **Editorial Table** from the drop-down list.

Editorial Table is the custom table that you created earlier.

7　In the **Group** box, select **No Group** from the drop-down list.

8　In the **Filter** box, select **Incomplete Editing Tasks** from the drop-down list.

Incomplete Editing Tasks is the custom filter that you created earlier.

TIP All views are either task-centric or resource-centric views. The specific tables, groups, and filters listed in the drop-down lists in the View Definition dialog box depend on the type of view you selected in the Screen box in step 5. For example, with Task Sheet selected in the Screen field, only filters that apply to tasks, such as the Critical filter, are available in the Filter field. In addition, the specific elements available vary by view type. For example, the Table and Group options are not available if you select the Calendar view type in the Screen field shown earlier.

9　Make sure that the **Show in menu** check box is selected.

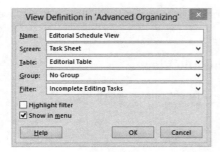

10 Click **OK** to close the **View Definition in** dialog box.

The new view appears and should be selected in the More Views dialog box.

11 Make sure that *Editorial Schedule View* is selected, and then click **Apply**.

Project applies the new view.

	Task Name	Editorial Focus	Duration	Start	Finish	Resource	Add Ne
1	▷ **Editorial staff mee**		**60.13 days**	**Mon 4/13/15**	**Mon 7/6/15**		
17	Content edit	Full developmenta	15 days	Mon 4/6/15	Thu 4/30/15	Carole Poland	
18	Author review (	Incorp must-fix issu	12 days	Thu 4/30/15	Mon 5/18/15	Tad Orman,Copy	
19	Handoff to Edit(		0 days	Mon 5/18/15	Mon 5/18/15	Carole Poland	
20	◢ **Editorial**		**29.13 days**	**Mon 5/18/15**	**Fri 6/26/15**		
21	Organize manu!	Address outstandir	5.13 days	Mon 5/18/15	Mon 5/25/15	Hany Morcos,Da	
22	Copyedit	Style Guide compli.	11.25 days	Mon 5/25/15	Tue 6/9/15	Copyeditors[200	
23	Author review (	Incorp must-fix issu	10 days	Tue 6/9/15	Tue 6/23/15	Tad Orman,Copy	
24	Copyedit incorp	Incorp must-fix issu	5.13 days	Fri 6/19/15	Fri 6/26/15	Carole Poland,D	

EDITORIAL SCHEDULE VIEW

The name of the custom view appears here.

Only uncompleted editorial tasks are now displayed, and the fields are presented in the way that you want them. Also, Project added *Editorial Schedule View* to the Other Views list in the Task Views group on the View tab. The new view appears under the Custom label, so it is always easily accessible in this plan.

Because of the housekeeping adjustment that you performed earlier in this chapter, the new custom view is not available in other plans. However, when you create your own custom views, you probably will want them available in any plan, so we'll change the display setting back to the default. That way, any custom views that you create in the future will be available in any plan you work with.

12   Click the **File** tab, and then click **Options**.

The Project Options dialog box appears.

13   Click **Advanced**, and under **Display**, select the **Automatically add new views, tables, filters, and groups to the global** check box.

14   Click **OK** to close the **Project Options** dialog box.

➡ CLEAN UP   Close the Advanced Organizing file.

Key points

- Common ways of organizing data in Project include sorting, grouping, and filtering. In all cases, Project never deletes the data; it simply changes what is displayed and how it appears.

- Project includes many built-in sort orders, groupings, and filters, and you can also create your own.

- Whereas sorting and filtering rearrange or selectively show only some data in a plan, grouping adds summary values or *roll-ups* of values, such as costs, based on whatever interval you choose.

- Tables are the primary elements of most views in Project. Project includes several built-in tables, and you can also create your own.

- You work with data in Project via views. Views can contain tables, groups, filters, and in some cases graphical charts. The Gantt Chart view, for example, consists of a table on the left and a timescaled chart on the right.

- Project contains many built-in views, and you can also create your own.

- By default, any new views, tables, filters, and groups you create in one plan are also available in all other plans you work with in Project. This behavior is controlled by the setting in the Project Options dialog box.

13

Chapter at a glance

Baseline

Update a baseline prior to tracking actual work, page 300.

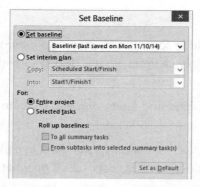

Work

Enter actual work values for tasks and assignments, page 305.

	Task Name	Work	Baseline	Variance	Actual	Remainin
0	◢ **Children's Book Sch**	**2,317.5 hrs**	**2,317.5 hrs**	**0 hrs**	**219 hrs**	**2,098.5**
1	▷ Editorial staff mee	45.5 hrs	45.5 hrs	0 hrs	7 hrs	38.5
15	◢ **Acquisition**	**444 hrs**	**444 hrs**	**0 hrs**	**212 hrs**	**232**
16	Manuscript rece	0 hrs	0 hrs	0 hrs	0 hrs	0
17	◢ Content edit	120 hrs	120 hrs	0 hrs	120 hrs	0
	Carole Pola	120 hrs	120 hrs	0 hrs	120 hrs	0
18	◢ Original art revi	164 hrs	164 hrs	0 hrs	92 hrs	72
	Hany Morcc	82 hrs	82 hrs	0 hrs	46 hrs	36
	Jane Dow	82 hrs	82 hrs	0 hrs	46 hrs	36

Timephased

Enter timephased actual work for tasks and assignments, page 312.

Details	5/10	5/17	5/24	June 5/31	6/7	6/14	6/21	6
Work			36h	87h	80h	71.75h	50h	8
Act. W			36h	87h	80h	48h		
Work			36h	27h				
Act. W			36h	27h				
Work			12h	9h				
Act. W			12h	9h				
Work			24h	18h				
Act. W			24h	18h				
Work				60h	80h	48h		
Act. W				60h	80h	48h		
Work				60h	80h	48h		
Act. W				60h	80h	48h		
Work						23.75h	50h	2
Act. W								

Reschedule

Interrupt work on the project to restart after the date you specify, page 317.

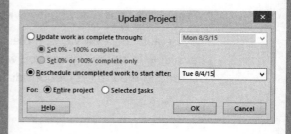

Tracking progress on tasks and assignments

IN THIS CHAPTER, YOU WILL LEARN HOW TO

- Update a previously saved baseline plan.

- Record actual work for tasks and assignments.

- Record actual work by time period.

- Interrupt work on a task, and reschedule the remaining work.

Building, verifying, and communicating a sound plan might take much or even most of your time as a project manager. However, *planning* is only the first phase of managing your projects. After the planning is completed, the implementation of the project starts—carrying out the plan that was previously developed. Ideally, projects are implemented exactly as planned, but this is seldom the case. In general, the more complex the plan and the longer its duration, the more opportunity there is for variance to appear. *Variance* is the difference between what you intended to happen (as recorded in the plan) and what actually happened (as recorded by your tracking efforts).

Properly tracking *actual* work and comparing it against the original plan enables you to identify variance early and adjust the incomplete portion of the plan when necessary. If you completed Chapter 8, "Tracking progress," you were introduced to the simpler ways of *tracking actuals* in a plan. These include recording the percentage of a task that has been completed as well as its actual start and finish dates. These methods of tracking progress are fine for many projects, but Microsoft Project 2013 also supports more detailed ways of tracking.

In this chapter, you track task-level and assignment-level *work* totals and work per time period, such as work completed per week or per day. Information distributed over time is commonly known as *timephased*, so tracking work by time period is sometimes referred to as *tracking timephased actuals*. This is the most detailed level of tracking progress available in Project.

As with simpler tracking methods, tracking timephased actuals is a way to address the most basic questions of managing a project:

- Are tasks starting and finishing as planned? If not, what will be the impact on the project's finish date?
- Are resources spending more or less time than planned to complete tasks?
- Is it taking more or less money than planned to complete tasks?

As a project manager, you must determine what level of tracking best meets the needs of your plan and stakeholders. As you might expect, the more detailed the tracking level, the more effort required from you and the resources assigned to tasks. This chapter exposes you to the most detailed tracking methods available in Project.

In this chapter, you work with different means of tracking work and handling incomplete work. You begin, however, by updating the project baseline.

PRACTICE FILES Before you can complete the exercises in this chapter, you need to copy the book's practice files to your computer. A complete list of practice files is provided in "Download the practice files" at the beginning of this book. For each exercise that has a practice file, simply browse to where you saved the book's practice file folder.

IMPORTANT If you are running Project Professional with Project Web App/Project Server, take care not to save any of the practice files you work with in this book to Project Web App (PWA). For more information, see Appendix C, "Collaborating: Project, SharePoint, and PWA."

Updating a baseline

If you completed Chapter 8, you saved a baseline for a plan. Recall that a *baseline* is a collection of important values in a plan, such as the planned start dates, finish dates, and costs of *tasks*, *resources*, and *assignments*. When you save (or set) a baseline, Project takes a "snapshot" of the existing values and saves it in the plan for future comparison.

Keep in mind that the purpose of the baseline is to record what you expected the plan to look like at one point in time. As time passes, however, you might need to change your expectations. After saving an initial baseline plan, you might need to fine-tune the plan by adding or removing tasks or assignments or making other adjustments. To keep an accurate baseline for later comparison, you have several options:

- Update the baseline for the entire project This simply replaces the original baseline values with the currently scheduled values.

- Update the baseline for selected tasks This does not affect the baseline values for other tasks or resource baseline values in the plan.

- Save a second or subsequent baseline You can save up to 11 baselines in a single plan. The first one is called *Baseline*, and the rest are Baseline 1 through Baseline 10.

The scenario: At Lucerne Publishing, the planning for the new children's book project has undergone some additional fine-tuning. This includes some adjustments to task durations and a new task in the Acquisition phase. Because of these changes, you need to capture a new baseline before work begins.

In this exercise, you compare the plan as it is currently scheduled with the baseline plan and update the baseline for the plan.

SET UP You need the Advanced Tracking A_Start file located in your Chapter14 practice file folder to complete this exercise. Open the Advanced Tracking A_Start file, and save it as Advanced Tracking A.

1   On the **View** tab, in the **Task Views** group, click the down arrow below the **Gantt Chart** button and then click **Tracking Gantt**.

The Tracking Gantt view appears.

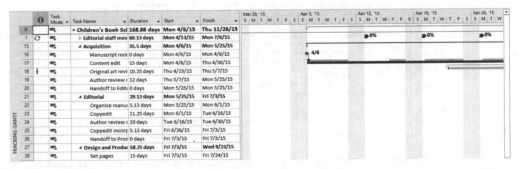

In the chart portion of this view, the tasks as they are currently scheduled appear as blue bars (if they are not *critical tasks*) or red bars (if they are critical tasks). Below them, the baseline values of each task appear as gray bars.

14

TIP In Gantt chart views, the colors, patterns, and shapes of the bars represent specific things. To see what any item on the Gantt chart represents, just point your mouse pointer at it and a description will appear in a ScreenTip. To see a complete legend of Gantt chart items and their formatting, on the Format tab, in the Bar Styles group, click Format and then click Bar Styles.

2   In the **Task Name** column, click the name of task 18, *Original art review*.

3   On the **Task** tab, in the **Editing** group, click **Scroll to Task**.

TIP Remember that to select a task quickly, even a task you can't see in the current view, press Ctrl+G. Then in the ID field of the Go To dialog box, enter a task number, and then click OK.

The Tracking Gantt view scrolls to display the Gantt bar for task 18, *Original art review*. This task was added to the plan after the initial baseline was saved. As you can see in the Tracking Gantt view, this task has no baseline bar, indicating that it has no baseline values. In addition, the additional task's duration has shifted its successor tasks off of their baselines.

To get a broader look at the plan's baseline, you'll adjust the zoom level.

4   On the **View** tab, in the **Zoom** group, in the **Timescale** box, click **Weeks**.

You can see that currently none of the later tasks in the plan match their baselines.

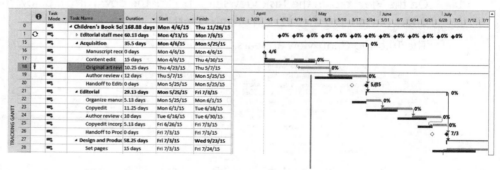

This task was added to the plan after its initial baseline was saved, so this task has no baseline bar.

To conclude this exercise, you will resave the baseline for the plan. Doing so will update all baseline information for tasks, resources, and assignments prior to tracking progress.

TIP This plan includes a previously saved baseline that you will now overwrite. That's fine at this stage of the new children's book project, where the planning is complete and you'd like to have the most up-to-date baseline before recording any actual work. However, after work has been recorded, you should be careful about overwriting any previously saved baseline values. Once you overwrite a baseline, the original values are replaced and cannot be retrieved. Saving additional baselines is often a better strategy after work on the project has begun.

5   On the **Project** tab, in the **Schedule** group, click **Set Baseline**, and then click **Set Baseline**.

The Set Baseline dialog box appears.

6   Make sure that the **Set Baseline** option is selected. In the **For** area, make sure that the **Entire project** option is selected. Note that the "last saved" date you see may differ.

TIP To update a baseline just for selected tasks, you can click Selected Tasks under the For label. When you do this, the options under Roll Up Baselines become available. You can control how baseline updates should affect the baseline values for summary tasks. For example, you could resave a baseline for a subtask and update its related summary task baseline values if desired. To remove a baseline, on the Project tab, in the Schedule group, click the Set Baseline button and then click Clear Baseline.

7   Click **OK** to update the baseline.

Project alerts you that you are about to overwrite the previously saved baseline values.

8   Click **Yes**.

Project updates the baseline values for the plan.

14

After resaving the baseline for the entire project, the baseline start, finish, and duration values (among others) match the scheduled values.

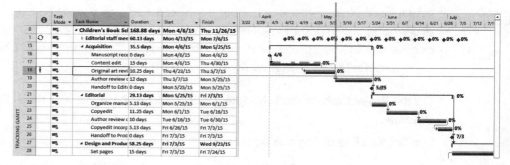

Task 18 now has a baseline, and all of the other tasks' baseline values now match their scheduled values. At this point, you have accounted for the tasks that will be in the plan. You are ready to move to the next stage of your plan, tracking actual progress.

 CLEAN UP Close the Advanced Tracking A file.

Saving interim plans

After you start tracking actual values or any time you adjust your plan, you might want to take another snapshot of the current start and finish dates. You can do this with an interim plan. Like a baseline, an *interim plan* is a set of current values from the plan that Project saves with the file. Unlike the baseline, however, an interim plan saves only the start and finish dates of tasks, not resource or assignment values. You can save up to 10 different sets of interim dates in a plan. (If you find that you need multiple snapshots of scheduled values in addition to start and finish dates, you should instead save additional baselines.)

Depending on the scope and duration of your projects, you might want to save an interim plan at any of the following junctures:

- At the conclusion of a major phase of work
- At preset time intervals, such as weekly or monthly
- Just before or after entering a large number of actual values

To save an interim plan, on the Project tab, in the Schedule group, click Set Baseline and then click Set Baseline. In the Set Baseline dialog box, select the Set Interim Plan option.

Tracking actual and remaining values for tasks and assignments

If you completed Chapter 8, you entered actual start, finish, and duration values for individual tasks. For tasks that have resources assigned to them, you can enter actual and remaining work values for the task as a whole or for specific assignments to that task. To help you understand how Project handles the actual values you enter, consider the following:

- If a task has a single resource assigned to it, the actual work values you enter for the task or assignment apply equally to both the task and the resource. For example, if you record that the assignment has five hours of actual work, those values apply to the task and to the assigned resource.

- If a task has multiple resources assigned to it, the actual work values you enter for the task are distributed among or rolled down to the assignments according to their assignment units. This level of detail is appropriate if you aren't concerned about the details at the individual assignment level.

- If a task has multiple resources assigned to it, the actual work values you enter for one assignment are rolled up to the task. However, the new actual work values do not affect the other assignments' work values on the task. This level of detail is appropriate if details at the individual assignment level are important to you.

The scenario: At Lucerne Publishing, several of the tasks in the new children's book plan have more than one resource assigned. To get a better look at how your recording of actual work on such tasks affects assigned work, you'll switch to the Task Usage view and then record actuals.

In this exercise, you record task-level and assignment-level actuals and see how the information is rolled up or down between tasks and assignments.

 SET UP You need the Advanced Tracking B_Start file located in your Chapter14 practice file folder to complete this exercise. Open the Advanced Tracking B_Start file, and save it as Advanced Tracking B.

This version of the plan includes the updated baseline values you previously saved, as well as the first actuals reported against the first tasks in the Acquisition phase.

1   On the **View** tab, in the **Task Views** group, click **Task Usage**.

14

The Task Usage view appears. As you might recall from Chapter 9, "Advanced task scheduling," the two sides of the usage view are split by a vertical divider bar. The Task Usage view lists resources under the tasks to which they're assigned. This information appears in the table on the left side. On the right side, you see rows organized under a timescale. The rows on the right side show you the scheduled work values for each task or assigned resource. The Task Usage view color-codes the rows on the right side: task rows have a shaded background, and assignment rows have a white background.

2　In the **Task Name** column, click the name of task 18, *Original art review*.

3　On the **Task** tab, in the **Editing** group, click **Scroll to Task**.

The timephased grid on the right side of the view scrolls to display the first scheduled work for the task.

Next, you'll switch the table and details shown in the view.

4　On the **View** tab, in the **Data** group, click **Tables** and then click **Work**.

The Work table appears.

	Task Name	Work	Baseline	Variance	Actual	Remaining	Details	T	W	T	F
0	◢ **Children's Book Sch**	**2,317.5 hrs**	**2,317.5 hrs**	**0 hrs**	**127 hrs**	**2,190.5 hrs**	Work	8h	8h	20h	24h
1	▷ Editorial staff mee	45.5 hrs	45.5 hrs	0 hrs	7 hrs	38.5 hrs	Work				
15	◢ **Acquisition**	**444 hrs**	**444 hrs**	**0 hrs**	**120 hrs**	**324 hrs**	Work	8h	8h	20h	24h
16	Manuscript rece	0 hrs	0 hrs	0 hrs	0 hrs	0 hrs	Work				
17	◢ Content edit	120 hrs	120 hrs	0 hrs	120 hrs	0 hrs	Work	8h	8h	8h	8h
	Carole Polar	120 hrs	120 hrs	0 hrs	120 hrs	0 hrs	Work	8h	8h	8h	8h
18	◢ Original art revi	164 hrs	164 hrs	0 hrs	0 hrs	164 hrs	Work			12h	16h
	Hany Morcc	82 hrs	82 hrs	0 hrs	0 hrs	82 hrs	Work			6h	8h
	Jane Dow	82 hrs	82 hrs	0 hrs	0 hrs	82 hrs	Work			6h	8h
19	◢ Author review	160 hrs	160 hrs	0 hrs	0 hrs	160 hrs	Work				

This table includes the Actual Work and Remaining Work columns you will work with shortly, although they might not yet be visible. The values in the Work column are the task and assignment totals for scheduled work. Note that each task's work value is the sum of its assignment work values. For example, the work total for task 18, 164 hours, is the sum of Hany Morcos' 82 hours of work on the task and Jane Dow's 82 hours.

Next, you'll change the details shown on the timephased grid on the right side of the view.

5　On the **Format** tab, in the **Details** group, click **Actual Work**.

For each task and assignment, Project now displays the Work and Actual Work rows on the timephased grid on the right side of the view.

When you display the actual work details, the Act. Work row appears in the timephased grid for every assignment, task, and summary task.

	Task Name	Work	Baseline	Variance	Actual	Remaining	Details	T	W	T	F
0	⊿ **Children's Book Sch**	**2,317.5 hrs**	**2,317.5 hrs**	**0 hrs**	**127 hrs**	**2,190.5 hrs**	Work	8h	8h	20h	24h
							Act. W	8h	8h	8h	8h
1	▷ **Editorial staff mee**	**45.5 hrs**	**45.5 hrs**	**0 hrs**	**7 hrs**	**38.5 hrs**	Work				
							Act. W				
15	⊿ **Acquisition**	**444 hrs**	**444 hrs**	**0 hrs**	**120 hrs**	**324 hrs**	Work	8h	8h	20h	24h
							Act. W	8h	8h	8h	8h
16	Manuscript rece	0 hrs	0 hrs	0 hrs	0 hrs	0 hrs	Work				
							Act. W				
17	⊿ Content edit	120 hrs	120 hrs	0 hrs	120 hrs	0 hrs	Work	8h	8h	8h	8h
							Act. W	8h	8h	8h	8h
	Carole Polar	*120 hrs*	*120 hrs*	*0 hrs*	*120 hrs*	*0 hrs*	Work	8h	8h	8h	8h
							Act. W	8h	8h	8h	8h
18	⊿ Original art revi	164 hrs	164 hrs	0 hrs	0 hrs	164 hrs	Work			12h	16h
							Act. W				
	Hany Morco	*82 hrs*	*82 hrs*	*0 hrs*	*0 hrs*	*82 hrs*	Work			6h	8h
							Act. W				
	Jane Dow	*82 hrs*	*82 hrs*	*0 hrs*	*0 hrs*	*82 hrs*	Work			6h	8h
							Act. W				
19	⊿ Author review (	160 hrs	160 hrs	0 hrs	0 hrs	160 hrs	Work				

TASK USAGE

TIP You can change the details (that is, fields) shown in the timephased grid in a usage view. You can add or remove fields and change the formatting of the fields shown. For example, you can add the Baseline Cost field to the fields shown in the usage view and format it with a different colored background. To see the available fields and formatting options, on the Format tab, in the Details group, click Add Details.

In the timephased grid, you see the scheduled work values per day. If you add up the daily work values for a specific task or assignment, the total equals the value in the Work column for that task or assignment. In a usage view, you see work values at two different levels of detail: the total value for a task or assignment and the more detailed timephased level. These two sets of values are directly related.

Next, you'll enter task-level and assignment-level actual work values and see how they are reflected in the timephased details.

6   Using the mouse, drag the vertical divider bar to the right until you can see all the columns in the Work table.

TIP When the mouse pointer is in the correct position to drag the vertical divider bar, it changes to a two-headed arrow that points left and right. Double-clicking the vertical divider bar will snap it to the nearest column's right edge.

14

To see more or less of the table on the left and the
timephased grid on the right, drag the divider bar left or right.
Double-clicking the divider bar will snap it to the nearest column.

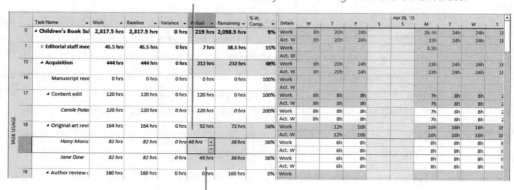

7   In the **Actual** column for task 18, *Original art review,* type or click **92h**, and then press
the Enter key.

Entering an actual value for the task causes Project
to distribute the actual values among the assigned
resources and adjust remaining work and other values.

Project highlights the most recently changed values.

Several important things occurred when you pressed Enter:

- Project applied change highlighting to the updated values in the table.

- The amount of actual work you entered was subtracted from the Remaining Work
column (labeled Remaining in the Project interface).

- The actual work was distributed to the two assignments on the task, resulting in 46 hours of actual work being recorded for one resource and 46 hours for the other resource. Likewise, the updated remaining work value was recalculated for each assignment.

- The updated actual and remaining work values were rolled up to the Acquisition summary and to the Project summary task.

- The actual work values were also redistributed to the task and assignment timephased values.

In the timephased grid side of the view, you can see the daily scheduled work and actual work values for the two resources through Thursday, April 30. Because you entered an actual work value for the entire task, Project assumes that the work was done as scheduled and records these timephased values for the resource assignments.

To conclude this exercise, you will enter actual work values at the assignment level and see the effect on the task.

8   In the **Actual** column for Hany Morcos' assignment to task 18 (which currently contains the value *46 hrs*), type or click **62h**, and then press Enter.

	Task Name	Work	Baseline	Variance	Actual	Remaining	% W. Comp.	Details	W	T	F
0	▲ Children's Book Sc	2,317.5 hrs	2,317.5 hrs	0 hrs	235 hrs	2,082.5 hrs	10%	Work	8h	20h	24h
								Act. W	8h	20h	24h
1	▷ Editorial staff mee	45.5 hrs	45.5 hrs	0 hrs	7 hrs	38.5 hrs	15%	Work			
								Act. W			
15	▲ Acquisition	444 hrs	444 hrs	0 hrs	228 hrs	216 hrs	51%	Work	8h	20h	24h
								Act. W	8h	20h	24h
16	Manuscript rece	0 hrs	0 hrs	0 hrs	0 hrs	0 hrs	100%	Work			
								Act. W			
17	▲ Content edit	120 hrs	120 hrs	0 hrs	120 hrs	0 hrs	100%	Work	8h	8h	8h
								Act. W	8h	8h	8h
	Carole Pola	120 hrs	120 hrs	0 hrs	120 hrs	0 hrs	100%	Work	8h	8h	8h
								Act. W	8h	8h	8h
18	▲ Original art revi	164 hrs	164 hrs	0 hrs	108 hrs	56 hrs	66%	Work		12h	16h
								Act. W		12h	16h
	Hany Morc	82 hrs	82 hrs	0 hrs	62 hrs	20 hrs	76%	Work		6h	8h
								Act. W		6h	8h
	Jane Dow	82 hrs	82 hrs	0 hrs	46 hrs	36 hrs	56%	Work		6h	8h
								Act. W		6h	8h
19	▲ Author review	160 hrs	160 hrs	0 hrs	0 hrs	160 hrs	0%	Work			

Entering actual work on this assignment updates the remaining work and related values on the task.

14

Hany's actual and remaining work values are updated, and those updates also roll up to the task and its summary task. (Project highlights the changed values.) However, the actual and remaining work values for Jane Dow, the other resource assigned to the task, are not affected.

9   Drag the vertical divider bar back to the left to see more of the updated timephased values for the task.

Task Name	Work	Baseline	Variance	Actual	Details	S	Apr 26, '15 S	M	T	W	T	F	S	May 3, '15 S	M	T
0 ▲ Children's Book Sc	2,317.5 hrs	2,317.5 hrs	0 hrs	235 hrs	Work			26.5h	24h	24h	18h	16h			19.5h	16h
					Act. W			23h	24h	24h	18h	8h			8h	
1 ▷ Editorial staff mee	45.5 hrs	45.5 hrs	0 hrs	7 hrs	Work			3.5h							3.5h	
					Act. W											
15 ▲ Acquisition	444 hrs	444 hrs	0 hrs	228 hrs	Work			23h	24h	24h	18h	16h			16h	16h
					Act. W			23h	24h	24h	18h	8h			8h	
16 Manuscript rece	0 hrs	0 hrs	0 hrs	0 hrs	Work											
					Act. W											
17 ▲ Content edit	120 hrs	120 hrs	0 hrs	120 hrs	Work			7h	8h	8h	2h					
					Act. W			7h	8h	8h	2h					
Carole Pola	120 hrs	120 hrs	0 hrs	120 hrs	Work			7h	8h	8h	2h					
					Act. W			7h	8h	8h	2h					
18 ▲ Original art revi	164 hrs	164 hrs	0 hrs	108 hrs	Work			16h	16h	16h	16h	16h			16h	16h
					Act. W			16h	16h	16h	16h	8h			8h	
Hany Morcc	82 hrs	82 hrs	0 hrs	62 hrs	Work			8h	8h	8h	8h	8h			8h	8h
					Act. W			8h	8h	8h	8h	8h			8h	
Jane Dow	82 hrs	82 hrs	0 hrs	46 hrs	Work			8h	8h	8h	8h	8h			8h	8h
					Act. W			8h	8h	8h	8h				8h	
19 ▲ Author review c	160 hrs	160 hrs	0 hrs	0 hrs	Work											

The actual work value entered in the table for the task and assignment is distributed across the timephased grid.

Again, Project assumes that the actual work value you entered for Hany was completed as scheduled; therefore, her work and actual work timephased values match through Monday, May 4.

✖ CLEAN UP Close the Advanced Tracking B file.

TIP You entered actual work values in this exercise, but you can also enter remaining work values or the percentage of work complete. All these values are related to each other—a change to one affects the others. You can update these values in the Work table or on the Tracking tab of the Assignment Information dialog box (when an assignment is selected).

Tracking a task's actual work-complete value is more detailed than entering a simple percentage-complete value on a task. However, neither method is as detailed as entering timephased actual work for tasks or assignments (as you will see in the next section). There's nothing wrong with tracking actual work at the task or assignment level (or simply entering a percentage-complete value, for that matter) if that level of detail meets your needs. In fact, whether you see the timephased details or not, Project always distributes any percentage complete or task-level or assignment-level actual work value you enter into corresponding timephased values, as you saw earlier. This is one reason why new Project users sometimes are surprised to encounter extremely precise values, such as 7.67 hours of work, scheduled for a particular day. If you generally understand the math that Project is following, however, you can figure out where such numbers come from. On the other hand, you might not care about this level of scheduling detail—and that's OK, too.

Entering actual costs manually

Whenever you've entered actual work values in this chapter, Project has calculated actual cost values for the affected task, its summary task, the resources assigned to the task, and the entire project. By default, Project calculates actual costs and does not allow you to enter them directly. In most cases, this is what we recommend and what is done with the practice files used in this book. However, if you want to enter actual cost values yourself in your own plans, follow these steps.

> **IMPORTANT** The following procedure is provided for your general information; however, do not follow this procedure now if you are completing the exercises in this book. Doing so will produce results that will not match those shown in this book.

1   On the **File** tab, click **Options**.
    The Project Options dialog box appears.

2   Click the **Schedule** tab.

3   Under the **Calculation options for this project** label, clear the **Actual costs are always calculated by Project** check box.

4   Click **OK**.

After automatic cost calculation is turned off, you can enter or import task-level or assignment-level actual costs in the Actual field. This field is available in several locations, such as the Cost table. You can also enter actual cost values daily or at another interval in any timescale view, such as the Task Usage or Resource Usage view. With a usage view displayed, on the Format tab, in the Details group, click Actual Cost.

14

Tracking timephased actual work for tasks and assignments

Entering *timephased* actuals requires more work on the project manager's part and might require more work from resources to inform the project manager of their daily or weekly actuals. However, using timephased actuals gives you far more detail about the project's task and resource status than the other methods used for entering actuals. Entering timephased values might be the best approach to take if you have a group of tasks or an entire project that includes the following:

- High-risk tasks

- Relatively short-duration tasks in which a variance of even one day could put the overall project at risk

- Tasks for which you'd like to develop or validate throughput metrics, or rates at which a given quantity of a deliverable can be completed over a given time period, such as *Copyedit 3000 words per day*

- Tasks in which sponsors or other stakeholders have an especially strong interest

- Tasks that require hourly billing for labor

When you need to track actual work at the most detailed level possible, use the timephased grid in the Task Usage or Resource Usage view. In either view, you can enter actual work values for individual assignments daily, weekly, or at whatever time period you want (by adjusting the timescale). For example, if a task has three resources assigned to it and you know that two resources worked on the task for eight hours one day and the third resource worked for six hours, you can enter these as three separate values on a timephased grid.

TIP If your organization uses a timesheet reporting system for tracking actual work, you might be able to use this timesheet data in Project as timephased actuals. You might not need to track at this level, but if resources complete timesheets for other purposes (billing other departments within the organization, for example), you can use their data and save yourself some work.

The scenario: At Lucerne Publishing, the Acquisition phase of work on the new children's book plan has been completed, and the Editorial phase has just begun. Because of the larger number of resources involved and the variability of the editorial work, these tasks are the riskiest ones so far in the project. To manage the actuals of these tasks in the most detailed way possible, you will record timephased actuals.

In this exercise, you enter some actuals for tasks, for assignments, and for specific time periods.

⊙ SET UP You need the Advanced Tracking C_Start file located in the Chapter14 practice file folder. Open the Advanced Tracking C_Start file, and save it as Advanced Tracking C.

1　Click the expand\collapse arrow next to task 15, *Acquisition*, to collapse this phase of the plan.

This phase of work has been completed.

2　In the **Task Name** column, click the name of task 22, *Organize manuscript for copyedit*, and then, on the **Task** tab, in the **Editing** group, click **Scroll to Task**.

Project scrolls the timephased grid to display the first scheduled work values of the Editorial phase.

	Task Name	Work	Baseline	Variance	Actual	Details	May 24, '15 S	M	T	W	T	F	S	May 31, '15 S	M	T	W
0	⊿ Children's Book Schedule	2,341.5 hrs	2,317.5 hrs	24 hrs	492.5 hrs	Work		11.5h	8h	12h	12h	12h			15.5h	12h	16h
						Act. W		11.5h	8h								
1	▷ Editorial staff meeting	45.5 hrs	45.5 hrs	0 hrs	24.5 hrs	Work		3.5h							3.5h		
						Act. W		3.5h									
15	▷ Acquisition	468 hrs	444 hrs	24 hrs	468 hrs	Work		8h	8h								
						Act. W		8h	8h								
21	⊿ Editorial	400 hrs	400 hrs	0 hrs	0 hrs	Work				12h	12h	12h			12h	12h	16h
						Act. W											
22	⊿ Organize manuscript for copyedit	60 hrs	60 hrs	0 hrs	0 hrs	Work				12h	12h	12h			12h	12h	
						Act. W											
	Dan Jump	20 hrs	20 hrs	0 hrs	0 hrs	Work				4h	4h	4h			4h	4h	
						Act. W											
	Hany Morcos	40 hrs	40 hrs	0 hrs	0 hrs	Work				8h	8h	8h			8h	8h	
						Act. W											
23	⊿ Copyedit	180 hrs	180 hrs	0 hrs	0 hrs	Work											16h
						Act. W											
	Copyeditors	180 hrs	180 hrs	0 hrs	0 hrs	Work											16h
						Act. W											
24	▷ Author review	100 hrs	100 hrs	0 hrs	0 hrs	Work											

The first timephased actual work values you will enter are at the task level and not for specific assignments.

3　In the timephased grid, click the cell at the intersection of the Wednesday, May 27 column and the task 22 actual work row. The actual work row is directly below the work row, which contains the value *12h*.

TIP If you point to the name of a day on the timescale, Project will display the full date of that day in a ScreenTip. You can change the formatting of the timescale to control the time period in which you enter actual values in the timephased grid. For example, you can format the timescale to show weeks rather than days; when you enter an actual value at the weekly level, that value is distributed over the week.

4　Type **9h**, and then press the Tab key.

14

Here is the first timephased actual work value you entered.

As soon as you entered the first actual value for the task, the scheduled work value changed to match it. Both work and actual work values rolled up to the summary task levels and were distributed among the specific assignments to the task. You can see this happen in the timephased grid on the right and the table on the left.

5   In the Thursday, May 28 actual work cell, type **15h**, and then press Tab.

TIP When entering actual work, you do not need to include the "h" abbreviation (to denote hours). You can simply enter the number and Project will record it as hours. Hours is the default work value for data entry. If you want, you can change this. Click the File tab and then click Options. On the Schedule tab of the Project Options dialog box, in the Work Is Entered In box, select the default time increment you want.

6   For task 22, enter the following actual work values for the dates listed:

Date	Actual Hours
Friday, May 29	12
Monday, June 1	12
Tuesday, June 2	15

	Task Name	Work	Baseline	Variance	Actual	Details	May 24, '15 S	M	T	W	T	F	S	May 31, '15 S	M	T	W
0	⊿ Children's Book Schedule	2,344.5 hrs	2,317.5 hrs	27 hrs	555.5 hrs	Work		11.5h	8h	9h	15h	12h			15.5h	15h	16h
						Act. W		11.5h	8h	9h	15h	12h			12h	15h	
1	▷ Editorial staff meeting	45.5 hrs	45.5 hrs	0 hrs	24.5 hrs	Work		3.5h							3.5h		
						Act. W		3.5h									
15	▷ Acquisition	468 hrs	444 hrs	24 hrs	468 hrs	Work		8h	8h								
						Act. W		8h	8h								
21	⊿ Editorial	403 hrs	400 hrs	3 hrs	63 hrs	Work				9h	15h	12h			12h	15h	16h
						Act. W				9h	15h	12h			12h	15h	
22	⊿ Organize manuscript for copyedit	63 hrs	60 hrs	3 hrs	63 hrs	Work				9h	15h	12h			12h	15h	
						Act. W				9h	15h	12h			12h	15h	
	Dan Jump	21 hrs	20 hrs	1 hr	21 hrs	Work				3h	5h	4h			4h	5h	
						Act. W				3h	5h	4h			4h	5h	
	Hany Morcos	42 hrs	40 hrs	2 hrs	42 hrs	Work				6h	10h	8h			8h	10h	
						Act. W				6h	10h	8h			8h	10h	
23	⊿ Copyedit	180 hrs	180 hrs	0 hrs	0 hrs	Work											16h
						Act. W											
	Copyeditors	180 hrs	180 hrs	0 hrs	0 hrs	Work											16h
						Act. W											
24	⊿ Author review	100 hrs	100 hrs	0 hrs	0 hrs	Work											

This step concludes the actual work recorded at the task level. Next, you'll enter actual work values on a task at the assignment level.

For task 23, *Copyedit*, you have weekly actual work values from the assigned resource. The copyeditors have completed the task. For this task, you'll adjust the timescale to record weekly actual values.

7   On the **View** tab, in the **Zoom** group, in the **Timescale** box, click **Weeks**.

8   Enter the following actual work values into the timephased grid for the Copyeditors' assignment to task 23, *Copyedit*:

Date (Week of)	Actual Hours
May 31	60
June 7	80
June 14	48

	Task Name	Work	Baseline	Variance	Actual	Details	5/10	5/17	5/24	June 5/31	6/7	6/14	6/21	July 6/28
21	⊿ Editorial	411 hrs	400 hrs	11 hrs	251 hrs	Work			36h	87h	80h	71.75h	50h	82.75h
						Act. W			36h	87h	80h	48h		
22	⊿ Organize manuscript for copyedit	63 hrs	60 hrs	3 hrs	63 hrs	Work		•	36h	27h				
						Act. W			36h	27h				
	Dan Jump	21 hrs	20 hrs	1 hr	21 hrs	Work			12h	9h				
						Act. W			12h	9h				
	Hany Morcos	42 hrs	40 hrs	2 hrs	42 hrs	Work			24h	18h				
						Act. W			24h	18h				
23	⊿ Copyedit	188 hrs	180 hrs	8 hrs	188 hrs	Work				60h	80h	48h		
						Act. W				60h	80h	48h		
	Copyeditors	188 hrs	180 hrs	8 hrs	188 hrs	Work				60h	80h	48h		
						Act. W				60h	80h	48h		
24	⊿ Author review of copyedit	100 hrs	100 hrs	0 hrs	0 hrs	Work						23.75h	50h	26.25h
						Act. W								

The resource's actual work values were rolled up to the task's actual work values. The original work values were saved in the baseline in case you need to refer to them later.

14

TIP In this exercise, you saw how task and assignment values are directly related; an update to one directly affects the other. However, you can break this relationship if you want. Doing so enables you to record progress for resource assignments, for example, and manually enter actual values for the tasks to which those resources are assigned. You normally should not break this relationship unless you have special reporting needs within your organization—for example, you must follow a status reporting methodology based on something other than the actual values recorded for assignments in plans. To break this relationship, do the following. On the File tab, click Options. In the Project Options dialog box, click the Schedule tab and then under the Calculation options for this project label, clear the Updating Task Status Updates Resource Status check box. This setting applies to the entire plan you have open at the time; you cannot apply it to only some tasks within a plan.

 CLEAN UP Close the Advanced Tracking C file.

Project management focus: Collecting actuals from resources

The view you used in the previous exercise is similar to a time card. In fact, to enter assignment-level actual work values, you might need some form of paper time card or its electronic equivalent. Several methods are used to collect such data from resources, assuming that you need to track actual and remaining work at this level of detail. Some collection methods include the following:

- **Collect actual values yourself** This method is feasible if you communicate with only a small group of resources on a frequent basis, such as a weekly status meeting. It's also a good opportunity to talk directly to the resources about any blocking issues or surprises they might have encountered (either positive or negative) while performing the work.

- **Collect actuals through a formal status reporting system** This technique might work through the already-existing hierarchy of your organization and serve additional purposes besides project status reporting.

Regardless of the data collection methods you might use, be aware that resources might have some concern about how their actual work values might reflect on their overall performance. You might need to communicate to resources that schedule actuals help in managing the project, but performance evaluation is a business management focus, not a project management one.

Speaking of time cards, depending on how your organization operates you might want to explore Project Professional's interoperability with SharePoint and Project Web App (PWA) online services. For more information, see Appendix C, "Collaborating: Project, SharePoint, and PWA."

Rescheduling incomplete work

During the course of a project, work might occasionally be interrupted for a specific task or for the entire project. Should this happen, you can have Project reschedule the remaining work to restart after the date you specify.

When you reschedule incomplete work, you specify the date after which work can resume—the rescheduled date. Here is how Project handles tasks in relation to the rescheduled date:

- If the task does not have any actual work recorded for it prior to the rescheduled date and does not have a constraint applied, the entire task is rescheduled to begin after that date.

- If the task has some actual work recorded prior to the rescheduled date but none after it, the task is split so that all remaining work starts after the rescheduled date. The actual work is not affected.

- If the task has some actual work recorded for it prior to, as well as after, the rescheduled date, the task is not affected.

The scenario: At Lucerne Publishing, work on the Editorial phase of the new children's book plan has been completed. The team has started work on the next phase, Design And Production. However, you need to troubleshoot a delay in work caused by an unforeseen problem.

In this exercise, you reschedule uncompleted work.

 SET UP You need the Advanced Tracking D_Start file located in the Chapter14 practice file folder. Open Advanced Tracking D_Start file, and save it as Advanced Tracking D.

The plan is currently in the Task Usage view. Next, you'll switch to the Gantt Chart view.

1   On the **View** tab, in the **Task Views** group, click the down arrow below the **Gantt Chart** button, and then click **Gantt Chart**.

2   Scroll the Gantt Chart view up so that the *1st Pages review* (task 30) appears near the top of the view.

3   In the **Task Name** column, click the name of task 31, *Proofread and index*.

Task 31, *Proofread and index* currently has two days of actual work completed and several days of scheduled work remaining.

Progress bars indicate the portion
of the task that has been completed.

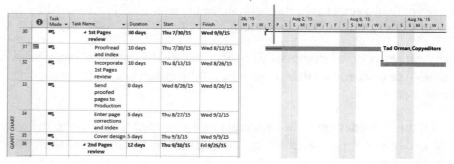

You have learned that over the weekend of August 1, a water pipe burst in the proofreaders' office. None of the project's equipment or material was damaged, but the cleanup will delay work until Wednesday, August 5. This effectively stops work on the proofreading task for a few days. Next, you will reschedule incomplete work so that the project can begin again on Wednesday.

4   On the **Project** tab, in the **Status** group, click **Update Project**.

The Update Project dialog box appears.

5   Select the **Reschedule uncompleted work to start after** option, and in the text box, type or select 8/4/15.

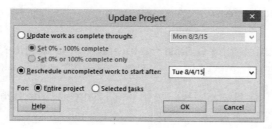

6   Click **OK** to close the **Update Project** dialog box.

Project splits task 31 so that the incomplete portion of the task is delayed until Wednesday.

Rescheduling work for the plan causes Project to split the task and then reschedule the remainder of it (and all subsequent tasks) after the date you specified.

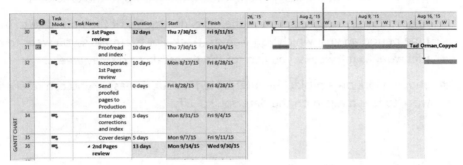

As you can see, although the duration of task 31 remains 10 working days, its finish date and subsequent start dates for successor tasks have been pushed out. Although you addressed a specific problem, in doing so, you created other problems in the remainder of the project. You will address this and other problems in the plan in later chapters.

Here are a few other things to keep in mind when tracking progress:

- You can turn off Project's ability to reschedule incomplete work on tasks for which any actual work has been recorded. On the File tab, click Options. In the Project Options dialog box, click the Schedule tab, and then, under the Scheduling Options For This Project label, clear the Split In-Progress Tasks check box.

- If you use status dates for reporting actuals, Project supports several options for controlling the way completed and incomplete segments of a task are scheduled around the status date. You can see the options by doing the following: On the File tab, click Options. In the Project Options dialog box, click the Advanced tab, and then, under the Calculation Options For This Project label, adjust the settings Move End Of Completed Parts After Status Date Back To Status Date and the three other check boxes below it.

✖ CLEAN UP Close the Advanced Tracking D file.

14

Key points

- Saving a baseline saves a large set of task, resource, and assignment values in a plan. Saving an interim plan, however, saves only the start and finish dates of tasks.

- If you track work at the task level, work rolls down to the assignments. Conversely, if you track work at the assignment level, work rolls up to the task level.

- In usage views, you can change the time increments of the timescale to match the time period against which you want to track. For example, if you want to record actual work as full weeks, you can set the timescale to display weeks.

- Should work on a project be interrupted for some reason, you can reschedule the work to begin again on the date you specify.

Chapter at a glance

Compare

Compare actual progress against the baseline plan, page 324.

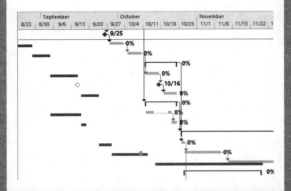

Task

See overbudget tasks, page 330.

Task Name	Fixed	Fixed Cost	Total Cost	Baseline	V
0 ▲ Children's Book Sch	$0.00	Prorated	$112,723.50	$97,588.00	
1 ▷ Editorial staff meeting	$0.00	Prorated	$2,223.00	$2,223.00	
15 ▲ Acquisition	$0.00	Prorated	$18,804.00	$18,264.00	
16 Manuscript rece	$0.00	Prorated	$0.00	$0.00	
17 Content edit	$0.00	Prorated	$6,300.00	$6,300.00	
18 Original art revi	$0.00	Prorated	$8,364.00	$8,364.00	
19 Author review	$0.00	Prorated	$4,140.00	$3,600.00	
20 Handoff to Edit	$0.00	Prorated	$0.00	$0.00	
21 ▲ Editorial	$0.00	Prorated	$16,201.00	$15,670.00	
22 Organize manu:	$0.00	Prorated	$3,213.00	$3,060.00	
23 Copyedit	$0.00	Prorated	$8,460.00	$8,100.00	
24 Author review	$0.00	Prorated	$918.00	$900.00	
25 Copyedit incorp	$0.00	Prorated	$3,610.00	$3,610.00	
26 Handoff to Proc	$0.00	Prorated	$0.00	$0.00	
27 ▲ Design and Produc	$0.00	Prorated	$60,743.50	$46,679.00	
28 Set pages	$0.00	Prorated	$7,590.00	$7,590.00	
29 Interior illustrat	$0.00	Prorated	$15,234.50	$13,050.00	

Resource

See overbudget resources, page 333.

Resource Name	Cost	Baseline	Variance	Actual Cost	F
Copyeditors	$20,718.00	$13,500.00	$7,218.00	$20,718.00	
Hany Morcos	$25,432.25	$22,066.25	$3,366.00	$16,654.75	
Dan Jump	$11,740.25	$8,644.75	$3,095.50	$9,399.75	
Luis Sousa	$15,456.00	$14,000.00	$1,456.00	$9,856.00	
Carole Poland	$11,182.50	$11,182.50	$0.00	$8,767.50	
Color Setting Ser	$0.00	$0.00	$0.00	$0.00	
Jane Dow	$18,848.50	$18,848.50	$0.00	$12,776.50	
Jun Cao	$546.00	$546.00	$0.00	$294.00	
Printing Service	$0.00	$0.00	$0.00	$0.00	
Tad Orman	$0.00	$0.00	$0.00	$0.00	
Travel	$3,500.00	$3,500.00	$0.00	$0.00	
Bound galley pro	$300.00	$300.00	$0.00	$0.00	

Stoplight

Use customized fields and formulas to create a stoplight view, page 336.

	Baseline	Variance	Actual	Remaining	Overbudget	A
3.50	$97,588.00	$15,135.50	$78,466.50	$34,257.00		
3.00	$2,223.00	$0.00	$1,197.00	$1,026.00		
4.00	$18,264.00	$540.00	$18,804.00	$0.00		
0.00	$0.00	$0.00	$0.00	$0.00		
0.00	$6,300.00	$0.00	$6,300.00	$0.00	😐	
4.00	$8,364.00	$0.00	$8,364.00	$0.00	😐	
0.00	$3,600.00	$540.00	$4,140.00	$0.00	☹	
0.00	$0.00	$0.00	$0.00	$0.00		
1.00	$15,670.00	$531.00	$16,201.00	$0.00		
3.00	$3,060.00	$153.00	$3,213.00	$0.00	😐	
0.00	$8,100.00	$360.00	$8,460.00	$0.00	😐	
3.00	$900.00	$18.00	$918.00	$0.00	😐	
0.00	$3,610.00	$0.00	$3,610.00	$0.00	😐	
0.00	$0.00	$0.00	$0.00	$0.00		

Viewing and reporting project status

IN THIS CHAPTER, YOU WILL LEARN HOW TO

- Determine which tasks were started or completed late.

- View task costs at summary and detail levels.

- Examine resource costs and variance.

- Use custom fields to create a stoplight view that illustrates each task's cost variance.

After a project's *baseline* has been set and work has begun, the primary focus of the project manager shifts from planning to collecting, updating, and analyzing project performance details. For most projects, these performance details boil down to three primary questions or vital signs:

- How much *work* was required to complete a task?

- Did the *task* start and finish on time?

- What was the cost of completing the task?

Comparing the answers to these questions against the baseline provides the project manager and other *stakeholders* with a good way to measure the project's progress and to determine when corrective action might be necessary.

Where the scheduled or actual project performance differs from the baseline plan, you have variance. *Variance* is usually measured as time, such as days behind schedule, or as cost, such as dollars over budget. After initial project planning is complete, many project managers spend most of their time identifying, investigating, and, in many cases, responding to variance. However, before you can respond to variance, you must first identify it. That is the subject of this chapter.

Communicating project status to key stakeholders, such as customers and sponsors, is arguably the most important function of a project manager and one that might occupy much of your time. Although the perfect flow of communications cannot guarantee a project's success, a project with poor communications flow is almost guaranteed to fail.

A key to communicating project status properly is knowing the following:

- Who needs to know the project's status, and for what purpose?
- What format or level of detail do these people need?

The time to answer these questions is in the initial planning phase of the project. After work on the project is under way, your main communications task will be reporting project status. This can take several forms:

- Status reports that describe where the project is in terms of cost, scope, and schedule (the three sides of the *project triangle,* as described in Appendix A, "A short course in project management")
- Progress reports that document the specific accomplishments of the project team
- Forecasts that predict future project performance

In this chapter, you'll look at project status in terms of schedule variance and costs.

PRACTICE FILES Before you can complete the exercises in this chapter, you need to copy the book's practice files to your computer. A complete list of practice files is provided in "Download the practice files" at the beginning of this book. For each exercise that has a practice file, simply browse to where you saved the book's practice file folder.

IMPORTANT If you are running Project Professional with Project Web App/Project Server, take care not to save any of the practice files you work with in this book to Project Web App (PWA). For more information, see Appendix C, "Collaborating: Project, SharePoint, and PWA."

Identifying tasks that have slipped

When tasks start or finish earlier or later than planned, schedule variance is the result. One cause of schedule variance is delays in starting or finishing tasks. You certainly want to know about tasks that started late or future tasks that might not start as scheduled. It's also helpful to identify completed tasks that did not start on time to try to determine why this occurred.

There are different ways to view tasks with variance, depending on the type of information you want:

- Apply the Tracking Gantt view to compare tasks' baseline dates graphically with their actual or scheduled dates. (To do this, on the View tab, in the Task Views group, click the down arrow below the Gantt Chart button and then click Tracking Gantt.)

- Apply the Detail Gantt view to show graphically each task's slippage from baseline. (To do this, on the View tab, in the Task Views group, click Other Views, click More Views, and then double-click Detail Gantt.)

- Apply the Variance table to a task view to see the number of days of variance for each task's start and finish dates. (To do this, on the View tab, in the Data group, click Tables and then click Variance.)

- Filter for delayed or slipping tasks with the Slipped/Late Progress, Slipping Tasks, or Late Tasks filter. (To do this, on the View tab, in the Data group, in the Filter box, select the filter that you want to apply.)

Project management focus: Is variance ever a good thing?

In project management, we generally look for variance that can have an adverse effect on a project, such as variance that pushes out the finish date or increases the cost of a project. However, the term *variance* refers to any difference between planned and actual schedule events—even differences that have a helpful effect, such as an earlier finish date or a lower-than-expected cost. Should you have the good fortune of managing a project that experiences such helpful variance, the techniques described here will help you identify the beneficial variance as well as any adverse variance. Your focus as a project manager is basically the same regardless of the nature of the variance—watch for it, and when it does occur, communicate it and its effects to project sponsors and other stakeholders and (if it's adverse variance) mitigate against it according to the nature of the project.

The scenario: At Lucerne Publishing, work on the children's book plan is well underway. You have encountered some variance from plan—in other words, actual work has not always matched the plan as captured in its baseline. You'd like to get a better look at this variance in the plan.

In this exercise, you use views and filters to identify variance on tasks and the plan as a whole. To begin your analysis of tasks that have slipped, you'll start at the highest level—the project summary information.

SET UP You need the Reporting Status_Start file located in your Chapter15 practice file folder to complete this exercise. Open the Reporting Status_Start file, and save it as Reporting Status.

1   On the **Project** tab, in the **Properties** group, click **Project Information**.

The Project Information dialog box appears.

2   Click **Statistics**.

The Project Statistics dialog box appears.

Project Statistics for 'Reporting Status'			
	Start		Finish
Current	Mon 4/6/15		Thu 12/24/15
Baseline	Mon 4/6/15		Thu 11/26/15
Actual	Mon 4/6/15		NA
Variance	0d		20.13d

	Duration	Work	Cost
Current	189d	2,722.1h	$112,723.50
Baseline	168.88d	2,317.5h	$97,588.00
Actual	115.52d	1,865.1h	$78,466.50
Remaining	73.48d	857h	$34,257.00

Percent complete:
Duration: 61%   Work: 69%   Close

In this dialog box, you can see (among other things) that the new book plan at Lucerne Publishing currently has substantial schedule variance on the finish date. The overall project finish date has slipped out by just over 20 days.

3   Click **Close** to close the **Project Statistics** dialog box.

For the remainder of this exercise, you will use various techniques to examine the specific task variance.

4   On the **View** tab, in the **Task Views** group, click the down arrow below the **Gantt Chart** button and then click **Tracking Gantt**.

Project displays the Tracking Gantt view.

5   On the **View** tab, in the **Zoom** group, click the down arrow next to the **Timescale** box and then click **Weeks**.

The timescale adjusts to show more of the plan.

6   In the **Task Name** column, click the name of task 33, *Send proofed pages to Production*, and scroll the Tracking Gantt view up so that task 33 appears near the top of the view.

7   On the **Task** tab, in the **Editing** group, click **Scroll to Task**.

TIP You can also right-click the task name and in the shortcut menu that appears, click Scroll To Task.

In the chart portion of this view, the tasks as they are currently scheduled appear as blue bars (if they are not on the *critical path*) or red bars (if they are on the critical path). In the lower half of each task's row, the baseline start and finish dates of each task appear as gray bars.

A gray bar represents the original (baseline) schedule in the Tracking Gantt view.

A blue or red bar represents the task as it is currently scheduled or when it was completed.

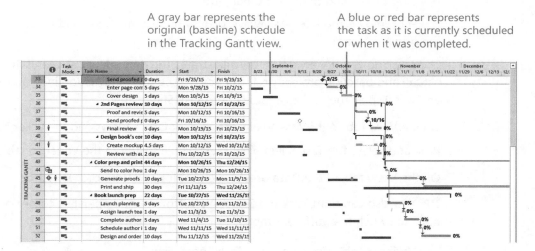

By comparing the currently scheduled Gantt bars with the baseline Gantt bars, you can see what tasks started later than planned or took longer to complete.

TIP To see details about any bar or other item in a Gantt Chart view, position the mouse pointer over it. After a moment, a ScreenTip appears with details.

To focus on only the slipping tasks, you will apply a filter.

8   On the **View** tab, in the **Data** group, click the down arrow next to the **Filter** box (it initially contains *[No Filter]*), and then click **More Filters**.

The More Filters dialog box appears. In this dialog box, you can see all the predefined filters for tasks (when in a task view) and resources (when in a resource view) that are available to you.

9   Click **Slipping Tasks**, and then click **Apply**.

Project filters the task list to show only uncompleted tasks that, as they are now scheduled, have slipped from their baseline schedule.

Note the gaps in the task ID numbers. Tasks 2 through 26, for example, do not appear with the filter applied because they are already complete.

At this point in the schedule, the scheduled start date of the uncompleted tasks has slipped quite a bit. Most of these tasks' scheduled Gantt bars are formatted red to indicate that they are critical, meaning that any delay in completing these tasks will delay the project's finish date.

10   On the **View** tab, in the **Data** group, click the arrow next to **Filter** (it now contains *[Slipping tasks]*) and then click **Clear Filter**.

Project removes the filter. As always, displaying or removing a filter has no effect on the original data.

The Tracking Gantt view graphically illustrates the difference between scheduled, actual, and baseline project performance. To see this information in a table format, you will display the Variance table in the Task Sheet view.

11   On the **View** tab, in the **Task Views** group, click **Other Views** and then click **Task Sheet**.

Project displays the Task Sheet view. Next, you'll switch to the Variance table.

12   On the **View** tab, in the **Data** group, click **Tables** and then click **Variance**.

TIP You also can right-click the Select All button in the upper-left corner of the active table to switch to a different table.

The Variance table appears in the Task Sheet view.

	Task Mode	Task Name	Start	Finish	Baseline Start	Baseline Finish	Start Var.	Finish Var.
0		⊿ Children's Book	Mon 4/6/15	Thu 12/24/15	Mon 4/6/15	Thu 11/26/15	0 days	20.13 days
1		▷ Editorial staff	Mon 4/13/15	Thu 8/6/15	Mon 4/13/15	Mon 7/6/15	0 days	23 days
15		▷ Acquisition	Mon 4/6/15	Tue 5/26/15	Mon 4/6/15	Mon 5/25/15	0 days	1.5 days
21		⊿ Editorial	Wed 5/27/15	Mon 7/6/15	Mon 5/25/15	Fri 7/3/15	1.5 days	0.78 days
22		Organize m:	Wed 5/27/15	Tue 6/2/15	Mon 5/25/15	Mon 6/1/15	1.5 days	1.38 days
23		Copyedit	Wed 6/3/15	Wed 6/17/15	Mon 6/1/15	Tue 6/16/15	1.38 days	0.63 days
24		Author revi:	Wed 6/17/15	Wed 7/1/15	Tue 6/16/15	Tue 6/30/15	0.63 days	0.83 days
25		Copyedit in	Mon 6/29/15	Mon 7/6/15	Fri 6/26/15	Fri 7/3/15	0.78 days	0.78 days
26		Handoff to I	Mon 7/6/15	Mon 7/6/15	Fri 7/3/15	Fri 7/3/15	0.78 days	0.78 days
27		⊿ Design and Pro	Mon 7/6/15	Fri 10/23/15	Fri 7/3/15	Wed 9/23/15	0.78 days	22.13 days
28		Set pages	Mon 7/6/15	Mon 7/27/15	Fri 7/3/15	Fri 7/24/15	0.78 days	0.78 days
29		Interior illu:	Mon 7/6/15	Wed 7/29/15	Fri 7/3/15	Fri 7/24/15	0.78 days	3.13 days
30		⊿ 1st Pages re	Thu 7/30/15	Fri 10/9/15	Fri 7/24/15	Fri 9/4/15	3.13 days	25.13 days
31		Proofrea:	Thu 7/30/15	Fri 8/28/15	Fri 7/24/15	Fri 8/7/15	3.13 days	15.13 days
32		Incorpor:	Mon 8/31/15	Fri 9/25/15	Fri 8/7/15	Fri 8/21/15	15.13 days	25.13 days

In this table, you can view the scheduled, baseline, and variance values per task.

Project management focus: Getting the word out

If you work in an organization that is highly focused on projects and project management, chances are that standard methods and formats already exist within your organization for reporting project status. If not, you might be able to introduce project status formats that are based on clear communication and effective project-management principles.

Techniques you can use in Project to help you report project status include the following:

- Print the Project Overview report. (To do this, on the Report tab, in the View Reports group, click Dashboards and then click Project Overview.) For more information, see Chapter 7, "Formatting and sharing your plan," and Chapter 18, "Advanced report formatting."

- If you have Microsoft Excel or Microsoft Visio, print a status-focused visual report. (To do this, on the Report tab, in the Export group, click Visual Reports.) For more information, see Chapter 20, "Sharing information with other programs."

- Copy Project data to other applications—for example, to copy the Gantt Chart view, use Copy Picture. (To do this, on the Task tab, in the Clipboard group, click the down arrow next to the Copy button.) For more information, see Chapter 20.

- Export Project data in other formats. (To do this, on the File tab, click Export and then click Create PDF/XPS Document, or click Save Project As File and then select the format you want.) For more information, see Chapter 20.

- Share Project information with others via SharePoint and Project Web Access (PWA). For more information, see Appendix C: "Collaborating: Project, SharePoint, and PWA."

Here are some additional tips and suggestions for viewing slipped tasks:

- You can see the criteria that most filters use to determine which tasks or resources they will display or hide. On the View tab, in the Data group, in the Filter box, click More Filters. In the More Filters dialog box, click a filter and then click Edit. In the Filter Definition dialog box, you can see the tests applied to various fields for the filter.

- You can quickly display late tasks—tasks that are late in relation to whatever status date you set. To set a status date, on the Project tab, in the Status group, click Status Date. Then on the Format tab, in the Bar Styles group, select the Late Tasks check box. The Gantt bars of tasks that were scheduled to be completed by the status date but are incomplete are formatted dark gray.

- The Slipping Tasks report describes tasks that are off schedule. To view a Slipping Tasks report, on the Report tab, in the View Reports group, click In Progress and then Slipping Tasks.

- If you saved a baseline in your plan, you can show baseline and slippage bars on the chart portion of a Gantt Chart view. On the Format tab, in the Bar Styles group, click Baseline or Slippage, and then select the baseline values you want.

- In this exercise, you viewed variance for a task. To see variance for assignments to a task, switch to the Task Usage view and then apply the Variance table (to see scheduled variance) or the Work table (to see work variance).

Examining task costs

The schedule's status (determining if tasks start and finish on time), although critical to nearly all projects, is only one indicator of overall project health. For projects that include *cost* information, another critical indicator is cost variance: Are tasks running over or under budget? Task costs in Project consist of fixed costs applied directly to tasks, resource costs derived from assignments, or both. When tasks cost more or less than planned to complete, cost variance is the result. Evaluating cost variance enables you to make incremental budget adjustments for individual tasks to avoid exceeding your project's overall budget.

Although tasks and resources (and their costs) are directly related, it's informative to evaluate each individually.

The scenario: At Lucerne Publishing, you've seen the overall scope of cost variance for the new children's book plan. Next you'll focus on the specific tasks that have incurred the highest variance.

In this exercise, you view task cost variance. You'll start by displaying the Cost table.

1   On the **View** tab, in the **Data** group, click **Tables** and then click **Cost**.

The Cost table appears in the Task Sheet view.

	Task Name	Fixed Cost	Fixed Cost Accrual	Total Cost	Baseline	Variance	Actual	Remaining
0	▲ Children's Book Sch	$0.00	Prorated	$112,723.50	$97,588.00	$15,135.50	$78,466.50	$34,257.00
1	▷ Editorial staff mee	$0.00	Prorated	$2,223.00	$2,223.00	$0.00	$1,197.00	$1,026.00
15	▷ Acquisition	$0.00	Prorated	$18,804.00	$18,264.00	$540.00	$18,804.00	$0.00
21	▲ Editorial	$0.00	Prorated	$16,201.00	$15,670.00	$531.00	$16,201.00	$0.00
22	Organize manus	$0.00	Prorated	$3,213.00	$3,060.00	$153.00	$3,213.00	$0.00
23	Copyedit	$0.00	Prorated	$8,460.00	$8,100.00	$360.00	$8,460.00	$0.00
24	Author review o	$0.00	Prorated	$918.00	$900.00	$18.00	$918.00	$0.00
25	Copyedit incorp	$0.00	Prorated	$3,610.00	$3,610.00	$0.00	$3,610.00	$0.00
26	Handoff to Prod	$0.00	Prorated	$0.00	$0.00	$0.00	$0.00	$0.00
27	▲ Design and Produc	$0.00	Prorated	$60,743.50	$46,679.00	$14,064.50	$42,264.50	$18,479.00
28	Set pages	$0.00	Prorated	$7,590.00	$7,590.00	$0.00	$7,590.00	$0.00
29	Interior illustrat	$0.00	Prorated	$15,234.50	$13,050.00	$2,184.50	$15,234.50	$0.00
30	▲ 1st Pages reviev	$0.00	Prorated	$26,280.00	$13,860.00	$12,420.00	$19,440.00	$6,840.00
31	Proofread an	$0.00	Prorated	$7,200.00	$900.00	$6,300.00	$7,200.00	$0.00
32	Incorporate 1	$0.00	Prorated	$12,240.00	$6,120.00	$6,120.00	$12,240.00	$0.00

In this table, you can see each task's baseline cost, scheduled cost (in the Total Cost column), actual cost, and cost variance. The variance is the difference between the baseline cost and the scheduled cost. Of course, costs aren't scheduled in the same sense that work is scheduled; however, costs derived from work resources (excluding fixed costs and costs associated with material and cost resources) are derived directly from the scheduled work.

Task 0 is the project summary task; its cost values are the project's cost values, and they match the values you would see in the Project Statistics dialog box. These values include the following:

- The current total cost value is the sum of the actual (that is, completed) and remaining (uncompleted) cost values.

- The baseline cost value is the project's planned cost when its baseline was set.

- The actual cost is the cost that has been incurred so far.

- The remaining cost is the difference between the current cost and actual cost.

Next, you'll focus on the top-level costs.

2   On the **View** tab, in the **Data** group, click **Outline** and then click **Level 1**.

Project hides all subtasks and nested summary tasks, leaving only the top-level tasks visible.

Looking at the Variance column, you can see that the *Design and Production* phase (task 27) accounts for nearly all the project's variance.

To conclude this exercise, you will use filters to help you zero in on tasks that have cost variance.

3   On the **View** tab, in the **Data** group, click **Outline** and then click **All Subtasks**.

Project expands the task list to show all subtasks.

4   On the **View** tab, in the **Data** group, click the down arrow next to the **Filter** box and then click **More Filters**.

5   In the **More Filters** dialog box, click **Cost Overbudget** and then click **Apply**.

Project filters the task list to show only tasks that had actual and scheduled costs greater than their baseline costs. Scanning the task list, you can see that tasks 31 and 32 both incurred substantial variance.

	Task Name	Fixed Cost	Fixed Cost Accrual	Total Cost	Baseline	Variance	Actual	Remaining
0	◢ **Children's Book Sch**	$0.00	Prorated	$112,723.50	$97,588.00	$15,135.50	$78,466.50	$34,257.00
15	◢ **Acquisition**	$0.00	Prorated	$18,804.00	$18,264.00	$540.00	$18,804.00	$0.00
19	Author review c	$0.00	Prorated	$4,140.00	$3,600.00	$540.00	$4,140.00	$0.00
21	◢ **Editorial**	$0.00	Prorated	$16,201.00	$15,670.00	$531.00	$16,201.00	$0.00
22	Organize manus	$0.00	Prorated	$3,213.00	$3,060.00	$153.00	$3,213.00	$0.00
23	Copyedit	$0.00	Prorated	$8,460.00	$8,100.00	$360.00	$8,460.00	$0.00
24	Author review c	$0.00	Prorated	$918.00	$900.00	$18.00	$918.00	$0.00
27	◢ **Design and Produc**	$0.00	Prorated	$60,743.50	$46,679.00	$14,064.50	$42,264.50	$18,479.00
29	Interior illustrat	$0.00	Prorated	$15,234.50	$13,050.00	$2,184.50	$15,234.50	$0.00
30	◢ **1st Pages reviev**	$0.00	Prorated	$26,280.00	$13,860.00	$12,420.00	$19,440.00	$6,840.00
31	Proofread an	$0.00	Prorated	$7,200.00	$900.00	$6,300.00	$7,200.00	$0.00
32	Incorporate 1	$0.00	Prorated	$12,240.00	$6,120.00	$6,120.00	$12,240.00	$0.00

6   On the **View** tab, in the **Data** group, click the arrow next to the **Filter** button and then click **Clear Filter**.

Project removes the filter.

What caused the task cost variance in the new book project? Because this project's costs are almost entirely derived from work performed by resources, you can conclude that more work than was originally scheduled has been required to complete the tasks to date.

As we noted earlier, task and resource costs are closely related; in most cases, task costs are mostly or fully derived from the costs of resources assigned to tasks. Examining resource costs is the subject of the next exercise.

Here are some additional tips and suggestions for working with cost data:

■   To see tasks that are over budget, you can use the Task Cost Overview report. To view this report, on the Report tab, in the View Reports group, click Costs and then click Task Cost Overview.

- If you have Excel, you can use the Budget Cost Report. To create the Budget Cost Report, on the Report tab, in the Export group, click Visual Reports. On the Assignment Usage tab of the Visual Reports dialog box, click Budget Cost Report and then click View.

- Apply the Late/Overbudget Tasks Assigned To filter for a specific resource. To do this, on the View tab, in the Data group, click the arrow next to Filter and then click More Filters.

- Display work variance in the Work table in a task view. To do this, on the View tab, in the Data group, click Tables and then click Work. Remember that for a plan where most costs are derived from work resources, examining work variance is one way to examine cost variance.

- You can compare timephased baseline and scheduled work in a usage view. For example, in the Task Usage view, on the Format tab, in the Details group, click Baseline Work.

- In this exercise, you viewed cost variance for a task. To see cost variance over time for assignments to a task, switch to the Task Usage view and then apply the Cost table. While in a usage view, you can also show Cost, Baseline Cost, and Actual Cost details via the Add Details dialog box. On the Format tab, in the Details group, select the options you want.

Examining resource costs

Project managers sometimes focus on resource costs as a means of measuring progress and variance within a project. However, resource cost information also serves other people and other needs. For many organizations, resource costs are the primary, or even the only, costs incurred while completing projects, so closely watching resource costs might directly relate to the financial health of an organization. It might not be a project manager, but instead an executive, cost accountant, or *resource manager* who is most interested in resource costs on projects as they relate to organizational costs.

Another common reason to track resource costs is for billing either within an organization (for example, billing another department for services your department has provided) or externally. In either case, the resource cost information stored in plans can serve as the basis for billing out your department's or organization's services to others.

The scenario: At Lucerne Publishing, expenses in the new children's book plan are derived, for the most part, from the costs of resource assignments. You've already seen the task costs, so next you'll focus on resource cost variance.

In this exercise, you use different tables and sorting options to see resource cost variance.

1   On the **View** tab, in the **Resource Views** group, click **Resource Sheet**.

The Resource Sheet view appears.

2   On the **View** tab, in the **Data** group, click **Tables**, and then click **Cost**.

The Cost table appears.

	Resource Name	Cost	Baseline	Variance	Actual Cost	Remaining
1	Carole Poland	$11,182.50	$11,182.50	$0.00	$8,767.50	$2,415.00
2	Color Setting Ser	$0.00	$0.00	$0.00	$0.00	$0.00
3	Copyeditors	$20,718.00	$13,500.00	$7,218.00	$20,718.00	$0.00
4	Dan Jump	$11,740.25	$8,644.75	$3,095.50	$9,399.75	$2,340.50
5	Hany Morcos	$25,432.25	$22,066.25	$3,366.00	$16,654.75	$8,777.50
6	Jane Dow	$18,848.50	$18,848.50	$0.00	$12,776.50	$6,072.00
7	Jun Cao	$546.00	$546.00	$0.00	$294.00	$252.00
8	Luis Sousa	$15,456.00	$14,000.00	$1,456.00	$9,856.00	$5,600.00
9	Printing Service	$0.00	$0.00	$0.00	$0.00	$0.00
10	Tad Orman	$0.00	$0.00	$0.00	$0.00	$0.00
11	Travel	$3,500.00	$3,500.00	$0.00	$0.00	$3,500.00
12	Bound galley pro	$300.00	$300.00	$0.00	$0.00	$300.00

In the Cost table, you can see each resource's cost, baseline cost, and related cost values. In most cases here, the cost values for work resources are derived from each resource's cost rate multiplied by the work on their assignments to tasks in the plan.

Currently, the resource sheet is sorted by resource ID. Next, you will sort it by resource cost.

3   Click the **AutoFilter** arrow in the **Cost** column heading, and in the menu that appears, click **Sort Largest to Smallest**.

Project sorts the resources by cost from highest to lowest. Note that the resources are sorted according to the values in the Cost column, which is the sum of their actual (or historical) costs, and their remaining (or expected) costs.

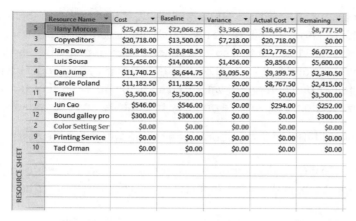

	Resource Name	Cost	Baseline	Variance	Actual Cost	Remaining
5	Hany Morcos	$25,432.25	$22,066.25	$3,366.00	$16,654.75	$8,777.50
3	Copyeditors	$20,718.00	$13,500.00	$7,218.00	$20,718.00	$0.00
6	Jane Dow	$18,848.50	$18,848.50	$0.00	$12,776.50	$6,072.00
8	Luis Sousa	$15,456.00	$14,000.00	$1,456.00	$9,856.00	$5,600.00
4	Dan Jump	$11,740.25	$8,644.75	$3,095.50	$9,399.75	$2,340.50
1	Carole Poland	$11,182.50	$11,182.50	$0.00	$8,767.50	$2,415.00
11	Travel	$3,500.00	$3,500.00	$0.00	$0.00	$3,500.00
7	Jun Cao	$546.00	$546.00	$0.00	$294.00	$252.00
12	Bound galley pro	$300.00	$300.00	$0.00	$0.00	$300.00
2	Color Setting Ser	$0.00	$0.00	$0.00	$0.00	$0.00
9	Printing Service	$0.00	$0.00	$0.00	$0.00	$0.00
10	Tad Orman	$0.00	$0.00	$0.00	$0.00	$0.00

This sort quickly tells you who are cumulatively the most and least costly resources (as indicated in the Cost column), but it doesn't help you see variance patterns. You will do that next.

4   Click the **AutoFilter** arrow in the **Variance** column heading, and in the menu that appears, click **Sort Largest to Smallest**.

Project re-sorts the resources by cost variance from highest to lowest.

	Resource Name	Cost	Baseline	Variance	Actual Cost	Remaining
3	Copyeditors	$20,718.00	$13,500.00	$7,218.00	$20,718.00	$0.00
5	Hany Morcos	$25,432.25	$22,066.25	$3,366.00	$16,654.75	$8,777.50
4	Dan Jump	$11,740.25	$8,644.75	$3,095.50	$9,399.75	$2,340.50
8	Luis Sousa	$15,456.00	$14,000.00	$1,456.00	$9,856.00	$5,600.00
1	Carole Poland	$11,182.50	$11,182.50	$0.00	$8,767.50	$2,415.00
2	Color Setting Ser	$0.00	$0.00	$0.00	$0.00	$0.00
6	Jane Dow	$18,848.50	$18,848.50	$0.00	$12,776.50	$6,072.00
7	Jun Cao	$546.00	$546.00	$0.00	$294.00	$252.00
9	Printing Service	$0.00	$0.00	$0.00	$0.00	$0.00
10	Tad Orman	$0.00	$0.00	$0.00	$0.00	$0.00
11	Travel	$3,500.00	$3,500.00	$0.00	$0.00	$3,500.00
12	Bound galley pro	$300.00	$300.00	$0.00	$0.00	$300.00

With the resource list sorted by cost variance, you can quickly zero in on resources with the greatest variance—Copyeditors in this case.

5   On the **View** tab, in the **Data** group, click **Sort**, and then click **by ID.**

Project re-sorts the resources by ID.

Note that the dollar amount of variance, while important, doesn't tell you the whole story. What would be useful to know is what tasks had the highest percentage of variance. A task with a $1,000 baseline and $1,200 actual cost has a lower percentage of variance than does a cost with a $100 baseline and $200 actual cost. In complex projects, understanding what tasks are prone to greater percentages of variance can help you avoid similar problems in the future. In the next section, you will see one way to begin to analyze variance in this way.

Here are some additional tips and suggestions for working with resource costs:

- You can use the Cost Overview report to see resources who are over budget. To do this, on the Report tab, in the View Reports Group, click Dashboards and then click Cost Overview.

- You can also see timephased cost values in a usage view. For example, in the Resource Usage view, on the Format tab, in the Details group, click Add Details. In the Details Styles dialog box, show the Baseline Cost and Cost fields. This also works in the Task Usage view.

- If you have Excel, you can use the Resource Cost Summary Report. To do this, on the Report tab, in the Export group, click Visual Reports. On the Resource Usage tab of the Visual Reports dialog box, click Resource Cost Summary Report and then click View.

Reporting project cost variance with a stoplight view

There are many different ways to report a project's status in terms of task or budget variance or other measures. There is no shortage of features in Project that support reporting project status, but the main point to keep in mind is that the method by which you report project status is less a technical question than a communications question. For example, what format and level of detail do your stakeholders need to see? Should project sponsors see aspects of a project's performance that are different than those seen by its resources? These questions are central to the project manager's job. Fortunately, as noted earlier, Project is a rich communications tool you can use to construct the type of project status information that best meets the needs of your stakeholders.

Next, you focus on creating what is often called a *stoplight report*. This status report represents key indicators for tasks, such as schedule or budget status, as a simple red, yellow, or green light. Such status reports are easy for anyone to understand, and they quickly provide a general sense of the health of a project. Strictly speaking, what you'll create here is not a report in Project, so we'll call it a stoplight *view* instead.

15

TIP This exercise uses custom fields and formulas. These are powerful features in Project and you'll find they have applicability for many other needs beyond the stoplight report we show here.

The scenario: At Lucerne Publishing, you conclude that the best way to help the team working on the new children's book plan to better understand cost variance is to employ a red/yellow/green stoplight style of view.

In this exercise, you edit a view using custom fields and formulas to visually focus on the cost variance of tasks.

1   On the **View** tab, in the **Task Views** group, click **Other Views** and then click **Task Sheet**.

Project displays the Task Sheet view. It currently contains the Cost table.

To save you time, we have customized a field in this Project file containing a formula that evaluates each task's cost variance. Next, you will view the formula to understand what it does and then view the graphical indicators assigned to the field.

2   On the **Format** tab, in the **Columns** group, click **Custom Fields**.

The Custom Fields dialog box appears.

3   In the **Type** box located in the upper-right corner of the dialog box, click **Number** in the drop-down list.

4   In the Field list box, click **Overbudget (Number3)**. This is the customized field we set up for you.

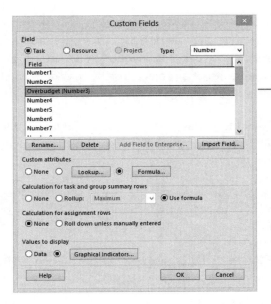

The Number3 field has been renamed "Overbudget" and customized with a formula and graphical indicators.

5   Under **Custom attributes**, click **Formula**.

The Formula dialog box appears.

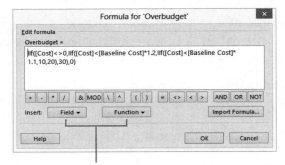

When writing a formula, use these buttons to insert Project fields or functions into your formula.

This formula evaluates each task's cost variance. If the task's cost is 10 percent or less above baseline, the formula assigns the number 10 to the task. If the cost is between 10 percent and 20 percent above baseline, it is assigned a value of 20. If the cost is more than 20 percent above baseline, it receives a 30. These values of 10, 20, or 30 appear in the Number3 field customized to be *Overbudget*.

6   Click **Cancel** to close the **Formula** dialog box.

7   In the **Custom Fields** dialog box, under **Values to display**, click **Graphical Indicators**.

The Graphical Indicators dialog box appears. Here, you specify a unique graphical indicator to display, depending on the value of the field for each task. Again, to save you time, the indicators are already selected.

Depending on the value returned by the formula, Project will display one of these three graphical indicators in the Overbudget column.

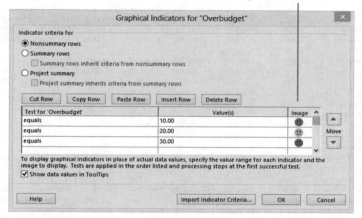

8   Click the first cell under the **Image** column heading (it contains a green smiley face), and then click the drop-down arrow.

Here, you can see the many graphical indicators you can associate with the values of fields.

9   Click **Cancel** to close the **Graphical Indicators** dialog box, and then click **Cancel** again to close the **Custom Fields** dialog box.

10   In the **Task Name** column, click the expand\collapse arrow next to the name of task 1, the *Editorial staff meeting* recurring summary task.

The recurring task list collapses to show just the recurring summary task.

To conclude this exercise, you will display the Overbudget (Number3) column in the Cost table.

11   On the right side of the table, click the **Add New Column** column heading.

A list of available fields appears.

12   In the list of fields, click **Overbudget (Number3)** in the drop-down list.

You will also see the same customized field named *Number3 (Overbudget)* in the list of fields.

TIP   When selecting items from a list like this, you can begin typing the name of the item you want and, when its full name appears, select it.

Project displays the Overbudget column in the Cost table.

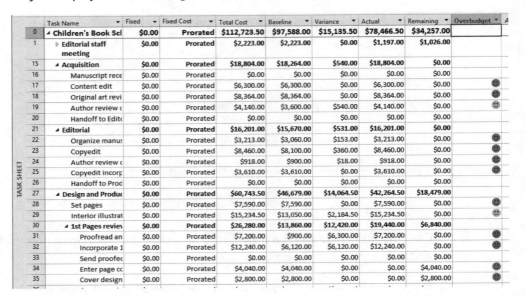

		Task Name	Fixed	Fixed Cost	Total Cost	Baseline	Variance	Actual	Remaining	Overbudget	A
	0	◢ Children's Book Sch	$0.00	Prorated	$112,723.50	$97,588.00	$15,135.50	$78,466.50	$34,257.00		
	1	▷ Editorial staff meeting	$0.00	Prorated	$2,223.00	$2,223.00	$0.00	$1,197.00	$1,026.00		
	15	◢ Acquisition	$0.00	Prorated	$18,804.00	$18,264.00	$540.00	$18,804.00	$0.00		
	16	Manuscript rece	$0.00	Prorated	$0.00	$0.00	$0.00	$0.00	$0.00		
	17	Content edit	$0.00	Prorated	$6,300.00	$6,300.00	$0.00	$6,300.00	$0.00	☺	
	18	Original art revi	$0.00	Prorated	$8,364.00	$8,364.00	$0.00	$8,364.00	$0.00	☺	
	19	Author review (	$0.00	Prorated	$4,140.00	$3,600.00	$540.00	$4,140.00	$0.00	☺	
	20	Handoff to Edit(	$0.00	Prorated	$0.00	$0.00	$0.00	$0.00	$0.00		
	21	◢ Editorial	$0.00	Prorated	$16,201.00	$15,670.00	$531.00	$16,201.00	$0.00		
	22	Organize manus	$0.00	Prorated	$3,213.00	$3,060.00	$153.00	$3,213.00	$0.00	☺	
	23	Copyedit	$0.00	Prorated	$8,460.00	$8,100.00	$360.00	$8,460.00	$0.00	☺	
	24	Author review (	$0.00	Prorated	$918.00	$900.00	$18.00	$918.00	$0.00	☺	
	25	Copyedit incorp	$0.00	Prorated	$3,610.00	$3,610.00	$0.00	$3,610.00	$0.00	☺	
	26	Handoff to Prod	$0.00	Prorated	$0.00	$0.00	$0.00	$0.00	$0.00		
	27	◢ Design and Produ(	$0.00	Prorated	$60,743.50	$46,679.00	$14,064.50	$42,264.50	$18,479.00		
	28	Set pages	$0.00	Prorated	$7,590.00	$7,590.00	$0.00	$7,590.00	$0.00	☺	
	29	Interior illustral	$0.00	Prorated	$15,234.50	$13,050.00	$2,184.50	$15,234.50	$0.00	☺	
	30	◢ 1st Pages reviev	$0.00	Prorated	$26,280.00	$13,860.00	$12,420.00	$19,440.00	$6,840.00		
	31	Proofread an	$0.00	Prorated	$7,200.00	$900.00	$6,300.00	$7,200.00	$0.00	☺	
	32	Incorporate 1	$0.00	Prorated	$12,240.00	$6,120.00	$6,120.00	$12,240.00	$0.00	☺	
	33	Send proofec	$0.00	Prorated	$0.00	$0.00	$0.00	$0.00	$0.00		
	34	Enter page cc	$0.00	Prorated	$4,040.00	$4,040.00	$0.00	$0.00	$4,040.00	☺	
	35	Cover design	$0.00	Prorated	$2,800.00	$2,800.00	$0.00	$0.00	$2,800.00	☺	

TIP   To see a graphical indicator's numeric value in a ScreenTip, just point to the indicator.

As each task's cost variance changes, so do the graphical indicators according to the ranges specified in the formula. This is a handy format for identifying tasks whose cost variance is higher than you'd like, as indicated by the yellow or red indicators. You can see that tasks 31 and 32, and consequently their summary task 30, experienced both a high dollar amount of variance and a high percentage above baseline, as indicated by the red sad face indicators.

Up to now, you've identified schedule and budget variance in a task view and budget variance in a resource view—each an important measure of project status. This is a good time to remind yourself that the final qualifier of project status is not the exact formatting of the data in Project, but the needs of your project's stakeholders. Determining what these needs are requires your good judgment and communication skills.

✖ CLEAN UP Close the Reporting Status file.

Key points

- Schedule variance is caused by tasks that have slipped from their planned start or finish dates (as recorded in a baseline). You can use a combination of views, tables, filters, and reports to identify which tasks have slipped and caused variance.

- Schedule and cost variance are closely related—if a plan has one, it likely has the other. As with schedule variance, you can apply a combination of views, tables, filters, and reports to locate cost variance.

- You can use formulas and graphical indicators in custom fields to create a highly customized view, such as a stoplight view, to communicate key project health indicators to your stakeholders.

Chapter at a glance

Resolve

Resolve missed deadlines by rescheduling tasks, page 345.

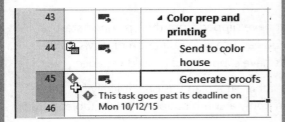

Reduce

Add additional resources to reduce task durations, page 352.

	Incorporate	10 days	Fri 8/28/15	Thu 9/10/15
You added resources to this task. Do you want to:				
○ Reduce duration but keep the same amount of work.				
◉ Increase the amount of work but keep the same duration.				
○ Reduce the hours resources work per day (units), but keep the same duration and work.				
	Enter page corrections and index	5 days	Fri 9/11/15	Thu 9/17/15
	Cover design	5 days	Fri 9/18/15	Thu 9/24/15
	◢ 2nd Pages review	10 days	Fri 9/25/15	Thu 10/8/15
	Proof and review	5 days	Fri 9/25/15	Thu 10/1/15
	Send proofed pages to Production	0 days	Thu 10/1/15	Thu 10/1/15
	Final review	5 days	Fri 10/2/15	Thu 10/8/15

Substitute

Replace resources with less expensive resources, page 353.

Replace Resource

Replace: Hany Morcos

With:

Resource Name	Units	Cost
Hany Morcos		$22,746.25
Bound galley proofs		$300.00
Carole Poland		$11,182.50
Color Setting Services		$0.00
Copyeditors		$17,838.00
Dan Jump		$7,512.25
Jane Dow		$21,884.50

OK
Cancel

Inactivate

Inactivate tasks (Project Professional) or delete tasks (Project Standard) to reduce overall project scope, page 357.

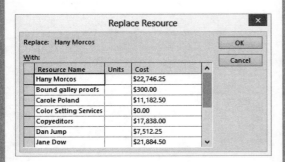

Getting your project back on track

IN THIS CHAPTER, YOU WILL LEARN HOW TO

- Address a missed deadline by adjusting task details such as task relationships and resource assignments.

- Reduce cost and overallocation by replacing resources assigned to tasks.

- Reduce project scope by deleting or inactivating tasks.

After work has started on a project, addressing *variance* is not a one-time event, but instead is an ongoing effort by the project manager. The specific way in which you should respond to variance depends on the type of variance and the nature of the project. In this chapter, we'll focus on some of the many variance problems that can arise during a project as work progresses. We'll frame these problems around the *project triangle*, described in detail in Appendix A, "A short course in project management."

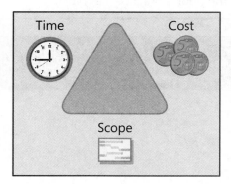

In short, the project triangle model frames a project in terms of *time* (or duration), *cost* (or budget), and *scope* (the project work required to produce a satisfactory *deliverable*). In this model time, cost, and scope are interconnected; therefore, changing one element can affect the other two. For purposes of identifying, analyzing, and addressing problems in project management, you'll find it useful to fit problems into one of these three categories.

In virtually any project, one of these factors will be more important than the other two. The most important factor is sometimes called the *driving constraint* because meeting it drives your actions as a project manager. For example, for a project that must be concluded by a specific date, you might need to make cost and scope compromises to meet the deadline. Working with the project triangle provides you with a good method to analyze the trade-offs that nearly always must be made. Just as importantly, it gives you a clear way of explaining the pros and cons of trade-offs to the project's *resources, sponsors,* and other *stakeholders.*

The specific issues that we'll focus on in this chapter are not necessarily the most common problems you'll face in your own projects. Because every project is unique, there's no way to anticipate specifically what you'll run into. However, we've attempted to highlight the most pressing issues at the midpoint of the new children's book project at Lucerne Publishing that we have been discussing throughout this book and apply solutions to common problems. You've already worked with most of the features used in this chapter, but here your intent is different—getting the plan back on track. In this chapter, you will apply a variety of strategies to address time, cost, and scope issues that have occurred in a project.

PRACTICE FILES Before you can complete the exercises in this chapter, you need to copy the book's practice files to your computer. A complete list of practice files is provided in "Download the practice files" at the beginning of this book. For each exercise that has a practice file, simply browse to where you saved the book's practice file folder.

IMPORTANT If you are running Project Professional with Project Web App/Project Server, take care not to save any of the practice files you work with in this book to Project Web App (PWA). For more information, see Appendix C, "Collaborating: Project, SharePoint, and PWA."

Troubleshooting time and schedule problems

Schedule variance will almost certainly appear in any lengthy project. Maintaining control over the schedule requires that the project manager know when variance has occurred and to what extent, and then take timely corrective action to stay on track. To help you identify when variance has occurred, the new children's book plan includes the following:

16

- A deadline date applied to a time-sensitive task
- A project baseline against which you can compare actual performance

The deadline date and project baseline will help you troubleshoot time and schedule problems in Project.

The scenario: At Lucerne Publishing, the new children's book plan has encountered enough schedule variance that corrective actions are required.

In this exercise, you address a missed deadline and shorten the durations of some tasks on the *critical path*.

 SET UP You need the Back on Track_Start file located in your Chapter16 practice file folder to complete this exercise. Open the Back on Track_Start file, and save it as Back on Track.

To begin troubleshooting the time and schedule issues, you'll get a top-level view of the degree of schedule variance in the plan to date.

1   On the **Project** tab, in the **Properties** group, click **Project Information**.

The Project Information dialog box appears.

2   Click **Statistics**.

	Start		Finish
		Project Statistics for 'Back on Track'	✕
	Start		Finish
Current	Mon 4/6/15		Fri 12/11/15
Baseline	Mon 4/6/15		Thu 11/26/15
Actual	Mon 4/6/15		NA
Variance	0d		11.13d
	Duration	Work	Cost
Current	180d	2,588.5h	$108,551.50
Baseline	168.88d	2,317.5h	$97,588.00
Actual	87.54d	1,375.5h	$62,714.50
Remaining	92.46d	1,213h	$45,837.00

Percent complete:
Duration: 49%   Work: 53%

[Close]

As you can see, the new book plan has both schedule variance and cost variance. The schedule variance is listed at the intersection of the Finish column and Variance row. Also note that in terms of overall duration, this plan is about 50 percent complete.

3   Click **Close** to close the **Project Statistics** dialog box.

The Statistics dialog box includes the project's finish date. However, to monitor the finish date as you work on the schedule, you can keep your eye on the Finish date for task 0, the project summary task.

	ⓘ	Task Mode ▾	Task Name ▾	Duration ▾	Start ▾	Finish ▾	F	S	Apr 5, '15 S	M	T
0		⭢	◢ Children's Book Schedule	180 days	Mon 4/6/15	Fri 12/11/15					
1	⟳	⭢	▷ Editorial staff meeting	83.13 days	Mon 4/13/15	Thu 8/6/15					

Note the current project finish date in task 0's Finish field. You know that this date must be pulled in to meet your book printing date. Before you address the overall project duration, you'll examine the missed deadline for the *Generate proofs* task.

4   In the **Task Name** column, click the name of task 45, *Generate proofs*.

5   On the **Task** tab, in the **Editing** group, click **Scroll to Task**.

TIP To select a task quickly, even a task you can't see in the current view, press Ctrl+G and, in the ID field of the Go To dialog box, enter a task number, and then click OK.

6   Point to the missed deadline indicator in the **Indicators** column for task 45, *Generate proofs*.

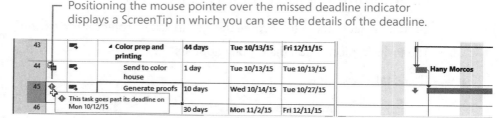

Positioning the mouse pointer over the missed deadline indicator displays a ScreenTip in which you can see the details of the deadline.

43		⭢	◢ Color prep and printing	44 days	Tue 10/13/15	Fri 12/11/15		
44		⭢	Send to color house	1 day	Tue 10/13/15	Tue 10/13/15		Hany Morcos
45		⭢	Generate proofs	10 days	Wed 10/14/15	Tue 10/27/15		
46				30 days	Mon 11/2/15	Fri 12/11/15		

This task goes past its deadline on Mon 10/12/15

Enough changes to the schedule have occurred to cause the scheduled completion of this task to move out beyond its deadline date of October 12. Next, you'll format the view to better see tasks on the *critical path*—that is, the tasks that are driving the finish date of the plan.

7   On the **View** tab, in the **Zoom** group, in the **Timescale** box, click **Weeks**.

8   On the **Format** tab, in the **Bar Styles** group, click **Critical Tasks**.

For tasks on the critical path, Project formats their task bars red.

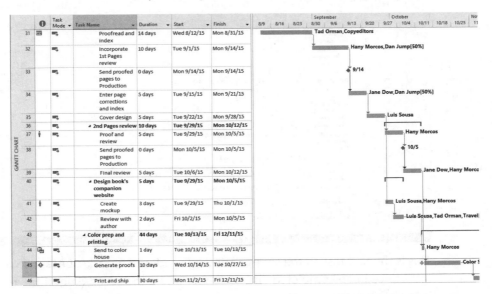

With the view displayed this way, you can see that task 45 and many of its predecessor tasks are on the critical path.

To continue addressing the missed deadline on task 45, you'll focus on its driven successor and driving predecessor tasks by using the Task Path feature.

9   With task 45 still selected, on the **Format** tab in the **Bar Styles** group, click **Task Path** and then click **Driving Predecessors**.

10   On the **Format** tab in the **Bar Styles** group, click **Task Path** and then **Driven Successors**.

Project applies a dark orange format to the task bars of tasks currently driving the schedule of task 45. You'll focus on these tasks to pull in the scheduled finish date of task 45.

11   In the **Task Name** column, select the name of task 31, *Proofread and index*.

12   On the **Task** tab, in the **Editing** group, click **Scroll to Task**.

The Gantt bar for task 31 comes into view.

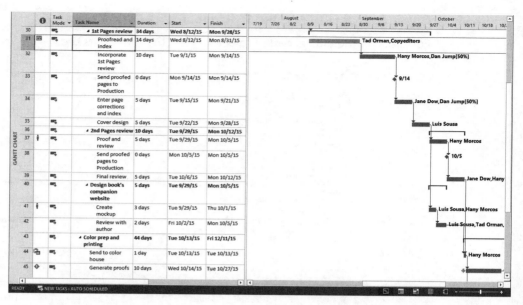

This is the first task in the series of driving predecessor tasks for task 45. Earlier tasks have been completed and no longer affect the scheduling of the remaining incomplete tasks.

The new children's book's author, Tad Orman, and a copyeditor are assigned to the task. After consulting with the assigned resources, you all agree that task 31 can be completed in a slightly shorter duration: 12 days.

13   In the **Duration** field of task 31, type **12d**, and then press the Enter key.

Project reduces the duration of the task and reschedules the affected successor tasks, including task 45 and the project finish date.

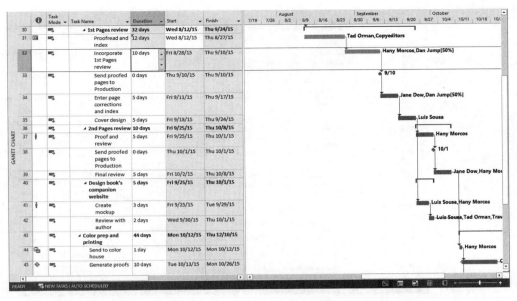

	ⓘ	Task Mode	Task Name	Duration	Start	Finish
30		⭢	▲ 1st Pages review	32 days	Wed 8/12/15	Thu 9/24/15
31	▦	⭢	Proofread and index	12 days	Wed 8/12/15	Thu 8/27/15
32		⭢	Incorporate 1st Pages review	10 days	Fri 8/28/15	Thu 9/10/15
33		⭢	Send proofed pages to Production	0 days	Thu 9/10/15	Thu 9/10/15
34		⭢	Enter page corrections and index	5 days	Fri 9/11/15	Thu 9/17/15
35		⭢	Cover design	5 days	Fri 9/18/15	Thu 9/24/15
36		⭢	▲ 2nd Pages review	10 days	Fri 9/25/15	Thu 10/8/15
37	ⓘ	⭢	Proof and review	5 days	Fri 9/25/15	Thu 10/1/15
38		⭢	Send proofed pages to Production	0 days	Thu 10/1/15	Thu 10/1/15
39		⭢	Final review	5 days	Fri 10/2/15	Thu 10/8/15
40		⭢	▲ Design book's companion website	5 days	Fri 9/25/15	Thu 10/1/15
41	ⓘ	⭢	Create mockup	3 days	Fri 9/25/15	Tue 9/29/15
42		⭢	Review with author	2 days	Wed 9/30/15	Thu 10/1/15
43		⭢	▲ Color prep and printing	44 days	Mon 10/12/15	Thu 12/10/15
44	▤	⭢	Send to color house	1 day	Mon 10/12/15	Mon 10/12/15
45	◆	⭢	Generate proofs	10 days	Tue 10/13/15	Mon 10/26/15

This adjustment isn't enough to fix task 45's missed deadline, however.

Task 32 should now be selected. For this task, you and the assigned resources agree that adding an additional resource should reduce the task's duration.

14 Ensure that task 32 is selected, and on the **Resource** tab, in the **Assignments** group, click **Assign Resources**.

The Assign Resources dialog box appears, with the names of the resources currently assigned to task 32 at the top of the Resource Name column.

15 In the **Assign Resources** dialog box, in the **Resource Name** column, click Jane Dow, and then click **Assign**.

After assigning the additional resource, you need to tell Project how it should adjust the scheduling of the task.

16 Click the **Action** indicator in the **Task Name** field of task 32 (the small triangle in the upper-left corner of the field), and then click the **Action** button that appears.

The Action list appears.

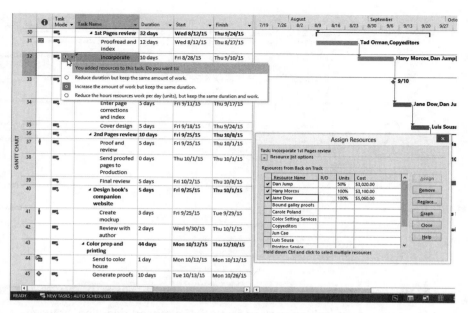

17   Click **Reduce duration but keep the same amount of work.**

Project reduces the duration of task 32 from 10 days to 6 days. Because of the Action option you chose, Project kept the amount of work on the task the same, but that work is now distributed among the three assigned resources rather than the two resources.

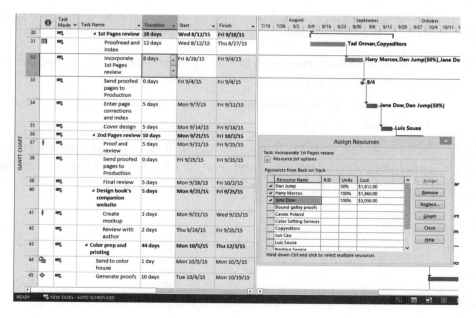

18   Click **Close** in the **Assign Resources** dialog box.

Checking the deadline indicator and the Gantt bar for task 45, you see that these actions have moved the completion date of task 45 closer to its deadline, but it's not there yet.

Looking over the remaining tasks that are predecessors of task 45, you see that tasks 34 and 35 have a finish-to-start relationship and different resources assigned. After consulting with the assigned resources, you decide these tasks could be completed in parallel. Next, you'll change their relationship type.

19   Scroll the table portion of the **Gantt Chart** view to the right to show the **Predecessors** column.

20   In the **Predecessors** field for task 35, type **34SS** and then press Enter.

Project changes the task relationship type to start-to-start.

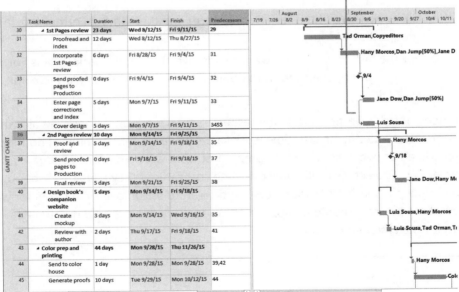

Changing the predecessor relationship between these tasks to start-to-start decreases the overall duration of the plan because these tasks are on the critical path.

Now that these two tasks have a start-to-start relationship, the successor task's start date is moved in by five days. Checking the deadline indicator on task 45, you see that the missed deadline indicator is gone; you've sufficiently pulled in task 45's finish date (for now at least). The project's finish date has been correspondingly adjusted because of these schedule changes to tasks on the critical path.

This is an important deadline on task 45, so you plan to closely monitor the progress on its predecessor tasks as work progresses.

21 On the **Format** tab, in the **Bar Styles** group, click **Task Path,** and then click **Remove Highlighting.**

Reduce task durations by assigning resource overtime hours

One way to reduce a task's duration is to add overtime to the assigned resource. The trade-off might be additional costs, especially if the resource has an overtime pay rate. To add overtime to an assignment, follow these steps.

1 On the **Task** tab, in the **Properties** group, click **Details.**
The Task Details Form appears below the Gantt Chart view.

2 Click anywhere in the **Task Details Form** and then on the **Format** tab, in the **Details** group, click **Work.**

3 For the task to which you want to add overtime, in the **Task Details Form,** enter the number of overtime work hours you want in the **Ovt. Work** column, and then click **OK.**

When you add overtime work, the resource's total work on the task remains the same. After entering an overtime work value, however, that number of hours will be scheduled as overtime. The same amount of work will be performed, but in a shorter time span. Project also will apply overtime cost rates, if they have been set up, to the overtime portion of the assignment. If you plan to assign overtime hours for which an overtime pay rate should be applied, make sure you have a valid overtime pay rate set up for the assigned resource.

Troubleshooting cost and resource problems

In projects where you entered cost information for resources, you might find that you must fine-tune resource and assignment details to address cost or budget problems. Although this might not be your intention, changing resource assignment details not only affects costs, but it can affect task durations as well.

The scenario: At Lucerne Publishing, in addition to schedule variance the new children's book plan has some cost variance. As it is currently scheduled, the plan will end up costing about $11,000 more than planned, or about 11 percent over budget. Recall from Chapter 15, "Viewing and reporting project status," that the new book plan's cost variance is the result of some longer-than-expected task durations, and the additional work increased the costs of the assigned resources. To address cost variance in this project, you'll focus on resource costs. While examining resource cost issues, you'll also look for opportunities to address any resource overallocation problems that have crept into the plan.

In this exercise, you examine resource cost values and replace one resource assigned to a task with another resource.

1   On the **View** tab, in the **Resource Views** group, click **Resource Sheet**.

You will use the Resource Sheet view to identify your most costly resources for the remaining tasks—costly not in hourly pay rate, but in the total expense in this plan based on their assignments.

2   On the **View** tab, in the **Data** group, click **Tables**, and then click **Cost**.

The Cost table appears in the Resource Sheet view.

	Resource Name	Cost	Baseline	Variance	Actual Cost	Remaining
1	Carole Poland	$11,182.50	$11,182.50	$0.00	$8,767.50	$2,415.00
2	Color Setting Services	$0.00	$0.00	$0.00	$0.00	$0.00
3	Copyeditors	$17,838.00	$13,500.00	$4,338.00	$13,518.00	$4,320.00
4	Dan Jump	$7,512.25	$8,644.75	($1,132.50)	$3,359.75	$4,152.50
5	Hany Morcos	$22,746.25	$22,066.25	$680.00	$11,818.75	$10,927.50
6	Jane Dow	$21,884.50	$18,848.50	$3,036.00	$12,776.50	$9,108.00
7	Jun Cao	$286.00	$546.00	($260.00)	$154.00	$132.00
8	Luis Sousa	$17,920.00	$14,000.00	$3,920.00	$12,320.00	$5,600.00
9	Printing Service	$0.00	$0.00	$0.00	$0.00	$0.00
10	Tad Orman	$0.00	$0.00	$0.00	$0.00	$0.00
11	Travel	$3,500.00	$3,500.00	$0.00	$0.00	$3,500.00
12	Bound galley pro	$300.00	$300.00	$0.00	$0.00	$300.00

At this point, about half the project's duration has elapsed, so the most expensive resources overall might not be the most expensive resources for the work not yet completed. To identify the most expensive resources for the remaining work, you'll sort the table.

3   Click the **AutoFilter** arrow in the **Remaining** column heading, and in the menu that appears, click **Sort Largest to Smallest**.

	Resource Name	Cost	Baseline	Variance	Actual Cost	Remaining
5	Hany Morcos	$22,746.25	$22,066.25	$680.00	$11,818.75	$10,927.50
6	Jane Dow	$21,884.50	$18,848.50	$3,036.00	$12,776.50	$9,108.00
8	Luis Sousa	$17,920.00	$14,000.00	$3,920.00	$12,320.00	$5,600.00
3	Copyeditors	$17,838.00	$13,500.00	$4,338.00	$13,518.00	$4,320.00
4	Dan Jump	$7,512.25	$8,644.75	($1,132.50)	$3,359.75	$4,152.50
11	Travel	$3,500.00	$3,500.00	$0.00	$0.00	$3,500.00
1	Carole Poland	$11,182.50	$11,182.50	$0.00	$8,767.50	$2,415.00
12	Bound galley pro	$300.00	$300.00	$0.00	$0.00	$300.00
7	Jun Cao	$286.00	$546.00	($260.00)	$154.00	$132.00
2	Color Setting Services	$0.00	$0.00	$0.00	$0.00	$0.00
9	Printing Service	$0.00	$0.00	$0.00	$0.00	$0.00
10	Tad Orman	$0.00	$0.00	$0.00	$0.00	$0.00

You can see that Hany Morcos and Jane Dow have the largest remaining cost values at this point in the plan's duration. Managing costs for these two resources is one way you can help limit additional cost variance. Note also that Hany's name is formatted red, indicating that she is overallocated.

4   On the **View** tab, in the **Task Views** group, click **Gantt Chart**.

Project displays the Gantt Chart view. Next, you'll look at the tasks to which Hany and Jane are assigned.

5   If necessary, drag the vertical divider bar to the right to display the **Resource Names** column, and then click the **AutoFilter** arrow in the **Resource Names** column heading.

6   In the menu that appears, click **(Select All)** to clear all the resource names, and then select *Hany Morcos* and *Jane Dow*.

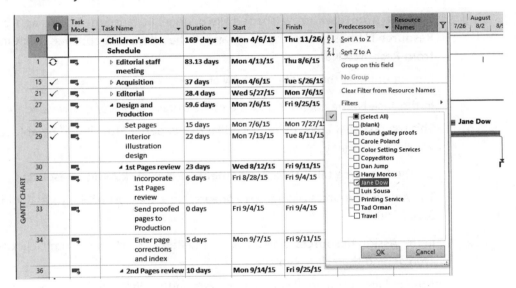

7   Click **OK**.

Project filters the task list to display tasks to which Hany or Jane is assigned.

8   Scroll the Gantt Chart view down to show later tasks.

	ℹ️	Task Mode ▾	Task Name ▾	Duration ▾	Start ▾	Finish ▾	Predecessors ▾	Resource Names	▼
36		🔾	◢ 2nd Pages review	10 days	Mon 9/14/15	Fri 9/25/15			
37	ℹ️	🔾	Proof and review	5 days	Mon 9/14/15	Fri 9/18/15	35	Hany Morcos	
38		🔾	Send proofed pages to Production	0 days	Fri 9/18/15	Fri 9/18/15	37	Hany Morcos	
39		🔾	Final review	5 days	Mon 9/21/15	Fri 9/25/15	38	Jane Dow,Hany I	
40		🔾	◢ Design book's companion website	5 days	Mon 9/14/15	Fri 9/18/15			
41	ℹ️	🔾	Create mockup	3 days	Mon 9/14/15	Wed 9/16/15	35	Luis Sousa, Hany Morcos	

Looking at the uncompleted tasks, you can spot Hany Morcos's overallocation: she's assigned to tasks 37 and 41, which overlap. That is why the red *overallocated resource* indicators appear in the Indicators column for these tasks.

You could fix Hany's overall allocation by resource leveling, but that is likely to extend the project's finish date and won't help reduce the project's overall cost. Instead, you'll replace Hany with a less expensive resource on one of her assignments.

9   Click the **AutoFilter** arrow (shaped like a funnel because the filter is applied) in the **Resource Names** column heading, and in the menu that appears, click **Clear Filter from Resource Names**.

Project unfilters the task list to show all tasks.

10   In the **Task Name** column, click the name of task 37, *Proof and review*.

This is a task that a less experienced (and cheaper) editor should be able to handle, so you'll replace Hany.

11   On the **Resource** tab, in the **Assignments** group, click **Assign Resources**.

The Assign Resources dialog box appears. Note the cost of Hany's assignment to task 37: $1,550.

12   In the **Assign Resources** dialog box, in the **Resource Name** column, click *Hany Morcos*, and then click **Replace**.

The Replace Resource dialog box appears. In this dialog box, you see the total cost per resource, based on their cost rates and assignments to tasks in the plan.

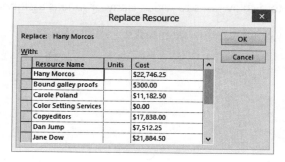

13   In the **Resource Name** column in the **Replace Resource** dialog box, click *Jun Cao*, and then click **OK**.

Project replaces Hany with Jun on this assignment.

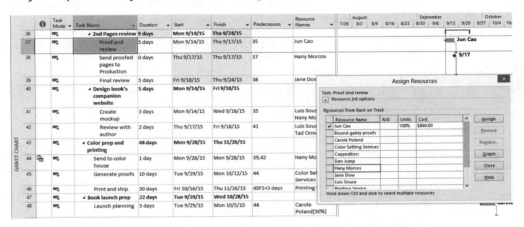

Jun's lower cost on the assignment, $880, appears in the Assign Resources dialog box. Note also that the red *overallocated resource* indicators no longer appear in the Indicators column; you have resolved Hany's overall allocation. Finally, note also that the finish date of task 37 was moved in by one day. This is due to Jun's "four by ten" working calendar that you set up in Chapter 5, "Setting up resources."

14   In the **Assign Resources** dialog box, click **Close**.

Troubleshooting scope-of-work problems

A project's scope should include all the work required—and only the work required—to deliver the product of the project successfully to its intended customer. After project work has started, managing its scope usually requires making trade-offs: trading time for money, quality for time, and so on. You might have the goal of never making such trade-offs, but a more realistic goal might be to make the best-informed trade-offs possible.

The scenario: At Lucerne Publishing, you just consulted with the management (that is, the project sponsors). You've been asked to shave about $5,000 from the remaining tasks in the new children's book plan. This plan's finish date is fine as is, but the actual cost has gone somewhat over budget. You need to reduce work to reduce the remaining costs.

In this exercise, you view tasks' remaining costs and remove some tasks from the plan.

1   On the **View** tab, in the **Data** group, click **Tables**, and then click **Cost**.

Your focus here is on the tasks not yet completed, so you'll filter the task list.

2   On the **View** tab, in the **Data** group, click the down arrow next to the **Filter** box (it initially contains *[No Filter]*) and then click **Incomplete Tasks**.

Project filters the task list to show only the tasks that are not yet complete, plus their summary tasks.

Task Name	Fixed Cost	Fixed Cost Accrual	Total Cost	Baseline	Variance	Actual	Remaining
0 Children's Book Schedule	$0.00	Prorated	$107,499.50	$97,588.00	$9,911.50	$62,714.50	$44,785.00
1 Editorial staff meeting	$0.00	Prorated	$1,963.00	$2,223.00	($260.00)	$1,057.00	$906.00
27 Design and Production	$0.00	Prorated	$55,779.50	$46,679.00	$9,100.50	$26,652.50	$29,127.00
30 1st Pages review	$0.00	Prorated	$17,868.00	$13,860.00	$4,008.00	$0.00	$17,868.00
31 Proofread and index	$0.00	Prorated	$4,320.00	$900.00	$3,420.00	$0.00	$4,320.00
32 Incorporate 1st Pages review	$0.00	Prorated	$6,708.00	$6,120.00	$588.00	$0.00	$6,708.00
33 Send proofed pages to	$0.00	Prorated	$0.00	$0.00	$0.00	$0.00	$0.00
34 Enter page corrections and index	$0.00	Prorated	$4,040.00	$4,040.00	$0.00	$0.00	$4,040.00
35 Cover design	$0.00	Prorated	$2,800.00	$2,800.00	$0.00	$0.00	$2,800.00
36 2nd Pages review	$0.00	Prorated	$5,425.00	$6,345.00	($920.00)	$0.00	$5,425.00
37 Proof and review	$0.00	Prorated	$880.00	$1,800.00	($920.00)	$0.00	$880.00
38 Send proofed pages to	$0.00	Prorated	$0.00	$0.00	$0.00	$0.00	$0.00
39 Final review	$0.00	Prorated	$4,545.00	$4,545.00	$0.00	$0.00	$4,545.00
40 Design book's companion website	$0.00	Prorated	$5,834.00	$5,834.00	$0.00	$0.00	$5,834.00
41 Create mockup	$0.00	Prorated	$2,610.00	$2,610.00	$0.00	$0.00	$2,610.00
42 Review with author	$0.00	Prorated	$3,224.00	$3,224.00	$0.00	$0.00	$3,224.00

One set of tasks in the plan that could be cut without affecting the result of the new book plan is task 40 and its subtasks, *Design book's companion website*. The remaining cost of this work is more than the $5,000 you've been asked to cut from the plan. After consulting with the project's sponsors, you all agree that this looks like a good set of tasks to remove from the plan.

3   Select the name of task 40, the summary task *Design book's companion website*.

4   Do one of the following:

- If you are running Project Professional, continue with step 5.

- If you are running Project Standard, skip ahead to step 6.

TIP Not sure which edition of Project you have? Here's one easy way to tell. The Project application title bar includes "Project Professional" or "Project Standard." You can also see your edition identified in the Account screen of the Backstage view. (To check this, click File, click Account, and then look for your edition name on the right side of the Account pane.)

5   On the **Task** tab, in the **Schedule** group, click **Inactivate**.

Project inactivates the summary task and its subtasks.

In Project Professional, inactivated tasks appear like this.

These inactivated tasks will remain in the plan, but they have no scheduling or cost impact now. Note that the Remaining cost value for task 0, the *project summary task*, and for task 27, the *Design and Production* summary task, are correspondingly reduced.

NOTE Project Professional users should skip to the end of this procedure. Project Standard users proceed from step 4 directly to step 6.

6   With the name of task 40 selected, right-click and in the shortcut menu that appears, click **Delete Task**.

A Planning Wizard message might appear, asking you to verify that you want to delete this summary task and its subtasks. If it appears, make sure that **Continue** is selected and then click OK.

Project deletes the summary task and its subtasks and renumbers the remaining tasks.

After deleting tasks, subsequent tasks are renumbered.

	Task Name	Fixed Cost	Fixed Cost Accrual	Total Cost	Baseline	Variance	Actual	Remaining	August 7/26	8/2	8/9	8/16	8/23	September 8/30	9/6	9/13	9/20	9/27
0	**Children's Book Schedule**	$0.00	Prorated	$101,665.50	$97,588.00	$4,077.50	$62,714.50	$38,951.00										
1	▷ **Editorial staff meeting**	$0.00	Prorated	$1,963.00	$2,223.00	($260.00)	$1,057.00	$906.00										
27	◢ **Design and Production**	$0.00	Prorated	$49,945.50	$46,679.00	$3,266.50	$26,652.50	$23,293.00										
30	◢ **1st Pages review**	$0.00	Prorated	$17,868.00	$13,860.00	$4,008.00	$0.00	$17,868.00										
31	Proofread and index	$0.00	Prorated	$4,320.00	$900.00	$3,420.00	$0.00	$4,320.00						Tad Orman,Copyeditors				
32	Incorporate 1st Pages review	$0.00	Prorated	$6,708.00	$6,120.00	$588.00	$0.00	$6,708.00						Hany Morcos,Dan Jump[				
33	Send proofed pages to	$0.00	Prorated	$0.00	$0.00	$0.00	$0.00	$0.00						9/4				
34	Enter page corrections and index	$0.00	Prorated	$4,040.00	$4,040.00	$0.00	$0.00	$4,040.00						Jane Dow,Dan Jun				
35	Cover design	$0.00	Prorated	$2,800.00	$2,800.00	$0.00	$0.00	$2,800.00						Luis Sousa				
36	◢ **2nd Pages revie**	$0.00	Prorated	$5,425.00	$6,345.00	($920.00)	$0.00	$5,425.00										
37	Proof and review	$0.00	Prorated	$880.00	$1,800.00	($920.00)	$0.00	$880.00							Jun Cao			
38	Send proofed pages to	$0.00	Prorated	$0.00	$0.00	$0.00	$0.00	$0.00							9/17			
39	Final review	$0.00	Prorated	$4,545.00	$4,545.00	$0.00	$0.00	$4,545.00								Jane Do		
40	◢ **Color prep and printing**	$0.00	Prorated	$5,310.00	$5,310.00	$0.00	$0.00	$5,310.00										
41	Send to color house	$0.00	Prorated	$310.00	$310.00	$0.00	$0.00	$310.00									Han	
42	Generate proofs	$5,000.00	End	$5,000.00	$5,000.00	$0.00	$0.00	$5,000.00										
43	Print and ship	$0.00	Prorated	$0.00	$0.00	$0.00	$0.00	$0.00										

Note that the Remaining cost value for task 0, the *project summary task,* and for task 27, the *Design and Production* summary task, are correspondingly reduced.

You confer with the project sponsors, who are pleased that you can wrap up the new book project at a lower cost. Although completing the remaining work within the given time and cost constraints will be a challenge, you're optimistic about the project's future performance given your project management skills and knowledge of Project.

❌ CLEAN UP Close the Back on Track file.

Key points

- When addressing variance in a plan, you'll find it useful to evaluate your plan (and variance) in terms of time, cost, and scope: the three sides of the project triangle.

- When addressing schedule problems, focus your remedies on tasks on the critical path; these drive the finish date of the project.

- When addressing cost or scope problems, focus on expensive resources—especially on their longer assignments.

In-Depth and Special Subjects

17 Applying advanced formatting
and printing   363

18 Advanced report formatting   388

19 Customizing Project   416

20 Sharing information with other programs   442

21 Consolidating projects and resources   468

Chapter at a glance

Define

Add more details to a Gantt chart view, page 364.

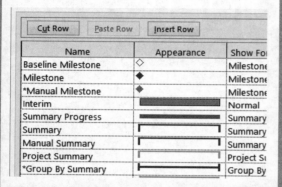

Customize

Customize text and task bars in a Timeline view, page 371.

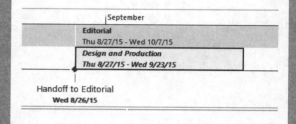

Change

Change the details in a Network Diagram view, page 373.

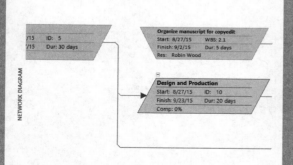

Export

Print views, and generate PDF or XPS files, page 381.

Applying advanced formatting and printing

IN THIS CHAPTER, YOU WILL LEARN HOW TO

- Customize a Gantt chart view.

- Format a Timeline view.

- Adjust details shown in nodes of a Network Diagram view.

- Add additional bar types to a Calendar view.

- Adjust printing options, and generate a PDF or XPS snapshot of views.

This chapter introduces you to some of the more advanced formatting features in Microsoft Project 2013. A well-formatted plan can be valuable when communicating details to *resources,* customers, and other *stakeholders.* Some of the formatting capabilities in Project are similar to those of a style-based word processor, such as Microsoft Word, in which defining a style once affects all content in the document to which that style has been applied. In Project, you can use styles to change the appearance of a specific type of Gantt bar, such as a summary bar, throughout a plan. Other formatting options introduced in this chapter focus on direct formatting of tasks and formatting some of the more commonly used views. In this chapter, you'll apply some of Project's more advanced formatting features to views.

PRACTICE FILES Before you can complete the exercises in this chapter, you need to copy the book's practice files to your computer. A complete list of practice files is provided in "Download the practice files" at the beginning of this book. For each exercise that has a practice file, simply browse to where you saved the book's practice file folder.

IMPORTANT If you are running Project Professional with Project Web App/Project Server, take care not to save any of the practice files you work with in this book to Project Web App (PWA). For more information, see Appendix C, "Collaborating: Project, SharePoint, and PWA."

Formatting a Gantt chart view

You can format specific items (a *milestone,* for example) in a *Gantt chart view* to change the appearance of that item. If you completed Chapter 7, "Formatting and sharing your plan," you worked with Gantt chart styles and direct formatting of Gantt bars. In this section, you will work with bar styles to change the visual appearance of specific types of Gantt bars (such as summary tasks) and other elements (such as deadline indicators) in ways that the Gantt chart styles cannot. The format changes you make apply only to the active view.

TIP Remember that several views are Gantt chart views, even though only one view is specifically called *the Gantt Chart view.* Other Gantt chart views include the Detail Gantt, Leveling Gantt, Multiple Baselines Gantt, and Tracking Gantt. The term *Gantt chart view* generally refers to a type of presentation that shows Gantt bars organized along a timescale.

In addition to changing the formatting of items that can appear in a Gantt chart view (such as a task's Gantt bar), you can add or remove items. For example, it might be useful to compare baseline, interim, and scheduled plans in a single view. Doing so helps you evaluate the schedule adjustments you have made.

Scenario: At Lucerne Publishing, you're managing a book project that is now underway. For this project, you are tracking progress closely and have found value in showing the team a view that compares current progress with a baseline plan. Now you'd like to add an interim plan to this view because the interim plan is more timely than the original baseline.

In this exercise, you customize a Gantt chart view with a custom bar style.

 SET UP You need the Advanced Formatting_Start file located in your Chapter17 practice file folder to complete this exercise. Open the Advanced Formatting_Start file, and save it as Advanced Formatting.

To begin, you will display the Tracking Gantt view.

1   On the **View** tab, in the **Task Views** group, click the arrow below the **Gantt Chart** button, and then click **Tracking Gantt**.

Project displays the Tracking Gantt view.

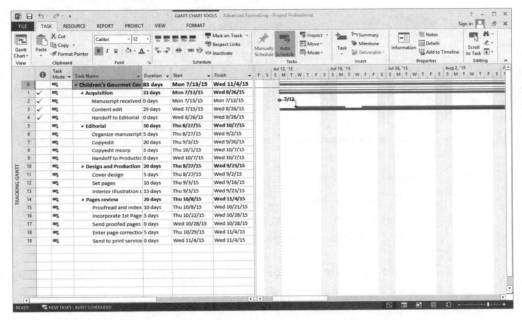

Next, you will customize this view. You will add the interim plan bars to the view.

2   On the **Format** tab, in the **Bar Styles** group, click **Format** and then click **Bar Styles**.

The Bar Styles dialog box appears. In this dialog box, the formatting changes you make to a particular bar type or other element apply to all such bars or elements in the Gantt chart. All of these bar and element types are listed in the Name column in the Bar Styles dialog box.

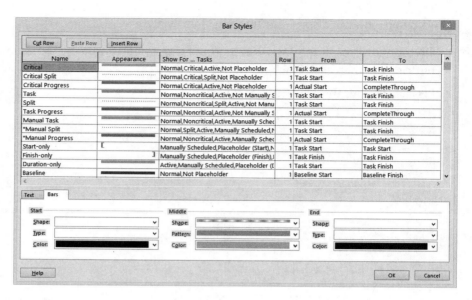

TIP You can also display this dialog box by double-clicking the background of the chart portion of a Gantt chart view or by right-clicking in the background and selecting Bar Styles from the shortcut menu.

3   Scroll down the list of the bars, and in the **Name** column, click **Summary Progress**.

4   Click **Insert Row**.

Project inserts a row for a new bar type in the table. Project draws Gantt bars in the order in which they are listed in the Bar Styles dialog box.

5   In the new cell in the **Name** column, type **Interim**.

Interim is the name of the new bar type that will appear on the chart portion of the view.

TIP The names of task bars will appear in the legend of printed Gantt chart views. If you do not want a task bar name to appear in the legend, type an asterisk (*) at the beginning of the task bar name. For example, if you want to prevent *Interim* from appearing in the legend, you enter its name here as ***Interim***. In the Bar Styles dialog box, you can see that the Manual Milestone task bar name (among others) is prefaced with an asterisk, so it does not appear in the legend of the printed Gantt chart view.

6   In the same row, click the cell under the **Show For...Tasks** column heading, and then click **Normal** on the drop-down list.

The Show For...Tasks value indicates the type of task the bar will represent (such as a normal task, a summary task, or a milestone) or the status of the task (such as critical or in progress).

7   Click the cell under the **Row** column heading, and in the drop-down list, click **2**.

This causes Project to display multiple rows of Gantt bars for each task in the view. Each task can have up to four bar rows.

TIP Project draws bars and other elements on a bar row in the order in which they are listed in the Bar Styles dialog box. This introduces the possibility of one bar obscuring another bar (or other element). If you don't get the results you want, look at the order of items in the Bar Styles dialog box.

8   Click the cell under the **From** column heading, and in the drop-down list, click **Start1**.

9   Click the cell under the **To** column heading, and then in the drop-down list, click **Finish1**.

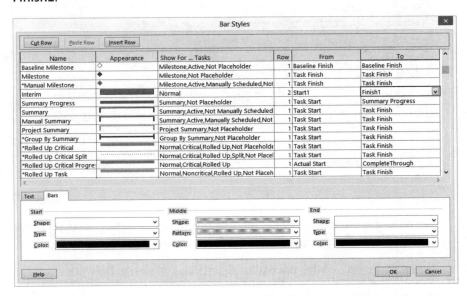

The From and To values represent the start and end points for the bar. The *Start1* and *Finish1* items are the fields in which the first interim plan values were previously set for you in the plan. The current start date and finish date of each task in the plan were saved to these fields when the interim plan was set. If you completed

Chapter 14, "Tracking progress on tasks and assignments," you have already been introduced to interim plans.

You have now instructed Project to display the first interim plan's start and finish dates as bars. Next, focus your attention on the lower half of the Bar Styles dialog box. There you will change the visual appearance of the new bar style.

10   Make sure the *Interim* bar you just created is still selected. Under the **Middle** label, in the **Shape** box ensure the full-height bar (the second option from the top of the list) is selected.

11   In the **Pattern** box, click the solid bar, the second option from the top of the list.

12   Click the **Color** box and, under **Standard Colors**, click green.

> **TIP** Point to a color to see its name in a ScreenTip.

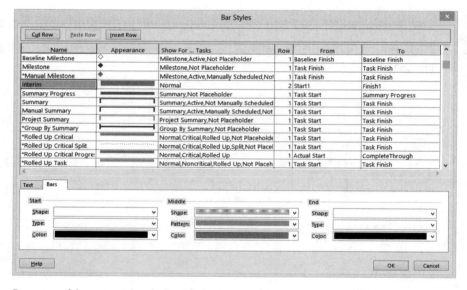

Because this customized view focuses on the interim plan, next you'll format the interim bars to show their start and finish dates.

13   In the lower half of the **Bar Styles** dialog box, click the **Text** tab.

14   In the **Left** box, click **Start1** in the drop-down list.

> **TIP** When selecting items from a list like this, you can often begin typing the name of the item you want, and when its full name appears, select it. For example if you type **s**, Project shows the values that begin with the letter *s*. If you then type **t**, Project shows the values that begin with the letters *st*.

15   In the **Right** box, click **Finish1** in the drop-down list.

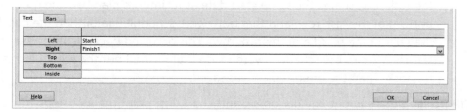

Selecting these values will display the Start1 and Finish1 dates on either side of the interim bars.

16   Click **OK** to close the Bar Styles dialog box.

Project displays the green interim bars on the Tracking Gantt view.

With multiple rows of bars now displayed per task, it can be difficult to visually connect task names to their bars. To remedy this, you will add horizontal gridlines to the chart portion of the view so that you can more easily associate Gantt bars with their tasks.

17   On the **Format** tab, in the **Format** group, click **Gridlines**, and then click **Gridlines**.

18   Under **Lines to change**, leave **Gantt Rows** selected, and in the **Type** box under **Normal**, select the small dashed line (the fourth option), and then click **OK**.

Project draws dashed lines across the chart portion of the Gantt Chart view.

To conclude this exercise, you will zoom out to get a better look at the overall plan.

19   On the **View** tab, in the **Zoom** group, click the arrow next to the **Timescale** box and click **Weeks**.

20   In the **Task Name** column, click the name of task 3, *Content edit*.

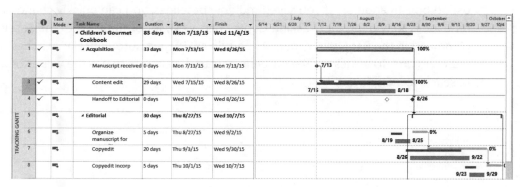

Here you can see that the completed task 3 (shown as a blue bar in the upper part of the task row) shares the same start date as its interim plan bar (the green bar at the bottom of the task row) and that both were scheduled later than the baseline (the gray bar in the middle of the task row). This occurred because, after the baseline was set, changes to the schedule were made that pushed out the scheduled start date of the task. Then the interim plan was saved.

TIP To see details about any bar on a Gantt chart, just point the mouse pointer at the bar. Its details will appear in a ScreenTip.

Yet more formatting options

Project supports several additional Gantt chart formatting features besides the ones you worked with in this section. If you want to explore other formatting options, look at these commands on the Format tab:

- **The Text Styles button in the Format group**   For formatting text associated with a specific task type, such as summary task text

- **The Layout button in the Format group**   For formatting link lines and Gantt bars' appearance

- **The Baseline and Slippage commands in the Bar Styles group**   For quickly switching which of the 11 sets of baseline bars and slippage lines (Baseline, Baseline1 through Baseline10) are shown in the chart portion of a Gantt chart view

All of the options you select in the Bar Styles group of the Format tab (other than the Format command itself) are represented in the Bar Styles dialog box. You can change the visual appearance of critical tasks, slack, and other such items via the Bar Styles dialog box. In addition, if you saved multiple baselines, you can quickly change which baseline is shown (on the Tracking Gantt Chart view, for example) with the Baseline command in the Bar Styles group. As you do so, Project automatically switches the From and To values for the baseline bars and elements to use the values of the baseline you displayed.

Formatting a Timeline view

As you might recall from Chapter 2, "A guided tour of Project," and Chapter 7, the *Timeline view* is a handy way of seeing the "big picture" of the plan. If you completed Chapter 7, you customized a Timeline view and adjusted the visual display of some tasks, such as switching the display of a task from a bar to a callout. You might find that the default text formatting of the Timeline view meets your needs, but you're also able to customize its look. As with the Gantt chart views, you can format entire categories of items (such as all milestone dates) with text styles or apply direct formatting to a specific item you choose.

Scenario: At Lucerne Publishing, you've found that the team working on the children's gourmet cookbook project likes the Timeline view. Some of these people have said the milestone date values are too small, so you'll make them more prominent. While you're at it, you'll apply other formatting changes in the Timeline view as well.

In this exercise, you format text and task bar elements in the Timeline view.

1　On the **View** tab, in the **Split View** group, select the **Timeline** check box.

Project displays the Timeline view. This Timeline view has been populated for you with some tasks from the plan.

2　Click anywhere in the **Timeline** view, and then click the **Format** tab.

This contextual tab dynamically changes based on the active view or selected item.

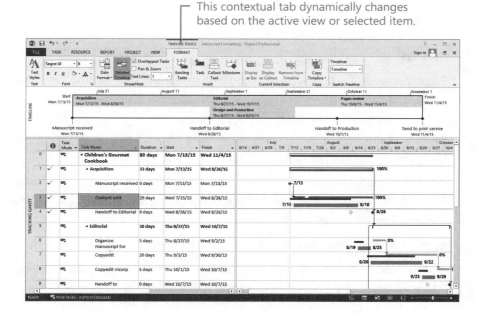

Putting the focus on the timeline causes the commands on the Format tab to change. Remember that the Format tab is contextual; it adjusts based on what is currently selected.

First, you will adjust the formatting of an entire category of text values in the Timeline view.

3   On the **Format** tab, in the **Text** group, click **Text Styles**.

The Text Styles dialog box appears. With this dialog box, you can alter the formatting of all occurrences of a specific type of information in the view.

4   In the **Item to Change** box, click **Milestone Date**.

5   In the **Font style** box, click **Bold**.

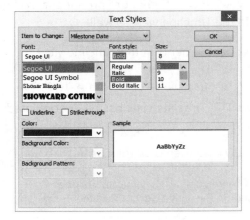

6   Click **OK**.

Project applies the text style change to all milestone dates in the Timeline view.

Next, you'd like to visually distinguish the *Design and Production* task in the timeline. You'll do so through direct formatting, instead of a style-based format change as you made in the preceding steps.

7   In the **Timeline** view, click the *Design and Production* task bar.

A selection border appears around the task bar, indicating that it is selected.

8   On the **Format** tab, in the **Font** group, click **Italic**.

Project italicizes the task bar's label (the task name) and its dates.

9   On the **Format** tab, in the **Font** group, click the arrow next to the **Background Color** button (it looks like a tipping paint can) and then, under **Standard Colors,** click yellow.

Project changes the task bar's color to yellow.

Now that you've applied the formatting you want, you'll temporarily hide the Timeline view.

10   On the **View** tab, in the **Split View** group, clear the **Timeline** check box.

Project hides the Timeline view. (The information in the view is not lost; it's just hidden for now.)

Because the Timeline view is simpler than most other views in Project, it has fewer formatting options.

Formatting a Network Diagram view

In traditional project management, a *network diagram* is a standard way of representing project activities and their relationships. Tasks are represented as boxes, or *nodes*, and the relationships between tasks are drawn as lines connecting the nodes. Unlike a Gantt chart, which is a timescaled view, a network diagram enables you to view project activities in a manner more closely resembling a flowchart format. This is useful if you'd like to place more focus on the relationships between activities rather than on their durations and sequence.

As with Gantt chart views, Project provides rich formatting options for the Network Diagram view. For example, you can change the overall layout of the Network Diagram view to group nodes by time period. In this section, you will customize the information that appears within nodes and node shape. If you're a heavy-duty network diagram user, you'll want to explore the formatting options in greater detail.

Scenario: At Lucerne Publishing, you've found the Network Diagram view helps the project team more clearly focus on task relationships rather than the sequence of the tasks. You decide to adjust the formatting of the Network Diagram view.

In this exercise, you change what information appears in task boxes and their shapes in the Network Diagram view.

1   In the **Task name** column, click the name of task 7, *Copyedit*.

    When you switch to the Network Diagram view, you'll find task 7 visible on the right side of your screen.

2   On the **View** tab, in the **Task Views** group, click **Network Diagram**.

    The Network Diagram view appears. In this view, each task is represented by a box or node, and each node contains several pieces of information (or fields) about the task.

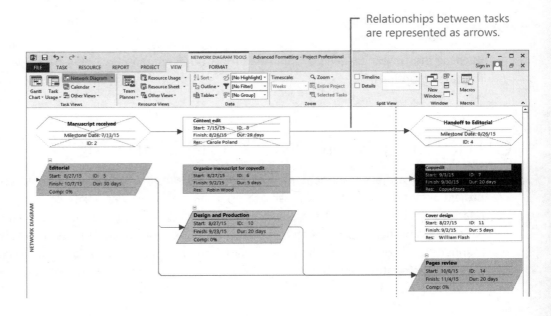

Relationships between tasks are represented as arrows.

Nodes with an X drawn through them represent completed tasks. Nodes with parallelogram shapes represent summary tasks.

In this exercise, you'd like to replace the task ID values with the *Work Breakdown Structure (WBS)* codes. Unlike task ID numbers, WBS codes indicate each task's location in the hierarchy of the plan.

3   On the **Format** tab, in the **Format** group, click **Box Styles**.

Recall that commands on the Format tab change depending on the type of active view; the Format tab is a contextual tab.

The Box Styles dialog box appears.

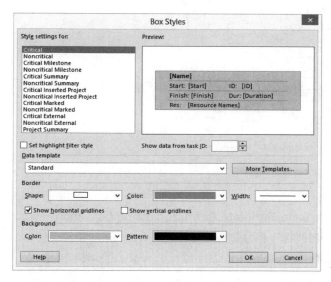

In the Style Settings For list, you can see all the task box styles available in Project.

Currently, the Network Diagram view has the Standard template applied to several of the box styles, such as *Critical*. In this context, *templates* determine what fields appear in boxes (nodes) as well as their layout (not to be confused with file templates). Next, you will create a copy of this template to customize, leaving your Standard template unaffected.

4   Click **More Templates**.

The Data Templates dialog box appears.

5   In the **Templates in "Network Diagram"** list, make sure that **Standard** is selected, and then click **Copy**.

The Data Template Definition dialog box appears. In the copy of the Standard template, you will replace the ID value with the Work Breakdown Structure (WBS) code value in the upper-right corner of the node.

6   In the **Template name** box, type Standard with WBS.

7   Below **Choose cell(s)**, click **ID**. This is the field you will replace.

8   Click the arrow and in the drop-down list of fields that appears, click **WBS**.

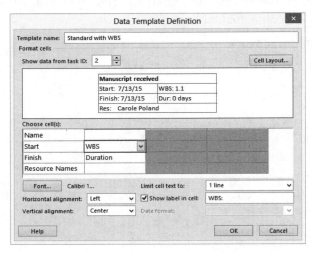

9   Click **OK** to close the **Data Template Definition** dialog box, and then click **Close** to close the **Data Templates** dialog box.

Next, you will update box styles for several task types at once.

10   In the **Box Styles** dialog box, under **Style settings for**, select **Critical**, and while holding down the Shift key, click **Noncritical Milestone**.

The four types of subtasks are selected.

11   In the **Data template** box, select **Standard with WBS** from the drop-down list.

12   In the **Shape** box, select the last shape in the list.

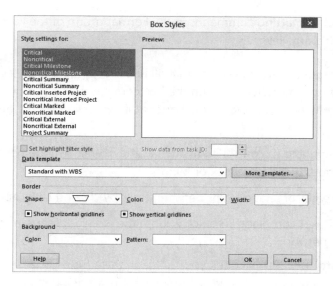

13   Click **OK** to close the **Box Styles** dialog box.

Project applies the revised box style to task boxes in the Network Diagram view.

After you reformat the box styles in the Network Diagram view,
the WBS code replaces the task ID and the box shape changes.

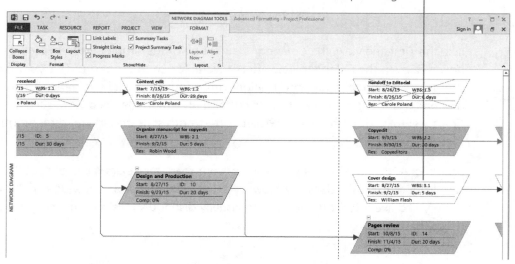

Now, for these box styles, the WBS value appears in the upper-right corner of each box rather than the Task ID and changes the shapes of the boxes for the task types you selected in the preceding steps.

Here are some additional formatting commands in the Format group of the Format tab that apply to the Network Diagram view:

- In the Network Diagram view, you can format all boxes with the Box Styles command, or you can format just the active box with the Box command. This is similar to the Bar Styles and Bar commands available on the Format tab when you have a Gantt chart view displayed.

- Use the Layout command to control items such as the overall arrangement of task boxes by time period, such as by week or by month.

- Show or hide the types of relationships between tasks by clicking Link Labels.

- Use the Collapse Boxes command to quickly zoom the Network Diagram view out to show more of the network.

TIP If you have Microsoft Visio 2007 or later, you can generate a Visio visual report that is similar to a network diagram view. Visio visual reports are pivot diagrams you can customize. For more information about visual reports, see Chapter 20, "Sharing information with other programs."

Formatting a Calendar view

Like the Timeline view, the *Calendar view* is one of the simpler views available in Project; however, even the Calendar view offers several formatting options. This view is especially useful for sharing schedule information with resources or stakeholders who prefer a traditional "month-at-a-glance" format rather than a more detailed view, such as the Gantt Chart view. As with other views, Project offers both style-based and direct formatting of the Calendar view.

Scenario: At Lucerne Publishing, some of your team members have told you they like the simplicity of the Calendar view. However, the default Calendar view doesn't include everything you'd like it to, and you want to visually distinguish tasks on the critical path from those that aren't.

In this exercise, you display summary tasks and reformat critical tasks in the Calendar view.

1   On the **View** tab, in the **Task Views** group, click **Calendar**.

The Calendar view appears.

The Calendar view resembles a traditional "month-at-a-glance" calendar and displays tasks as bars spanning the days on which they are scheduled to occur.

This view displays several weeks at a time, and it draws task bars on the days on which tasks are scheduled. The visible weeks are indicated by the orange blocks in the monthly calendars on the left side of the view.

The Calendar view currently includes the project summary task and subtask bars, but not summary task bars. You'll display those next.

2   On the **Format** tab, in the **Format** group, click **Bar Styles**.

The Bar Styles dialog box appears.

3   In the **Task type** box, click **Summary**.

4   In the **Bar type** box, click **Line** in the drop-down list.

You'll see the summary tasks displayed as lines in the Calendar view shortly, but while you're in the Bar Styles dialog box you'll next change the formatting of critical tasks. Currently, the Calendar view formats critical and noncritical tasks the same; you will change this.

5   In the **Task type** box, click **Critical**.

6   Click the **Color** box and, under **Standard Colors**, click red.

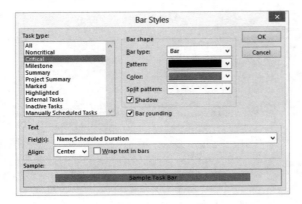

7   Click **OK** to close the **Bar Styles** dialog box.

Project applies the format options to the Calendar view. The summary task lines appear below the subtask bars. Next, you'll adjust the layout of the summary task lines so that they appear above the subtask bars.

8   On the **Format** tab, in the **Layout** group, click **Layout Now**.

Project updates the Calendar view so that subtask bars appear below their summary task lines.

Note the down arrows that appear next to many dates. These indicate that some task bars are not able to fit in the current height of the week rows. You'll adjust this next.

9   On the **Format** tab, in the **Layout** group, click **Adjust Week Height**.

Project adjusts the height of the week rows to show all task bars.

After you reformat the Calendar view, critical tasks appear red and summary tasks appear as lines.

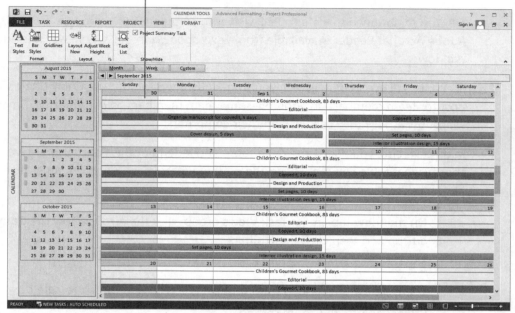

As with the other views you customized in this chapter, the Calendar view has additional formatting options available on the Format tab.

Printing and exporting views

Project offers customization options for printing views beyond what you worked with in Chapter 7. Because views such as the Gantt Chart view are often shared with resources and other project stakeholders, you might find that you need to add additional details to the views you print.

When printing views, you can choose from a wide range of options. For example, you can customize headers and footers, specify what will print in the legend, and include specific options such as task or resources notes.

The printing and page layout options you can adjust vary with the type of view that is currently displayed. Simpler views, like the Resource Sheet view, have fewer printing and page layout options than do more complex views, like the Gantt Chart view.

Sometimes, you might need to produce a high-fidelity snapshot of a view for online viewing. To this end, Project supports easy generation of PDF and XPS format files.

TIP You might need to install a PDF viewer to complete this exercise. A free version of Adobe Acrobat Reader is available from *www.adobe.com*. An XPS viewer is included with Windows.

Scenario: At Lucerne Publishing, you frequently need to print the Gantt Chart view to post for team members. In addition, some team members have requested Timeline-view snapshots as files they can view on their computers.

In this exercise, you adjust the page setup and legend of the Gantt Chart view, and you specify what table columns to include on the printed view. You then generate a PDF or XPS file of the Timeline view.

1   On the **View** tab, in the **Task Views** group, click the arrow below the **Gantt Chart** button and then click **Gantt Chart**.

The Gantt Chart view appears.

2   On the **View** tab, in the **Zoom** group, click **Weeks** in the **Timescale** box.

Project adjusts the zoom setting.

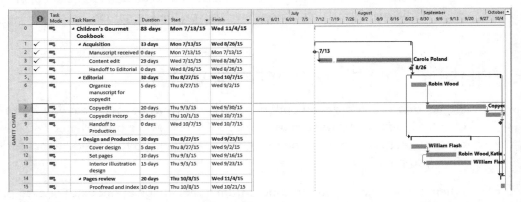

If you completed Chapter 7, you've already seen the Gantt Chart view in the Print Preview window in the Backstage. There, you adjusted some print options, like printing a specific date range. Here, you'll explore some additional printing options.

3 On the **File** tab, click **Print**.

The Print screen appears in the Backstage with the Gantt Chart in the preview. As currently set up, this view will require two letter-size pages to print. Note the *1 of 2* status message below the print preview.

TIP If you have a plotter selected as your default printer, or you have a different page size selected, what you see in the print preview review screen might differ from what's shown in this exercise.

4 Under **Settings**, click **Page Setup**. This link appears at the bottom of the controls, to the left of the print preview.

The Page Setup dialog box appears. Next, you'll adjust the settings so that the full Gantt Chart view will print on a single page.

5 Make sure the **Page** tab is visible, and then under **Scaling**, click **Fit to** and type or select 1 page wide by 1 tall.

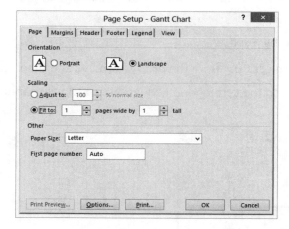

Next, you will customize what appears in the Gantt chart's legend.

6 In the **Page Setup** dialog box, click the **Legend** tab.

7 On the **Legend** tab are three alignment tabs. Click the **Left** tab.

Here, you can see the text and field codes that appear in the legend.

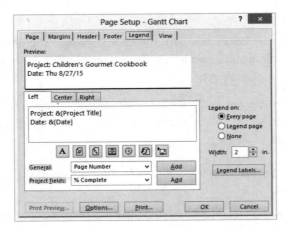

Project will print the project title and current date on the left side of the legend. You also want to print the plan's estimated cost value in the legend.

8   On the **Left** tab, click at the end of the second line of text, and then press the Enter key.

9   Type **Total Cost:** followed by a space.

10   In the **Project fields** box, select **Cost** from the drop-down list, and then click **Add**.

Project adds the cost code to the Left legend text, and the cost value appears in the Preview.

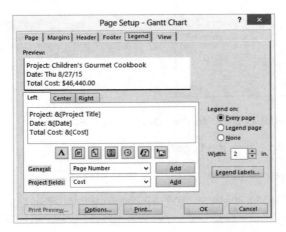

To conclude the page setup customization, you'll specify what columns from the table in the Gantt Chart view get printed.

11   Click the **View** tab.

12   Click **Print all sheet columns**, and then click **OK** to close the **Page Setup** dialog box.

Project applies the changes you specified in the Page Setup dialog box. To get a closer look, zoom in on the legend.

13   In the **Print Preview** screen, click the lower-left corner of the page with the magnifying-glass pointer.

Project zooms in to show the page at a legible resolution.

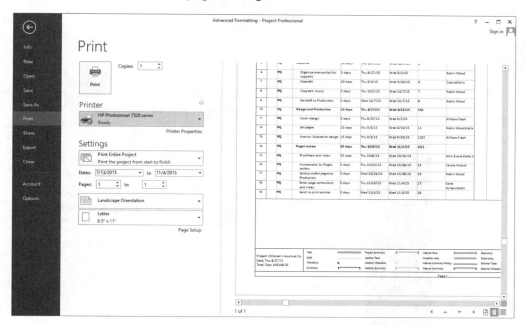

Next, you'll shift focus from output formatting options to output file types. Two common file formats of printed output are Portable Document Format (PDF) and XML Paper Specification (XPS). PDF represents an Adobe Acrobat document. XPS is a format supported by Microsoft. Both formats provide a high-fidelity online representation of what would appear on a printed page. To conclude this exercise, you'll generate a PDF or XPS output file of the Timeline view.

14   Click the Back button to exit the Backstage.

15   On the **View** tab, in the **Split View** group, select the **Timeline** check box.

Project displays the same Timeline view you customized earlier in this chapter.

16   Click anywhere in the **Timeline** view to put the focus on it.

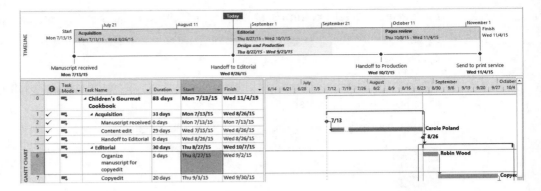

17   On the **File** tab, click **Export**.

The Export screen includes options for sharing the plan. Note the explanation of PDF and XPS documents appears on the right side of the screen.

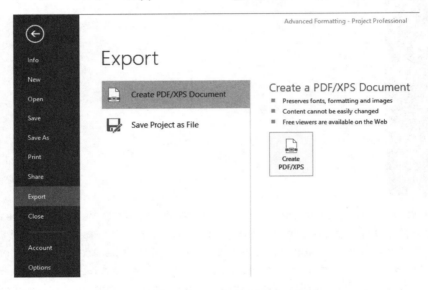

18   On the right side of the screen, click **Create PDF/XPS**.

The Browse dialog box appears. Use the file name and location given in the dialog box.

19   In the **Save as type** box, select either **PDF Files** or **XPS Files** (depending on what format you want to see), and then click **OK**.

The Document Export Options dialog box appears.

20   Click **OK** to use the default settings.

Project generates the PDF or XPS document.

21   In File Explorer, navigate to the Chapter17 folder and double-click the PDF or XPS document you created.

You can share details from your plans with team members and other project stakeholders. When doing so, give consideration to both the appropriate level of detail to share and the format in which you share it.

✖ CLEAN UP Close the Advanced Formatting file.

Key points

- Use the Bar Styles dialog box to add additional bar types or other elements, such as an interim plan, to a Gantt chart view.

- Use the Bar Styles dialog box to change the appearance of a specific type of Gantt bar, such as all summary tasks.

- In the Timeline view, you can directly modify text or all text styles, such as all task names, with the commands in the Font and Text groups on the Format tab.

- Nodes represent tasks and summary tasks in the Network Diagram view. You can customize the information that appears in a node.

- The Calendar view is especially helpful for those who prefer a traditional "month-at-a-glance" format.

- You can adjust page layout and legend text for Gantt chart views in the Backstage.

- Use the PDF or XPS formats for sharing project details that approximate on the screen what one can print.

Chapter at a glance

Format

Customize tables in reports, page 390.

MILESTONES DUE
Milestones that are coming soon.

Name	Finish	Baseline Finish
Handoff to Production	Wed 10/7/15	Fri 9/25/15
Send proofed pages to Production	Wed 10/28/15	Fri 10/16/15
Send to print service	Wed 11/4/15	Fri 10/23/15

Visualize

Customize charts in reports, page 399.

RESOURCE STATS
Work status for all work resources.

	Carole Poland	Copyedit ors	John Evans	Katie Jordan	Robin Wood	William Flash
Remaining Work	40 hrs	104 hrs	80 hrs	144 hrs	104 hrs	64 hrs
Actual Work	232 hrs	56 hrs	0 hrs	56 hrs	96 hrs	96 hrs
Baseline Work	240 hrs	160 hrs	80 hrs	200 hrs	200 hrs	160 hrs

Choose

Create custom reports with your choice of fields, page 406.

Style

Apply styles to charts and tables in custom reports, page 414.

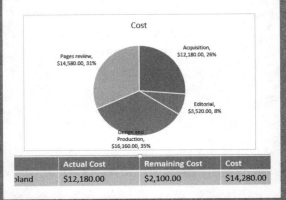

Advanced report formatting

IN THIS CHAPTER, YOU WILL LEARN HOW TO

- Change the content and formatting of tables in a report.

- Change a chart's layout and content.

- Create a custom report with chart and table elements.

This chapter continues the focus on advanced formatting and customization features introduced in the previous chapter. This chapter focuses on reports.

As you might recall from "Customizing reports" in Chapter 7, "Formatting and sharing your plan," Microsoft Project 2013 replaces the old tabular reports feature with an entirely new way of visualizing your Project data. The new reports feature includes a dynamic mix of tables, charts, and textual content, and it's highly customizable.

TIP If you're looking for information on visual reports, see "Generating visual reports with Excel and Visio" in Chapter 20, "Sharing information with other programs."

To begin, let's compare *reports* and *views*. Any report or view focuses on just a subset of your plan's data. Every report and view included with Project is designed to help you better visualize some aspect of your plan. You normally need to work with multiple reports and views over time to manage the aspects of your plan that matter most to you.

For example, if your project is primarily deadline-driven, you'll get the best insight into your plan by working with *timescaled* views such as the Gantt chart views, the Timeline and usage views, and reports such as Upcoming Tasks, Critical Tasks, and Late Tasks.

There are important differences between reports and views, however. Throughout this book, you've worked in views both to enter and modify schedule data (such as task names and resource assignments) and to see schedule details (such as which resources are assigned to what tasks). With reports, however, you can't directly change your plan's data. You can't add or delete tasks or change resource assignments, for example. What reports excel at is giving you more options for discovering and sharing key aspects of your plan in formats that are visually compelling. What's more, you can customize reports to include just the information you want, presented the way you want.

TIP Project includes a set of instructional tools designed as reports. On the Report tab, in the View Reports group, click Getting Started and then click the report you want. You'll also find more information about reports in Project's online help. Click the Help button (which looks like a question mark) in the upper-right corner of the Project window, and in the Help Search box, type **Create a Project report**.

Reports can contain two main elements: tables and charts. In addition, reports can include other elements such as text boxes, images (such as photographs), and shapes. In this chapter, you will format and customize both table and chart elements, and create a custom report that includes a mix of elements.

PRACTICE FILES Before you can complete the exercises in this chapter, you need to copy the book's practice files to your computer. A complete list of practice files is provided in "Download the practice files" at the beginning of this book. For each exercise that has a practice file, simply browse to where you saved the book's practice file folder.

IMPORTANT If you are running Project Professional with Project Web App/Project Server, take care not to save any of the practice files you work with in this book to Project Web App (PWA). For more information, see Appendix C, "Collaborating: Project, SharePoint, and PWA."

Formatting tables in a report

As with views, tables in reports use Project field labels as column headings and display field values in the rows. The *field* labels (such as *Duration*) and values (such as *20 days*) are the same labels and values you see in views and dialog boxes throughout Project. In fact, many of the tables included in reports are similar to tables found in views, such as the Entry table.

When you select any table in a report, the Field List pane appears. In this pane, you control what fields are included in the selected table. In the Field List pane, you can also apply *filtering*, *grouping*, and *sorting* of the table rows and, for task fields, change the outline levels of what tasks get displayed. Fields in Project are organized into task fields and resource fields. You will work with the Field List pane in the following exercise.

When you select a table in a report, in addition to the Field List pane appearing, the two Table Tools contextual tabs, Design and Layout, also appear on the ribbon:

- **The Design tab** Contains commands to add or remove a header row, change the table's formatting, apply table styles (color schemes), and apply WordArt styles to selected text in the table.

- **The Layout tab** Contains commands you use to adjust row height and column width, adjust the alignment of content in the table's cells, and make other table size adjustments.

In addition, whenever you view a report the Report Tools Design contextual tab appears. You'll work with this tab later in this chapter when you create a custom report.

The scenario: At Lucerne Publishing, the team working on the children's gourmet cookbook as well as the project's sponsors like the Project Overview report for its concise project status that can be seen at a glance. Because the cookbook plan includes a baseline, you want to include the baseline finish values of upcoming milestones in the report. You also like how the Project Statistics dialog box shows % Complete and % Work Complete side by side, and you'd like to add this to the report as well.

In this exercise, you change the content and formatting of tables in a report.

 SET UP You need the Advanced Reporting_Start file located in your Chapter18 practice file folder to complete this exercise. Open the Advanced Reporting_Start file, and save it as Advanced Reporting.

1   On the **Report** tab, in the **View Reports** group, click **Dashboards** and then click **Project Overview**.

Project displays the Project Overview report.

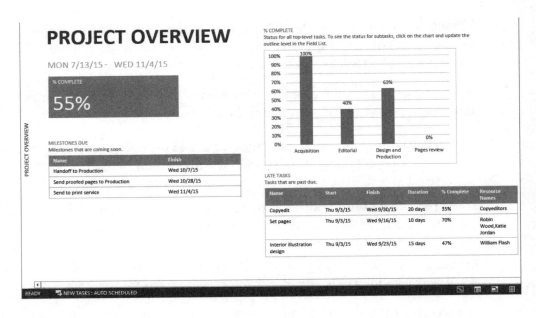

This is a handy report that conveys the vital statistics of a plan. To begin your customizations of this report, you'll add the Baseline Finish field to the Milestones Due table.

2   Click anywhere in the *Milestones Due* table in the lower-left corner of the report.

Project displays the Field List pane.

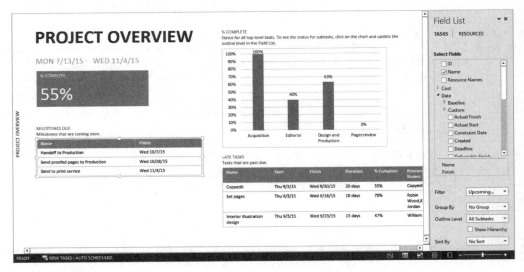

TIP If the Field List pane did not appear when you clicked in the Milestones Due table, try this. On the Table Tools Design tab, in the Show/Hide group, click Table Data. This commands toggles the display of the Field List pane on or off.

In the Field List pane, take a moment to scroll through the list of items under the Select Fields heading. As you can see, the selected fields *Name* and *Finish* match the fields included in the Milestones Due table. (The selected field names are also listed below the Select Fields box.) In addition, this table has the Upcoming Milestones filter applied (which might be truncated to *Upcoming...*) in the Filter box in the lower part of the Field List pane. If this filter were not applied, the table would include the names and finish dates of all tasks in the plan. With the filter applied, however, only uncompleted milestone tasks are displayed. Note that the filter, group, outline, and sort options available with a report table are similar to those you can apply to a view.

Because you plan to add a field (or column) to the table, you'll need to resize the table later so that it will fit correctly in the report. Next, you'll note the table's current width.

3   On the **Table Tools Layout** tab, in the **Table Size** group, note the current width.

Now you're ready to add the Baseline Finish field to the table. The Field List pane organizes Project's fields in a hierarchy, so you'll work through the hierarchy structure to get to the field you want. Because the Baseline Finish field is a baseline field that contains a date value, you'll look in the Baseline category.

4   In the **Select Fields** box, in the **Fields List** pane, under **Date**, click the expand/collapse arrow next to **Baseline** to expand the Baseline fields list.

5   In the **Baseline** fields list, click **Baseline Finish**.

Project adds the Baseline Finish field to the table.

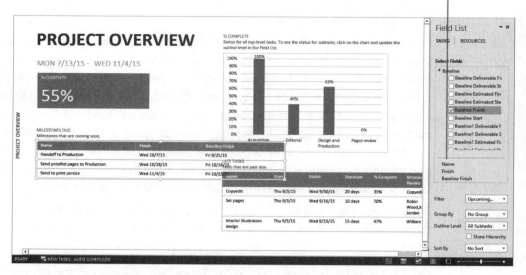

The names of selected fields appear here.

Because the Upcoming Milestones filter is applied to this table, only the Baseline Finish values for upcoming milestones are displayed in the table.

With the Baseline Finish column added to the table, it is now too wide. You'll address this next.

6   On the **Table Tools Layout** tab, in the **Table Size** group, in the **Width** box type or select 4.4 and then press the Enter key.

TIP If you don't immediately see your formatting change applied in the report, try this: click in the background of the report to deselect the selected table or chart.

Project resizes the table close to its original width.

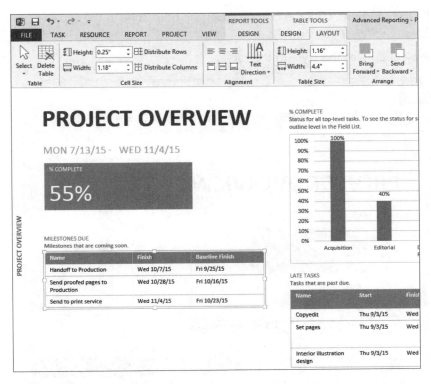

TIP Other ways you can change the width of the table include double-clicking the column dividers so that they adjust to accommodate the content of the column, or dragging the handle on the right edge of the table to the left. Feel free to experiment with these techniques.

Now that the table contains the fields you want, you'll next apply a table style to give it a different look.

7   On the **Table Tools Design** tab, in the **Table Styles** group, click the **More** button to display the gallery of table styles.

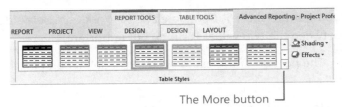

The More button

8   Under **Medium**, click the orange style (the third style in the top row; its ToolTip is *Medium Style 1 – Accent 2*).

Project applies the style to the table.

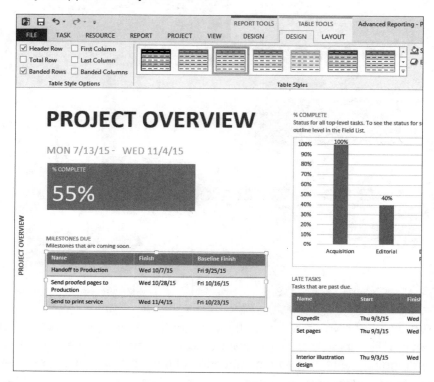

Next, you'll turn your attention to the large orange % Complete box in the upper-left corner of the report. This element is also a table, but it contains just one column, the % Complete field. Recall from earlier that you can include Project fields only in tables, so using a single-column table (that is, the cell that contains the field's value plus the field name as the label) is a smart way to give visual focus to a single value like % Complete.

For this report, you want to show % Complete and % Work Complete side by side. The difference between the two values is subtle but important:

- **% Complete**   The portion of the plan's overall scheduled duration that has elapsed so far

- **% Work Complete**   The portion of the plan's total scheduled work that has been completed so far

9   Click anywhere in the *% Complete* table.

Note that the selected fields, filter, and outline level in the Field List pane are different for this table.

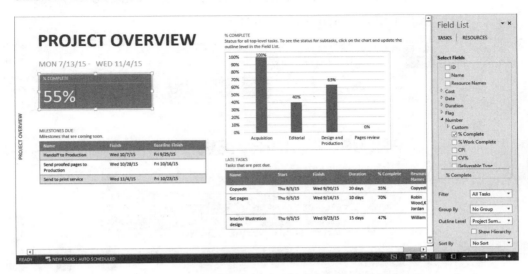

Because this is a single-column table, only the % Complete field for the project summary task is displayed. Note the value in the Outline Level box in the Field List pane: Project Summary (which might be truncated to *Project Sum...*).

10   In the **Select Fields** box, under **Number**, select **% Work Complete**.

Project adds the % Work Complete field to the table, although it's not visible right now because this table's text is formatted white (as is the report background).

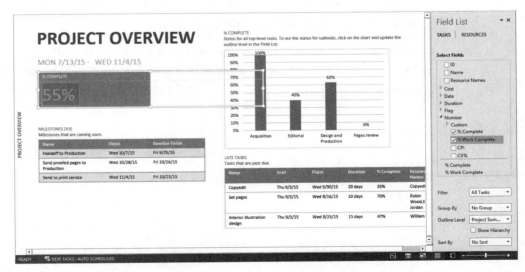

Next, you will change the color formatting of the table.

11   On the **Table Tools Design** tab, in the **Table Styles** group, click **Shading** and then in the top row under **Theme Colors**, click **Orange** (its ToolTip is *Orange – Accent 2*).

Project applies orange fill to the table.

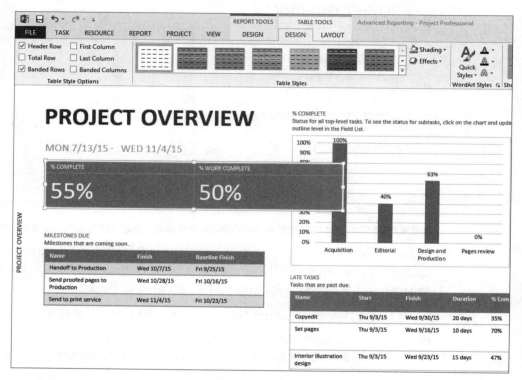

To conclude this exercise, you'll resize the table.

12   Click and drag the handle on the right side of the table to the left until this table's width approximately matches the width of the *Milestones Due* table below it.

Project resizes the table.

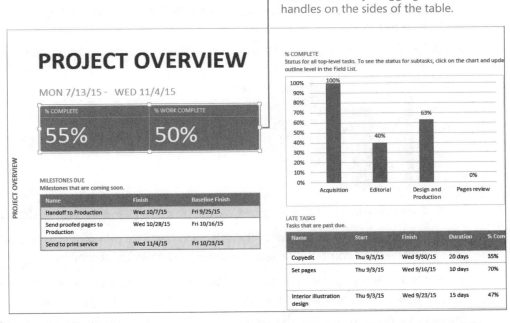

Resize a table by dragging the handles on the sides of the table.

This section introduced you to table formatting in a report. In the next section, you'll focus on chart formatting.

Formatting charts in a report

Project's reports give you charting capabilities comparable to what you'd previously expect to find in an application like Excel. In Project, you can now create a variety of chart types including column, line, pie, and bar charts. Project has included the Resource Graph view (a bar chart showing work allocation per resource) for several versions. With the addition of charts in reports, however, you have much more to work with.

When you select a chart in a report, in addition to the Field List pane appearing, the two Chart Tools contextual tabs, Design and Format, also appear on the ribbon. Note that these are different contextual tabs than appear when a table is selected in a report:

- **The Design tab**   Contains commands to change the chart's layout and style, and include elements such as data labels.

- **The Format tab**   Contains commands to format chart elements such as data series, add and style graphic shapes such as text boxes to a chart, and apply WordArt effects to selected text.

In addition, whenever you select a chart, three floating contextual commands appear:

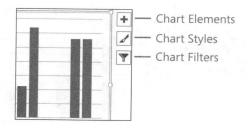

- **Chart elements**   Let you quickly add or remove elements such as data labels
- **Chart styles**   Let you switch the selected chart to a different chart style (basically color and fill combinations) and change the chart's color scheme
- **Chart filters**   Let you add or remove the specific data series (which correspond to Project fields) and data categories (which correspond to specific tasks or resources)

These three floating commands give you quick access to some of the features on the Design tab. You use the Chart Filters' options to include or exclude data categories (specific tasks or resources) from a chart. This feature is especially handy, and one you will use in the following exercise.

The scenario: At Lucerne Publishing, the project team and management like the Resource Overview report for its concise reporting of actual and remaining work per resource. You'd like to change some of the content included in the report and change how it appears.

In this exercise, you change the content and formatting of charts in a report.

1   On the **Report** tab, in the **View Reports** group, click **Resources** and then click **Resource Overview**.

Project displays the Resource Overview report.

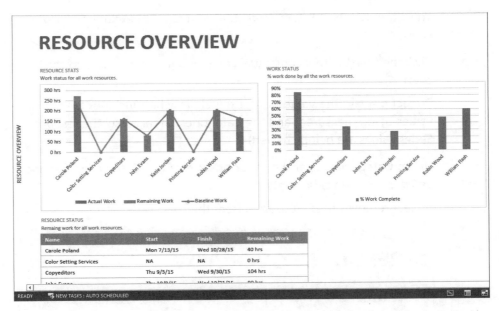

This report includes two charts and a table. Note that both of the charts include resources who have no work values. You'll remove these resources from the first chart.

2 Click anywhere in the *Resource Stats* chart.

Project displays the three floating contextual commands for this chart, as well as the Field List pane. In addition, the contextual tabs in the ribbon are updated.

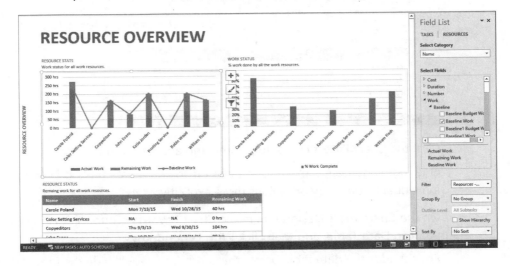

You'll use the Chart Filters contextual command to exclude two resources from this chart.

3   Click the **Chart Filters** contextual command just to the right of the Resource Stats chart.

Project displays the Values list for this chart, which includes the Series values (the values being measured) and the Categories (in this case, the resources for whom the Series values are being charted).

4   Under **Categories**, clear the check boxes for *Color Setting Services* and *Printing Service*, and then click **Apply**.

Project removes these resources from the chart.

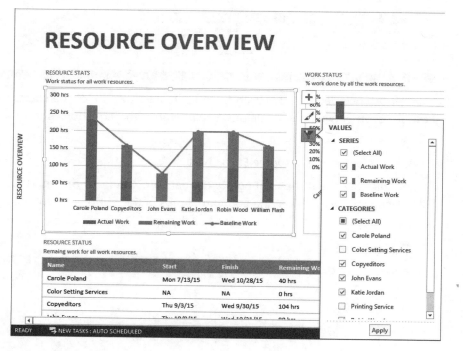

5   Click the **Chart Filters** contextual command again to dismiss it.

One more addition to make to this chart is to add a data table that exposes the individual resources' work values more explicitly.

6   On the **Chart Tools Design** tab, in the **Chart Layouts** group, click **Add Chart Element**, point to **Data Table**, and then click **With Legend Keys**.

Project adds the data table below the chart. Next, you'll hide the (now redundant) legend below the data table.

7   On the **Chart Tools Design** tab, in the **Chart Layouts** group, click **Add Chart Element**, point to **Legend**, and then click **None**.

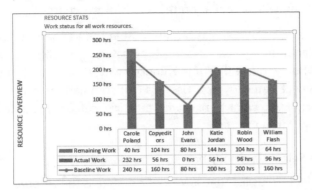

Next, you will use the features in the Field List pane to change the order in which resource names appear in the Work Status chart. As you do so, you'll explore some other settings in the Field List pane.

8   Click anywhere in the *Work Status* chart.

9   In the Field List pane, click the arrow in the **Select Category** box.

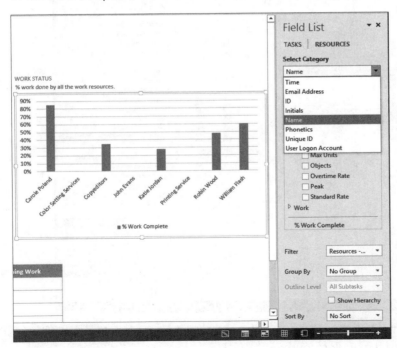

Recall from earlier in the chapter that "Category" in the context of a chart means the type of values that will be displayed in the chart. For this chart, the selected category is the names of resources, which appear on the X-axis of the chart.

TIP Although the Time category value is not applicable to this chart, it is unique and merits some explanation. You can use the Time category to show values (such as work) over time. When you use the Time category with a chart, an Edit command appears next to the Select Category box. Use this Edit command to adjust the timescale in your chart. If you want to play with the Time category settings, a good report to view is the Milestone report.

10   Click the arrow in the **Select Category** box again to close it.

You can see in the Select Fields list that % Work Complete is the resource field for which Project will show the values per category (in this case, resource names). These values are delineated on the Y-axis of the chart, and the specific values per resource appear per column.

11   Click the arrow in the **Filter** box.

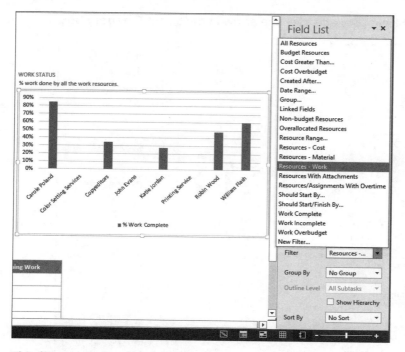

This filter excludes all values other than work resources. Next, you'll adjust the sort order of the work resources.

12   In the **Sort By** box, click **% Work Complete**.

      Project sorts the work resource names in ascending order from lowest to highest %
      Work Complete values. Next, you'll switch this to descending order.

13   Just to the right of the **Sort By** box, click the **Ascending/Descending** sort order
      button.

      Project re-sorts the work resource names in descending order.

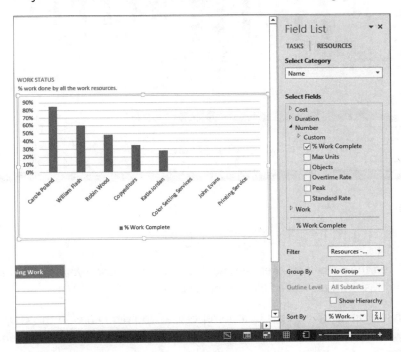

      To conclude this exercise, you'll display data labels on the bars in the chart.

14   On the **Chart Tools Design** tab, in the **Chart Layouts** group, click **Add Chart Element**,
      point to **Data Labels**, and then click **Outside End**.

      Project adds the % Work Complete values per column (that is, per work resource) in
      the chart.

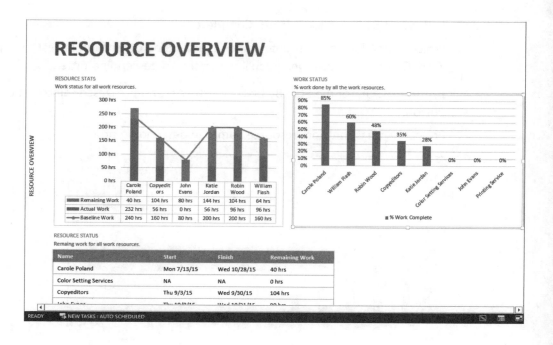

Creating a custom report

If you completed the preceding exercises, you've worked with both table and chart elements using task and resource fields in reports.

In addition to customizing Project's built-in reports as you did earlier in this chapter, you can create custom reports. Custom reports can include any mix of report elements (charts and tables), text boxes, and graphics that you like. In fact, you can combine task and resource information together in a single report to convey insights not possible elsewhere in Project.

In this section, you'll create a custom report for the gourmet cookbook project. When creating your own custom reports, you'll want to dig deeper into the commands on the Report Tools Design tab. You use these commands to select the report elements you want, apply themes, and control page setup options.

The scenario: At Lucerne Publishing, you are sometimes asked for project cost details in terms of both summary tasks (or phase) and resources. You'll create a custom report that includes the mix of cost information you want.

In this exercise, you create a custom report that includes a chart and a table.

1   On the **Report** tab, in the **View Reports** group, click **New Report.**

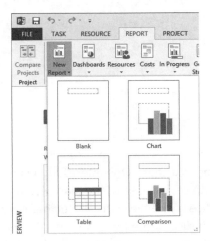

These options let you start either with a blank report or with an initial table or chart. The Comparison option creates a new report that contains two identical charts, with the expectation that you'll customize one or both.

2   Click **Blank**.

The Report Name dialog box appears. The name you enter will be the title at the top of the report and will appear on the Custom menu (in the View Reports group, on the Report tab) so that you can view this report later.

3   In the **Name** field, type Gourmet Cookbook Cost Summary and then click **OK**.

Project creates the new blank report.

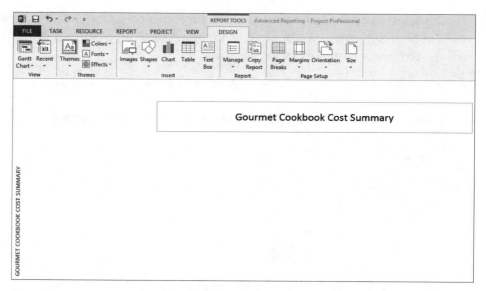

The first element you'll add to the report is a chart. One interesting way of expressing the cost of this plan is as a pie chart, with each phase of the plan (*Acquisition, Editorial*, and so on) represented as a slice of the pie chart. To further clarify how much each phase costs, you'll label each slice of the pie chart with the name, cost, and percentage of the total cost of that phase. This gives you a unique all-up view of the project cost.

4   On the **Report Tools Design** tab, in the **Insert** group, click **Chart**.

The Insert Chart dialog box appears.

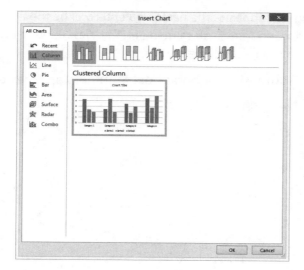

Take a moment to browse through the types of charts supported.

5 Click **Pie**, and then click **OK**.

Project adds a new pie chart to the report and displays the Field List pane.

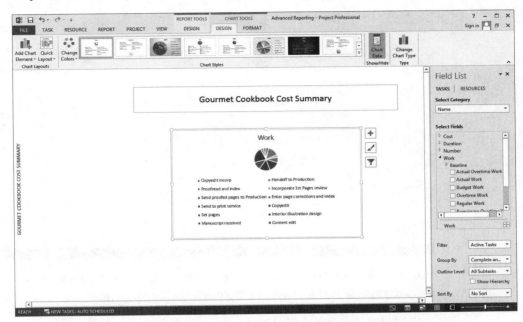

The default new pie chart does not contain the values you want, so you'll change those.

6 In the Field List pane, in the **Select Fields** box, click the expand/collapse arrow next to **Cost** to expand the **Cost** field list, and then select the **Cost** check box.

Next, you'll remove the field you don't want included in the chart.

7 In the **Select Fields** box, under the Work fields list, clear the **Work** check box.

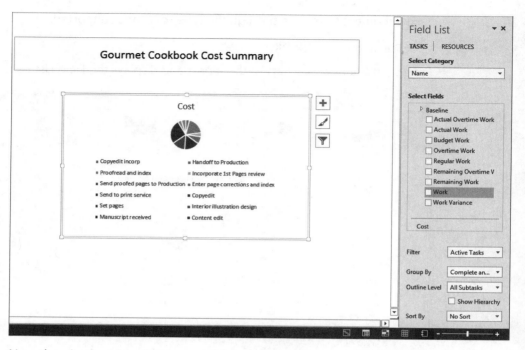

Now the pie chart has the correct field applied, but not for the top-level summary tasks to represent the phases of the plan. You'll change that next.

8   In the **Filter** box, select **All Tasks**.

9   In the **Group By** box, select **No Group**.

10   In the **Outline Level** box, select **Level 1**.

Now the pie chart includes one slice per top-level phase (the Level 1 outline level), and each slice is proportionally sized to represent that phase's percentage of the plan's total cost.

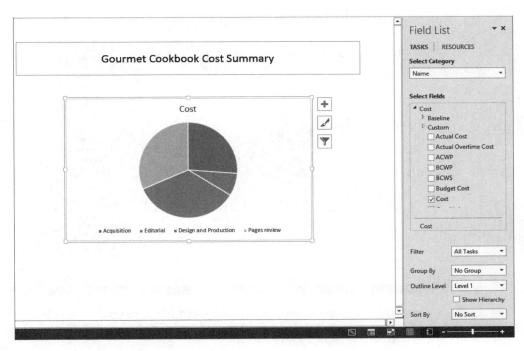

Next, you'll add data labels to the slices.

11   On the **Chart Tools Design** tab, in the **Chart Layouts** group, click **Add Chart Element**, point to **Data Labels**, and then click **More Data Label Options**.

> **TIP** You can also click the Chart Elements floating contextual command, click Data Labels, and then click More Options.

The Format Data Labels pane appears.

12   Under **Label Options**, click (to check) the following boxes: **Category Name** and **Percentage**. Leave the other selected values checked.

13   Under **Label Position**, select **Outside End**.

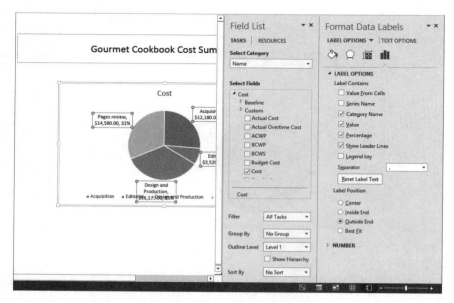

Next, you'll hide the legend below the chart because you've included the Category Name values per slice.

14   Close the **Format Data Labels** pane.

15   On the **Chart Tools Design** tab, in the **Chart Layouts** group, click **Add Chart Element**, point to **Legend**, and then click **None**.

Your screen should look similar to the following illustration.

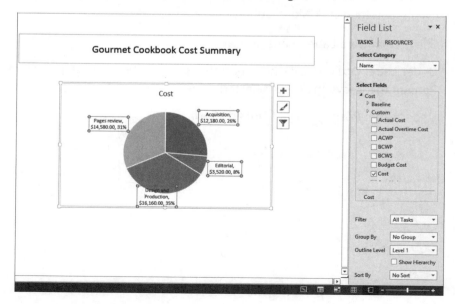

Next, you'll add a table to convey the cost values per resource.

16   Click anywhere outside of the chart to deselect it.

17   On the **Report Tools Design** tab, in the **Insert** group, click **Table**.

Project adds a table to the report.

18   Drag the table below the pie chart.

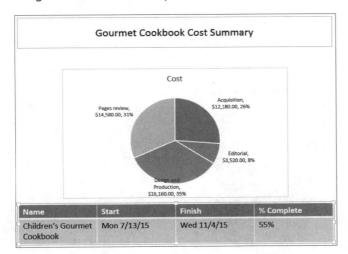

Now you'll change the fields included in the table.

19   At the top of the **Field List** pane, click **Resources**.

This table will contain resource fields.

The default resource table already includes the resource names in the first column, but not the cost values you want. You'll add those next.

20   Below the **Select Fields** box, right-click **Finish**, and in the shortcut menu that appears click **Remove Field**.

21   Right-click **Start**, and in the shortcut menu that appears click **Remove Field**.

Note that as you add or remove fields in the Field List pane, the table is updated to reflect the selected fields.

22   In the **Select Fields** box, click the expand/collapse arrow next to **Cost** to expand the **Cost** field list, and then click the following fields in the order listed:

- **Actual Cost**
- **Remaining Cost**
- **Cost**

To quickly reorder or remove fields, right-click the field name here.

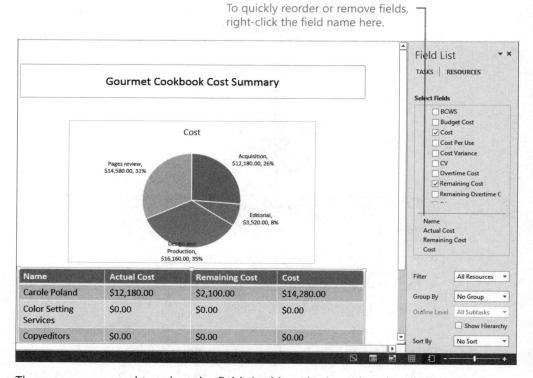

The reason you need to select the fields in this order is so that they'll be added as columns from the left to right in the same order. Because cost is the sum of the actual cost and remaining cost, it's most logical to add it last so that it appears in the rightmost column.

TIP You can also reorder fields in a table by dragging the field names that appear below the Select fields box into the order you want.

To conclude this exercise, you'll apply a table style.

23   On the **Table Tools Design** tab, in the **Table Styles** group, in the table style box, click the orange style (the third style in the box; its ToolTip is *Medium Style 2 – Accent 2*).

Project applies the style to the table.

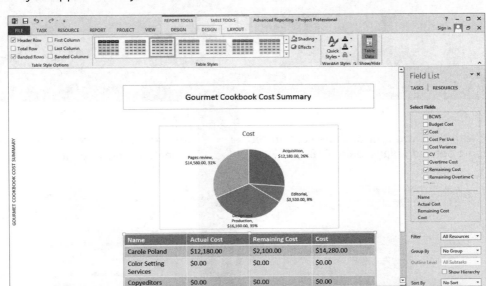

As with all reports, the field values included in this custom report will automatically be updated as the underlying cost and schedule data changes in the plan.

TIP Custom reports reside within the plan in which they were created and are not available in other plans. To make a custom report available in any plan you work with in Project, use the Organizer to copy it to the Global template. For more information about the Organizer, see Chapter 19, "Customizing Project."

❌ CLEAN UP **Close the Advanced Reporting file.**

Key points

- Reports in Project help you visualize your data with a mix of tables, charts, and other elements.

- You use the Field List pane to control which fields are included in a table and how they are organized.

- Project supports a wide range of chart types, including column, line, pie, and bar.

- You can create a custom report with a mix of table and chart elements showing task or resource fields.

Chapter at a glance

Share

Work with the Organizer to share customized elements between plans, page 418.

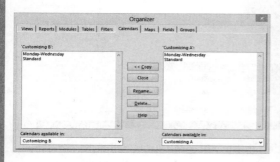

Record

Record a VBA macro to perform often-repeated actions, page 423.

Code

Edit VBA macro code in the Visual Basic Editor, page 429.

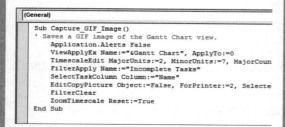

Customize

Create your own custom tab in the ribbon, page 434.

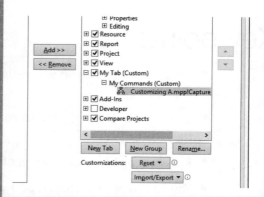

Customizing Project   19

IN THIS CHAPTER, YOU WILL LEARN HOW TO

- Copy a customized element, such as a calendar, from one plan to another by using the Organizer.

- Record and play back a macro.

- Edit a macro in the Visual Basic for Applications (VBA) Editor.

- Customize the Quick Access Toolbar and the ribbon.

This chapter describes some of the ways you can customize Microsoft Project 2013 to suit your own preferences. Like most other Microsoft Office applications, Project uses the *ribbon interface*, which offers good customization options. Project has other customization features, such as the Organizer and global template, that are unique to it. In addition, Project has customization features, such as recording Microsoft Visual Basic for Applications (VBA) macros, that are similar to other Microsoft Office applications.

> **IMPORTANT** Some of the actions you perform in this chapter can affect your overall settings in Project regardless of the specific plan you are using. To keep your Project environment unaffected or at the "factory settings" throughout this chapter, we include steps to undo some actions.

PRACTICE FILES Before you can complete the exercises in this chapter, you need to copy the book's practice files to your computer. A complete list of practice files is provided in "Download the practice files" at the beginning of this book. For each exercise that has a practice file, simply browse to where you saved the book's practice file folder.

> **IMPORTANT** If you are running Project Professional with Project Web App/Project Server, take care not to save any of the practice files you work with in this book to Project Web App (PWA). For more information, see Appendix C, "Collaborating: Project, SharePoint, and PWA."

Sharing custom elements between plans

Project uses a *global template*, named Global.mpt, to provide the default views, tables, reports and other elements you see in Project. The very first time you display a view, table, or similar element in a plan, it is copied automatically from the global template to that plan. Thereafter, the element resides in the plan. Any subsequent customization of that element in the plan (for example, changing the fields displayed in a table) applies to only that one plan and does not affect the global template. The global template is installed as part of Project, and you normally don't work with it directly.

Initially, the specific definitions of all views, tables, and other elements listed here are contained in the global template. For example, the fact that the default Usage table contains one set of fields and not others is determined by the global template. The list of elements provided by the global template includes the following:

- Views
- Reports
- Tables
- Filters
- Calendars
- Groups

In addition, you can copy modules (VBA macros), import/export maps, and custom fields to the global template or between plans.

When you customize an element like a view, the customized element remains in the plan in which it was customized. With views and tables, you have the option of updating the version of that element in the global template with your customized view or table. If you create a new element, however, such as a new view, that new element is copied to the global template and thereafter becomes available in all other plans you might work with.

One exception, however, is calendars. When you create a custom calendar, it remains just in the plan in which it was created. A customized standard calendar that meets your needs in one plan could redefine working times in other plans in ways you do not intend. For this reason, Project has a feature you can use to share custom calendars (and other elements) between plans in a controlled way. That feature is the *Organizer*.

The complete list of elements you can copy between plans with the Organizer was listed previously and is indicated by the names of the tabs in the Organizer dialog box, which you will see shortly.

You could use Project extensively and never need to touch the global template. However, when you do work with the global template, you normally do so through the Organizer. Some actions you can accomplish relating to the global template include the following:

- Create a customized element, such as a custom calendar, and make it available in all plans you work with by copying the custom calendar into the global template.

- Replace a customized element, such as a view or table, in a plan by copying the original, unmodified element from the global template to the plan in which you've customized the same element.

- Copy one customized element, such as a custom report, from one plan to another.

The settings in the global template apply to all plans you work with in Project. Because we don't want to alter the global template that you use, in this exercise, we'll focus on copying customized elements between two plans. Keep in mind, though, that the general process of using the Organizer shown here is the same whether you are working with the global template and a plan or two plans.

IMPORTANT In the Organizer, when you attempt to copy a customized view, table, or other element from a plan to the global template, Project alerts you as to whether you will overwrite that element with the same name in the global template. If you choose to overwrite it, that customized element (such as a customized view) will be available in all new plans and any other plans that do not already contain that element. If you choose to rename the customized element, it becomes available in all plans but does not affect the existing elements already stored in the global template. It's generally a good idea to give your customized elements unique names, such as *Custom Gantt Chart*, so that you can keep the original element intact.

The scenario: At Lucerne Publishing, you previously created a calendar to apply to a task in one plan that can be started only on certain weekdays. Another plan includes the same type of task with the same calendar requirements. You'd like to use the task calendar in this other plan.

In this exercise, you will use the Organizer to copy a custom calendar from one plan to another.

You need multiple files located in your Chapter19 practice file folder to complete this exercise.

1   Open **Customizing B_Start** and save it as Customizing B.

2   Next, open **Customizing A_Start** and save it as Customizing A.

The Customizing A plan contains a custom calendar named *Monday-Wednesday* that you created in Chapter 9, "Advanced task scheduling."

3   Scroll the **Gantt Chart** view vertically until task 44, *Send to color house,* is visible, and then point the mouse pointer at the task calendar icon in the **Indicators** column.

	ⓘ	Task Mode ▾	Task Name ▾	Duration ▾	Start ▾	Finish ▾	F	S	Apr S
43		⊞,	⊿ Color prep and printing	44 days	Tue 10/6/15	Fri 12/4/15			
44		⊞,	Send to color	1 day	Tue 10/6/15	Tue 10/6/15			
45			fs	10 days	Wed 10/7/15	Tue 10/20/15			
46		⊞,	Print and ship	30 days	Mon 10/26/15	Fri 12/4/15			

The calendar 'Monday-Wednesday' is assigned to the task.

This task uses the custom calendar, so it can occur only on a Monday, Tuesday, or Wednesday. You'd like to use this calendar in the Customizing B plan.

4   On the **File** tab (and if the Info screen is not already visible), click **Info**. Then click **Organizer**.

The Organizer dialog box appears.

5   Click several of the tabs in the dialog box to get a look at the types of elements you can manage with the Organizer, and then click the **Calendars** tab.

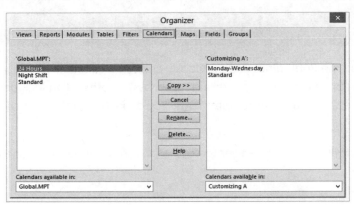

As you can see, most tabs of the Organizer dialog box have a similar structure: elements in the global template appear on the left side of the dialog box, and the elements that have been used in the active plan at any time (for example, views displayed) appear on the right.

Selecting an element on the left side of the dialog box and then clicking the Copy button will copy that element to the plan listed on the right. Conversely, selecting an element on the right side of the dialog box and then clicking the Copy button will copy that element to the file listed on the left (the global template, by default).

6   From the **Calendars available in** drop-down list on the left side of the **Organizer** dialog box, select **Customizing B**.

This plan appears in the list because it is open in Project.

The side of the dialog box in which you've selected an element determines the direction in which you copy the element.

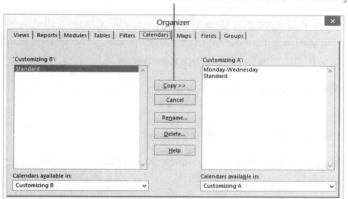

As you can see, the Customizing B plan (on the left) does not have the Monday-Wednesday custom calendar, and the Customizing A plan (on the right) does.

7   In the list of calendars on the right side of the dialog box, click **Monday-Wednesday**.

Notice that the two arrow symbols (>>) in the Copy button switch direction (<<) when you select an element on the right side of the dialog box.

8   Click **Copy**.

Project copies the custom calendar from the Customizing A plan to the Customizing B plan.

After clicking the Copy button, the Monday-Wednesday calendar is copied from the Customizing A plan to the Customizing B plan.

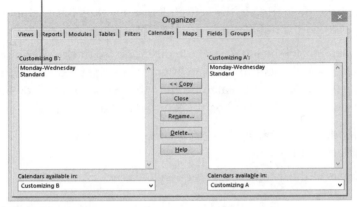

9   Click **Close** to close the **Organizer** dialog box.

TIP In this exercise, you used the Organizer to copy a custom calendar from one plan to another. If you want to make a custom calendar available in all plans, use the Organizer to copy it into the global template instead.

To conclude this exercise, you apply the custom calendar to a task in the Customizing B plan.

10   Click the Back button to exit the Backstage view.

11   On the **View** tab, in the **Window** group, click **Switch Windows**, and then click **2 Customizing B**.

Project switches to the Customizing B plan, which is the plan to which you just copied the custom calendar.

12   Select the name of task 19, *Send to color house*.

Note that this 1-day task is currently scheduled to occur on a Thursday.

13   On the **Task** tab, in the **Properties** group, click **Information**.

The Task Information dialog box appears.

14   Click the **Advanced** tab.

As you can see in the Calendar box, the default for all tasks is "None."

15   In the **Calendar** box, select **Monday-Wednesday** from the list of available base
calendars, and then click **OK** to close the dialog box.

Project applies the Monday-Wednesday calendar to task 19 and reschedules the
task to start on Monday, the next working day on which the task can occur. A task
calendar icon appears in the Indicators column.

16   Point to the task calendar icon.

The task calendar indicator's ScreenTip reminds you that this task has a task calendar
applied to it. Note that the Monday-Wednesday calendar was not available in this plan until
you copied it via the Organizer.

As you customize views, tables, and other elements, you might find the Organizer to be a
useful feature for managing your customized elements and the built-in elements in Project.

❌ CLEAN UP Close the Customizing B file. The Customizing A file should remain open.

Recording macros

Many activities you perform in Project can be repetitive. To save time, you can record a
macro that captures keystrokes and mouse actions for later playback. The macro is recorded in Microsoft Visual Basic for Applications (VBA), the built-in macro programming
language of Microsoft Office. You can do sophisticated things with VBA, but you can record
and play back simple macros without ever directly seeing or working with VBA code.

The macros you create are stored in the global template by default, so they are available to you whenever Project is running. The plan for which you originally created the macro need not be open to run the macro in other plans. You can also use the Organizer to copy macros between plans. For example, you can use the Organizer to copy the VBA module (which contains the macro) from the global template to another plan to give it to a friend.

What kinds of repetitive activities might you want to capture in a macro? Here's one example. Creating a graphic-image snapshot of a view is a great way to share project details with others. However, it's likely that the details you initially capture will become obsolete quickly as the plan is updated. Capturing updated snapshots can be a repetitive task that is ideal for automation through a macro. When this task is automated, you can quickly generate a new GIF image snapshot of a plan and save the GIF image to a file. From there, you could attach the GIF image file to an email message, publish it to a website, insert it into a document, or share it in other ways.

The scenario: At Lucerne Publishing, you frequently generate a GIF image snapshot of a plan for sharing with the team. You'd like to automate this task.

In this exercise, you record and run a macro.

1   On the **View** tab of the Customizing A plan, in the **Macros** group, click the down arrow below the **Macros** button, and then click **Record Macro**.

The Record Macro dialog box appears.

2   In the **Macro name** box, type Capture_GIF_Image.

> **TIP** Macro names must begin with a letter and cannot contain spaces. To improve the readability of your macro names, you can use an underscore (_) in place of a space. For example, rather than naming a macro **CaptureGIFImage**, you can name it **Capture_GIF_Image**.

For this macro, we will not use a shortcut key. When recording other macros, note that you cannot use a Ctrl+ combination that is already reserved by Project, so combinations like Ctrl+F (the keyboard shortcut for Find) and Ctrl+G (Go To) are unavailable. When you close the dialog box, Project alerts you whether you need to choose a different key combination.

3   In the **Store macro in** box, click **This Project** to store the macro in the active plan.

When a macro is stored in a plan, the macro can be used by any plan when the plan that contains the macro is open. The default option, *Global File*, refers to the global template. When a macro is stored in the global template, the macro can be used by any plan at any time because the global template is open whenever Project is running. In this exercise, because we don't want to customize your global template, you'll store the macro in the active plan.

4   In the **Description** box, select the current text and replace it by typing Saves a GIF image of the Gantt Chart view.

The description is useful to help identify the actions that the macro will perform.

5   Click **OK**.

Project begins recording the new macro. Project does not literally record and play back every mouse movement and passing second; it records only the results of the keystrokes and mouse actions that you make. Do not feel that you have to rush to complete the recording of the macro.

6   On the **View** tab, in the **Task Views** group, click the down arrow below the **Gantt Chart** button, and then click **Gantt Chart**.

Even though the plan is already showing the Gantt Chart view, including this step in the macro thereby records the action so that, if the plan is initially in a different view, the macro switches to the Gantt Chart view.

7   On the **View** tab, in the **Zoom** group, in the **Timescale** box, click **Thirds of Months**.

Project adjusts the timescale to display more of the project.

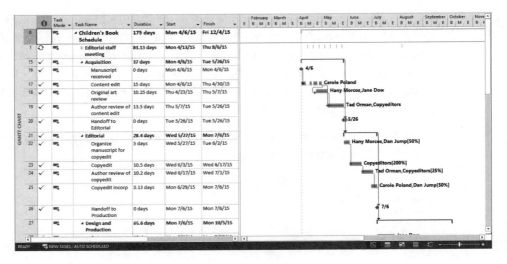

8   Click the **Task Name** column heading.

This selects all tasks to be copied.

9   On the **Task** tab, in the **Clipboard** group, click the arrow next to **Copy**, and then click **Copy Picture**.

The Copy Picture dialog box appears.

10 Under **Render image**, click **To GIF image file**, and then click **Browse**.

11 In the **Browse** dialog box, navigate to the **Chapter19** folder, and then click **OK**.

12 Back in the **Copy Picture** dialog box, under **Copy**, click **Selected Rows**.

13 Under **Timescale**, in the **From** box, type or select **4/6/15**, and in the **To** box, type or select **12/4/15**.

This date range matches the plan's current start and finish date. You can see these dates for task 0, the *project summary task*.

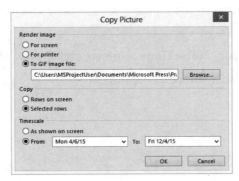

14   Click **OK** to close the **Copy Picture** dialog box.

Project saves the GIF image.

15   On the **View** tab, in the **Zoom** group, click **Zoom** and then click **Zoom**.

16   In the **Zoom** dialog box, click **Reset**, and then click **OK**.

Now you are ready to stop recording.

17   On the **View** tab, in the **Macros** group, click the down arrow below the **Macros** button, and then click **Stop Recording**.

Next, you will run the macro to see it play back.

18   On the **View** tab, in the **Macros** group, click **Macros** button.

The Macros dialog box appears.

19   In the **Macro name** box, click **Customizing A.mpp!Capture_GIF_Image**, and then click **Run**.

The macro begins running, but it pauses as soon as Project generates a confirmation message to replace the existing GIF image file (the one you just created while recording the macro).

IMPORTANT Your security-level setting in Project affects Project's ability to run macros that you record or receive from others. You might not have set the security level directly, but it might have been set when you installed Project or by a system policy within your organization.

20 Click **Overwrite** to overwrite the previously created GIF image file.

The macro resaves the GIF image. Next, you'll see the results of the macro's actions.

21 In Windows Explorer (in Windows 7) or File Explorer (in Windows 8), navigate to the **Chapter19** folder and double-click the **Customizing A** GIF image file to open it in your image editor or viewer application.

The GIF image appears in your image-viewer application.

22 Close your image-viewing application, and then switch back to the Customizing A plan in Project.

A macro like this one could be very useful if you needed to recapture a plan's snapshot frequently.

Editing macros

Once you've recorded a macro, it might work perfectly fine as you recorded it or it might benefit from some adjustments to its code. By editing the macro's code, you can give the macro functionality that you cannot capture when recording the macro, such as dismissing an alert. A macro's code resides in a VBA module, and you work with the code in the Visual Basic for Applications environment, commonly called the *VBA Editor*.

TIP The VBA language and VBA Editor are standard in many Microsoft Office applications, including Project. Although the specific details of each program differ, the general way in which you use VBA in each is the same. VBA automation is a powerful tool you can master, and that knowledge can be used in many Microsoft programs.

The scenario: At Lucerne Publishing, you've recorded a macro to capture a repetitive task. As handy as the Capture_GIF_Image macro is to use, it can be improved. Remember that when you ran it in the previous exercise, you had to confirm that Project should overwrite the existing GIF image. Because the intent of the macro is to capture the most current information, you always want to overwrite the older information. You can change the macro code directly to accomplish this

In this exercise, you work in the VBA Editor to fine-tune and enhance the macro you recorded in the previous exercise and then run it.

1   On the **View** tab, in the **Macros** group, click **Macros** button.

2   Under **Macro name**, click **Customizing A.mpp!Capture_GIF_Image**, and then click **Edit**.

    Project loads the module that contains the macro in the VBA Editor.

This VBA code was generated when Project recorded your macro.

A full explanation of the VBA language is beyond the scope of this book, but we can walk you through some steps to change the behavior of the previously recorded macro. You might also recognize some of the actions you recorded earlier by the names used in the VBA code.

3   Click at the beginning of the line **ViewApplyEx Name:="&Gantt Chart", ApplyTo:=0**, and press the Enter key.

4   Click in the new line you just created, press the Tab key, and type the following:

```
Application.Alerts False
```

This line of code will suppress the prompt you received when running the macro and accept the default option of replacing the existing GIF image file with the same name.

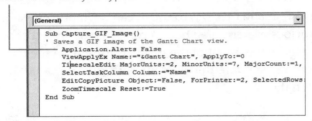

Here is the text you typed.

TIP Note that as you were typing, selection boxes and ScreenTips might have appeared. The VBA Editor uses such tools and feedback to help you enter text in a module correctly.

5   In the line that begins with **EditCopyPicture**, select the date and time **"4/6/15 8:00 AM"** (including the quotation marks) that follows **FromDate:=** and type the following:

```
ActiveProject.ProjectStart
```

This VBA code describes the project start date of the active project.

Here is the text string you typed
to return the project start date.

```
(General)                                                      Capture_GIF_Image
Sub Capture_GIF_Image()
' Saves a GIF image of the Gantt Chart view.
    Application.Alerts False
    ViewApplyEx Name:="&Gantt Chart", ApplyTo:=0
    TimescaleEdit MajorUnits:=2, MinorUnits:=7, MajorCount:=1, MinorCount:=1, TierCount:=2
    SelectTaskColumn Column:="Name"
    EditCopyPicture Object:=False, ForPrinter:=2, SelectedRows:=1, FromDate:=ActiveProject.ProjectStart, ToDate:="12/4/15 5:00 F
    ZoomTimescale Reset:=True
End Sub
```

This causes the macro to get the current start date of the active plan for the GIF image that the macro creates.

6   In the same line, select the date and time **"12/4/15 5:00 PM"** (including the quotation marks) that follows **ToDate:=** and type the following:

```
ActiveProject.ProjectFinish
```

Here is the text string you typed
to return the project finish date.

This causes the macro to get the current finish date of the active plan for the GIF image that the macro creates. Now, if the plan's start or finish date changes, the date range used when copying the GIF image will change as well.

Next, you'll add new macro capabilities while in the VBA Editor.

7   Click at the beginning of the line **SelectTaskColumn**, and press Enter.

8   Click in the new line you just created and type the following:

```
FilterApply Name:="Incomplete Tasks"
```

This line of code will apply the Incomplete Tasks filter to the current view.

9   Click at the beginning of the line **ZoomTimescale Reset:=True**, and press Enter.

10   Click in the new line you just created and type the following:

```
FilterClear
```

This line of code will clear the Incomplete Tasks filter from the current view.

Here are the two lines of text
you added to this macro.

11 On the **File** menu in the VBA Editor, click **Close and Return to Microsoft Project**.

The VBA Editor closes, and you return to the plan.

You could run the updated macro now, but first, you'll record some progress on tasks. That way, you'll see how the macro will filter the new progress and adjust what is captured in the GIF image.

12 Click the name of task 31, *Proofread and index*.

13 On the **Task** tab, in the **Schedule** group, click the down arrow to the right of the **Mark on Track** button and then click **Update Tasks**.

The Update Tasks dialog box appears.

14 In the **Actual dur** field, type **16d**, and then click **OK**.

Next, you'll record partial progress on another task.

15 Click the name of task 32, *Incorporate 1st Pages review*.

16 On the **Task** tab, in the **Schedule** group, click the down arrow to the right of the **Mark on Track** button and then click **Update Tasks**.

17 In the **Actual dur** field, type **5d**, and then click **OK**.

	❶	Task Mode ▾	Task Name ▾	Duration ▾	Start ▾	Finish ▾	14 T	W
27		▬	◢ Design and Production	67.6 days	Mon 7/6/15	Wed 10/7/15		
28	✓	▬	Set pages	15 days	Mon 7/6/15	Mon 7/27/15		
29	✓	▬	Interior illustration design	22 days	Mon 7/13/15	Tue 8/11/15		
30		▬	◢ 1st Pages review	31 days	Wed 8/12/15	Wed 9/23/15		
31	✓	▬	Proofread and index	16 days	Wed 8/12/15	Wed 9/2/15		
32		▬	Incorporate 1st Pages review	10 days	Thu 9/3/15	Wed 9/16/15		
33		▬	Send proofed pages to Production	0 days	Wed 9/16/15	Wed 9/16/15		
34		▬	Enter page corrections and index	5 days	Thu 9/17/15	Wed 9/23/15		

Now you are ready to rerun the macro.

18 On the **View** tab, in the **Macros** group, click the **Macros** button.

19 Under **Macro name**, click **Customizing A.mpp!Capture_GIF_Image**, and then click **Run**.

The macro runs, and this time, you are not prompted to overwrite the previously saved file as you were in the previous exercise. To verify that the macro ran correctly, you'll view the updated GIF image in your image application.

20 In Windows Explorer (in Windows 7) or File Explorer (in Windows 8), navigate to the **Chapter19** folder, and double-click the **Customizing A GIF** image file to open it in your image editor or viewer application.

The GIF image appears in your image application. Depending on your image application, you might be able to zoom in on the image to get a better look.

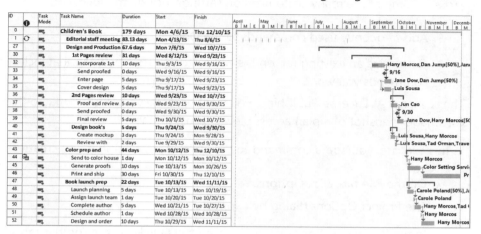

The updated screen shot includes the updated project finish date and displays only incomplete tasks because the macro applied the Incomplete Tasks filter. (Note that task 31, which is now completed, does not appear.) Now you can run the macro as frequently as needed to capture the most up-to-date information.

21 Close your image-viewing application, and then switch back to the Customizing A plan in Project.

Here are some additional tips for working with VBA macros in Project.

- VBA is a rich and well-documented programming language. If you would like to take a closer look at VBA in Project, try this: On the View tab, in the Macros group, click the arrow below the Macros button, and then click Visual Basic. In the Microsoft Visual Basic for Applications window, on the Help menu, click Microsoft Visual Basic For Applications Help.

- While working in a module, you can get help on specific items such as objects, properties, and methods. Click a word, and then press the F1 key.

- To close the VBA Editor and return to Project, on the File menu, click Close and Return to Microsoft Project.

Customizing the ribbon and Quick Access Toolbar

As with other Office applications, you have several choices concerning how to work with Project. Some of the many customization settings include the following:

- Add frequently used commands to the Quick Access Toolbar.
- Customize an existing tab on the ribbon, or create a new tab that includes any commands you want.

The scenario: At Lucerne Publishing, you want to make your custom macro that generates a GIF image snapshot of a plan accessible via a custom tab.

In this exercise, you add a command to the Quick Access Toolbar and create a custom tab.

1   On the **File** tab, click **Options**.

The Project Options dialog box appears.

2   In the **Project Options** dialog box, click the **Quick Access Toolbar** tab.

TIP You can also click the drop-down arrow on the right edge of the Quick Access Toolbar and then click More Commands.

3   On the left side of the dialog box, in the **Choose commands from** box, click **Commands Not in the Ribbon**.

Project displays the list of commands that are not currently accessible from the ribbon. Take a moment to look through this list for commands you would like quick access to.

4   In the list of commands (in the large box on the left side of the dialog box), click **Go To**, and then click **Add**.

Project adds the Go To command to the right side of the dialog box.

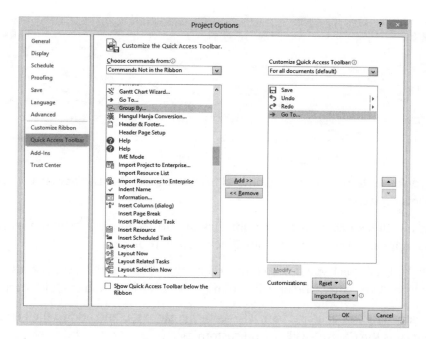

The Go To command is a handy way to navigate to a specific task ID and scroll the timescale in the Gantt Chart view, all in one action.

5   Click **OK** to close the **Project Options** dialog box.

Project adds the Go To command to the Quick Access Toolbar.

The Go To command now appears on the Quick Access toolbar

Now try out the Go To command by doing the following steps:

6   On the **Quick Access Toolbar**, click **Go To**.

7   In the **Go To** dialog box, type **43** in the **ID** box and then click **OK**.

TIP In the Go To dialog box, you can also enter a date value in the Date field to scroll the Gantt Chart's timescale to a specific date.

Project jumps to task 43 and scrolls the chart portion of the Gantt Chart view to display its Gantt bar.

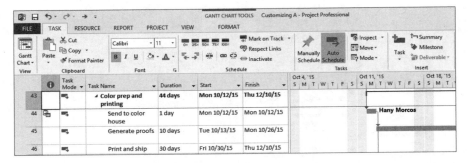

If you'd like to remove the command from the Quick Access Toolbar, complete the following step.

8   On the **Quick Access Toolbar**, right-click the **Go To** button and, in the shortcut menu that appears, click **Remove from Quick Access Toolbar**.

> **TIP** You can quickly add any command on the ribbon to the Quick Access toolbar. Right-click the command and, in the shortcut menu, click Add to Quick Access Toolbar.

To conclude this exercise, you will create a custom tab and add to the tab a command that runs the Capture_GIF_Image custom macro.

9   On the **File** tab, click **Options**.

10   In the **Project Options** dialog box, click the **Customize Ribbon** tab.

Project displays options for customizing the ribbon.

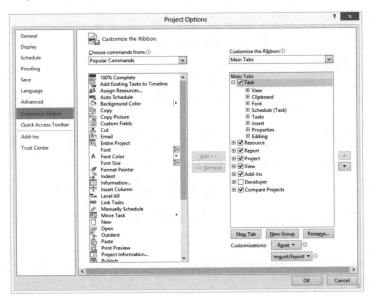

Here, you can get access to the commands and features supported by Project.

11   On the right side of the dialog box, under **Main Tabs**, select the **View** item (but don't clear its check box) and then click **New Tab**.

Project creates a new tab and group below (which on the ribbon will be to the right of) the View tab.

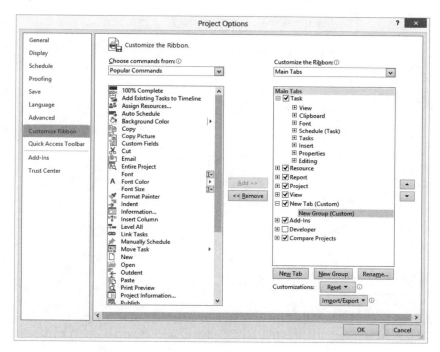

12   On the right side of the dialog box, under **Main Tabs**, select the **New Tab (Custom)** item (but don't clear its check box) and then click **Rename**.

The Rename dialog box appears.

13   In the **Display name** field, type My Tab and then click **OK**.

14   Click the **New Group (Custom)** item, and then click **Rename**.

The Rename dialog box appears.

15   In the **Display name** field, type My Commands and then click OK.

Now you are ready to add the custom macro to the new tab.

16   On the left side of the dialog box, in the **Choose commands from** box, click **Macros**.

The name of the custom macro appears.

17   Select the name of the **Customizing A.mpp!Capture_GIF_Image** macro, and then click **Add**.

Project adds the macro item to your custom group.

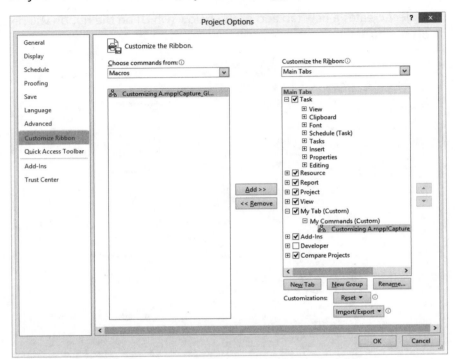

Next, you will rename the macro command and assign it an icon.

18   On the right side of the dialog box, select the name of the **Customizing A.mpp!Capture_GIF_Image** macro, and then click **Rename**.

19   In the **Display name** field, type Copy GIF, and in the **Symbol** box, select the picture image (sixth from the left in the second row).

Select this image.

20   Click **OK** to close the **Rename** dialog box, and then click **OK** to close the **Project Options** dialog box.

Project adds your custom tab to the interface.

21   Click the **My Tab** tab.

The custom tab and command now appear in the ribbon.

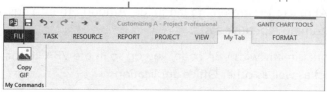

22   On the **My Tab** tab, in the **My Commands** group, click **Copy GIF**.

Project runs the macro. If you want to, navigate to the Chapter19 folder to view the GIF image.

Finally, you will remove the custom ribbon to undo this customization.

23   Right-click the **My Tab** tab, and in the shortcut menu that appears, click **Customize the Ribbon**.

24   On the right side of the **Project Options** dialog box, right-click **My Tab (Custom)**, and in the shortcut menu that appears, click **Remove**.

TIP You can also click the Reset button to undo all ribbon and Quick Access Toolbar customizations that might have been made to your copy of Project.

25   Click **OK** to close the **Project Options** dialog box.

Project has removed the custom tab.

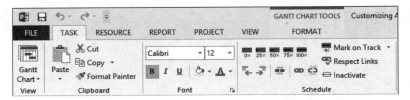

❌ CLEAN UP Close the Customizing A file.

Key points

- In Project, elements such as custom calendars are managed through the global template via the Organizer.

- Project, like many other Microsoft Office applications, uses the Visual Basic for Applications (VBA) macro programming language. Among other things, macros enable you to automate repetitive tasks.

- If you want to work directly with VBA code, you do so in the VBA Editor, which is included in Project as well as other Office applications.

- You can customize the Quick Access Toolbar and tabs in Project to include the commands and features that interest you the most.

Chapter at a glance

Copy

Copy Project data, including column headings, to other programs, page 444.

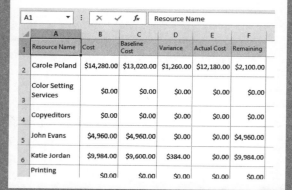

Import

Import data from other programs to Project, page 449.

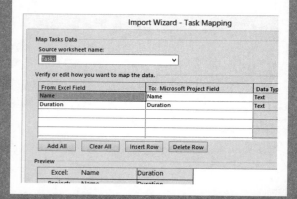

Export

Export Project data to other file formats, page 454.

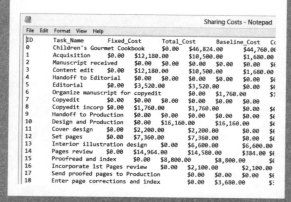

Visualize

Create a visual report to represent schedule details in Excel or Visio, page 460.

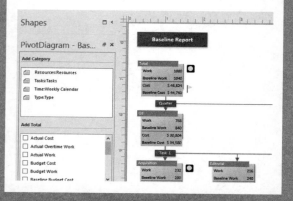

Sharing information with other programs

20

IN THIS CHAPTER, YOU WILL LEARN HOW TO

- Copy and paste tabular data from Project to another program.

- Use Project to open a file produced in another program.

- Save Project data to other file formats using import/export maps.

- Generate Excel and Visio documents using the Visual Reports feature.

In this chapter, you focus on various ways of getting data into and out of Microsoft Project 2013. In addition to the standard Microsoft Windows copy and paste features with which you might be familiar, Project offers a variety of options for importing and exporting data.

Throughout this chapter, you'll see the following terms:

- The *source program* is the program from which you copy information.

- The *destination program* is the program to which you paste information.

PRACTICE FILES Before you can complete the exercises in this chapter, you need to copy the book's practice files to your computer. A complete list of practice files is provided in "Download the practice files" at the beginning of this book. For each exercise that has a practice file, simply browse to where you saved the book's practice file folder.

IMPORTANT If you are running Project Professional with Project Web App/Project Server, take care not to save any of the practice files you work with in this book to Project Web App (PWA). For more information, see Appendix C, "Collaborating: Project, SharePoint, and PWA."

Copying Project data to other programs

Project supports copying information out of and pasting information into Project. However, because Project information is highly structured, there are a few things to note.

When copying data from Project into other applications, you have some options for the results that you get:

- You can copy information (such as task names and dates) from a table in Project and paste it as structured tabular data in spreadsheet applications like Microsoft Excel, or as a table in word-processor applications that support tables, like Microsoft Word. In most cases, the table's column headings for the data you copied will also be pasted, and the summary/subtask hierarchy will be indicated by the subtasks being indented.

- You can copy text from a table in Project and paste it as tab-delimited text in text editor applications that do not support tables, like WordPad or Notepad.

- When pasting information from Project into an email application such as Microsoft Outlook, you probably will get tabular results if your email application supports the Hypertext Markup Language (HTML) format.

- You can create a graphic-image snapshot of the active view and paste the image into any application that supports graphic images. You worked with the Copy Picture feature (on the Task tab) in Chapter 7, "Formatting and sharing your plan."

    TIP Many Windows programs—such as Word, Excel, and PowerPoint—have a Paste Special feature. This feature provides you with more options for pasting data from Project into the destination program. For example, you can use the Paste Special feature in Word to paste formatted or unformatted text, a picture, or a Microsoft Project Document Object (an OLE object). You can also choose to paste only the data or paste it with a link to the source data in Project. When pasted with a link, the destination data in Project can be updated whenever the source data is changed.

You also have options when pasting data from other programs into Project:

- You can paste text (such as a list of task or resource names) into a table in Project. For example, you can paste a range of cells from Excel or a group of paragraphs from Word into Project. You can paste a series of task names that are organized in a vertical column from Excel or Word into the Task Name column in Project, for instance.

- You can paste a graphic image or an OLE object from another program into a graphical portion of a Gantt Chart view. You can also paste a graphic image or an OLE object into a task, resource, or assignment note and into a form view such as the Task or Resource Form view.

TIP Pasting text as multiple columns into Project requires some planning. First, make sure that the order of the information in the source program matches the order of the columns in the Project table. You can either rearrange the data in the source program to match the column order in the Project table or vice versa. Second, make sure that the columns in the source program support the same types of data (text, numbers, dates, and so on) as do the columns in Project.

The scenario: At Lucerne Publishing, you already used the Copy Picture feature in Project to create snapshots of schedule details you can then share with others. However, the resulting graphic image is not editable as textual content. You'd like to share textual content such as task and resource lists from Project with other Office applications.

In this exercise, you will copy tabular data from Project and paste it into Excel and Word.

TIP The following exercise uses Word and Excel. If you do not have access to one or both of these programs, you can experiment with pasting tabular data from Project into other applications. In general, you should get the expected pasting results if your destination application supports the HTML format.

 SET UP You need the Sharing_Start file located in your Chapter20 practice file folder to complete this exercise. Open the Sharing_Start file, and save it as Sharing.

To begin, you'll copy some task names, durations, and start and finish dates from Project to Word.

1   In the **Entry** table on the left side of the **Gantt Chart** view, select from the name of task 5, *Editorial*, through task 13's finish date, *Wed 9/23/15*.

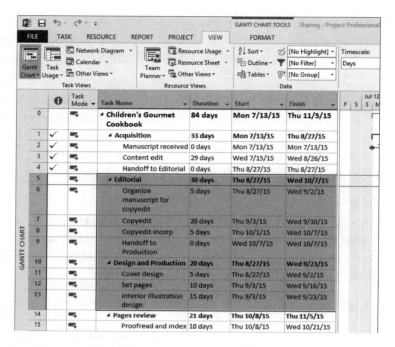

TIP One quick and easy way to select this range is to click the name of task 5, hold down the Shift key, and then click the finish date of task 13.

2   On the **Task** tab, in the **Clipboard** group, click **Copy**.

Project copies the selected range to the Clipboard.

3   Start Word (or a comparable word-processor application), create a new document, and then paste the Clipboard contents into the new document.

If you have Word 2013, your screen should look similar to the following illustration.

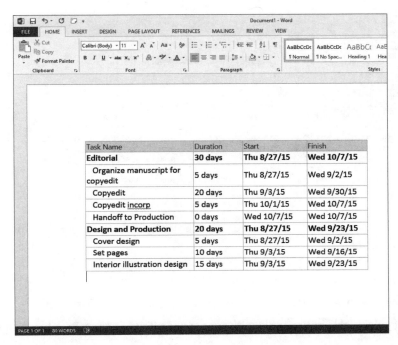

Pasting into Word generated a formatted table. The column headings from Project are included in the table, and the summary task and subtask outline structure from Project has been indicated as well.

Next, you'll paste tabular data from Project into a spreadsheet application.

4 Start Excel (or a comparable spreadsheet application), and create a new workbook.

Now you will copy resource cost details from Project to Excel.

5 Switch back to Project.

6 On the **View** tab, in the **Resource Views** group, click **Resource Sheet**.

The Resource Sheet view replaces the Gantt Chart view.

7 On the **View** tab, in the **Data** group, click **Tables** and then click **Cost**.

This is the resource cost information you'd like to paste into Excel.

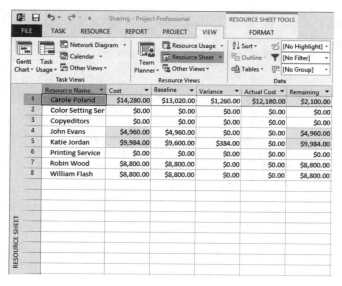

8   Click the **Select All** button in the upper-left corner of the **Cost** table.

Project selects the entire table, although only cells that contain values will be copied.

Click the Select All button to select the entire table.

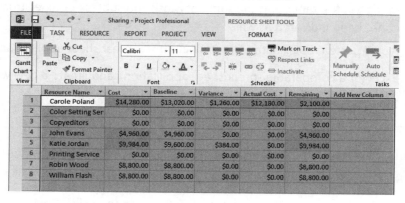

9   On the **Task** tab, in the **Clipboard** group, click **Copy**.

Project copies the selected range to the Clipboard.

10   Switch back to Excel and then paste the Clipboard contents into the new workbook.

In Excel, if necessary, widen any columns that don't display the data values and instead display pound signs (##). If you have Excel 2013, your screen should look similar to the following illustration:

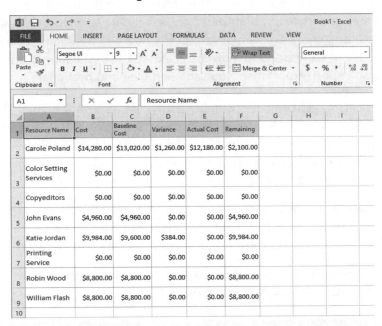

As with pasting into Word, note that pasting into Excel generated the correct column headings. The values from Project are also given the correct formatting (such as currency) in Excel.

11 Close Word and Excel without saving changes, and then switch back to Project.

The pasting of rich tabular data into Word or Excel does not work the same way in all applications. If you pasted the same data into Notepad, for example, the result would be tab-delimited data and no column headings. Feel free to experiment with this.

Opening other file formats in Project

Information that you need to incorporate into a plan in Project can come from a variety of sources. A task list from a spreadsheet or resource costs from a database are two examples. You might want to use the unique features of Project to analyze data from another program. For example, many people keep to-do lists and simple task lists in Excel, but accounting for basic scheduling issues, such as distinguishing between working and nonworking time, is impractical in Excel.

When saving data to or opening data from other formats, Project uses maps (also called *import/export maps* or *data maps*) that specify the exact data to import or export and how to structure it. You use import/export maps to specify how you want individual fields in the source program's file to correspond to individual fields in the destination program's file. After you set up an import/export map, you can use it over and over again.

TIP If you have Excel installed on your computer, open the workbook named Sample Task List in the Chapter20 folder. This is a file you will import into Project. The important things to note about the workbook are the names and order of the columns, the presence of a header row (the labels at the top of the columns), and that the data is in a worksheet named "Tasks." When you are finished with the workbook, close it without saving the changes.

The scenario: At Lucerne Publishing, a colleague has sent you an Excel workbook that contains her recommended tasks and durations of activities for some work that Lucerne Publishing might do in the future. You'd like to import this data into Project.

In this exercise, you open an Excel workbook in Project and set up an import/export map to control how the Excel data is imported into Project.

IMPORTANT Project 2013 has a security setting that might prevent you from opening files from previous versions of Project or files in other nondefault formats. You'll change this setting to complete the following activity and then restore it to its original setting.

1   In Project, on the **File** tab, click **Options**.

     The Project Options dialog box appears.

2   Click **Trust Center**.

3   Click **Trust Center Settings**.

     The Trust Center dialog box appears.

4   Click **Legacy Formats**.

5   Under **Legacy Formats**, click **Prompt when loading files with legacy or non-default file format**.

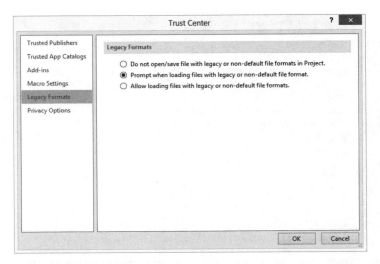

6　Click **OK** to close the **Trust Center** dialog box, and then click **OK** again to close the **Project Options** dialog box.

With this change to Project's Trust Center settings completed, you're ready to import an Excel workbook.

7　Click the **File** tab, and then click **Open**.

8　Navigate to the Chapter20 practice file folder.

9　In the file type box (initially labeled **Projects**), select **Excel Workbook** in the drop-down list.

TIP While scrolling through the file type box, you can see the file formats that Project can import. If you work with programs that can save data in any of these file formats, you can import their data into Project.

10　Select the **Sample Task List** file, and then click **Open**.

The Import Wizard appears. This wizard helps you import structured data from a different format to Project.

11　Click **Next**.

The second page of the Import Wizard appears.

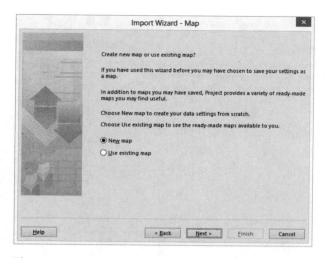

The Import Wizard uses maps to organize the way that structured data from another file format is imported into Project. For this exercise, you will create a new map.

12   Make sure that **New map** is selected, and then click **Next**.

The Import Mode page of the Import Wizard appears.

13   Make sure that **As a new project** is selected, and then click **Next**.

The Map Options page of the Import Wizard appears.

14   Select the **Tasks** check box, and make sure that **Import includes headers** is selected as well.

Headers here refer to column headings.

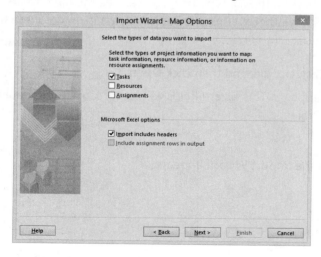

15   Click **Next**.

The Task Mapping page of the Import Wizard appears. Here, you identify the source worksheet within the Excel workbook and specify how you want to map the data from the source worksheet to Project fields.

16   In the **Source worksheet name** box, select **Tasks**.

Tasks is the name of the sheet in the Excel workbook. Project analyzes the header row names from the worksheet and suggests the Project field names that are probable matches. If Project was not able to match column names or types correctly, you could change the mapping to other fields here.

On this page of the Import Wizard, you specify how Project should import data from other file formats—in this case, an Excel workbook.

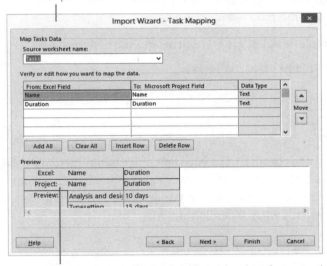

Use the Preview area to see how the data from another file format will be mapped to Project fields, based on the settings you choose above.

17   Click **Next**.

The final page of the Import Wizard appears. Here, you have the option of saving the settings for the new import map, which is useful when you anticipate importing similar data into Project in the future. This time, you'll skip this step.

18   Click **Finish**.

Project imports the Excel data into a new plan. (The dates you see on the timescale will differ from those shown because Project uses the current date as the project start date in the new file.)

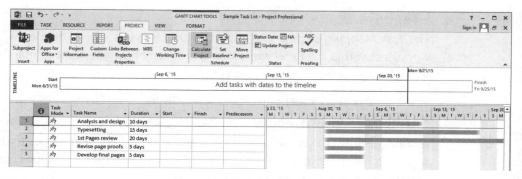

Unless you changed the default scheduling setting for new tasks, the task list is manually scheduled.

This is a simple task list with just task names and durations. The process for importing more complex structured data is similar, however.

19   Close the new Sample Task List file without saving the changes.

The Sharing plan remains open in Project.

Saving to other file formats from Project

Pasting Project data into other programs as you did earlier might be fine for one-time or infrequent needs, but this technique might not work as well if you must export a large volume of data from Project. Instead, you can save Project data in different file formats, which can be accomplished in various ways, including the following:

- You can save the entire project as Extensible Markup Language (XML) format for structured data exchange with other applications that support XML.

- You can save only the data you specify in a different format. The supported formats include Excel workbook and tab-delimited or comma-delimited text. When saving to these formats, you choose the format in which you want to save, pick a built-in export map (or create your own), and export the data.

TIP You can also save the active view to an archival format such as XPS or PDF that preserves layout and formatting but is generally not editable. For more information, see Chapter 17, "Applying advanced formatting and printing."

The scenario: At Lucerne Publishing, a financial planner has requested some book project cost data. You'd like to give this data to the financial planner, but the financial planner uses a budget program that cannot work directly with Project files. You decide to provide her with cost data as tab-delimited text, which will allow her the greatest flexibility when importing the data into her budget program.

In this exercise, you save project data to a text file using a built-in export map.

1   On the **File** tab, click **Export**.

2   Click **Save Project as File**.

Under Save Project As File, you can see some of the supported file types.

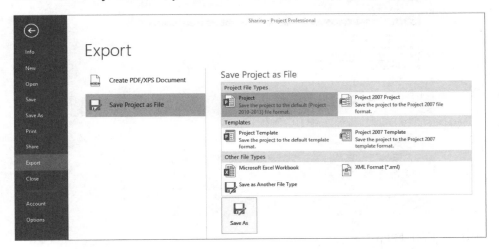

3   Under **Other File Types**, click **Save as Another File Type** and then click **Save As**.

4   Navigate to the Chapter20 practice file folder.

5   In the **File name** box, type Sharing Costs.

6   In the **Save as type** box, click **Text (Tab delimited)** from the list, and then click **Save**.

A confirmation dialog box appears because Project is now attempting to save to a nondefault file format.

7   Click **Yes**.

The Export Wizard appears.

TIP When you use import/export maps, it makes no difference what current view is displayed in Project. The current view does not affect what data can or cannot be exported.

8   Click **Next**.

The second page of the Export Wizard appears.

9   Click **Use existing map**, and then click **Next**.

10   Under **Choose a map for your data**, select **Cost data by task**.

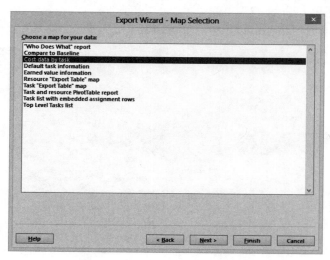

11   Click **Next**.

On the Map Options page of the wizard, you can see your options for the types of data to export, the delimiter between data values (tab, space, or comma), and other options. This time you'll use the default options.

12   Click **Next**.

Use these buttons to control what fields will be exported.

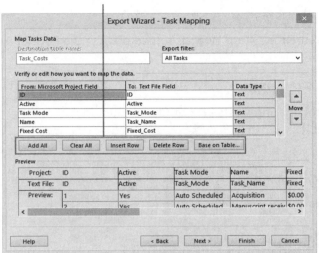

Here, you can see the detailed field mapping to be applied for this export. Next, you will customize what data to export. You'll remove two of the fields from the export.

13   In the **From** column, click **Active**.

14   Click **Delete Row**.

Next, you'll remove the second field.

15   In the **From** column, click **Task Mode**.

16   Click **Delete Row**.

Project removes the Task Mode field from the export list and updates the Preview pane below.

17   Click **Finish**.

Project saves the text file. To view it, you will open the file in Notepad.

18   Do one of the following:

- If you are running Windows 7 or earlier, do this: on the **Start** menu, click **All Programs**, and in the **Accessories** program group, click **Notepad**.

- If you are running Windows 8, do this: from the Start screen, type notepad, and in the Apps results list, click or tap **Notepad**.

Notepad starts.

TIP You can also navigate to the Chapter20 folder and double-click the Sharing Costs text file.

19   In Notepad, make sure that **Word Wrap** is turned off. (On the **Format** menu, **Word Wrap** should not be selected.)

20   On the **File** menu, click **Open**.

21   Open the document **Sharing Costs** in your Chapter20 folder.

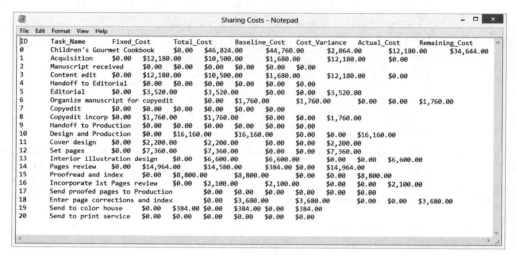

In this file, the fields are separated by tabs. It might not be easy for you to read, but this format is imported easily into virtually any data-crunching program.

22   In Notepad on the **File** menu, click **Exit**.

Notepad closes, and you return to Project.

To conclude this exercise, you'll restore the Trust Center settings.

23   On the **File** tab, click **Options**.

24   Click **Trust Center**, and then click **Trust Center Settings**.

25   Click **Legacy Formats**.

26   Under **Legacy Formats**, click **Do not open/save file with legacy or non-default file formats in Project**.

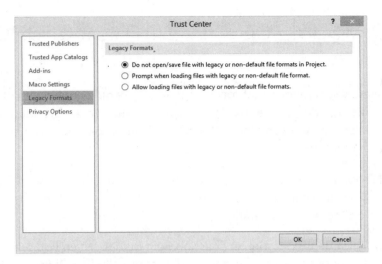

27   Click **OK** to close the **Trust Center** dialog box, and then click **OK** again to close the
      Project Options dialog box.

Working with files from previous versions of Project

Project 2000, 2002, and 2003 shared a common file format that could be opened by
any version of Project from 2000 to 2003. In other words, if you were using Project
2000, 2002, or 2003, you didn't need to pay attention to the Project file format across
these three versions of Project.

To accommodate the new functionality introduced in a new product release, Project
2007 introduced its own file format, as did Project 2010. Project 2010 and 2013 share
the same file format.

When running Project 2013, you might find you need to share plans with users of
previous versions of Project. One strategy is to save in Microsoft Project 2000–2003
format or Microsoft Project 2007 format. (These are both file formats listed in the Save
As Type box in the Save As dialog box.) However, some data relating to new features
in Project 2013 will be changed or discarded when saved in an older format. Manually
scheduled tasks, for example, will be converted to automatically scheduled tasks in
Project 2007 and earlier.

To learn more about file formats and Project versions, click the Help button (which
looks like a question mark) in the upper-right corner of the Project window, and in the
Help Search box, type Supported file formats.

Generating visual reports with Excel and Visio

Project can generate visual reports that focus on sharing schedule details with other applications. Specifically, you can use the Visual Reports feature to export data from Project to either Excel or Microsoft Visio and, once the data is there, visually represent schedule details in compelling formats.

TIP Some visual reports (especially those that are generated in Excel) are similar to the built-in reports now available in Project 2013. You might find the visual reports beneficial when you want to do more complex data analysis in Excel.

A visual report can include task, resource, or assignment details. When you select a visual report in Project, it generates a highly structured database, called an *Online Analytical Processing (OLAP) cube*, from your plan. Project then starts either Excel or Visio (depending on the visual report you selected), loads and organizes the data used by that application, and generates a graphical representation of that data (an Excel chart or a Visio diagram). The specific results you obtain depend on the type of visual report you choose:

- Excel visual reports use the PivotTable and PivotChart features in Excel. You can format the chart and modify the details in the PivotTable report from which the chart is derived. PivotTable reports are well suited to analyzing and summarizing the large volumes of data that plans can contain. You can create Excel visual reports with Excel 2003 or later.

- Visio visual reports use the PivotDiagrams feature in Visio. PivotDiagrams are well suited for presenting hierarchical data and can complement Project very well. Not only can you customize the visual report as a Visio diagram, but you can also filter and rearrange the data from which the diagram is derived. Visio visual reports require Visio 2007 or later.

Project includes several Excel and Visio visual report templates. You can also create your own visual reports from scratch or modify one of the supplied templates. Visual reports can be beneficial to any Project user. If you are already familiar with Excel PivotTables or you are a Visio power user, and you have the need to analyze and present Project data, you'll find visual reports especially interesting.

The scenario: At Lucerne Publishing, a colleague is handy with both Excel and Visio. She's asked you for some Project data that she can work with in both applications.

In this exercise, you generate both Excel and Visio visual reports.

IMPORTANT If the computer on which you are now working does not have Excel 2003 or later installed, you cannot complete this exercise. If this is the case, skip to the Visio-specific portion of this section.

1   On the **Report** tab, in the **Export** group, click **Visual Reports**.

The Visual Reports dialog box appears. If you don't have Excel or Visio installed, what you see might differ.

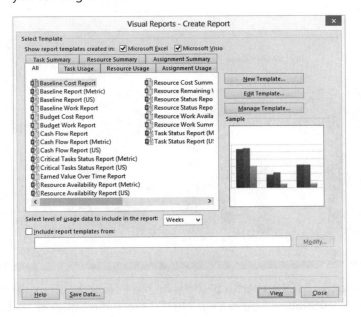

This dialog box groups visual reports in a number of ways: all reports; only Excel or only Visio reports; and task, resource, or assignment details (divided into summary and usage reports). The dialog box includes a simplified preview of the type of graphic (chart or diagram) associated with each visual report. If you want to, you can click the various tabs in the dialog box to see how the visual reports are organized.

The first visual report you'll generate is Excel-based.

2   Click the **Resource Summary** tab.

3   Click **Resource Remaining Work Report** and then click **View**.

Project generates the data required by this report, starts Excel, and creates the report.

4   If the **PivotChart Fields** pane does not automatically appear, click anywhere in the chart.

You might need to adjust the zoom level to view the entire chart.

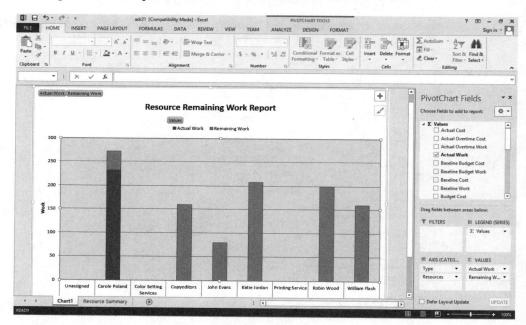

The PivotTable on which the chart is based is on the Resource Summary sheet. If you are familiar with PivotTables, you can view that sheet and modify the PivotTable settings if you want.

TIP PivotTables is a powerful feature in Excel. To learn more, search for **PivotTable** in Excel Help.

5   When you are through working with the Excel chart, close Excel without saving the changes.

To conclude this exercise, you will generate a Visio-based visual report.

> **IMPORTANT** If the computer on which you are now working does not have Visio 2007 or later installed, you cannot complete this exercise. If this is the case, skip to the end of this section.

In Project, the Visual Reports dialog box should still be displayed.

6   Click the **Assignment Usage** tab.

7   Click **Baseline Report (US),** and then click **View.**

Project generates the data required by this report, starts Visio, and creates the Baseline Report diagram. Your view should look similar to the following illustration:

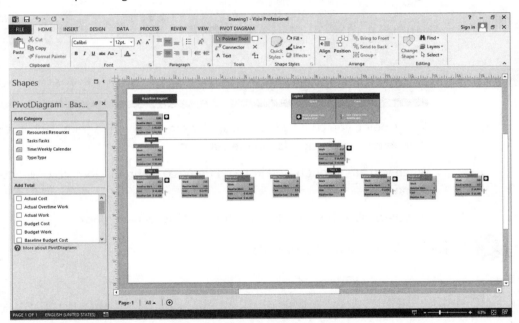

Next, you'll take a closer look at the items in this diagram.

8   Do either of the following:

- In Visio 2007, on the View menu, point to Zoom, and then click 100%.

- In Visio 2010 or 2013, in the Zoom slider, set the zoom level to 100%.

9   If necessary, adjust the vertical and horizontal scroll bars until you can see the diagram details.

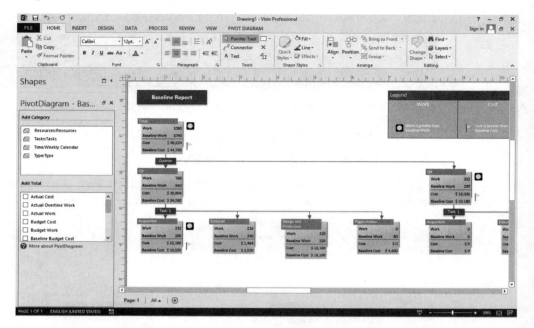

At this point, you could adjust the settings in the PivotDiagram pane in Visio to change the details included in the diagram.

10   When you are through working with the Visio diagram, close Visio without saving the changes.

11   In Project, click **Close** to close the **Visual Reports** dialog box.

✖ CLEAN UP Close the Sharing file.

Key points

- You can both copy from and paste into Project, just as you can with most other Windows applications. However, when pasting data into a table in Project, take care to ensure that the data you want ends up in the correct fields and field types.

- When opening other data formats in Project, Project uses import maps to help organize the imported data into the right structure for a Project table.

- Project supports saving data to common structured data formats, such as XML.

- Visual reports help you export Project data to nicely formatted Excel charts and Visio diagrams.

20

Chapter at a glance

Share

Share resources from a central resource pool across several plans, page 468.

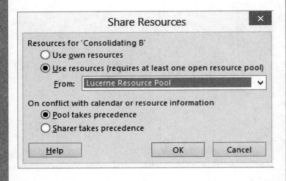

Manage

Manage resources and assignments across multiple plans, page 474.

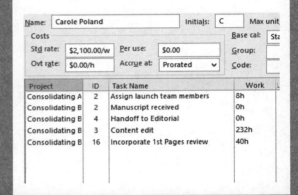

Consolidate

Create a consolidated plan for a bird's-eye view across multiple plans, page 493.

Link

Link tasks across different plans, page 496.

Consolidating projects and resources

21

IN THIS CHAPTER, YOU WILL LEARN HOW TO

- Create a resource pool to share resources across multiple plans.

- Look at resource allocation across multiple plans.

- Change resource assignments in a sharer plan, and see the effects in a resource pool.

- Change a resource's working time in a resource pool, and see the effects in a sharer plan.

- Make a specific date nonworking time in a resource pool, and see the effects in the sharer plan.

- Create a plan, and make it a sharer plan for a resource pool.

- Change sharer plan assignments, and update a resource pool.

- Insert plans to create a consolidated plan.

- Link tasks between two plans.

In the previous exercises in this book, you've generally worked with a single plan at a time. Although this might be your main focus in Project much of the time, chances are you or your organization will need to coordinate people, work, and deliverables across multiple projects. This chapter introduces you to the powerful features in Project that can help you optimize your resources, consolidate multiple plans into a single consolidated plan, and create dependencies between plans.

As you complete the exercises in this chapter, you will need to open and close more practice files than was required in previous chapters. In some cases, you'll take additional steps to see in one plan the results of actions you completed in another plan.

Creating a resource pool

When managing multiple projects, you might find that it's common for *work resources* (people and equipment) to be assigned to more than one project at a time. It might become difficult to coordinate the work resources' time among the multiple projects, especially if those projects are managed by different people. For example, an editor at a book publishing firm might have task *assignments* for a new book, a promotional website, and a press release—three projects proceeding simultaneously. In each plan, the editor might be *fully allocated* or even *underallocated*. However, if you add all her tasks from these plans together, you might discover that she has been overallocated or assigned to work on more tasks than she can handle at one time. When working with cost resources in multiple plans, you might want to see not only the cost per plan associated with a cost resource, but the cumulative costs across plans as well. Likewise, when working with material resources in multiple plans, you'd see cumulative consumed material resources in whatever unit of consumption you've used.

A *resource pool* can help you see how resources are utilized across multiple plans. The resource pool is a plan from which other plans draw their resource information. It contains information about all resources' task assignments from all plans linked to the resource pool. You can change resource information—such as maximum units, cost rates, and nonworking time—in the resource pool, and all linked plans will use the updated information.

The plans that are linked to the resource pool are called *sharer plans*. The following is one way of visualizing a resource pool and sharer plans.

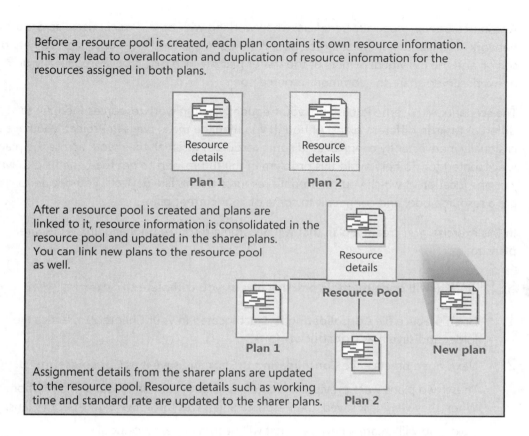

Before a resource pool is created, each plan contains its own resource information. This may lead to overallocation and duplication of resource information for the resources assigned in both plans.

Resource details
Plan 1

Resource details
Plan 2

After a resource pool is created and plans are linked to it, resource information is consolidated in the resource pool and updated in the sharer plans. You can link new plans to the resource pool as well.

Resource details
Resource Pool

Plan 1

New plan

Assignment details from the sharer plans are updated to the resource pool. Resource details such as working time and standard rate are updated to the sharer plans.

Plan 2

If you manage just one project with resources that are not used in other plans, a resource pool provides you no benefit. However, if your organization plans to manage multiple plans, setting up a resource pool enables you to do the following:

- Enter resource information, such as nonworking time, in any of the sharer plans or in the resource pool so that it is available in other sharer plans.

- View resources' assignment details from multiple plans in a single location.

- View assignment costs per resource across multiple plans.

- View cumulative costs for work and cost resources across multiple plans.

- View cumulative consumption values for material resources across multiple plans.

- Find resources who are overallocated across multiple plans, even if those resources are underallocated in individual plans.

21

A resource pool is especially beneficial when working with other Project users across a network. In those cases, the resource pool is stored in a central location, such as a network server, and the individual owners of the sharer plans (which might be stored locally or on a network server) share the common resource pool.

The scenario: At Lucerne Publishing, you frequently assign work resources (people) to different tasks in different plans. Although you manage those plans in Project, you have occasionally inadvertently overallocated some resources when all their work across the plans is accounted for. To help avoid this problem in the future, and to get the benefits of having just one location at which you can update resource details like days off, you decide to create a resource pool and connect it to some of your current plans.

In this exercise, you create a plan that will become a resource pool and link two sharer plans to it.

→ SET UP **You will open multiple practice files as you complete this exercise.**

1   Open practice file **Consolidating A_Start** located in your Chapter21 practice file folder and save it as Consolidating A.

2   Next, open practice file **Consolidating B_Start** and save it as Consolidating B.

     These two plans were previously created, and both contain resource information. When they were last saved, the Resource Sheet was the active view in both plans.

     Next, you will create a new plan that will become a resource pool.

3   On the **File** tab, click **New,** and then click **Blank project**.

     Project creates a new plan, with the Gantt with Timeline view displayed.

4   On the **File** tab, click **Save As**.

5   Navigate to the **Chapter21** folder.

6   In the **File name** box, type Lucerne Resource Pool, and then click **Save**.

     TIP You can give a resource pool any name you want, but it is a good idea to indicate that it is a resource pool in the file name.

7   On the **View** tab, in the **Resource Views** group, click **Resource Sheet**.

     The Resource Sheet view replaces the Gantt Chart view.

8   On the **View** tab, in the **Window** group, click **Arrange All**.

Project arranges the three plan windows within the Project window.

Prior to being linked to a resource pool, some resource names and other details are duplicated in these plans.

Title bar

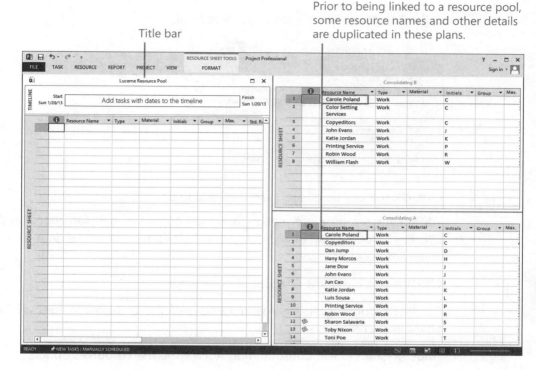

TIP You do not need to arrange the project windows in this way to create a resource pool, but it is helpful to see the results as they occur in this section.

Looking at the resource names in the two plans (Consolidating A and Consolidating B), you can see that several of the same resources appear in both plans. These include *Carole Poland, Copyeditors, John Evans,* and others. None of these resources are overallocated in either plan.

9   Click the title bar of the **Consolidating B** window.

10 On the **Resource** tab, in the **Assignments** group, click **Resource Pool**, and then click **Share Resources**.

The Share Resources dialog box appears.

11   Under **Resources for 'Consolidating B'**, select the **Use resources** option.

The Use Resources From list contains the open plans that can be used as a resource pool.

12   In the **From** box, click **Lucerne Resource Pool**.

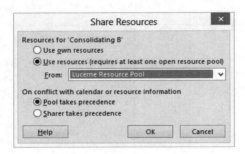

13   Click **OK** to close the **Share Resources** dialog box.

You see the resource information from the Consolidating B plan appear in the Lucerne Resource Pool plan. Next, you will set up the Consolidating A plan as a sharer plan with the same resource pool.

14   Click the title bar of the **Consolidating A** window.

15   On the **Resource** tab, in the **Assignments** group, click **Resource Pool**, and then click **Share Resources**.

16   Under **Resources for 'Consolidating A'**, click the **Use resources** option.

17   In the **From** list, make sure that **Lucerne Resource Pool** is selected.

Lucerne Resource Pool is selected by default. The Consolidating A plan is already a sharer plan, and Project won't allow a sharer plan to be a resource pool for another plan.

18   Under **On conflict with calendar or resource information**, make sure that the **Pool takes precedence** option is selected.

Selecting this option causes Project to use resource information (such as cost rates) in the resource pool rather than in the sharer plan, if it finds any differences between the two plans.

19   Click **OK** to close the **Share Resources** dialog box.

You see the resource information from the Consolidating A plan appear in the resource pool.

After these two sharer plans have been linked to the resource pool, the combined resource information appears in all files.

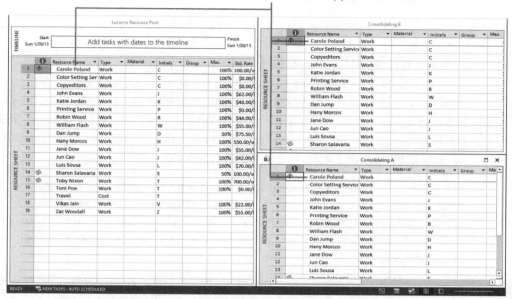

The resource pool contains the resource information from both sharer plans. Project will consolidate resource information from the sharer plans based on the name of the resource. *John Evans*, for example, is listed only once in the resource pool, no matter how many sharer plans list him as a resource.

IMPORTANT Project cannot match variations of a resource's name—for example, *John Evans* from one sharer plan and *J. Evans* from another. For this reason, you should develop a convention for naming resources in your organization and then stick with it.

TIP If you decide that you do not want to use a resource pool with a plan, you can break the link. To do this, in the sharer plan, on the Resources tab, click Resource Pool and then click Share Resources. Under Resources For *<Current Project Name>*, select the Use Own Resources option.

Now you can see how resources are assigned across multiple projects. By linking new plans to the resource pool, resource information will instantly be available in the new plan. (You'll do this in the next section.)

Again, note that you do not have to arrange the plan's windows as you did in this exercise to link the sharer plans to the resource pool. However, in this section it was helpful to see the results as they occurred.

Creating a dedicated resource pool

Any plan, with or without tasks, can serve as a resource pool. However, it is a good idea to designate as the resource pool a plan that does not contain tasks. This is because any project with tasks will almost certainly conclude at some point, and you might not want assignments for those tasks (with their associated costs and other details) to be included indefinitely in the resource pool.

Moreover, a dedicated resource pool without tasks can enable people, such as *line managers* or resource managers, to maintain some information about their resources, such as nonworking time, in the resource pool. These people might not have a role in project management, and they will not need to deal with task-specific details in the resource pool.

Viewing assignment details in a resource pool

One of the most important benefits of using a resource pool is that it allows you to see how resources are allocated across plans. For example, you can identify resources that are overallocated across the multiple plans to which they are assigned.

Let's look at a specific example. As you might have noticed in the previous section, the resource Carole Poland, who was not overallocated in either of the individual plans, did appear overallocated after Project accounted for all her assignments across the two plans. When Carole's assignments from the two sharer plans were combined, they exceeded her capacity to work on at least one day. Although Carole most likely was aware of this problem, the project manager might not have known about it without setting up a resource pool (or hearing about the problem directly from Carole).

The scenario: At Lucerne Publishing, you'd like to use your newly created resource pool to look for any resource overallocations across the two sharer plans.

In this exercise, you view assignments across plans in the resource pool.

1 Double-click the title bar of the **Lucerne Resource Pool** window.

The resource pool window is maximized to fill the Project window. In the resource pool, you can see all the resources from the two sharer plans. To get a better view of resource usage, you will change views.

2 On the **View** tab, in the **Resource Views** group, click **Resource Usage**.

The Resource Usage view appears.

3 In the **Resource Name** column, if it's not already selected, click the name of resource 1, *Carole Poland*.

4 On the **Task** tab, in the **Editing** group, click **Scroll to Task**.

The timephased details on the right side of the view scroll horizontally to show Carole Poland's earliest task assignments. The red numbers (for example, 16 hours on July 20) indicate a day on which Carole is overallocated. Next, you will display the Resource Form to get more detail about Carole's assignments.

5 On the **View** tab, in the **Split View** group, click **Details**.

The Resource Form appears below the Resource Usage view.

6 If necessary, drag the vertical divider between the **Project** and **ID** columns in the Resource Form to the right until you can see the full content in the **Project** column.

21

In this combination view, you can see both the resource's assigned tasks and details about each assignment.

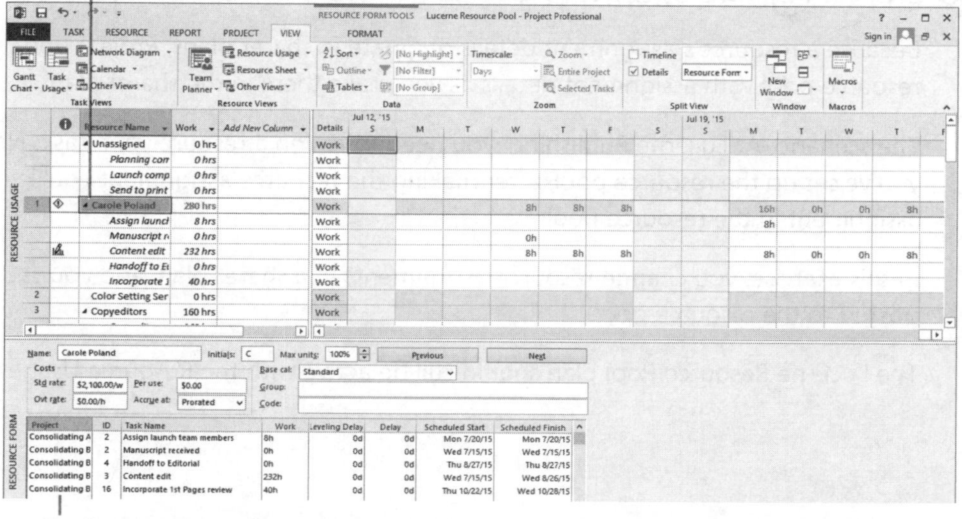

The Resource Form shows assignments across multiple projects when using a resource pool.

In this combination view, you can see all resources in the resource pool and their assignments (in the upper pane), as well as the selected resource's details (in the lower pane) from all sharer plans. You can see, for example, that the *Assign launch team members* task to which Carole is assigned is from the Consolidating A project and the *Content edit* task is from the Consolidating B project. Carole was not over-allocated in either project, but she is overallocated when you see her assignments across plans in this way.

If you want, click different resource names in the Resource Usage view to see their assignment details in the Resource Form.

7   On the **View** tab, in the **Split View** group, clear the **Details** check box.

> **TIP** In a resource pool, the Resource Form is just one way to see the details of specific assignments from sharer plans. You can also add the Project or Task Summary Name column to the table portion of the Resource Usage view. Doing so will show you which project each task assignment is from and that assignment's summary task name.

In this exercise, you viewed resource assignments across plans in the resource pool. As you add or change assignments, you'll always see the most current assignment information in the resource pool and across the sharer plans.

Updating assignments in a sharer plan

Because a resource's assignment details originate in sharer plans, Project updates the resource pool with assignment details as you make them in the sharer plan.

The scenario: At Lucerne Publishing, you need to assign a resource to a task. Now that you've set up the resource pool, after making the resource assignment you'll verify the assignment in the resource pool.

In this exercise, you change resource assignments in a sharer plan, and you see the changes posted to the resource pool.

The Lucerne Resource Pool plan should still be active with the Resource Usage view applied.

1   In the **Resource Name** column heading, select Resource 13, *Luis Sousa*.

You can see that Luis has no task assignments in either sharer plan. (Luis has no assignments listed below his name.) Next, you will assign Luis to a task in one of the sharer plans, and you will see the result in the resource pool as well as in the sharer plan.

2   On the **View** tab, in the **Window** group, click **Switch Windows** and then click **Consolidating A**.

Project displays the Consolidating A plan. Currently, it has the Resource Sheet view displayed.

3   On the **View** tab, in the **Task Views** group, click **Gantt Chart**.

The Gantt Chart view appears.

4   On the **Resource** tab, in the **Assignments** group, click **Assign Resources**.

The Assign Resources dialog box appears.

5   In the **Task Name** column, click the name of task 5, *Design and order marketing material*.

6   In the **Resource Name** column in the **Assign Resources** dialog box, click **Luis Sousa**, and then click **Assign**.

Project assigns Luis to the task.

21

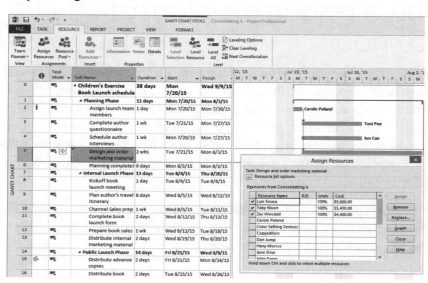

7 Click **Close** to close the **Assign Resources** dialog box.

8 On the **View** tab, in the **Window** group, click **Switch Windows**, and then click **Lucerne Resource Pool**.

9 Make sure that resource 13, *Luis Sousa*, is selected, and then, on the **Task** tab, in the **Editing** group, click **Scroll to Task**.

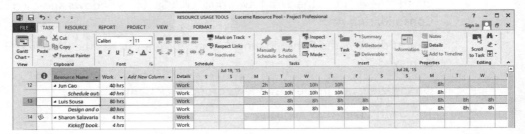

As expected, Luis Sousa's new task assignment appears in the resource pool.

When the resource pool is open in Project, any changes you make to resource assignments or other resource information in any sharer plans immediately show up in all other open sharer plans and the resource pool. You don't need to switch between sharer plans and the resource pool, as you did in this section, to verify the updated resource assignments.

Updating a resource's information in a resource pool

Another important benefit of using a resource pool is that it gives you a central location in which to enter resource details, such as cost rates and working time. When a resource's information is updated in the resource pool, the new information is available in all the sharer plans. This can be especially useful in organizations with a large number of re-sources working on multiple projects. In larger organizations, people such as line managers, resource managers, or staff in a *program office* are often responsible for keeping general resource information up to date.

The scenario: At Lucerne Publishing, William Flash has told you that he will be unavailable to work on September 3 and 4 because he plans to attend a workshop. You'd like to record this calendar exception just once in the resource pool.

In this exercise, you update a resource's working time in the resource pool, and see the changes in the sharer plans.

1   In the Lucerne Resource Pool plan, select the name of resource 8, *William Flash*.

2   Scroll the timephased portion of the view horizontally to the right until William's assignments for the week of August 30 appear.

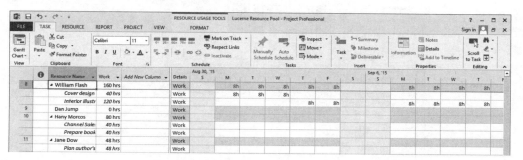

3   On the **Project** tab, in the **Properties** group, click **Change Working Time**.

      The Change Working Time dialog box appears.

4   In the **For calendar** box, make sure that *William Flash* is selected.

      William's resource calendar appears in the Change Working Time dialog box. William has told you that he will not be available to work on Thursday and Friday, September 3 and 4.

5   On the **Exceptions** tab in the **Change Working Time** dialog box, click in the first row under **Name** and type William at workshop.

      The description for the calendar exception is a handy reminder for you and others who might view the plan later.

6   Click in the **Start** field, and type or select 9/3/15.

7   Click in the **Finish** field, type or select 9/4/15, and then press the Enter key.

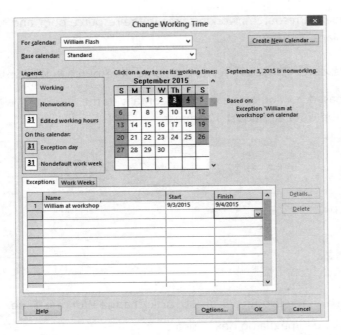

8 Click **OK** to close the **Change Working Time** dialog box.

Now William has no work scheduled on these two days (he did previously).

Because September 3 and 4 have been set
as nonworking days for this resource, no work
is scheduled on these days and they are
formatted as nonworking days for this resource.

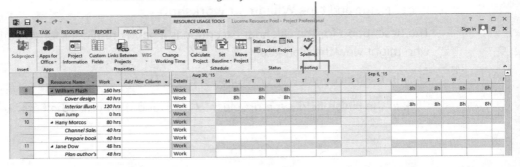

To verify that William's nonworking time setting was updated in the sharer plans, you
will look at his working time in one of those plans.

9 On the **View** tab, in the **Window** group, click **Switch Windows**, and then click
Consolidating A.

10   On the **Project** tab, in the **Properties** group, click **Change Working Time.**

The Change Working Time dialog box appears.

11   In the **For calendar** box, click **William Flash**.

On the Exceptions tab, you can see that September 3 and 4 are flagged as nonworking days for William; the change to this resource's working time in the resource pool has been updated in the sharer plans.

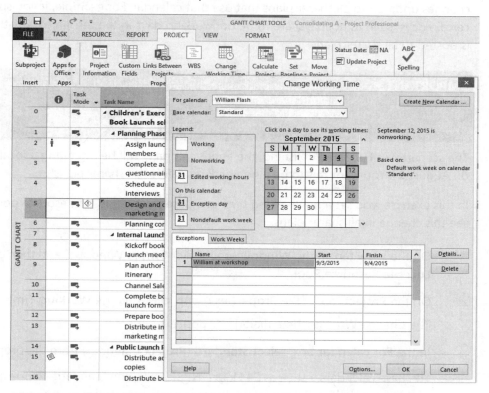

TIP To scroll the calendar quickly to September 2015 in the Change Working Time dialog box, just select the exception name or the Start or Finish date for William's exception.

12   Click **Cancel** to close the **Change Working Time** dialog box.

Updating all plans' working times in a resource pool

In the previous exercise, you changed an individual resource's working time in the resource pool, and you saw the change posted to a sharer plan. Another powerful capability of a resource pool enables you to change working times for a base calendar and see the changes updated to all sharer plans that use that calendar. For example, if you specify that certain days (such as holidays) are to be nonworking days in the resource pool, that change is posted to all sharer plans.

> **IMPORTANT** By default, all sharer plans share the same base calendars, and any changes you make to a base calendar in one sharer plan are reflected in all other sharer plans through the resource pool. If you have a specific sharer plan for which you want to use different base calendar working times, change the base calendar that sharer plan uses.

The scenario: At Lucerne Publishing, the entire company will be attending a local book fair on August 17. You want this to be a nonworking day for all sharer plans.

In this exercise, you set a nonworking time in a base calendar in the resource pool, and you see this change in all sharer plans.

1   On the **View** tab, in the **Window** group, click **Switch Windows**, and then click **Lucerne Resource Pool**.

2   On the **Project** tab, in the **Properties** group, click **Change Working Time**.

    The Change Working Time dialog box appears.

3   In the **For calendar** box, select **Standard (Project Calendar)** from the drop-down list.

    TIP Base calendars—such as 24 Hours, Night Shift, and Standard—appear at the top of the list in the For Calendar box. Resource calendar names appear below the base calendars.

    Changes in working time to the Standard base calendar in the resource pool affect all plans that are sharer plans of the resource pool.

4   On the **Exceptions** tab in the **Change Working Time** dialog box, click in the first row under **Name** and type Local book fair.

5   Click in the **Start** field and type or select **8/17/15**, and then click the **Finish** field.

    Project fills in the same value in the Finish Date field.

August 17 is set as a nonworking day in the resource pool.

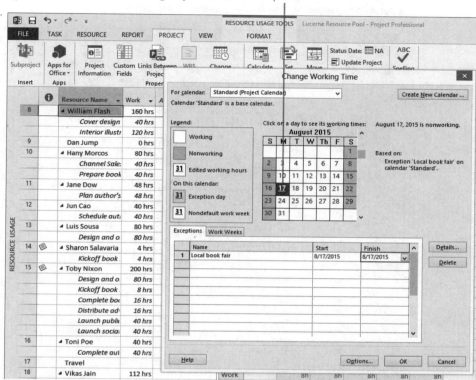

6   Click **OK** to close the **Change Working Time** dialog box.

To verify that this change to the Standard base calendar in the resource pool was up-dated in the sharer plans, you will look at working times in one of the sharer plans.

7   On the **View** tab, in the **Window** group, click **Switch Windows**, and then click **Consolidating A**.

8   On the **Project** tab, in the **Properties** group, click **Change Working Time**.

The Change Working Time dialog box appears.

9   In the **For calendar** box, make sure that **Standard (Project Calendar)** is selected in the drop-down list.

Note the *Local book fair* exception on August 17. All plans that are sharer plans of the same resource pool will see this change in this base calendar.

In the sharer plans linked to the resource pool, August 17
is set as a nonworking day in the Standard base calendar.

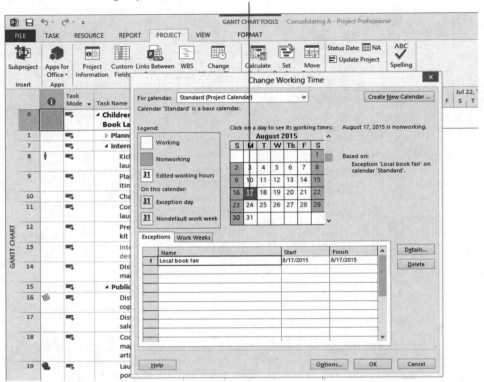

10   Click **Cancel** to close the **Change Working Time** dialog box.

If you want, you can switch to the Consolidating B plan and verify that August 17 is
also a nonworking day for that project.

11   Close and save changes to all open plans, including the resource pool.

IMPORTANT When working with sharer plans and a resource pool, you need to understand that
when you open a sharer plan, you must also open the resource pool if you want the sharer plan
to be updated with the most recent changes to the resource pool. For example, assume that you
change the project calendar's working time in the resource pool, save it, and close it. If you later
open a sharer plan but do not also open the resource pool, that sharer plan will not reflect the
updated project calendar's working time.

Linking new plans to a resource pool

You can make a plan a sharer plan for a resource pool at any time: when initially entering the plan's tasks, after you assign resources to tasks, or even after work begins. After you set up a resource pool, you might find it helpful to make sharer plans of all new plans, along with the sharer plans already created. In that way, you get used to relying on the resource pool for resource information.

A definite time-saving advantage of creating new plans as sharer plans of a resource pool is that your resource information is instantly available. You do not have to reenter any resource data.

The scenario: At Lucerne Publishing, you're about to start a plan for a new project. You'd like this new plan to be a sharer plan of your resource pool so that it gets the resource information already in the resource pool.

In this exercise, you create a plan and make it a sharer plan for the resource pool.

➡️ SET UP **You will open multiple practice files as you complete this exercise.**

1   In the Backstage view, click **Open**.

The Open screen appears.

2   Navigate to the Chapter21 folder, and open **Lucerne Resource Pool**.

   TIP Alternatively, you can select the file name from the Recent Projects list on the Open screen.

   When you open the resource pool file, Project prompts you to select how you want to open it.

   > **IMPORTANT** The default option is to open the resource pool as read-only. You might want to choose this option if you and other Project users are sharing a resource pool across a network. That way, you won't prevent other Project users from updating the resource pool. If you store the resource pool locally, however, you should open it as read-write.

3   Click the second option to open the resource pool as read-write.

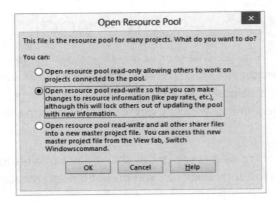

4   Click **OK**.

The resource pool opens with the Resource Usage view displayed.

When working with a resource pool, you might want to see a list of its sharer plans (especially if other Project users access the same resource pool file). You'll do so next.

5   On the **Resource** tab, in the **Assignments** group, click **Resource Pool**, and then click **Share Resources**.

The Share Resources dialog box appears. The Sharing Links path values you see might differ from those shown here.

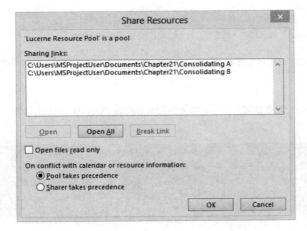

Because the resource pool is the active plan, the Share Resources dialog box contains the paths and filenames of its sharer plans. If you ever wanted to break a link to a sharer plan, you can do so here.

6   Click Cancel to close the Share Resources dialog box.

Next, you'll look at the list of resources in the resource pool. You'd expect these same resources to become available to any new plan you make a sharer of this resource pool.

7   On the **View** tab, in the **Resource Views** group, click **Resource Sheet**.

The Resource Sheet view appears. This is the information that will become available to the new plan you make a sharer plan of this resource pool.

8   On the **File** tab, click **New**, and then click **Blank project**.

Project creates a new plan.

9   On the **File** tab, click **Save As**.

10 Navigate to the Chapter21 folder.

The Save As dialog box appears.

11 In the **File name** box, type Consolidating C, and then click **Save**.

12 On the **Resource** tab, in the **Assignments** group, click **Assign Resources**.

The Assign Resources dialog box is initially empty because you have not yet entered any resource information in this plan.

13 On the **Resource** tab, in the **Assignments** group, click **Resource Pool** and then click **Share Resources**.

The Share Resources dialog box appears.

14 Under **Resources for 'Consolidating C'**, select the **Use resources** option.

15 Make sure that **Lucerne Resource Pool** is selected in the **From** box, and then click **OK** to close the **Share Resources** dialog box.

In the Assign Resources dialog box, you see all the same resource names appear that you saw in the resource pool.

21

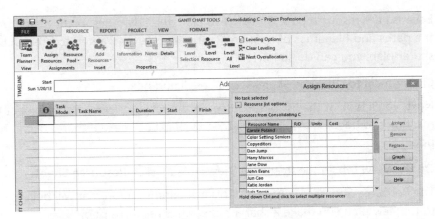

Now these resources are ready to be assigned to new tasks in this project.

16   Click **Close** to close the **Assign Resources** dialog box.

17   On the **File** tab, click **Close**. When prompted, click **Yes** to save your changes.

The Consolidating C plan closes, and the Lucerne Resource Pool remains open.

18   On the **File** tab, click **Close**. When prompted, click **Yes** to save your changes to the resource pool.

IMPORTANT You save changes to the resource pool because it records the names and locations of its sharer plans.

TIP A sharer plan's assignment information is duplicated in its resource pool. If a sharer plan is deleted, its assignment information remains in the resource pool. To clear this assignment information from the resource pool, you must break the link to the sharer plan. To do this, open the resource pool as read-write. On the Resource tab, in the Assignments group, click Resource Pool, and then click Share Resources. In the Share Resources dialog box, click the name of the now-deleted sharer plan and click Break Link. Note that what you see in the Share Resources dialog box for a resource pool differs from what you see for all other types of plans.

Changing sharer plan assignments and updating a resource pool

If you are sharing a resource pool with other Project users across a network, whoever has the resource pool open as read-write prevents others from updating resource information, such as standard cost rates, or making other plans sharers of that resource pool. For this reason, you should open the resource pool as read-only, and use the Update Resource Pool command only when you need to update the resource pool with assignment information. This command updates the resource pool with new assignment information; once that is done, anyone else who opens the resource pool will see the latest assignment information.

In this chapter, you are working exclusively with the resource pool and sharer plans locally. If you are going to share a resource pool with other Project users over a network, you need to understand the updating process. This exercise introduces you to that process.

The scenario: At Lucerne Publishing, you'd like to try out the Project commands to push assignment updates from a sharer plan to the resource pool. If you later decide to give other Project users access to this resource pool, you'll know how to update it on demand.

In this exercise, you change assignments in a sharer plan and then send updated assignment information to the resource pool.

 SET UP You need multiple practice files to complete this exercise.

1 In the Backstage view, click **Open**.

2 Navigate to the Chapter21 folder, and open the **Consolidating A** file.

   Because this plan is a sharer plan linked to a resource pool, Project gives you the options shown in the following illustration:

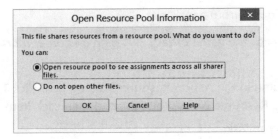

3   Click the **Open resource pool to see assignments across all sharer files** option, and then click **OK**.

> **TIP** Choosing the second option, Do Not Open Other Files, allows you to see assignments only in the sharer plan.

The resource pool opens as read-only behind the scenes. (If you want to verify this, look at the items in the Switch Windows command on the View tab.) Next, you will change some assignments in the sharer plan.

4   On the **Resource** tab, in the **Assignments** group, click **Assign Resources**.

The Assign Resources dialog box appears. First, you will assign a resource to a task.

5   In the **Task Name** column, click the name of task 3, *Complete author questionnaire*.

6   In the **Resource Name** column in the **Assign Resources** dialog box, click **Hany Morcos**, and then click **Assign**.

Project assigns Hany to the task.

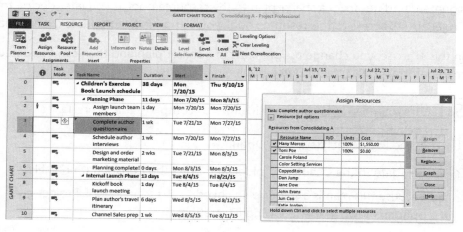

Next, you will remove a resource from a task.

7   In the **Task Name** column, click the name of task 5, *Design and order marketing material*.

8   In the **Resource Name** column in the **Assign Resources** dialog box, click **Toby Nixon** (located near the top of the **Resource Name** column), and then click **Remove**.

Project removes Toby from the task.

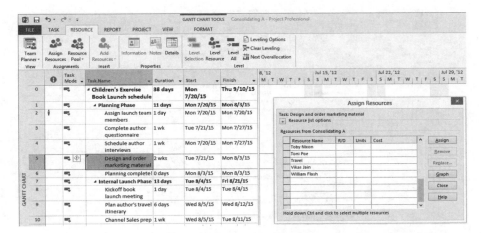

You have made two assignment changes in the sharer plan. Because the resource pool is open as read-only, those changes have not been saved permanently in the resource pool. Next, you will update the resource pool.

9   On the **Resource** tab, in the **Assignments** group, click **Resource Pool**, and then click **Update Resource Pool**.

Behind the scenes, Project updates the assignment information in the resource pool with the new details from the sharer plan and then saves the resource pool. Anyone else who opens or refreshes the resource pool now will see the updated assignment information.

> **IMPORTANT** Only assignment information is saved to the resource pool from the sharer plan. Any changes you make to resource details, such as maximum units, in the sharer plan are not saved in the resource pool when you update. When you want to change the resource details, open the resource pool as read-write. After it is open as read-write, you can change resource details in either the resource pool or the sharer plan, and the other plans will be updated.

Next, you will change another assignment in the sharer plan, close the sharer plan, and then update the resource pool.

10 In the **Task Name** column, click the name of task 8, *Kickoff book launch meeting.*

11 In the **Resource Name** column in the **Assign Resources** dialog box, click **Carole Poland**, and then click **Assign**.

Project assigns Carole to the task.

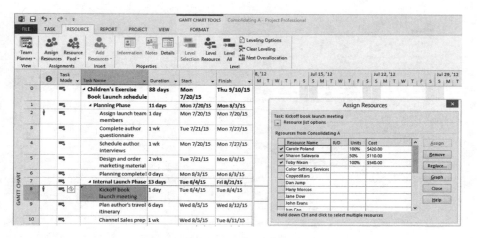

12   Click **Close** to close the **Assign Resources** dialog box.

13   On the **File** tab, click **Close**.

14   When prompted to save changes to the Consolidating A plan, click **Yes**.

Project determines that, because the resource pool was open as read-only, the latest assignment changes from the sharer plan have not been updated in the resource pool. You are offered the choices shown in the following message box.

15   Click **OK**.

Clicking OK causes Project to save the updated assignment information from the sharer plan to the resource pool, just as you did earlier in this section. The resource pool remains open as read-only.

16   On the **File** tab, click **Close** to close the resource pool.

Because the resource pool was opened as read-only, Project closes it without prompting you to save the changes.

TIP In addition to you pushing updates to your resource pool, other Project users who share the same resource pool can get the most current information themselves whenever they want. To do so, they select Refresh Resource Pool in the Resource Pool group on the Resources tab.

When sharing a resource pool with other Project users, be sure to update the resource pool with the latest assignment information. The updated assignments might affect resource allocations across other plans.

Consolidating plans

You likely will find yourself managing multiple plans that involve some of the same resources and might be related to the same overall goal or deliverable of an organization. Although a resource pool can help you manage resource details across different plans, it might not give you the level of control you want over tasks and relationships between plans. Or you might be coordinating with several people working on tasks at different times, sometimes in different locations, and frequently for different supervisors. In either case, you might need to produce a single "all-up" view of distinct but related plans.

A good way to pull together far-flung project information is to use a consolidated plan. This is a plan that contains other plans, called *inserted plans*. The inserted plans do not reside within the consolidated plan; rather, they are linked to it in such a way that they can be viewed and edited from it. If a plan is edited outside the consolidated plan, the updated information appears in the consolidated plan the next time it is opened.

TIP Consolidated plans are also known as **consolidated projects** or master projects, and inserted plans are also known as *subprojects*; however, this chapter uses the terms *consolidated* and *inserted* plans.

Using consolidated plans enables you to do the following:

- See all tasks from your organization's plans in a single view.

- Roll up information to higher levels of management. For example, you might insert a team's plan into the larger department's consolidated plan and then insert that plan into the larger organization's consolidated plan.

- Divide your project data into different plans to match the nature of your project, such as by phase, component, or location. Then you can pull the information back together into a consolidated plan for a comprehensive look at the whole plan.

- See all your plans' information in one location so that you can filter, sort, and group the data.

21

Consolidated plans use Project's outlining features. An inserted plan appears as a summary task in the consolidated plan, except that its summary Gantt bar is gray and an inserted project icon appears in the Indicators column. When you save a consolidated plan, you are also prompted to save any changes you made to inserted plans as well.

The scenario: At Lucerne Publishing, you occasionally need to look at information spread between closely related but distinct projects. To get an "all-up" view across plans, you decide to add them to a consolidated plan.

In this exercise, you create a new consolidated plan by inserting other plans.

SET UP You need multiple practice files to complete this exercise.

1   On the New screen of the Backstage view, click **Blank project**.

    Project creates a new plan. This plan will become the consolidated plan into which you insert other plans.

2   On the **Project** tab, in the **Insert** group, click **Subproject**.

    The Insert Project dialog box appears.

3   Navigate to the Chapter21 folder, and while holding down the Ctrl key, select **Consolidating A** and **Consolidating B**.

4   Click **Insert**.

    Project inserts the two plans into the consolidated plan as collapsed summary tasks.

5   On the **Task** tab, in the **Editing** group, click **Scroll to Task**.

    Project displays the Gantt bars of the collapsed inserted plans.

Note the Inserted Project icon in the Indicators column and gray summary task bars.

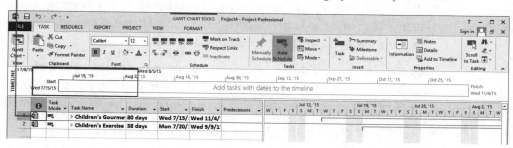

Next, you will save the new consolidated project.

6   On the **File** tab, click **Save As**.

7   Navigate to the Chapter21 folder.

8   In the **File name** box, type Lucerne Consolidated Projects, and then click **Save**.

Next, you will display the details of the two inserted plans.

9   On the **View** tab, in the **Data** group, click **Outline** and then click **All Subtasks**.

The Open Resource Pool Information box appears. Project asks whether you want to open the resource pool. Project hasn't actually loaded the content of the inserted plans yet, and showing the subtasks in the consolidated project is akin to opening them.

10   Make sure that **Open resource pool to see assignment across all sharer files** is selected, and then click **OK**.

Project expands the two plans. Note that the task IDs within both inserted plans start at 1, and the summary tasks representing the inserted plans are numbered 1 and 2.

Next, you'll look at the details of the inserted plans.

11   On the **View** tab, in the **Zoom** group, click **Entire Project**.

Project adjusts the timescale in the Gantt Chart so that the full duration of the two inserted plans is visible.

21

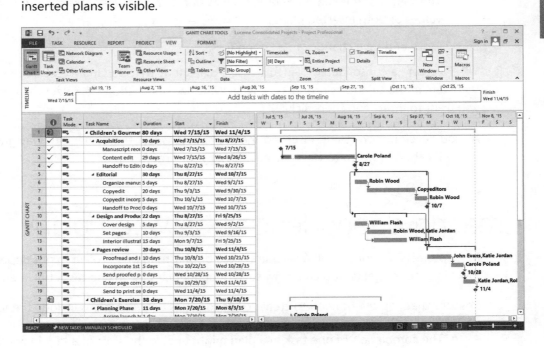

To conclude this exercise, you will display the project summary task of the consolidated plan.

12   On the **Format** tab, in the **Show/Hide** group, click **Project Summary Task**.

Project displays the consolidated plan's summary task.

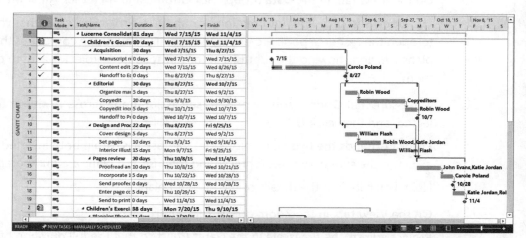

The values of this summary task, such as duration and work, represent the rolled-up values of both inserted plans.

13   Close and save changes to all open files.

TIP To create a consolidated plan and insert plans that are open in Project quickly, on the View tab, in the Windows group, click New Window. Under Projects, select the open plans you want to insert and then click OK.

As you develop more plans, inserting them into a consolidated plan in this way gives you a single location in which to view all activities of your organization.

Creating dependencies between plans

Most projects do not exist in a vacuum. Tasks or phases in one project might depend on tasks in other projects. You can show such dependencies by linking tasks between plans.

Reasons that you might need to create dependencies between plans include the following:

■ The completion of one task in a plan might enable the start of a task in another plan. For example, another project manager might need to complete an environmental impact statement before you can start to construct a building. Even if these two tasks are managed in separate plans (perhaps because separate departments of a development company are completing them), one plan has a logical dependency on the other.

- A person or a piece of equipment might be assigned to a task in one plan, and you need to delay the start of a task in another plan until that resource completes the first task. The two tasks might have nothing in common other than needing that resource.

Task relationships between plans look similar to links between tasks within a plan, except that external predecessor and successor tasks have gray task names and Gantt bars (sometimes referred to as *ghost tasks*). Such external tasks are not linked to tasks within the plan, only to tasks in other plans.

The scenario: At Lucerne Publishing, you have identified the deliverable of a task from one plan is required before a task in another plan can begin. You decide to create a cross-project link between these two plans.

In this exercise, you link tasks across two plans, and see the results in the plans as well as in a consolidated plan.

SET UP You will open multiple practice files as you complete this exercise.

1   In the Backstage view, click **Open**.

The Open screen appears.

2   Navigate to the Chapter21 folder, and open the **Consolidating B** file.

The Open Resource Pool Information box appears.

3   Click **Open resource pool to see assignment across all sharer files**, and then click **OK**.

Now you are ready to open a second file.

4   On the **File** tab, click **Open**.

5   Navigate to the Chapter21 folder, and open the **Consolidating A** file.

This time you are not prompted to open the resource pool because it was opened with the Consolidating B file.

6   In the **Task Name** column of the Consolidating A plan, click the name of task 12, *Prepare book sales kit*.

You need the book sales kit before you begin a task in the Consolidated B plan, so you will create a task dependency between the two plans.

7   On the **View** tab, in the **Window** group, click **Switch Windows**, and then click **Consolidating B**.

8   On the **View** tab, in the **Task Views** group, click **Gantt Chart**.

The Gantt Chart view appears.

9   Click the name of task 13, *Interior illustration design*.

10   On the **Task** tab, in the **Editing** group, click **Scroll to Task**.

Project scrolls the Gantt Chart view to display task 13.

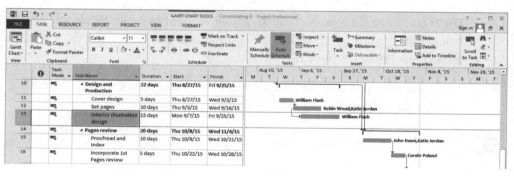

11   On the **Task** tab, in the **Properties** group, click **Information**.

The Task Information dialog box appears.

12   Click the Predecessors tab and, directly below the existing predecessor value *12* in the ID field, type **Consolidating A\12** and then press Tab.

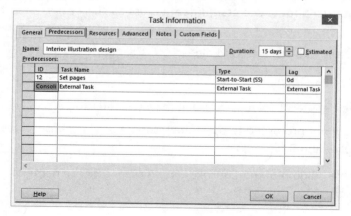

NOTE When you are creating an external predecessor link, Project requires the following format: *File Name\Task ID.*

Project supplies the value *External Task* for the new predecessor task's name and other values.

13   Click OK to close the Task Information dialog box.

Project inserts the external predecessor task named *Prepare book sales kit* into the project. The external task represents task 12 from the Consolidating A project.

The external predecessor task appears in the plan
to which it is linked with its task name in gray.

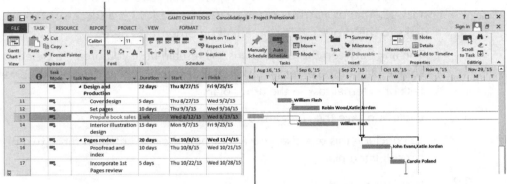

The external task's Gantt bar is gray.

TIP If you point to the external task's Gantt bar, Project displays a ScreenTip that contains details about the external task, including the full path to the external plan where the external predecessor task resides.

Next, you'll look at the external task in the Consolidating A plan.

14   On the **View** tab, in the **Window** group, click **Switch Windows**, and then click **Consolidating A**.

15   In the **Task Name** column, select the names of task 12, *Prepare book sales kit*, and task 13, *Interior illustration design*.

16   On the **View** tab, in the **Zoom** group, click **Selected Tasks**.

Project adjusts the chart portion of the Gantt Chart view to display the selected tasks.

21

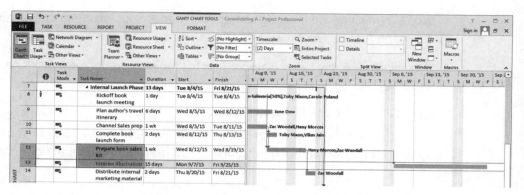

Here, you can see that task 12, *Prepare book sales kit*, is a predecessor for the external task 13, *Interior illustration design*. Because task 13 is a successor task with no other links to this project, it has no effect on other tasks here.

The link between these two plans will remain until you break it. Deleting a task in the source plan or the external task in the destination plan deletes the corresponding task or external task in the other plan.

17   Close and save the changes to all open files.

To conclude this exercise, you will display the link between these two plans in the consolidated plan.

18   In the Backstage view, click **Open**.

19   Navigate to the Chapter21 folder, and open the **Lucerne Consolidated Projects** file.

The Open Resource Pool Information box appears.

20   Click **Open resource pool to see assignment across all sharer files**, and then click **OK**.

21   In the **Children's Exercise Book Launch** schedule plan (the second inserted project), click the expand/collapse arrow next to the name of task 1, *Planning Phase* to collapse it.

Project collapses this phase. By doing this, you can see both the predecessor and successor tasks across the two inserted plans.

22   If necessary, scroll up until task 14 in the first inserted plan is visible.

You can see the link line between the *Prepare book sales kit* task in one inserted plan and the *Interior illustration design* task in the other inserted plan.

In the consolidated plan, the cross-plan link appears as a normal task link.

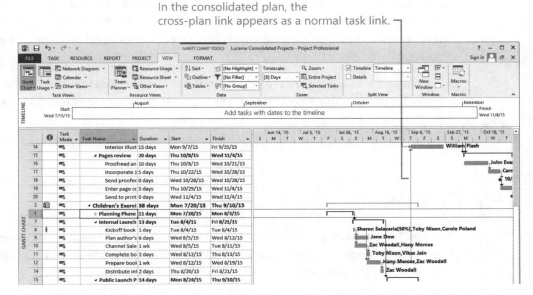

Because you are looking at a consolidated plan that shows the tasks from both plans, the cross-plan link does not appear as an external task.

The following are a few additional tips and suggestions for working with cross-plan links:

21

- You can turn off the display of external tasks if you want. To do this, on the File tab, click Options. In the Project Options dialog box, on the Advanced tab, under Cross Project Linking Options For *<File Name>*, clear the Show External Successors and Show External Predecessors check boxes.

- When viewing a consolidated plan, you can create cross-plan links quickly by clicking the Link Tasks button on the Task tab. Dragging the mouse between two task bars will do the same thing.

- Each time you open a plan with cross-plan links, Project prompts you to update the cross-plan links. You can suppress this prompt if you would rather not be reminded, or you can tell Project to accept updated data from the linked plan automatically. To do this, on the File tab, click Options. In the Project Options dialog box, on the Advanced tab, under Cross Project Linking Options For *<File Name>*, select the options you want.

- To delete a cross-plan link, do this: Go to the successor task first. On the Task tab, in the Properties group, click Information. In the Task Information dialog box, click the Predecessors tab. In the Predecessors box, select the external task link's ID and press Delete.

- To see and manage all links (external predecessors and external successors) into and out of a plan, on the Project tab, in the Properties group, click Links Between Projects.

 **CLEAN UP** Close all open files.

Key points

- If you have resource information duplicated in more than one plan, a resource pool is an excellent way to collect resource information across plans and spot problems, such as resource overallocation.

- In addition to indicating various resources' nonworking time in a resource pool, you can edit the project calendar in a resource pool (for example, marking holidays as nonworking time) and that information will be propagated to all sharer plans of the resource pool file.

- Resource assignment details from all sharer plans are available for viewing (but not editing) in the resource pool file.

- Consolidating plans into a single plan is useful when you want to see all the aggregate details in one place (the consolidated plan) and yet continue to work with the individual plans.

- When a task in one plan has a logical dependency on a task in another plan, you can link the two with a cross-plan link. This produces an external task (the predecessor or successor task) in both plans.

Appendices

A A short course in project management   505

B Developing your project-management
skills   513

C Collaborating: Project, SharePoint,
and PWA   516

D Using this book in a classroom   529

Throughout this book, we've included advice on how best to use Microsoft Project 2013 while following sound project-management practices. This appendix focuses on the basics of project management, regardless of any software tools you might use to help you manage projects. While project management is a broad, complex subject, in this appendix we focus on the *project triangle* model. In this model, you consider projects in terms of *time*, *cost*, and *scope*.

Understanding what defines a project

Succeeding as a project manager requires that you complete your projects on time, finish within budget, and make sure your customers are happy with what you deliver. That sounds simple enough, but how many projects have you heard of (or worked on) that were completed late, cost too much, or didn't meet the needs of their customers?

A Guide to the Project Management Body of Knowledge (published by the Project Management Institute)—referred to as the PMBOK and pronounced "pimbok"—defines a project as "a temporary endeavor undertaken to create a unique product or service." Let's walk through this definition to clarify what a project is—and what it is not.

TIP For more information about the Project Management Institute and the PMBOK, see Appendix B, "Developing your project-management skills."

First, a project is *temporary*. A project's duration might be just one week, or it might go on for years, but every project has an end date. You might not know that end date when the project begins, but it's out there somewhere in the future. Projects are not the same as ongoing operations, although the two have a great deal in common. *Ongoing operations*, as the name suggests, go on indefinitely; you don't establish an end date. Examples include most activities of accounting and human resources departments. People who run ongoing operations might also manage projects; for example, a manager of a human resources department for a large organization might plan a college recruiting fair. Yet, projects are distinguished from ongoing operations by an expected end date, such as the date of the recruiting fair.

Next, a project is an *endeavor*. *Resources*, such as people and equipment, need to do work. The endeavor is undertaken by a team or an organization, and therefore projects have a sense of being intentional, planned events. Successful projects do not happen spontaneously; some amount of preparation and planning happens first.

Finally, every project creates a *unique product* or *service*. This is the *deliverable* for the project and the reason that the project was undertaken. A refinery that produces gasoline does not produce a unique product. The whole idea, in this case, is to produce a standardized commodity; you typically don't want to buy gas from one station that is significantly different from gas at another station. On the other hand, commercial airplanes are unique products. Although all Boeing 787 Dreamliner airplanes might look the same to most of us, each is, in fact, highly customized for the needs of its purchaser.

By now, you might realize that much of the work that goes on in the world is project-oriented work. In fact, a substantial portion of your work might be focused on project management—even if that's not your job title.

Project management has been a recognized profession for many decades, but project-management work in some form has been occurring for as long as people have been doing complex work. When the Great Pyramids at Giza in Egypt were built, somebody somewhere was tracking resources, schedules, and specifications in some fashion.

TIP Project management is now a well-recognized profession in most industries. To learn more about organizations that train project managers and advance project management as a profession, see Appendix B.

The project triangle: Viewing projects in terms of time, cost, and scope

You can visualize project work in many ways, but our favorite method is what is sometimes called the *project triangle* or *triangle of triple constraints*.

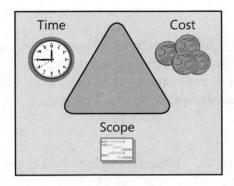

This theme has many variations, but the basic concept is that every project has some element of a time constraint, has some type of budget, and requires some amount of work to complete. (In other words, it has a defined scope.) The term *constraint* has a specific meaning in Project, but here we're using the more general meaning of "a limiting factor." Let's consider these constraints one at a time.

Time

Have you ever worked on a project that had a deadline? (Maybe we should ask whether you've ever worked on a project that did not have a deadline.) Limited *time* is the one constraint of any project with which we are all probably most familiar. If you're working on a project right now, ask your team members to name the date of the project deadline. They might not know the project budget or the scope of work in great detail, but chances are they all know their immediate deadlines, and probably also the overall project deadline.

The following are examples of time constraints:

- You are building a house and must finish the roof before the rainy season arrives.
- You are assembling a large display booth for a trade show that starts in two months.
- You are developing a new inventory-tracking system that must be tested and running by the start of the next fiscal year.

Since we were children, we have been trained to understand time. We carry wristwatches, paper organizers or electronic tablets, and other tools to help us manage time. For many projects that create a product or event, time is the most important constraint to manage.

Cost

You might think of cost simply in monetary terms, but in the context of projects, *cost* has a broader meaning: costs include all the resources required to carry out the project. Costs include the people and equipment doing the work, the materials being used, and all the other events and issues that require money or someone's attention in a project.

The following are examples of cost constraints:

- You signed a fixed-price contract to develop an e-commerce website for a client. If your costs exceed the agreed-upon price, your customer might be sympathetic, but he or she probably won't be willing to renegotiate the contract.

- The president of your organization has directed you to carry out a customer research project using only the staff and equipment in your department.

- You received a $5,000 grant to create a public art installation. You have no other funds.

For virtually all projects, cost is ultimately a limiting constraint; few projects can go over budget without eventually requiring corrective action.

Scope

You should consider two aspects of *scope*: product scope and project scope. Every successful project produces a unique product: a tangible item or service. Customers usually have some expectations about the features and functions of products they consider purchasing. *Product scope* describes the intended quality, features, and functions of the product, often in minute detail. Documents that outline this information are sometimes called *product specifications*. A service or event usually has some expected features as well. We all have expectations about what we'll do or see at a party, concert, or sporting event.

Project scope, on the other hand, describes the work required to deliver a product or service with the intended product scope. Project scope is usually measured in phases and tasks.

The following are examples of scope constraints:

- Your organization won a contract to develop an automotive product that has exact requirements—for example, physical dimensions measured to 0.01 millimeters. This is a product scope constraint that will influence project scope plans.

- You are constructing a building on a lot that has a height restriction of 50 feet.

- You can use only internal services to develop part of your product, and those services follow a product development methodology that is different from what you had planned.

Product scope and project scope are closely related. The project manager who manages project scope should also understand product scope or know how to communicate with those who do.

Time, cost, and scope: Managing project constraints

Project management gets most interesting when you must balance the time, cost, and scope constraints of your projects. The project triangle illustrates the process of balancing constraints because the three sides of the triangle are connected, and changing one side of a triangle affects at least one other side.

The following are examples of constraint balance:

- If the duration (time) of your project schedule decreases, you might need to increase budget (cost) because you must hire more resources to do the same work in less time. If you cannot increase the budget, you might need to reduce the scope because the resources you have cannot complete all the planned work in less time.

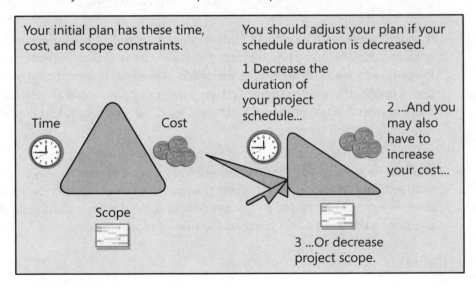

Your initial plan has these time, cost, and scope constraints.

Time   Cost

Scope

You should adjust your plan if your schedule duration is decreased.

1 Decrease the duration of your project schedule...

2 ...And you may also have to increase your cost...

3 ...Or decrease project scope.

If you must decrease a project's duration, make sure that overall project quality is not unintentionally lowered. For example, testing and quality control often occur last in a software development project; if project duration is decreased late in the project, those tasks might be the ones to suffer with cutbacks. You must weigh the benefits of decreasing the project duration against the potential downside of a deliverable of poorer quality.

- If the budget (cost) of your project decreases, you might need more time because you cannot pay for as many resources or for resources of the same efficiency. If you cannot increase the time, you might need to reduce project scope because fewer resources cannot complete all the planned work in the time remaining.

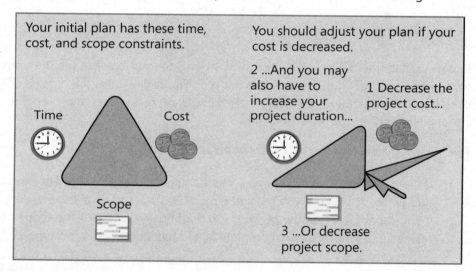

Your initial plan has these time, cost, and scope constraints.

Time

Cost

Scope

You should adjust your plan if your cost is decreased.

2 ...And you may also have to increase your project duration...

1 Decrease the project cost...

3 ...Or decrease project scope.

If you must decrease a project's budget, you could look at the *grades* of material resources for which you had budgeted. A lower-grade material is not necessarily a lower-quality material. So long as the grade of material is appropriate for its intended use, it might still be of high quality. Here's one example we can all relate to: fast food and gourmet are two grades of restaurant food, but you might find high-quality and low-quality examples of each.

You should also look at the costs of the human and equipment resources you planned to use. Can you hire less-experienced people for less money to carry out simpler tasks? Reducing project costs can lead to a poorer-quality deliverable, however. As a project manager, you must consider (or, more likely, communicate to the decision makers) the benefits versus the risks of reducing costs.

- If your project scope increases, you might need more time or resources (cost) to complete the additional work. When project scope increases after the project has started, it's called scope creep. Changing project scope midway through a project is not necessarily a bad thing; for example, the environment in which your project deliverable will operate might have changed or you've learned more about the nature of the work since beginning the project. Changing project scope is a bad thing only if the project manager doesn't recognize and plan for the new requirements—that is, when other constraints (cost, time) are not correspondingly examined and, if necessary, adjusted.

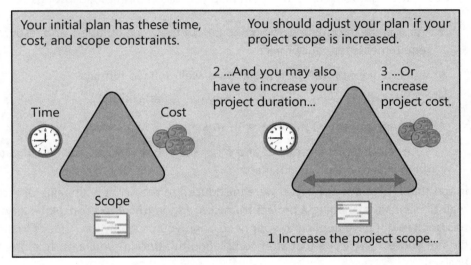

Your initial plan has these time, cost, and scope constraints.

Time

Cost

Scope

You should adjust your plan if your project scope is increased.

2 ...And you may also have to increase your project duration...

3 ...Or increase project cost.

1 Increase the project scope...

Time, cost, and scope are the three essential elements of any project. To succeed as a project manager, you should know how all three of these constraints apply to your projects and be able to communicate this to your stakeholders.

Here is our final word about the project triangle model. Like all simple models of complex subjects, this model is a useful learning tool but not always a reflection of the real world. If real projects always performed as the project triangle suggests that they should, you might see projects delivered late but at the planned cost or with the expected scope; or projects might be completed on time and with the expected scope, but at higher cost. In other words, you'd expect to see at least one element of the project triangle come in as planned. But the sad truth is that many projects, even with rigorous project management oversight, are delivered late, over budget, *and* with far less than the expected scope of functionality. You've probably participated in a few such projects yourself. Project management is a demanding field. Success in project management requires a rare mix of skills and knowledge about schedule practices and tools, as well as skill in the domain or industry in which a project is executed.

Managing your projects with Project

The best project-management tool in the world can never replace your good judgment. However, the right tool can and should help you accomplish the following:

- Track all the information you gather about the work, duration, and resource requirements for your project.

- Visualize your project plan in standard, well-defined formats.

- Schedule tasks and resources consistently and effectively.

- Exchange project information with *stakeholders* in a variety of ways.

- Communicate with resources and other stakeholders while leaving ultimate control in the hands of the project manager.

In the chapters of this book, you were introduced to the rich functionality of Project in a realistic context: managing a project from conception to completion. Not everything in this book might have applied to your needs, and you probably have needs that this book did not address. We hope that after completing this tutorial, you're off to a great start with Project!

Developing your project-management skills

B

If you completed most of or all the chapters in this book, you're well on your way to mastering Microsoft Project 2013. However, one book can get you only so far. To help further your knowledge of Project and project management, start with the sources listed in this appendix.

Joining a Project learning community

If there's one thing we can say about Project users, it's that they love to talk about the application and their work with it and to share ideas with others. Whether you work in a large organization or independently, you're likely to find a community of Project users nearby.

If you're in a large organization, especially one with a strong project-management focus, you might find an internal Project user group or support group there. Such groups often meet informally to provide peer training and support, critique plans, and share best practices. If such a group does not exist in your organization, perhaps you can start one.

In the public realm, there are many Project user groups around the world. These groups typically meet on a regular basis to share tips and tricks about Project. Joining a user group is a great way to broaden your exposure to Project usage; it also can be a great source for informal product support, training, and career networking.

The following are a few places where you can investigate Project user groups and related resources:

- The Microsoft Project User Group (MPUG) is the official industry association for Project. MPUG offers information about a variety of Project and project-management resources, as well as a directory of Project user groups around the world. Find it on the web at *www.mpug.com*.

- The Project area of the Microsoft Office Online website includes a variety of tools and information from Microsoft and other Project users to help you manage your projects.

Find it on the web at office.microsoft.com, and then navigate to the Project page.

- The Project Support area of the Microsoft Office Support website includes community questions and answers, downloads, and access to technical support specialists. Find it on the web at *office.microsoft.com/en-us/support*, and then navigate to the Project page or go directly to *support.microsoft.com/ph/931/en-us* for the Project Support page.

- The official Project Community offers help and discussions with other Project users, including Microsoft Most Valuable Professionals (MVPs). To get started, see *answers.microsoft.com/en-us/office/*.

- The Microsoft Project MVPs are independent Project experts (not Microsoft employees) officially given MVP status by Microsoft in recognition of their product expertise and work in helping the larger user community use Project successfully. MVPs frequently respond to questions in the Project Community forums. Find Project MVP information at *https://mvp.support.microsoft.com/communities/mvp.aspx*, and then navigate to the Project page.

- One of the authors of this book, Carl Chatfield, posts to a blog that focuses on Project, project management, and knowledge worker teams. Find the blog on the web at *www.projhugger.com*.

To showcase your Project expertise formally, you can become certified. Microsoft developed Microsoft Certified Technology Specialist (MCTS) certifications for Project and enterprise project-management solutions for Project 2010, and it might offer similar certifications for Project 2013. To learn about training opportunities and requirements for Project certification, look on the web at *www.microsoft.com/learning*.

Joining a project-management learning community

Perhaps more than other desktop programs, Project requires you to be involved in a specific formal activity: project management. Project management can be an exciting mix of technical, organizational, and social challenges. The Project Management Institute (PMI) is the leading organization of professional project management. PMI focuses on setting project-management standards, developing and offering educational programs, and certifying project managers. The most widely recognized PMI certification is the Project Management Professional (PMP) certification.

A Guide to the Project Management Body of Knowledge—published by the PMI and referred to as the PMBOK (pronounced "pimbok") describes generally accepted project-management practices, knowledge areas, and terminology. In addition, the PMI publishes the journals *Project Management Journal* and *PM Network*. You can learn more about the PMI on the web at *www.pmi.org*. If you are professionally invested in the practice of project management, you should be in the PMI.

Final words

There are, of course, many worthwhile commercial and nonprofit organizations dedicated to Project and project management besides those we have described here. Project enjoys a leading position in the diverse, sometimes contentious, but always interesting world of project management. Wherever you are in your own Project and project-management knowledge and career development, you can find a great variety of supporting organizations and peers today. The authors wish you the greatest success!

Collaborating: Project, SharePoint, and PWA

C

This appendix introduces you to some of the team-collaboration features available when you combine Microsoft Project 2013 Professional with Microsoft SharePoint 2013 or Project Web App (PWA). Although full coverage of Project's interoperability with SharePoint and PWA is beyond the scope of this book, we want to help you gain a basic understanding of the benefits these products offer beyond Project's capabilities on the desktop. We conclude the appendix with a discussion of Project Server–based Enterprise Project Management (EPM) and what capabilities EPM can add to your organization.

Because you might not have access to SharePoint or PWA, this appendix describes and illustrates these services but does not include hands-on activities with practice files. Each section concludes with a "Sources for more information" list of online resources you can investigate.

Introduction to sharing your plan with SharePoint

Project managers and teams benefit when they share information. With Project Professional 2013, you can synchronize tasks between Project and SharePoint 2013. You can either create the initial task list in Project and then synchronize it to a list in SharePoint or create the initial task list in SharePoint and then create a new Project plan based on the task list. Team members can view, edit, and report the status of their tasks in the SharePoint tasks list.

The following illustrations show you some of the key parts of working with a tasks list in SharePoint.

The Project Summary page includes a timeline, upcoming and late tasks, and other key details about the plan.

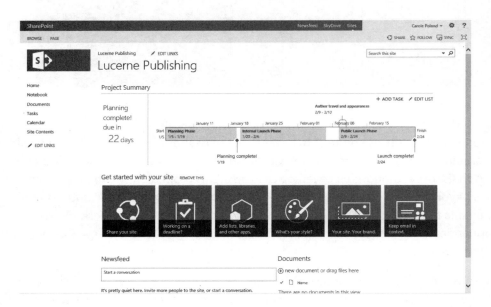

From the Project Summary page, you can share the plan, customize the site, and drill into the task list. Here's what a timeline and tasks list look like in SharePoint:

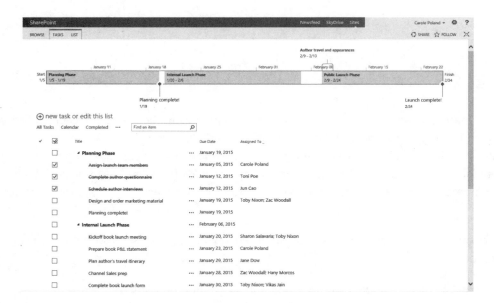

In SharePoint, you can track progress on a task or add new tasks, but no active scheduling occurs. You can even view your tasks list in other views, including a calendar and, as shown next, a Gantt Chart view.

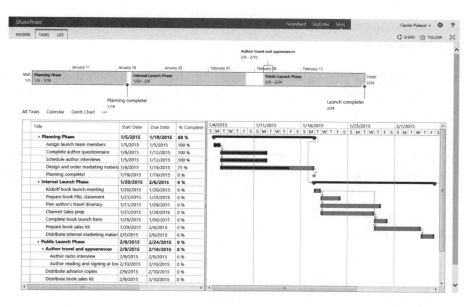

When the SharePoint tasks list is synchronized with Project, you can then take full advantage of the Project feature set and scheduling engine. Here you can see the SharePoint tasks list from the preceding illustration now shown in Project:

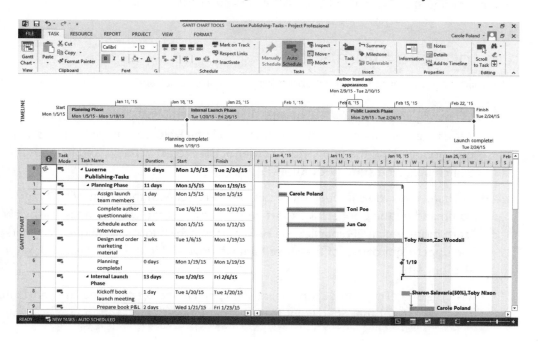

Project Professional users can think of task synchronization with SharePoint as serving two very useful purposes:

- You can create an initial tasks list in SharePoint and invite team members and other stakeholders to add tasks, durations, and other details in SharePoint. You can then open the list in Project and do scheduling work in Project. Then resynchronize back to SharePoint so that the team can see the results.

- You can create an initial tasks list in Project and then synchronize it with SharePoint. You can then invite team members and other stakeholders to adjust task details as needed. Then edit the list in Project for additional schedule fine-tuning.

In both cases, you use the scheduling engine in Project and the collaborative, multi-user capabilities of SharePoint—the best combination of the strengths of both products.

You can also convert a SharePoint task list into a PWA project (described in the next section). You might choose to do so, for example, when you find you need more detailed status tracking or workflow management of tasks.

This section introduced you to Project and SharePoint integration via task list synchronization. Depending on the collaborative practices and tools of your organization, you might find that Project and SharePoint together make a powerful combination.

Sources for more information

The following are some resources about Project Professional and SharePoint integration:

- In Project, you can share a plan with SharePoint in the Save As screen of the Backstage view. To learn more, in Project click the Help button (which looks like a question mark) in the upper-right corner of the Project window, and in the Help Search box, type sync with SharePoint.

- In SharePoint, you can open a tasks list with Project with the Open With Project command on the Connect & Export group of the List tab while in a tasks list view. To learn more, in SharePoint click the Help button (which looks like a question mark) in the upper-right corner of the SharePoint window, and in the Help Search box, type Project site.

- Visit the SharePoint product portal at *sharepoint.microsoft.com*, and then navigate to the tasks list or other SharePoint features that interest you.

- Members of the Project Engineering team have written some detailed posts on the Office Blog about Project and SharePoint task lists. Visit *blogs.office.com*, and then search for SharePoint task list.

Introduction to team collaboration with Project Web App

Project Web App (PWA) is the browser-based interface to Project Server. Project managers can use PWA in conjunction with the Project Professional application to build and manage projects. Others who can use PWA include:

- Team members who have task assignments
- Portfolio managers who collect and analyze data across multiple projects
- Site administrators who set up and manage access to PWA and create custom user experiences

Projects that can be managed in PWA can come from a variety of sources, including:

- Project Professional plans (MPP files)
- SharePoint task lists
- Created directly in PWA

A PWA project is stored in Project Server, and it can be edited by authorized stakeholders in PWA and by the project manager in Project.

At first glance, a tasks list in PWA might look similar to a SharePoint tasks list. PWA tasks lists offer much greater scheduling capabilities, however, and support the scheduling features in PWA and the full feature set of Project Professional.

The following illustrations show you some of the capabilities in PWA for project managers and team members.

The hub of PWA is the Home screen.

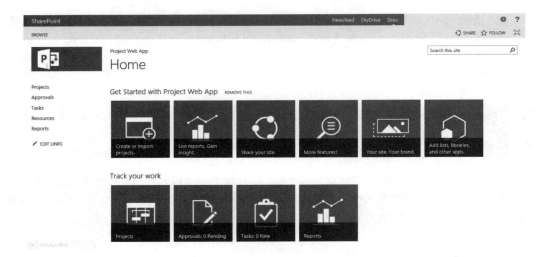

From here, you can manage your PWA site and drill down into your projects and tasks. Here is what a collection of projects, or a *portfolio*, looks like in the Project Center:

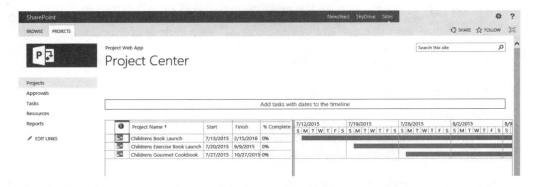

The commands on the Projects tab (shown next) indicate some of the actions you can perform. Important abilities include adding new projects to the portfolio, controlling access to projects, and changing how the list of projects appears.

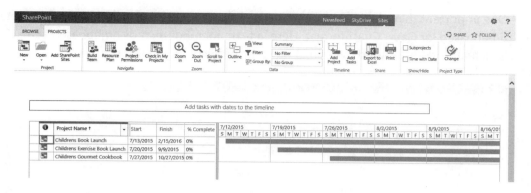

When you view a project, you get a familiar Gantt Chart with Timeline view very similar to what you would see in Project. In fact, you can see on the Task tab, in the following illustration, many of the same task-management features you saw in Project, including tracking progress and applying groups or filters.

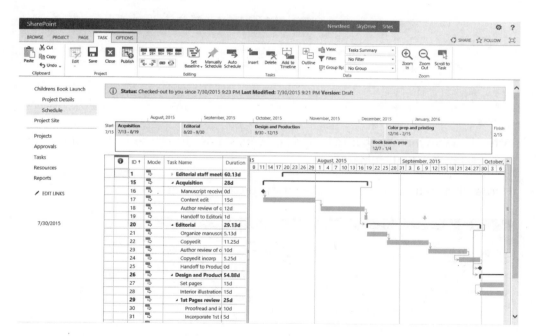

Next, we'll look at PWA from the perspective of a team member who has task assignments in a PWA project.

One important thing team members can use PWA for is to record work status in sheet, timephased, or Gantt Chart format. Here, a team member records timephased actuals (that is, actual work distributed over time) on some of her assigned tasks.

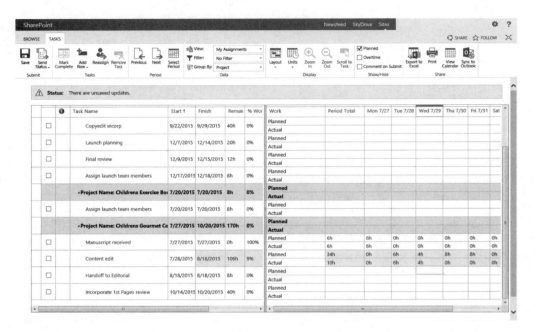

After the team member has recorded her work status, she can submit her status for approval by the project manager.

Here's what status updates look like for the project manager:

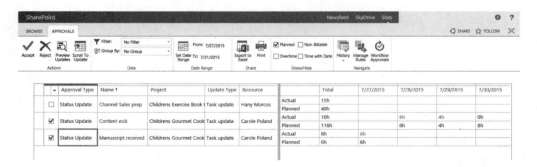

Team members can add comments to their status per task, which looks like this to the project manager:

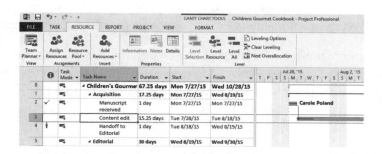

Once the project manager accepts the status updates, Project's scheduling engine responds to the progress reported by team members and any other changes made to the plan in PWA.

The next time the plan is published, all team members and other stakeholders will see the changes. This collaborative process continues throughout the life of the project.

Sources for more information

The following are some resources about Project Professional and PWA integration:

- If you have access to PWA, you can get an overview of supported activities in PWA's Help. Click the Help button (which looks like a question mark) in the upper-right corner of the PWA window, and explore the Help content.

- Visit the Project Server product portal at *office.microsoft.com/products*.

- See IT-Pro content about Project Server 2013 at *technet.microsoft.com/en-US/ projectserver*.

- Members of the Project Engineering team have written some detailed posts on the Office Blog about Project and SharePoint task lists. Visit *blogs.office.com*, and then search for PWA.

Introduction to Enterprise Project Management

The previous sections introduced you to some of the team collaboration features enabled by SharePoint and Project Web App (PWA). Behind PWA sits Project Server. Project Server is the cornerstone of the Microsoft Enterprise Project Management (EPM) solution. (We'll refer to this as *Project Server–based EPM*; you might also see the related label *Project Portfolio Management*, or PPM). The project-management functionality of Project Server-based EPM extends far beyond the desktop functionality of Project as you've practiced it in this book.

This section introduces some of the key differences between desktop project management and Project Server–based *Enterprise Project Management*. EPM is one of the more complex but potentially rewarding practices that a large organization can adopt.

Some organizational benefits of Project Server–based EPM include:

- Capturing your organization's best practices with regard to workflow models and resource skills in enterprise templates

- Gaining insight into resource workload and availability across all projects and other activities in your organization

- Developing consistent ways of describing and tracking project activities across your organization

- Collecting a broad range of data relating to projects and reporting this data in timely and informative ways

Although you might be the sole user of Project in your organization, the real "user" of EPM is the entire organization; thus, the software toolset is correspondingly more complex than Project running on a single computer. For this reason, fully addressing the details of EPM is far beyond the scope of this book. However, we want to introduce Project Server–based EPM here so that you can start to determine whether it can serve a useful role in your organization. For most organizations, we think the answer will be "Yes," but getting from an initial interest in Project Server–based EPM to a full implementation is a series of complex steps. We hope that this brief introduction can help you formulate some ideas of how Project Server–based EPM can improve your organization's performance.

If you've completed the previous chapters in this book, you have a good introduction to project management on the scale of a single project manager with projects that have dozens of resources working on hundreds of tasks. You might be practicing project management at this scale now. Indeed, with a resource pool and multiproject features, such as consolidated projects, a single project manager should be able to stay on top of several different projects in various stages of completion with Project running on a single computer.

Now, imagine dozens of project managers planning and tracking hundreds of projects, each with hundreds or even thousands of resources and tasks—all within a single organization. Project management at this scale requires a high degree of planning, coordination, and standardization. This is the realm of EPM: a large organization planning, coordinating, and executing a large number of projects simultaneously.

Think about any past or current experiences you've had working on projects in a large organization, and try to answer these questions:

- Were potential projects evaluated against the goals and objectives of the organization such that the projects selected for execution aligned well with the strategic goals of the organization?

- Were the projects defined and scoped in a consistent way that enabled apples-to-apples comparisons?

- Were resource assignments made with full knowledge of each resource's skills, location, and availability?

- Did the executive leadership of the organization have a clear picture of the status of each project?

If your answer to these questions is "No," the organization was probably not practicing EPM effectively. There is no question that many large organizations can gain great benefits by adopting EPM; however, this is no easy task, or they would have implemented EPM already. Succeeding with EPM requires a strong willingness from the leadership of the organization (executive sponsorship), a well-trained group of administrators, project and resource managers, and a software infrastructure (either on the premises or hosted via Project Online) capable of enabling it.

Sources for more information

The following are some resources to help with your evaluation, planning, and deployment of a Project Server–based EPM solution:

- Review all the relevant material on the Project Server area of the Office Online website. Find it on the web at *office.microsoft.com*, and then navigate to the Project Server page.

- Consider attending classroom training on EPM deployment from Microsoft Learning. Check the Microsoft Learning website for Project Server information: *www.microsoft.com/learning*.

- If you are in an organization that is relatively new to the project and portfolio-management discipline, consider working through the Project Server deployment process with a recognized Project partner. You can begin your search for a qualified partner firm here: *pinpoint.microsoft.com*.

We hope this brief introduction will give you and your organization a good start in exploring EPM tools and practices.

Using this book in a classroom

This book is suitable for various learning environments and needs, including:

- Individual self-paced training
- Instructor-led classroom training

If you are an instructor preparing training material for classroom delivery, this appendix offers some suggestions for how to best integrate this book into your syllabus or lesson plans.

Matching content to instructional needs

The following table describes the organization of this book and how you as an instructor can incorporate this book into your classroom training environment.

Book Level	Training Focus
Entire book	Assign for the duration of your course or the portion of the course that focuses on Microsoft Project 2013 skills development.
Part	Part 1, "Introduction to Microsoft Project," includes Chapters 1 and 2. Chapter 2 is an introduction to Project and is especially well suited to those who are new to Project.
	Part 2, "Simple scheduling basics," includes Chapters 3 through 8. These chapters cover a complete project life cycle and introduce simpler task, resource, assignment, formatting, and tracking features of Project. The chapters in Part 2 follow a logical sequence to build a plan and track progress. If your students have some experience with Project 2013, you can elect to skip Part 2.
	Part 3 (Chapters 9 through 16), "Advanced scheduling techniques," covers a complete project life cycle and introduces more advanced features and skills relating to task, resource, assignment, formatting, and tracking activities in Project. The chapters in Part 3 follow a logical sequence in which you fine-tune a plan, track progress, and respond to variance.
	Part 4 (Chapters 17 through 21), "In-depth and special subjects," covers some subjects that are not part of a project life cycle but are important for well-rounded training in Project. The chapters in Part 4 are not in any particular sequence and can be used in any order.

Book Level	Training Focus
Chapter	Each chapter is a complete learning solution that focuses on a major feature set of Project. Most chapters in this book require the use of at least one practice file and sometimes multiple practice files.
	If you have specific feature areas you want to cover, you can assign chapters based on subject matter. For example, if you want to focus on resource features in Project, you could assign Chapter 5, "Setting up resources," followed by Chapter 11, "Fine-tuning resource and assignment details," and possibly Chapter 21, "Consolidating projects and resources" (if you want to address resource pools).
	Several chapters include "Project management focus" sidebars, in which project-management principles or issues are brought up in the context of Project functionality. These sidebars are a great opportunity to broaden classroom discussions and activities to encompass project-management practices.
Section	Each chapter consists of several sections. At the beginning of each chapter, you will find the learning objectives addressed in that chapter. The objectives state the instructional goals for each section so that you and your students understand what skills they will master.
	In this book, the sections are strongly sequential within the chapter; students are expected to complete sections in the order in which they appear. If you need to assign just some sections of a chapter, check what state the chapter's practice file or files should be in at the start of each assigned section. In some cases, you might need to create section-specific versions of practice files.
Explanatory portion of section	Each section is roughly divided between an explanatory portion, which defines core concepts, and the hands-on activity (the enumerated procedure). When presenting core concepts to students, you might want to elaborate on the supplied content. For example, if you are teaching project management in an engineering course, you might want to provide more engineering-specific examples and terms in your explanation.
Hands-on activity per section	The hands-on activity per section is intended to be completed by students or by an instructor while observed by students. The procedures are heavily illustrated so that students can check their results against the illustrations.
	Students might work through the hands-on activities outside the classroom, or in the classroom if it is equipped with computers. For lab environments, you might find it helpful to pair up students so that one completes the hands-on activity while the other reads the instructions, and both discuss the results. They can then alternate roles between sections.
Practice files	This book includes instructions about downloading the practice files used in the hands-on activities throughout this book. If your practice files become unsuitable for new users (for example, students complete activities but overwrite the original practice files), you can reinstall fresh practice files from the web.

The sections and chapters in this book vary in terms of page count and, for the hands-on activities, completion time. For this reason, we recommend that you complete the activities yourself that you intend to assign to students so that you can better estimate how long the assignments should take. An experienced Project user should be able to complete any chapter in this book within one hour; a new Project user, however, might require substantially more time.

Depending on your classroom environment and training objectives, you might find a variety of instructional strategies to be effective, including:

- Instructor leads a lecture or discussion through the explanatory portion of a section and then demonstrates the hands-on activity in Project.

- Instructor leads a lecture and then assigns students to complete the hands-on activity at computers in the classroom or lab.

- Instructor leads a lecture and then assigns students to complete the hands-on activity outside the classroom.

- Instructor assigns the reading and completion of hands-on activities to students, to be completed outside the classroom.

These are just a few possible options.

Teaching project management with Project

A core principle of this book's instructional strategy is that success with Project is built on success with basic project-management practice. Although Project is a feature-rich application, mastery of its features alone is no guarantee of success in project management. For this reason, you will find material about project-management practice throughout this book. See, for example, the following:

- The many "Project management focus" sidebars throughout the chapters

- Appendix A, "A short course in project management"

- Appendix B, "Developing your project-management skills"

This book does not prescribe a specific project-management methodology, but in general aims to be in alignment with the Project Management Institute's (PMI's) *A Guide to the Project Management Body of Knowledge* (PMBOK) and generally accepted project-management practices.

That said, it is important to acknowledge that some core areas of project management are beyond the scope of activities performed with Project. Resource recruiting and procurement, for example, are critical activities for many projects, but they are not activities that Project directly supports. If your instructional context is more focused on Project features than project-management practice, you should explore this issue with your students so that they gain a fuller understanding of the broad domain of project management and where specifically Project can best support them.

Glossary

8/80 rule A general guideline regarding the estimation of task duration. Task durations between 8 hours (or one day) and 80 hours (10 working days, or two weeks) are generally sized to a manageable duration. See Chapter 4.

accrual The method by which a plan incurs the cost of a task or a resource. The three types of accrual are start, prorated, and end. See Chapter 10.

actual A detail about task progress recorded in a plan in Microsoft Project. Prior to recording actuals, the plan contains scheduled or planned information. Comparing planned project information to actuals helps the project manager better control project execution. See Chapters 8 and 14.

allocation The portion of the capacity of a resource devoted to work on a specific task. See Chapter 12.

assignment The matching of a work resource (a person or a piece of equipment) to a task. You can also assign a material or cost resource to a task, but those resources have no effect on work or duration. See Chapters 6 and 11.

AutoFilter In a table, a quick way to view or organize only the task or resource information that meets the criteria you choose. See Chapter 13.

automatically scheduled task A task for which Microsoft Project dynamically adjusts the start or finish date to account for schedule changes in a plan. See Chapter 4.

Backstage view The view accessed from the File tab and is standardized across most Office 2013 applications. This view contains customization and sharing options, as well as the essential commands for file management like Open, New, and Save. See Chapter 2.

base calendar A calendar that can serve as the project calendar or a task calendar. A base calendar also defines the default working times for resource calendars. Microsoft Project includes three base calendars named Standard, 24 Hours, and Night Shift. You can customize these, or you can use them as a basis for your own base calendar. See Chapter 3.

baseline The original plan, saved for later comparison with the revised or updated plan. The baseline includes the planned start and finish dates, durations and work values of tasks and assignments, as well as their planned costs. Plans can have up to 11 baselines. See Chapters 8, 14 and 15.

bottom-up planning A method of developing a plan that starts with the lowest-level tasks and organizes them into broad phases. See Chapter 4.

calendar The settings that define the working days and time for a plan, resources, and tasks. See Chapter 11.

Calendar view A simple view in Project that shows tasks in a "month-at-a-glance" layout. See Chapter 17.

consolidated project A plan in Microsoft Project that contains one or more inserted plans. The inserted plans are linked to the consolidated plan so that any changes to the inserted plans are reflected in the consolidated plan, and vice versa. A consolidated plan is also known as a *master project*. See Chapter 21.

constraint A restriction, such as Must Start On (MSO) or Finish No Later Than (FNLT), that you can place on the start or finish date of a task. See Chapter 9.

contour The manner in which a resource's work on a task is scheduled over time. Microsoft Project includes several predefined work contours that you can apply to an assignment. For example, a back-loaded contour schedules a small amount of work at the beginning of an assignment and then schedules increasing amounts of work as time progresses. You can also contour an assignment manually by editing work values in a usage view, such as the Resource Usage view. Applying a predefined contour or manually contouring an assignment causes Project to display a work contour icon in the Indicators column. See Chapter 11.

cost The resources required to carry out a plan, including the people who do the work, the equipment used, and the materials consumed as the work is completed. Cost is one side of the project triangle model. See Chapter 15 and Appendix A.

cost rate table The resource pay rates that are stored on the Costs tab of the Resource Information dialog box. You can have up to five separate cost rate tables per resource. See Chapter 11.

cost resource A type of resource used to represent financial costs associated with tasks in a plan. Use cost resources to account for standard categories of costs that you want to track in a plan, such as costs for travel or catering. A cost resource does no work and has no effect on the scheduling of a task to which it is assigned. See Chapters 5 and 6.

critical path A series of tasks that, if delayed, will push out the end date of a plan. See Chapters 10 and 15.

deadline A date value that you can enter for a task that indicates the latest date by which you want the task to be completed. If the scheduled completion date of a task is later than its deadline, Microsoft Project notifies you. The benefit of entering deadline dates is that they do not constrain tasks. See Chapter 10.

deliverable The final product, service, or event that a plan is intended to produce. See Chapter 4 and Appendix A.

dependency A link between a predecessor task and a successor task. A dependency controls the start or finish of one task relative to the start or finish of the other task. The most common dependency is finish-to-start (FS), in which the finish date of the predecessor task determines the start date of the successor task. See Chapter 4.

destination program The program into which you place the data when exchanging data between Microsoft Project and another program. See Chapter 20.

Driving predecessor A predecessor task that directly affects, or drives the scheduling of its successor task. See Chapter 9.

duration The span of working time that you expect it will take to complete a task. See Chapter 4.

effort-driven scheduling A scheduling method in which the work of a task remains constant regardless of the number of resources assigned to it. As resources are added to a task, the duration decreases, but the total work remains the same and is distributed among the assigned resources. Effort-driven scheduling is turned off by default, but it can be turned on for fixed-unit or fixed-duration tasks. Effort-driven scheduling is always turned on for fixed-work tasks. See Chapter 6.

elapsed duration The uninterrupted span of time that it will take to finish a task, based on a 24-hour day and a 7-day week. Elapsed duration is not limited by project, resource, or task calendars; it is continuous. See Chapter 4.

enterprise project management (EPM) Project management practiced in a formal, consistent way throughout an organization. See Appendix C.

Entry table The grid on the left side of the default Gantt Chart view. See Chapter 2.

export map The specifications for exporting fields from Microsoft Project to other file formats, such as Tab-delimited format. Project includes several export maps, which you can use as they are or modify. See Chapter 20.

field The lowest-level information about a task, resource, or assignment. See Chapter 2.

filtering In a view, a way to see or highlight only the task or resource information that meets the criteria you choose. See Chapter 13.

fixed consumption rate A fixed quantity of a material resource to be consumed in the completion of an assignment. See Chapter 11.

fixed cost A set amount of money budgeted for a task. This amount is independent of resource costs and task duration. See Chapter 10.

fixed duration A task type in which the duration value is fixed. If you change the amount of work that you expect a task to require, Microsoft Project recalculates the resource assignment's peak units for each resource. If you change duration or units, Project recalculates the work. See Chapter 9.

fixed units A task type in which a resource assignment's units value is fixed. If you change the duration of a task, Microsoft Project recalculates the amount of work scheduled for the task. If you change units or work, Project recalculates the duration. See Chapter 9.

fixed work A task type in which the work value is fixed. If you change the duration of the task, Microsoft Project recalculates the resource assignment's peak units for each resource. If you change units or work, Project recalculates the duration. See Chapter 9.

flexible constraint A constraint type that gives Microsoft Project the flexibility to change the start or finish dates (but not the duration) of a task. As Soon As Possible (ASAP) and As Late As Possible (ALAP) are examples of flexible constraints. See Chapter 9.

free slack The amount of time that a task can be delayed without delaying the start date of another task. See Chapter 10.

fully allocated The condition of a resource when the total work of his or her task assignments is exactly equal to his or her work capacity. See Chapter 12.

Gantt Chart view A predefined view in Microsoft Project consisting of a table (the Entry table by default) on the left and a graphical bar chart on the right that shows the plan over time. See Chapter 17.

Global template A template in Microsoft Project named Global.mpt that contains the default views, tables, filters, and other items that Project uses. See Chapter 19.

group A way to reorder task or resource information in a table and display summary values for each group. You can specify several levels of groups. (The term *group* is also used to refer to the Resource Group field, which is unrelated.) See Chapter 13.

Group field A resource field in which you can specify a group name (such as a department) with which you want to associate a resource. If you organize resources into groups, you can sort, filter, or group resources by group. See Chapter 13.

hyperlink A link to another file, a specific location in a file, a page on the Internet, or a page on an intranet. See Chapter 4.

import/export map A set of specifications for importing specific data to or from fields in Microsoft Project. Project includes several built-in maps, which you can modify or use as they are. Import and export maps are sometimes referred to as *data maps*. See Chapter 20.

inflexible constraint A constraint type that forces a task to begin or end on a certain date. Must Start On (MSO) and Must Finish On (MFO) are both inflexible constraints. See Chapter 9.

inserted plan In Microsoft Project, a plan that is inserted into another plan, called a *consolidated plan*. An inserted plan is also known as a *subproject*. See Chapter 21.

interim plan A task's start and finish values, saved for later comparison. Each plan in Microsoft Project can have, at most, 10 interim plans. See Chapter 14.

lag time A delay between tasks that have a task relationship. For example, lag time causes the successor task in a finish-to-start (FS) relationship to begin some time after its predecessor task concludes. See Chapter 9.

lead time An overlap between tasks that have a task relationship. For example, lead time causes the successor task in a finish-to-start (FS) relationship to begin before its predecessor task concludes. In Microsoft Project, you enter lead time as negative lag time. See Chapter 9.

line manager A manager of a group of resources; also called a *functional manager*. A line manager might also have project management skills and responsibilities, depending on the organization's structure. See Chapter 21.

link A logical relationship between tasks that controls sequence and dependency. In the Gantt Chart and Network Diagram views, links appear as lines between tasks. See Chapters 4 and 9.

macro A recorded or programmed set of instructions that carry out a specific action when initiated. Macros in Microsoft Project use Microsoft Visual Basic for Applications (VBA). See Chapter 19.

manually scheduled task A task for which Microsoft Project does not set a start or finish date or duration automatically. Such a task can include any type of value you want in most fields. See Chapter 4.

material resources The consumables that are used up as a plan progresses. As with work resources, you assign material resources to tasks. Unlike work resources, material resources have no effect on the total amount of work scheduled on a task. See Chapter 11.

maximum units The maximum capacity (as entered in the Max. Units field) of a resource to accomplish tasks. If you allocate the resource beyond its capacity, Microsoft Project alerts you that the resource is overallocated. See Chapters 5 and 6.

milestone A significant event that is reached within the plan or imposed upon the plan. In Microsoft Project, milestones normally are represented as tasks with zero duration. See Chapter 4.

negative slack The amount of time that tasks overlap due to a conflict between task relationships and constraints. See Chapter 9.

Network Diagram view A Project view that focuses on activities and their relationships. Tasks are represented as nodes and the relationships between tasks are drawn as lines connecting the nodes See Chapter 17.

Night Shift base calendar A base calendar included with Microsoft Project designed to accommodate an 11:00 P.M.–8:00 A.M. "graveyard" work shift. See Chapter 3.

noncritical tasks The tasks that have slack. Noncritical tasks can finish within their slack time without affecting the plan's completion date. See Chapter 10.

note The information (including linked or embedded files) that you want to associate with a task, resource, or assignment. See Chapters 4 and 5.

ongoing operation An activity that has no planned end date and is repetitive in nature. Examples include accounting, managing human resources, and some manufacturing tasks. See Chapter 1 and Appendix A.

Organizer In Microsoft Project, a dialog box with which you can copy views, tables, filters, and other items between the Global.mpt template and other plans or between two different plans. See Chapter 19.

outline A hierarchy of summary tasks and subtasks within Microsoft Project, usually corresponding to major phases of work. See Chapter 4.

overallocated The condition of resources when they are assigned to do more work than is their normal work capacity. See Chapter 5.

phase A sequence of tasks that represent a major portion of the plan's work. In Microsoft Project, phases are represented by summary tasks. See Chapter 4.

planning The first major phase of project management work. Planning includes all the work in developing a schedule up to the point where the tracking of actual work begins. See Chapter 14.

plan The Microsoft Project document type, also referred to as schedules, projects and MPPs.

Project's plans have a .MPP file extension. See Chapter 3.

Predecessor task A task whose start or end date determines the start or finish of another task or tasks, called *successor tasks*. See Chapters 4 and 9.

product scope The quality, features, and functions (often called *specifications*) of the deliverable of the plan. See Chapter 4 and Appendix A.

program office A department within an organization that oversees a collection of projects (such as producing wings and producing engines), each of which contributes to a complete deliverable (such as an airplane) and the organization's strategic objectives. Sometimes also called a program management office, or PMO. See Chapter 21.

progress bar A graphical representation on a bar in the Gantt Chart view that shows how much of a task has been completed. See Chapter 8.

project A temporary endeavor undertaken to create a unique product or service. See Chapter 1.

project calendar The base calendar that is used by the entire plan. The project calendar defines normal working and nonworking days and times. See Chapter 3.

project scope The work required to produce a deliverable with agreed-upon quality, features, and functions. See Chapter 4 and Appendix A.

project summary task A summary task that contains top-level information such as duration, work, and costs for the entire plan. The project summary task has a task ID of 0 and is displayed through the Show/Hide group of the Format tab. See Chapter 4.

project triangle A popular model of project management in which time, cost, and scope are represented as the three sides of a triangle. A change to one side will affect at least one of the other two sides. There are many variations on this model. See Chapter 16 and Appendix A.

Project Web App (PWA) The browser-based interface to Project Server, the foundation of Microsoft's Enterprise Project Management (EPM) and Project and Portfolio Management (PPM) solutions. See Appendix C.

recurring task A task that repeats at established intervals. You can create a recurring task that repeats for a fixed number of times or that ends by a specific date. See Chapter 10.

relationship The type of dependency between two tasks, visually indicated by a link line. The types of relationships include finish-to-start (FS), start-to-start (SS), finish-to-finish (FF), and start-to-finish (SF). Also known as a *link*, a *logical relationship*, a *task dependency*, or a *precedence relationship*. See Chapters 4 and 9.

report A view-like format that includes a dynamic mix of tables, charts and textual content, and is highly customizable. Microsoft Project includes several predefined reports, each focusing on specific aspects of your plan. You can also define your own reports. Another type of report is a *visual report*, which exports structured data to Microsoft Excel or Microsoft Visio for graphical representation and analysis. See Chapters 2, 7, and 18.

resource calendar The working and nonworking days and times of an individual work resource. See Chapter 5.

resource leveling A method of resolving resource overallocation by delaying the start date of an assignment or an entire task or splitting up the work on a task. Microsoft Project can level resources automatically, or you can do it manually. See Chapter 12.

resource manager A person who oversees resource usage in a plan's activities, specifically to manage the time allocation and costs of resources. A resource manager might also have project management skills and responsibilities, depending on the organization's structure. See Chapter 15.

resource pool In Microsoft Project, a plan that other plans use for their resource information. Resource pools contain information about resources' task assignments from all plans (called *sharer plans*) linked to the resource pool. See Chapter 21.

resources People, equipment, and material (and the associated costs of each) needed to complete the work on a plan. See Chapter 5.

ribbon interface A user interface design used by Microsoft Office applications. In the ribbon interface, commands are organized into groups and tabs for quick access. See Chapters 2 and 19.

risk An event that decreases the likelihood of completing the plan on time, within budget, and to specification (or, less likely, an opportunity to improve project performance). See Chapter 4.

scheduling formula A representation of how Microsoft Project calculates work, based on the duration and resource units of an assignment. The scheduling formula is Duration x Assignment Units = Work. See Chapters 6 and 9.

scope The products or services to be provided by a plan and the work required to deliver it. For planning, it's useful to distinguish between product scope and project scope. Scope is one side of the project triangle model. See Appendix A.

semi-flexible constraint A constraint type that gives Microsoft Project the flexibility to change the start and finish dates of a task within one date boundary. Start No Earlier Than (SNET), Start No Later Than (SNLT), Finish No Earlier Than (FNET), and Finish No Later Than (FNLT) are all semi-flexible constraints. See Chapter 9.

sequence The chronological order in which tasks occur. A sequence is ordered from left to right in most views that include a timescale, such as the Gantt Chart view. See Chapter 4.

sharer plan A plan that is linked to a resource pool. Sharer plans use resources from a resource pool. See Chapter 21.

shortcut menu A menu that you display by pointing to an item on the screen and then right-clicking. Shortcut menus contain only the commands that apply to the item to which you are pointing. See Chapter 2.

slack The amount of time that a task can be delayed without delaying a successor task (free slack) or the plan end date (total slack). Slack is also known as *float*. See Chapter 10.

sorting A way of ordering task or resource information in a view by the criteria you choose. See Chapter 13.

source program When exchanging data between Microsoft Project and another program, the program in which the data resided originally. See Chapter 20.

split An interruption in a task, represented in the Gantt bar as a dotted line between segments of a task. You can split a task multiple times. See Chapter 9.

sponsor An individual or organization that both provides financial support and champions the project team within the larger organization. See Chapters 6 and 16.

stakeholders The people or organizations that might be affected by project activities (those who "have a stake" in its success). These also include the resources working on the plan as well as others (such as customers) external to the plan's work. See Chapter 15.

Standard base calendar A base calendar included with Microsoft Project designed to accommodate an 8:00 A.M.–5:00 P.M., Monday through Friday work shift. See Chapter 3.

status date The date that you specify (not necessarily the current date) that determines how Microsoft Project calculates earned value data. See Chapter 8.

subtask A task that is indented below a summary task. Summary and subtasks make up a plan's outline structure. See Chapter 4.

successor task A task whose start or finish is driven by another task or tasks, called *predecessor tasks*. See Chapters 4, 9, and 10.

summary task A task that is made up of and summarizes the subtasks below it. In Microsoft Project, phases of a plan's work are represented by summary tasks. See Chapter 4.

table A spreadsheet-like presentation of a plan's data, organized in vertical columns and horizontal rows. Each column represents one of the many fields in Microsoft Project, and each row represents a single task or resource. In a usage view, additional rows represent assignments. See Chapter 13.

task An activity that has a starting and finishing point. A task is the basic building block of a plan. See Chapter 4.

task calendar The base calendar that is used by a single task. A task calendar defines working and nonworking times for a task, regardless of settings in the project calendar. See Chapter 9.

task ID A unique number that Microsoft Project assigns to each task in a plan. In the Entry table, the task ID appears in the far-left column. See Chapter 4.

task priority A numeric ranking between 0 and 1000 of a task's importance and appropriateness for resource leveling. Tasks with the lowest priority are delayed or split first if necessary. The default value is 500. See Chapter 12.

task type A setting applied to a task that determines how Microsoft Project schedules the task, based on which of the three scheduling formula values is fixed. The three task types are fixed units, fixed duration, and fixed work. See Chapter 9.

template In Microsoft Project, a file format that enables you to reuse existing plans as the basis for new plans. Project includes several templates that relate to a variety of industries, and you can create your own templates. See Chapter 2.

time The scheduled durations of individual tasks and the overall plan. Time is one side of the project triangle model. See Appendix A.

Timeline view A Project view in which you can display select tasks and milestones against a simple timeline. See Chapters 7 and 17.

throughput metric A measurement of the quantity of a deliverable that can be completed over a given time period, usually expressed as a ratio. For example, "paint one wall per day" describes a quantity of a deliverable (a painted wall) that can be produced in a given time period (a day). Note that the time period used in a metric is work, not elapsed duration. See Chapter 14.

timephased field A task, resource, or assignment value that is distributed over time. The values of timephased fields appear in the timescale grid on the right side of a view, such as the Task Usage or Resource Usage view. See Chapter 14.

timescale The timescale appears in a view, such as the Gantt Chart or Resource Usage view, as a band across the top of the grid and denotes units of time. To customize the timescale, do this: On the View tab, in the Zoom group, click the down arrow to the right of the Timescale box and then click Timescale. See Chapter 2.

top-down planning A method of developing a plan by identifying the highest-level phases or summary tasks before breaking them into lower-level components or subtasks. See Chapter 4.

total slack The amount of time that a task can be delayed without delaying the plan's end date. See Chapter 10.

tracking The second major phase of project management work. Tracking includes all the collecting, entering, and analyzing of actual performance values, such as work on tasks and actual durations. See Chapters 8 and 14.

underallocated The condition of resources when they are assigned to do less work than their normal work capacity. For example, a full-time resource who has only 25 hours of work assigned in a 40-hour work week is underallocated. See Chapter 12.

units A standard way of measuring the capacity of a resource to work when you assign the resource to a task in Microsoft Project. Units are one variable in the scheduling formula: Duration x Units = Work. See Chapter 5.

variable consumption rate A quantity of a material resource to be consumed that will change if the duration of the task to which it is assigned changes. See Chapter 11.

variance A deviation from the schedule or budget established by the baseline plan. See Chapters 14 and 15.

view A visual representation of the tasks or resources in your plan. The three categories of views are charts, sheets, and forms. Views enable you to enter, organize, and examine information in a variety of formats. See Chapters 2 and 13.

work The total scheduled effort for a task, a resource, a resource assignment, or an entire plan. Work is measured in person-hours and might not match the duration of the task. Work is one variable in the scheduling formula: Duration x Units = Work. See Chapters 4 and 6.

work breakdown structure (WBS) The identification of every task in a plan that reflects that task's location in the hierarchy of the plan. See Chapter 17.

work resources The people and equipment that do the work of the plan. See Chapters 5 and 11.

Index

8/80 rule, 62
% Complete field, 165, 396–397
% Work Complete field, 165, 396–397

A

accrual methods, 203–204
Actions list, 112–115, 194–195
Active Directory, importing resource details to, 6
actual costs, 267, 311. *See also* costs
actual work, 299, 308–309, 314. *See also* work
actuals, 152, 316, 319
    entering, 161–165, 308–309
    recording, 157–158
    tracking, 299, 305–310
Add Tasks To Timeline dialog box, 134–135
Add to Timeline command (Task tab), 136
Advanced Properties dialog box, 48
All Subtasks view, 214
allocation, 250–255. *See also* overallocation
apps for Office, 6
As Soon As Possible constraints, 200–201
Assign Resources command (Resources tab), 23
Assign Resources dialog box, 23, 105–110
    Cost field, 117–118
    cost values, entering, 98
    material resources, assigning, 236–237
    Replace button, 255
    Resource list, 118
    Units field, 255
Assignment Information dialog box, 227–231, 235
assignment notes, 79, 233
assignments, 103, 103–116, 120–121
    actual work values, 308–310
    adding and removing, 112–116
    contouring, 187, 229–234
    of cost resources, 116–118
    costs, 90, 106, 118
    delaying, 226–229, 261
    editing, 229
    overtime, adding, 352
    peak units, 191
    reassigning, 245–246
    recurring tasks, 206–208

Resource Names column, 109–110
    in sharer plans, 476–478, 489–493
    in Team Planner view, 241–246
    units value, 104, 192–193
    variance, viewing, 330
    viewing across plans, 474–476
    work values, manually editing, 232–233
Auto Schedule command (Task tab), 74–75
AutoFilter, 7, 278, 285–287
availability of resources, 218–221, 254

B

Backstage view, 7, 17–21
    SkyDrive access, 5
Bar command (Format tab), 131–132
Bar Styles command (Format tab), 132
Bar Styles dialog box, 26–27, 365–370
    Gantt charts, formatting, 128
base calendars, 45–46, 98, 188–190, 482–484
Baseline command, 370
baseline costs, 267
baseline plans, 152, 156
    multiple, 154–155, 301
    saving, 154–156, 302–304
    updating, 300–304
Blank Project template, 43
book, training and instruction with, 529–532
Box command (Format tab), 378
Box Styles command (Format tab), 378
Box Styles dialog box, 375
Budget Cost Report, 333
burdened rates, 93

C

Calendar view, 25, 378–381
calendars, 44
    base calendars, 45–46, 98, 188–190, 482–484
    custom, 418, 420–423
    exceptions, 46–47, 479–480
    project calendars, 45
    resource calendars, 93–98

callouts, displaying tasks as, 136
change highlighting, 8, 69, 184, 308
Change Working Time dialog box, 45–47, 479, 481–483
    base calendar, changing, 98
    base calendars, creating, 188
    Work Weeks tab, 189
    working-time exceptions, adding, 94–95
    working week days and times, modifying, 96–97
Chart Styles group, 139
charts
    contextual commands, 400
    data labels, 411–412
    Design tab, 399
    elements, adding, 402–403
    fields, adding and removing, 409–410
    filtering data, 400, 402
    Format tab, 400
    formatting, 138–139, 399–406
    legend, hiding, 412
    reports, adding to, 408–413
    Time category value, 404
    timescale, adjusting, 404
Chatfield, Carl, 514
Clear All Filters command (View tab), 287
Clear command (Task tab), 81
Clear Filter command (View tab), 290
Clear Group command (View tab), 284
collaboration features, 517–528
Collapse Boxes command, 378
color styles, 25–26
commands, 16, 22–27. See also individual command names
    adding to Quick Access Toolbar, 434–436
    keyboard shortcuts, 27
    split buttons, 24
completion percentages, 158–161, 165
connected services, 19
consolidated plans, 493
    capabilities of, 493
    creating, 494
    cross-plan links, creating, 501
    outlining features, 494
    project summary task, viewing, 495
    saving, 494–495
    task links, displaying, 500–501
constraints, 179–185
    balancing, 509–512
    cost, 508
    definition of, 507
    driving constraints, 344

    managing, 509–512
    Must Finish On, 200
    scope, 508–510
    As Soon As Possible, 200
    Start No Earlier Than, 205
    time, 507
contours, 229–234
    back-loaded, 230–231
    details, recording in notes, 233
    fixed-duration tasks and, 232
    flat (default), 230
    indicators, 231–232
Copy Picture dialog box, 141, 426
Copy Report command (Design tab), 144
Copy Timeline command (Format tab), 142–143
copying and pasting, 7. See also pasting
    to other programs, 444–449
Cost Overview report, 336
cost rate tables, 222–224
    changing, 234–235
    multiple pay rates, 223
cost resources, 8, 84, 203
    assigning, 116–118
    costs, 117
    setting up, 98–99
Cost table, 120, 162, 234–235, 267–269
    cost variance, 330–332
    resource costs, 334, 354–355
    usage view, 333
cost variance, 330–333
    graphical indicators, 339–340
    stoplight view, 336–341
    troubleshooting, 352–355
costs
    actual, 267
    assignment details, relationship with, 353
    baseline, 267
    calculation, 104
    as constraint, 508
    cost per use (set fee), 91, 225
    current (scheduled), 267
    displaying, 254
    entering, 202–204
    legends, adding to, 384
    planned, 117
    rates, 90–93
    remaining, 267
    resource costs, 85, 333–336
    timephased values, 336
    viewing, 118–122, 267–270

Create New Base Calendar dialog box, 188–189
critical path
    crashing, 208
    finish dates and, 268
    formatting, 210
    recalculation of, 210
    slack and, 208–201
    viewing, 208–210, 346–347
critical tasks, 268, 380
cross-plan links, 497–502
current (scheduled) costs, 267
Custom AutoFilter dialog box, 286
custom elements, sharing between plans, 418–423
Custom Fields dialog box, 337–338

D

data maps, 450, 452–453, 456
Data Template Definition dialog box, 376
Data Templates dialog box, 375–376
data types, 7
dates. *See also* finish dates; start dates
    deadlines, 184, 200–202, 507
    linking objects to, 134
deadlines, 184, 200–202, 507
Define Group Interval dialog box, 283
Define New View dialog box, 294
Delete Task command, 57
deliverables, 57, 506
dependencies, 54
    creating, 67–73
    between plans, creating, 496–502
    reasons for, 496–497
    scheduling and, 75
Design tab, 22, 35
destination programs, 441
Detail Gantt view, 209, 210, 325
Details dialog box, 95
dialog box launcher buttons, 26–27
Display AutoFilter command (View tab), 278
Document Export Options dialog box, 386–387
Drawing tool, 133–134
driving constraints, 344
driving predecessors, 170–172
Driving Predecessors command (Format tab), 171–172
duration, 54, 77–79, 505
    abbreviations for, 58
    actuals, recording, 163–165
    adjusting, 112–115, 194–195, 350
    contours and, 232

critical path, managing with, 210
    elapsed, 59–60
    elapsed time vs. work accomplished, 165
    entering, 58–63, 72
    estimating, 62–63
    manually setting, 211–214
    numerical values, 75
    of recurring tasks, 207
    reducing, 352
    Scheduled Duration value, 214
    split tasks, 187
    standard values, 59
    of summary tasks, 64, 211–214
    text values, 58–59, 62
    viewing, 118–122

E

effort-driven scheduling, 116, 191, 196
effort-driven tasks, 112–116
email
    copying Project data to, 442
    plans, sending, 19
Enterprise Project Management (EPM), 526–528
Entire Project view, 212
Entry table, 156, 175
equipment resources, 86. *See also* work resources
Excel
    importing data from, 449–452
    pasting Project data into, 445–447
    PivotTables, 458, 460
    saving projects as workbooks, 452
    visual reports, 8, 458–461
exceptions, working-time, 8, 45–47, 94–95, 479–480
Export Wizard, 455–457
exporting data, 19, 382, 385–387, 455–459
external tasks, 498–499, 501

F

Field List pane, 139, 390–391
    displaying, 392–393
    field hierarchy, 393
    resource names, reordering, 403–405
    selected field names, 393
fields
    % Complete field, 165, 396–397
    % Work Complete field, 165, 396–397
    custom, 7, 293
    sorting by, 279

file formats of Project, 459
Filter Definition dialog box, 288, 329
filtering
    AutoFilters, 7, 278, 285–287
    cost variance, 332–333
    custom filters, 287–289
    incomplete tasks, 358
    predefined filters, 285
    project details, 7, 284–290
    removing, 290
    by resource, 355
    resources by cost, 334–335
    slipping and late tasks, 325, 327–328
finish dates, 42, 77–79
    critical path and, 208, 268
    entering, 61
    Finish No Earlier Than constraint, 184
    interim plan, 304
    latest, 6
    of recurring tasks, 205, 207
    resource leveling and, 261
    Scheduled Finish dates, 214
    viewing, 119, 267–270
finish-to-finish (FF) task relationships, 67, 174
finish-to-start (FS) task relationships, 67, 173–175
fixed costs, 202–204
fixed-duration task type, 191
fixed-unit task type, 191
fixed-work task type, 191
flexible constraints, 179–180, 182
float, 208
forecasts, 324
Form views, 145
Format Bar dialog box, 131–132
Format Data Label pane, 411
Format tab, 22
    Bar Styles group, 128, 131
    Baseline and Slippage commands, 370
    contextual nature, 371–372
    Current Selection group, 136
    Details group, 100
    Drawings group, 134
    Format group, 133
    Gantt Chart Style group, 128–130
    Insert group, 134
    label, 29
    Layout button, 370
    Show/Hide group, 79
    Text Styles button, 370

formatting, 7
    Calendar view, 378–381
    charts, 399–406
    critical path and slack, 210
    direct, 372–373
    Gantt chart views, 127–134, 302, 364–370
    link lines, 370
    Network Diagram view, 373–378
    overallocation, 253–254
    style-based, 371–372
    summary data rows, 281
    tables, 390–399
    text, 370–373
    Timeline view, 371–373
Formula dialog box, 338
formulas, custom, 338
free slack, 208–210

G

Gantt, Henry, 127
Gantt bars
    color formatting, 170–173
    details, viewing, 370
    linking objects to, 133–134
    names, 366
    progress bars, 158, 160
    From and To values, 367–368
Gantt Chart button, 271
Gantt Chart Style group, 128–130
Gantt Chart view, 22, 24–27
    actuals, displaying, 163
    bar chart, 127
    baseline and slippage bars, 330
    baseline values, 156
    copying, 140–142
    customizing, 127–134
    Gantt bars, 128, 327
    horizontal gridlines, 132–133
    panning and zooming, 137
    Print Preview, 146–148
    printing options, 382–385
    project summary task, 79, 119
    Resource Names column, 109–110
    timescale, 28
Gantt chart views, 127, 364
    displaying, 271
    drawing on, 133–134
    formatting, 127–134, 302, 364–370
    gridlines, 369

Gantt with Timeline view, 127
global template, 415, 418, 419, 424–425
Go To command, 434–435
Go To dialog box, 182, 435
graphic images
        pasting into Project, 445
        snapshots, 424–428, 444
graphical indicators, 339–340
Graphical Indicators dialog box, 339
gridlines, formatting, 133
Group By dialog box, 284
grouping, 15
        group intervals, 283
        More Groups dialog box, 282
        project details, 280–284
        removing, 284
        resource groups, 281
Guide to the Project Management Body of Knowledge, A
        (Project Management Institute), 505, 515, 533

H
Help, 15, 210, 433
highlighting, 285
        change highlighting, 8, 184, 308
        critical path, 210
        task relationships, 170–173
hyperlinks, task, 79–81

I
images, copying, 141
import/export maps, 450, 452–453, 456
Import Wizard, 451–454
importing data, 451–454
Inactivate command (Task tab), 272
incomplete work, rescheduling, 317–319
Indent Task command (Task tab), 66
indicators
        Actions indicators, 113
        AutoFilter indicators, 287
        constraint indicators, 183
        contour indicators, 231–232
        deadline indicators, 200–202
        Inserted Project icon, 494
        missed deadline indicator, 346
        overallocation indicator, 240
        recurring task indicator, 206
        red exclamation point, 202

        task calendars, 190
        viewing, 118–122
Indicators column, 81
inflexible constraints, 179–180, 182
Information command, 178
Insert Chart dialog box, 408–409
Insert Hyperlink dialog box, 81
Insert Project dialog box, 494
inserted plans, 493–494
instruction with this book, 529–532
interim plans, 304, 367–369

K
keyboard shortcuts, 27

L
lag time, 174–175, 177
Late/Overbudget Tasks Assigned To filter, 333
Late Tasks filter, 325
Layout command (Format tab), 378
Layout dialog box, 187
Layout tab, 22, 36
lead time, 174–175, 178
learning communities, 513–515
legends, 383–384, 410
Level All button, 265
Level Resources dialog box, 259
Leveling Gantt view, 266
line managers, 474
Link The Selected Tasks command (Task tab), 69, 76–77
linking, 67–73
        cross-plan links, 497–500
        to Gantt bars or dates, 133–134
        managing, 502
        respecting, 73
Lync 2010, 86

M
macros
        adding to ribbon tabs, 437–438
        editing, 429–433
        recording, 423–428
Macros dialog box, 427
manually scheduled tasks, 7, 43, 54, 63, 71–72, 192, 242
        duration, 57–60
        indicator of, 55

manually scheduled tasks (*continued*)
    start and finish dates, 60–61
    summary tasks, 211–214
maps, import/export, 450, 452–453, 456
Mark On Track command (Task tab), 157
Mark Task As Milestone command, 64
master (consolidated) projects, 493
material costs, 236–237
material resources, 84
    assigning, 236–237
    consumption rates, 237
    grades of, 510
    per-unit costs, 226
    setting up, 225–226
    unit of measurement, 226
Max. Units field, 86–89, 93, 104
maximum units value, 218, 225, 238, 251
    adjusting, 219
Microsoft Enterprise Project Management (EPM),
    526–528
Microsoft Excel. *See* Excel
Microsoft Office Fluent interface, 6
Microsoft Office Online website Project area, 513–514
Microsoft Office Support website Project Support area,
    513–514
Microsoft Project 2013. *See* Project 2013
Microsoft Project MVPs, 513
Microsoft Project User Group (MPUG), 513
Microsoft SharePoint. *See* SharePoint
Microsoft Visio visual reports, 8, 378, 460–464
Microsoft Visual Basic for Applications (VBA). *See* VBA
    (Visual Basic for Applications)
milestones, 63–64, 136, 201–202
Mini Toolbars, 7–8, 16
missed deadlines, 346–352
More Filters dialog box, 288, 327–329
More Groups dialog box, 282
More Tables dialog box, 290–292
More Views dialog box, 209, 294
mouse input, 6
Must Finish On constraint, 200

N

negative slack, 184–185
Network Diagram view, 280, 373–378
network diagrams, 373
New Report command (Report tab), 407
nonworking days, 45–47
nonworking time, 161

Notepad, exporting data to, 455–459
notes, 79–81, 99–102

O

Office apps, 6. *See also* Excel
    Visio, 8, 378, 460–464
    Word, 446–447
Office blog, 521, 526
ongoing operations, 9, 505
Online Analytical Processing (OLAP) cube, 460
Open Resource Pool Information dialog box, 495
Open screen, 18, 485
Organizer, 18, 418–419
    Calendars tab, 420–421
    elements, copying to global template, 422
    elements, copying with, 421
    tabs in, 421
Other Views command, 32
Outdent Task command (Task tab), 66
Outline view, 212
output files, 385–387
overallocation, 218, 250
    addressing, 245–246
    day by day vs. hour by hour, 266
    manually resolving, 255–259
    from multiple assignments, 468
    navigating, 254
    resource leveling, 259–266
    resources, replacing, 356–357
    viewing, 240, 242, 253–254
overtime, 91, 222–223, 352

P

Page Setup dialog box, 383–384
pan and zoom controls, 137
password protection, 93
Paste Special feature, 444
pasting. *See also* copying and pasting
    into destination programs, 444, 446
    into Project, 444–445
pay rates, 90–93
    applying at different times, 223–225
    applying different rates, 234–235
    increases, entering, 223–225
    multiple, 221–223
PDF documents, 7, 19, 382, 385–387
peak, 192–193
peak units, 192–193

peak units field, 191
people resources, 86–87. *See also* work resources
percentage of work complete, 310
performance tracking, 152–165
phases, 64
PivotTables, 460, 462
planning, 65, 299
plans. *See also* projects
    % Complete field, 396–397
    % Work Complete field, 396–397
    baseline plans, 152, 154–156, 300–304
    consolidated and inserted plans, 493–496,
      500–501costs, checking, 267–270
    custom elements, sharing between, 418–423
    default views, 127
    dependencies between, creating, 496–500
    duration, viewing, 77–78
    emailing, 19
    exporting, 19
    file properties, setting, 48–49
    finish date, checking, 267–270
    indicators, viewing, 118–122
    information about, 18, 48–49
    interim plans, 304
    legends, 383–384
    new, 18
    nonworking days, setting, 45–47
    password protection, 93
    printing, 18
    resource allocation across, 474. *See also* resource
      pools
    resource pools, 468, 471–473.
    saving, 44–45
    scheduling, 42. *See also* scheduling
    sharer plans, 468–469. *See also* sharer plans
    sharing, 21, 517–521
    snapshots of, 424–428
    start date, setting, 43–45
    starting, 42–43
    tasks, linking across, 497–500
    templates, 20–21
    timescales, 28
    tracking. *See* tracking progress
PM Network, 515
PMBOK, 505, 515, 533
practice files, downloading, 13
predecessor tasks
    details, viewing, 176–177
    driving predecessors, 170–172

external, 498–499
    viewing, 170–173
Predecessors command (Format tab), 171
Presentation Styles, 129–130
Print Entire Project command, 147
print preview, 146–150, 383–385
Print Specific Dates command, 147
printing
    legends, 383–384
    page setup, 148–149, 383–385
    reports, 145–150
    scaling documents, 383
    views, 145–150
product scope, 57, 508–509
productivity, resource assignment and, 116
program offices, 478
progress, 158–161. *See also* tracking progress
progress bars, 158, 160, 318
progress reports, 324
Progress ScreenTips, 160–161
Project 2007, 8
Project 2010, 6–8
Project 2013, 3–4
    apps support, 6
    certifications, 514
    copying data to other programs, 444–449
    customization features, 417–440
    dynamic recalculation, 152
    dynamic updating, 162
    edition, identifying, 358
    features, 4–8
    file format, 459
    global template, 418
    opening other files formats in, 449–454
    project management, teaching with, 533–534
    project management with, 512
    Project Professional edition, 4. *See also* Project
      Professional
    Project Standard edition, 4
    saving other files formats, 454–459
    security settings, 450–451
    start screen, 14
    starting, 14
    touch input, 6
    visual interface, 6, 14–17
project calendars, 8, 45–47. *See also* calendars
Project Community, 514
project data
    copying and pasting, 7, 329, 444–449
    exporting, 329

project data (*continued*)
    filtering, 7, 284–290
    grouping, 280–284
    sharing, 329
    sorting, 276–280
Project Information dialog box, 43–44
    project calendar, selecting, 45–46
    start and finish dates, 78, 270
    statistics, 105, 326
    system clock setting, 221
Project learning communities, 513–514
project management, 9–10, 505–512
    actuals, collecting, 316
    cost management, 93
    deliverables, defining, 57
    effort-driven scheduling, 116
    large-scale, 526–528
    learning communities, 514–515
    planning, top-down and bottom-up, 65
    with Project, 49, 512
    project status, evaluating, 165
    project status, reporting, 329
    resource allocation, 250
    resource capacity, understanding, 238
    scope, 57
    task durations, 62–63
    teaching with Project, 533–534
    variance, 325
Project Management Institute (PMI), 514
Project Management Journal, 515
Project Online, 5
Project Options dialog box, 19
    automatically adding new resources and tasks, 92
    calculation options, 316, 319
    commands, adding quick access to, 434–435
    critical tasks, marking, 210
    cross-project linking options, 501
    Customize Ribbon tab, 436–437
    default views, setting, 127
    new views, tables, filters, and groups options, 282
    Schedule tab, 184
    scheduling options, 115, 319
    startup options, 14
Project Overview report, 329, 391–392
    formatting, 392–399
Project Pro for Office 365, 5
Project Professional, 4
    collaboration features, 517–528
    online services, interaction with, 317

Resource Leveling dialog box, 265
    tasks, inactivating, 271–272, 359
    Team Planner view, 241–246
project scope, 57, 357–360, 508–509
Project Server, 43, 521, 526–528
    product portal, 525
Project Statistics dialog box, 78, 122, 270
    duration, 78
    plan costs, 267
    schedule and cost variance, 326, 345–346
project status
    communicating to stakeholders, 323–324
    displaying, 119–122
    reporting, 329
    tracking, 323. *See also* tracking progress
    variance, 323
Project Summary Name column, 476
project summary tasks, 65, 119–120
    in consolidated plan, viewing, 496
    cost values, 331
    displaying, 79
    finish date, 346
    name, 268
Project tab, 22
    Properties group, 43, 45, 78, 94, 105
    Schedule group, 155
    Status group, 157
project triangle, 324, 343–344, 506–512
Project Web App (PWA), 521–526
    comments, 525
    Home screen, 522
    practice files and, 13
    Project Center, 522
    Projects tab, 522–523
    status updates, 524–525
    task list, 521
    team member view, 524
projects. *See also* plans
    blank, 15
    critical path, 208–210
    definition of, 9, 505
    deliverables, 57, 506
    duration, 505
    finish dates, 6
    master (consolidated) projects, 493
    new from existing projects, 21
    planning, 299
    resources, 506
Properties dialog box, 48–49, 80–81
PWA (Project Web App). *See* Project Web App (PWA)

Q

Quick Access toolbar, 15
    commands, adding, 434–435
    commands, removing, 436
    Undo command, 108

R

Record Macro dialog box, 424
Recurring Task Information dialog box, 205–206
recurring tasks, 204–208
    duration, 207
    hiding, 207
    resources, assigning, 206–208
    scheduling, 207
    viewing, 206
Relationship diagrams, 145
remaining costs, 267
remaining work values, 310–311
Remove Highlighting command (Format tab), 173
Replace Resource dialog box, 356–357
Report Name dialog box, 407
Report tab, 21–23, 390
Report Tools tab, 35
reports, 5, 33–36
    Budget Cost Report, 333
    charts in, 390, 408–413
    copying, 140–145
    Cost Overview report, 336
    custom, 137–139, 406–415
    exporting to Excel or Visio, 460–464
    global templates, 415
    naming, 407
    plan costs in, 267
    printing, 145–150
    progress reports, 324
    Project Overview report, 329
    Report Tools Design tab, 391
    resource capacity, viewing, 241
    Resource Cost Summary Report, 336
    Resource Overview report, 120–120
    status-focused, 329
    status reports, 324
    tables in, 390–399, 413–415
    Task Cost Overview report, 332
    visual, 8
    vs. views, 389–390
Reports feature, 126
Reset button, 439

resource allocation
    examining, 250–255
    fully allocated state, 250
    overallocated state, 250
    overallocation. *See* overallocation
    underallocated state, 250
resource calendars. *See also* calendars
    base calendar, changing, 98
    ignoring, 188
    working times, 93–98
resource capacity, 238–241
Resource Cost Summary Report, 336
resource costs, 333–336. *See also* costs
    tracking, 333
    variance, viewing, 334–336
Resource Form, 475-476
    notes, entering, 99–102
Resource Graph, 255, 260, 399
    resource capacity, viewing, 241
resource groups, 276, 278–279, 281–282
resource IDs, 276, 279
Resource Information dialog box
    Costs tab, 222–224
    Per Use Cost field, 225
    resource availability, 219–221
resource leveling, 259–266
Resource Leveling dialog box, 261, 263–265
    Level All button, 265
    overallocations, looking for, 263
    in Project Professional, 265
resource management, 84–85
resource notes, 79
Resource Overview report, 33–36, 120–120, 400–401
resource pools
    assignment details, viewing, 474–476
    assignment information, clearing, 486
    capabilities of, 469
    creating, 468–474
    dedicated plan for, 474
    naming, 470
    new plans, linking, 485–488
    opening, 485–486, 490
    precedence, 472
    read-only rights, 489, 492
    read-write rights, 489, 491
    refreshing, 492
    Resource Form, 475–476
    saving, 488
    sharer plans, updating, 484
    sharing over network, 489

resource pools (*continued*)
    storage location, 470
    Update Resource Pool command, 489, 491
    updating, 478–481, 491–493
    working times, updating all, 482–484
Resource Sheet view, 30, 87, 219, 262, 487
    cost data, 353–355
    Cost table, 334
    Cost/Use field, 91, 225
    Group column, 281
    Max. Units field, 221
    Ovt. Rate field, 92
    sorting, 277–280
    Std. Rate field, 91
    Summary table, 277
Resource Stats chart, 33, 121, 401–402
Resource Status table, 34–35, 121
Resource tab, 21, 105
Resource Usage view, 30–31, 475
    assignment details timescale, 251
    assignment values, displaying, 254
    Cost Rate Table field, 235
    Notes button, 233
    outline view, 251–252
    overallocations, editing, 256–259
    Project or Task Summary Name column, 476
    resource availability, viewing, 239–240
    tables, displaying, 254
    Usage table, 251
resource variance, 355–357
Resource Views group, 30–31
resources, 3
    adding, 88
    assigning, 31, 103
    assignments, viewing across plans, 475–476
    availability, 218–221
    cost resources, 8, 84, 98–99
    costs, 203, 225, 356–357
    custom fields for, 293
    details, importing, 6
    leveling, 187, 259–266
    managing, 6
    material resources, 84, 225–226, 236–237
    maximum capacity, 88–90
    naming conventions, 473
    notes, 99–102
    overallocation, 88, 90. *See also* overallocation
    overtime, adding, 352
    part-time, 94

pay rates, 90–93, 221–225, 234–235
reassigning, 245–246
for recurring tasks, 206–207
replacing, 356–357
in resource pools, updating, 478–481
selecting, 109
start and finish dates, viewing, 121
start time, delaying, 226–229
task status, relationship with, 315–316
unassigning, 107, 114
work resources, 84–93
working and nonworking times, 93–98
Respect Links command (Task tab), 73
ribbon, 6, 15, 21–27, 417
    collapsing and expanding, 21
    customizing, 7, 434–440
    Quick Access Toolbar commands, 434–436
    tabs, adding and removing, 436–440
    touch input mode, 22
risk, task durations and, 63

S

Save As Template dialog box, 21
Save Project As File command (File tab), 455
saving
    auto saving, 45
    file format, specifying, 459
Schedule table, 210
schedule variance, 324–330
    identifying, 326–328
    missed deadlines, troubleshooting, 346–352
    troubleshooting, 345–352
    viewing, 345–346
Scheduled Duration field, 214
Scheduled Finish field, 214
Scheduled Start field, 214
scheduling, 73–77
    automatically scheduled tasks, 73–74
    change highlighting, 69
    constraints and, 180–185
    dependencies and, 75
    details, viewing, 176
    drag-and-drop method, 241–246
    effort-driven, 112–116
    from finish date, 185
    formula for, 104, 111, 191
    lead and lag times, 68, 174–175
    linked tasks, 67–68

scheduling (*continued*)

    manually scheduled tasks. *See* manually scheduled tasks

    Must Finish On constraints, 200

    rescheduling, 187

    schedule variance, 324–330

    As Soon As Possible constraints, 200–201

    summary tasks, 211–214

    task types and, 191–196

scheduling modes, 55, 58

    automatic, 73–77

    changing, 74–76

    indicator of, 56

Scheduling Styles, 129

scope

    product vs. project, 508–509

    project scope, 57, 357–360, 508–509

    of work, managing, 357–360

scope creep, 511

ScreenTips

    assignment dates, 252

    dates, 313

    external tasks, 499

    Gantt bar details, 327, 370

    for splitting tasks, 185–186

    task calendars, 190

    task details, 243

    viewing, 183

Scroll To Task command (Task tab), 128, 178

Select All button, 277

selection

    with Ctrl key, 109

    in lists, 109

    Select All command, 448

    with Shift key, 446

semi-flexible constraints, 179–180

Set Baseline dialog box, 155, 303–304

Share Resources dialog box, 471–472

    Break Link option, 488

    Sharing Links path, 486

SharePoint

    calendar view, 519

    integration with, 8

    plans, sharing with, 517–521

    progress, tracking, 518

    Project Summary page, 518

    synchronizing with, 19

    tasks, 518–519

    timeline, 518

sharer plans, 468–469

    adding, 485–488

    assignments, changing, 489–493

    assignments, updating, 476–478

    base calendar, 482

    information, consolidating, 473

    link to resource pool, breaking, 473, 487–488

    opening, 484, 490

sharing

    custom elements, 418–423

    with SharePoint, 8, 19, 517–521

shortcut menus, 16

SkyDrive, 5

slack, 170, 172

    formatting, 210

    free and total, 208

    negative, 184–185

    viewing, 209–210

Slippage command, 370

Slipped/Late Progress filter, 325

Slipping Tasks filter, 325

Slipping Tasks report, 330

Sort By dialog box, 280

Sort command (View tab), 23–24

Sort dialog box, 278–279

sorting, 276–280

source programs, 443

split buttons, 24

Split Task command (Task tab), 185–186

split tasks, 185–187, 233

Split View group, 28, 31

split views, 100

stakeholders, 323–324

Standard base calendar, 93–94, 189

start dates, 42

    actuals, recording, 163–164

    delaying, 226–229

    interim plan, 304

    recording, 161

    of recurring tasks, 205, 207

    Scheduled Start dates, 214

    setting, 43–45, 61, 227–229

    Start No Earlier Than constraint, 184, 205

    viewing, 119

Start No Earlier Than constraint, 184, 205

start screen, 14

start-to-finish (SF) task relationships, 67, 174

start-to-start (SS) task relationships, 67, 174

Statistics dialog box, 346

status bar, 15–16
    Filter Applied label, 289
status dates, 319, 330
status reports, 324
stoplight reports, 337–340
subtasks, 120, 252, 444
successor tasks, 170–173
Successors command (Format tab), 172
summary data, 281
Summary table, 277
summary tasks, 64–67
    adding to Timeline view, 135–136
    duration, 211–214
    expand/collapse triangles, 212
    formatting, 379–380
    inactivating, 271–272
    linking to other tasks, 72
    manually scheduling, 211–214

T

Table Definition dialog box, 291
Table Tools tab, 35, 36
tables. *See also individual table names*
    % Complete field, 396–397
    % Work Complete field, 396–397
    active, 277
    charts, adding to, 402–403
    columns, adding and removing, 292
    copying and pasting data to and from, 444–449
    cost rate tables, 222–223
    Cost table, 120. *See also* Cost table
    creating, 290–292
    custom fields, 293, 337–340
    Deadline field, 202
    Design tab, 391
    displaying, 254
    field labels, 390
    Field List pane, 390–391
    field values, 390
    fields, adding, 393–397, 413
    fields, removing, 413
    fields, reordering, 414
    formatting, 390–399
    graphical indicators, 339–340
    laying out, 36
    Layout tab, 391
    pasting into Excel, 447–449
    pasting into Word, 446–447

    pasting text into, 444
    reports, adding to, 413–415
    resizing, 393–395, 398–399
    Resource Status table, 121
    Scheduled Duration field, 214
    Scheduled Finish field, 214
    Scheduled Start field, 214
    single-column, 396–397
    styles, applying, 395–396, 415
    switching among, 156
    Variance table, 325, 328, 330
    view, adjusting, 307–308
    Work table, 330
tabs, 15, 21–27
    adding to ribbon, 436–439
    in Backstage view, 18–19
    collapsing and expanding, 21
    Design tab, 22, 35, 399
    Format tab, 22, 400. *See also* Format tab
    groups, 15
    Layout tab, 22, 36
    macros, adding to, 437–438
    Project tab, 22, 522–523. *See also* Project tab
    removing from ribbon, 439–440
    Report tab, 21–23. *See also* Report tab
    Task tab, 21–22. *See also* Task tab
    View tab, 22–23. *See also* View tab
task calendars, 187–190, 422–423. *See also* calendars
task constraints, 179–185
    categories of, 179
    default start and end times, 184
    finish dates, scheduling from, 185
    indicators, 183
    negative slack, 184–185
    removing, 184
    task scheduling and, 180–182
    types of, 180
Task Cost Overview report, 332
Task Dependency dialog box, 175
Task Details Form, 352
Task Form, 31–32, 107
    cost values, entering, 98
    Effort driven option, 115
    lead and lag times, entering, 175
    task type information, 192
    Work details, 108
Task Information dialog box
    Calendar box, 190
    constraints, adjusting, 183

Task Information dialog box (*continued*)
    cross-plan link options, 502
    deadlines, entering, 201–202
    displaying, 178
    Effort Driven option, 115
    lead and lag times, entering, 175, 177
    linking tasks, 70
    Notes tab, 79–81
    Predecessors tab, 70
    task type information, 192, 195–196
Task Inspector pane, 8, 176, 183
task list synchronization, 517–520
Task Mode column, 56
task notes, 79–81
Task Path, 5, 170–173, 208
    Driving Predecessors command, 171–172, 347–348
    Predecessors command, 171
    Remove Highlighting command, 173
    Successors command, 172
task relationships, 68–69, 378
    adjusting, 178–179
    appearance of, 497
    lead and lag times, 174–175
    type, changing, 351–352
    viewing, 170–173
Task Sheet view, 30, 268
    Cost table, 330–331
    custom fields and formulas, 337–338
    Variance table, 156, 328
Task Summary Name column, 476
Task tab, 21–22
    Clipboard group, 141
    Editing group, 81, 128
    Insert group, 57, 63, 66
    Properties group, 80
    Schedule group, 66, 69, 159
    Tasks group, 74
task types, 191–196
    changing, 192, 195–196
    effort-driven scheduling and, 191, 196
    fixed duration, 191
    fixed units, 191
    fixed work, 191
Task Usage view, 31, 193–195, 227–228, 305–306
    Cost Rate Table field, 235
    Notes button, 233
    tasks, splitting, 233
Task Views group, 31

tasks, 3, 54
    actuals, 161–165, 308–309
    assignments, adding and removing, 112–116
    baseline, updating, 301, 303
    completion percentages, 158–161
    copying to other programs, 444
    cost resources, 8, 116–117
    costs, 90, 202–204, 332
    critical, 208–210, 268
    custom fields for, 293
    default settings, 114–115
    delaying, 261
    deleting, 57, 359–360
    dependencies, 54–60
    details, 32
    displaying as callouts, 136
    duration, 54, 58–63, 77–79
    effort-driven, 112–116
    finish date, 77–79. *See also* finish dates
    hyperlinks, 79–81
    ID numbers, 55, 276, 279
    inactivating, 8, 271–272, 359
    incomplete, 288–289, 358
    inserting, 57
    interrupting, 185–187
    late tasks, viewing, 330
    linking, 67–73, 173–179, 497–500
    location in plan hierarchy, 375
    manually scheduled, 192, 211–214, 242
    material resources, assigning, 236–237
    milestones, 63–64
    names, 55–57, 130–131
    outline structure, 64
    predecessors, 67, 70, 170–173, 176–177, 498–499
    priority, 263–264
    progress bars, 318
    progressing as scheduled, 157
    project summary, 65
    promoting and demoting, 66
    reassigning, 245–246
    recurring, 204–208
    rejoining splits, 187
    rescheduling, 317–319
    resource status, relationship with, 315–316
    resources, assigning and unassigning, 31, 103–116
    scheduled and unscheduled, 241
    scheduling. *See* scheduling
    scrolling to, 128–129
    selecting, 182

tasks (*continued*)
    slipped, 324–330
    splitting, 185–187, 233, 261
    status dates, 330
    subtasks, 64
    successors, 170–173
    summary, 64–67
    Timeline view, adding to, 134–136
    timephased actuals for, 313–315
    unassigned, 252
    Work Breakdown Structure codes, 375–377
    working time, adjusting, 187–190
team collaboration with PWA, 521–526
Team Planner view, 7, 241–246, 255
templates, 20–21, 43
text
    copying to other programs, 444
    formatting, 370–373
    pasting into Project, 444–445
Text Styles dialog box, 372
time constraints, 507
Timeline view, 7, 28, 36, 119–120
    copying, 142–144
    customizing, 134–137
    detailed format, 143
    exporting as PDF or XPS file, 385–387
    formatting, 371–373
    Gantt Chart view, panning and zooming, 137
    star and finish dates, 77–78
timephased actuals
    timesheet data as, 312
    tracking, 299, 312–316
timephased grid
    actuals, entering, 312
    cells, working with, 234
    details, displaying, 307
    duration, viewing, 228
    settings, adjusting, 252–253
    in Task usage view, 233
    Work and Actual Work rows, 306–307
    work values, 252
    zoom level, 240
timephased values, 154
timescale, 389
    adjusting, 28, 31, 245, 255, 313
Timescale box, 28
Timescale command (View tab), 31
total slack, 208
touch input, 6
    enabling, 22

Tracking Gantt view
    baseline dates vs. actual or scheduled dates, 325–327
    formatting, 365–370
    task baseline values, 301–302
    tasks as currently scheduled, 301
tracking progress, 152
    actuals, 161–165, 305–310
    level of, 153, 300
    plan as scheduled, 157–158
    Project updating process, 162
    resource costs, 333
    simple method, 161
    task completion percentage, 158–161
    timephased actuals, 299, 312–316
Tracking tables, 162
training with this book, 529–532
travel expenses, 98–99
Trust Center dialog box, 450–451

U

Undo command, 108
    multi-level, 8
Update Project dialog box, 157–158, 318
Update Resource Pool command, 489, 491
Update Task dialog box, 159, 163–164, 432
usage views, 31, 268, 307, 333, 336

V

variance, 299, 323
    addressing, 343
    cost variance, 330–333, 336–341
    schedule variance, 324–330
    start and finish date variance, 325
    work variance, 333
Variance table, 156, 325, 328, 330
VBA Editor, 423, 429–432
VBA (Visual Basic for Applications), 429, 433
    macros, recording, 423–426
View Definition dialog box, 295–296
View label, 16
View tab, 22–23
    Data group, 162
    Resource Views group, 30–31, 87
    Split View group, 28–29, 31, 107–108
    Task Views group, 31
    Zoom group, 28, 173

views, 27–32. *See also individual view names*
    active, 16
    All Subtasks view, 214
    AutoFilter arrows, 278, 285
    Backstage view, 7, 17–21
    built-in, 294
    Calendar view, 25
    columns, inserting, 194
    copying, 140–145
    creating, 294–297
    customizing, 127–137
    default views, 27, 127
    Detail Gantt view, 209
    display settings, 296–297
    Entire Project view, 212
    exporting; 385–387
    filtering data in, 285–290
    formatting, 364–381
    Gantt with Timeline view, 127
    graphic-image snapshots of, 444
    grouping data in, 280–284
    Leveling Gantt view, 266
    Network Diagram view, 280
    Outline view, 212
    printing, 145–150, 381–385
    Resource Graph view, 399
    Resource Sheet view, 30, 87, 219, 262, 487
    Resource Usage view, 475
    shortcuts, 15–16
    sorting data in, 276–280
    task-centric or resource-centric, 295
    Task Form view, 107–108
    Task Sheet view, 30, 268
    Task Usage view, 31, 193–195, 227–228
    Team Planner view, 7
    Timeline view, 7, 28–29, 36, 119–120
    timescaled, 389
    View labels, 16
    viewing, 32
    vs. reports, 389–390
Visio visual reports, 8, 378, 460–464
visual reports, 8, 460–464
Visual Reports dialog box, 461

W

what-if scenarios, 271–272
windows, arranging, 471
Windows Snipping Tool, 140
Word, pasting Project data into, 446–447

work. *See also* actual work
    adjusting, 194–195
    calculation of, 111–112
    effort-driven tasks, 112–116
    incomplete work, 317–319
    interrupting, 185–187
    manually editing, 232–233
    percentage of work complete, 310
    reducing, 258–259
    remaining work, 310–311
    rescheduling, 317–319
    sequence, 174–175
    start of, delaying, 226–229
    viewing, 118–122
work assignments, 31. *See also* assignments
Work Breakdown Structure (WBS) codes, 375–377
work contours, 229–233
Work details, 108
Work Overview reports, 138–139
    copying, 143–144
    printing, 148–150
work resources, 84. *See also* resources
    allocation of, 250–255
    assigning, 103–116
    availability, 85–86
    costs, 116, 510
    maximum units value (capacity), 88–90, 218–221
    multiple assignments in multiple projects, 468
    names, 85–88
    pay rates, 90–93
Work Status chart, 403–405
Work table, 162–163, 306, 330
work variance, 333
working capacity, 88–90
working time, 93–98
    adjusting, 187–190
    maximum units, 88–90
    in resource pools, updating, 479–484
working-time exceptions, 8, 45–47, 94–95

X

XML format, saving projects as, 454
XPS documents, 7, 19, 382, 385–387

Z

Zoom group, 28
zoom levels, 173, 240
Zoom Slider, 15–16, 28

About the authors

Tim Johnson

Tim's first connection with Project began as a product support professional at Microsoft, starting with Project 3.0. Later, Tim worked on the Project user assistance team, where he brought his firsthand knowledge of Project customers' issues to new learning solutions for Project. Tim remains involved in the computer industry and continues to look for ways to help customers better understand and use their computer applications.

Carl Chatfield

Carl is a content project manager at Microsoft. In this role, Carl develops technical product documentation and Web content for a variety of products and services. Carl also teaches software user assistance in the Human Centered Design and Engineering department at the University of Washington. Carl is a graduate of the master's program in Technical Communication at the University of Washington and is certified as a Project Management Professional (PMP) by the Project Management Institute. Carl blogs regularly about Microsoft Project, project management, and knowledge worker teams at *www.projhugger.com*.

Acknowledgments

The authors would like to thank some of the many people who supported us while writing this book. We thank our technical reviewer, Shawn Kim, Microsoft Services senior consultant, and Kate Simpson, Microsoft support engineer, for their timely and valuable expertise. We thank our project editor, Valerie Wooley of Microsoft Press, and our project manager, Steve Sagman of Waypoint Press, for their outstanding work. Finally, Carl would like to thank his many friends and mentors in the Puget Sound chapters of two fine organizations: the Microsoft Project User Group (MPUG) and the Project Management Institute (PMI).

Microsoft

How To Download Your ebook

To download your ebook, go to http://aka.ms/PressEbook and follow the instructions.

Please note: You will be asked to create a free online account and enter the access code below.

Your access code:

WPNHBDG

Microsoft Project 2013 Step by Step

Your PDF ebook allows you to:

- Search the full text
- Print
- Copy and paste

Best yet, you will be notified about free updates to your ebook.

If you ever lose your ebook file, you can download it again just by logging in to your account.

Need help? Please contact:
mspinput@microsoft.com

Now that you've read the book...

Tell us what you think!

Was it useful?
Did it teach you what you wanted to learn?
Was there room for improvement?

Let us know at http://aka.ms/tellpress

Your feedback goes directly to the staff at Microsoft Press,
and we read every one of your responses. Thanks in advance!